TEXT AND WORKBOOK

Leading and Managing Nonprofit Organizations

Third Edition

D0082553

Kendall Hunt
publishing company

Roger M. Weis, Ed.D. | Susan M. Muller, Ph.D. | Chapter One by Peter C. Weber, Ph.D.

Cover image © Shutterstock.com

Kendall Hunt
publishing company

www.kendallhunt.com
Send all inquiries to:
4050 Westmark Drive
Dubuque, IA 52004-1840

Previous editions published by eddie bowers publishing co., inc., 2015
Third Edition Copyright © 2017 by Kendall Hunt Publishing Company

ISBN 978-1-5249-2097-5

Published in the United States of America

This book is dedicated to my"favorite" grandchildren,
Riley and Ryder.
May you always make a positive difference
in the lives of others.

—*Roger M. Weis*

This book is dedicated with love to
my husband Ted,
my daughters Karen and Katie, and
my grandchildren Amber and Logan.

—*Susan M. Muller*

To Sindhu.

—*Peter C. Weber*

CONTENTS

3 Staff, Board, and Volunteers: Leading Effectively 99

4 Human Development, Competencies, Issues, and Trends..... 147

5 Program Development, Marketing, and Promotion 183

6 Financial Processes and Financial Development 225

7   **Risk Management** **277**

8   **Organizational Development: Building Capacity,
Impact, and Sustainability** **311**

9   **Career Planning and Professional Development** **331**

PREFACE

Most reports indicate there are 1.6 million different private nonprofit organizations in the United States and tens of thousands of new positions open in youth, human service, and other nonprofit organizations each year. The primary purpose of this introductory text is to present information relevant to a number of competencies required to be leaders/managers in these organizations. Another purpose is to provide opportunities to develop skills in these competency areas through classroom activities, simulations, and service learning projects. The competencies selected for discussion in the chapters to come were selected through numerous processes including surveys and reports developed by the Nonprofit Academic Centers Council (NACC) and the Nonprofit Leadership Alliance (NLA). The first chapter of the text discusses the history, purpose, and importance of the nonprofit sector throughout history. The next chapter presents theories, models, and studies on leadership and management and the development of each as well as discussing the connection between leadership, character, and ethics. Following this, Chapter 3 is an in-depth look at staff, board, and volunteer development. Chapter 4 includes information on various theories of human development essential to future leaders in the nonprofit sector and presents information on a number of trends and issues—important information to have prior to designing programs. Developing programs from beginning to end is covered in Chapter 5 and includes information on marketing and promotion of programs. Chapter 6 presents an overview of financial processes including accounting, budgeting, and financial development. The importance of risk management and developing a risk management plan, along with a discussion on the importance of insurance is covered in Chapter 7. Chapter 8 discusses different theories related to organizational development and support. The final chapter, Chapter 9, provides information on assessing oneself relative to a career in the nonprofit sector and information on developing effective resumes, cover letters, and interview and networking techniques.

The authors would like to acknowledge and express our appreciation for Maria Schuberger, our administrative assistant who worked tirelessly in helping to make this text a success, and to all of those who have gone before us in preparation for this generation of nonprofit enlightenment.

ABOUT THE AUTHORS

Roger M. Weis is Professor for the Nonprofit Leadership Studies program at Murray State University (MSU). He has twice been selected as student advisor of the year and was the first recipient of the Nonprofit Leadership Alliance's National Award for Excellence in Leadership and the first recipient of the Distinguished Service Learning and Civic Engagement Award at MSU. During his tenure, the program at MSU received numerous national and local awards for excellence in academics, leadership, service, and research and was the largest program in the country for quite some time. This is Dr. Weis's 14th book publication.

© Sherry McClain

Susan Marie Muller, Dean of Health Sciences at Stephens College, is a Master Certified Health Education Specialist (MCHES). She earned her doctorate in Health Education from the University of Maryland College Park and has 33 years of teaching experience including nine years as a middle and elementary school health instructor, and 24 years as a college professor. She has held several leadership positions over the past two decades, most notably as the Dean, College of Health Sciences and Human Services (HSHS) at Murray State University and as an academic department chairperson at Salisbury University.

© Susan Muller

Peter C. Weber is Assistant Professor and Director of Nonprofit Leadership Studies at Murray State University. He holds a doctorate in Philanthropic Studies from the Indiana University Lilly Family School of Philanthropy, as well as a Master in History and a Master in International Studies in Philanthropy and Social Innovation, both from the University of Bologna in Italy. His research focuses on the role of civil society and international philanthropy in building democratic practices of governance in fledgling democracies from both a historical and a contemporary perspective. He has published his work in peer-reviewed journals such as *Global Society, Voluntas, Nonprofit and Voluntary Sector Quarterly,* and the *Journal of Public Affairs Education.*

1

UNDERSTANDING THE NONPROFIT SECTOR

Working together collaboratively for common goals is rooted in American tradition and history. Emblematically, when he visited the United States in the early nineteenth century, French nobleman Alexis de Tocqueville (2006/1835–40) noted with surprise that

> Americans of all ages, all stations in life, and all types of disposition are forever forming associations. There are not only commercial and industrial associations in which all take part, but others of a thousand different types—religious, moral, serious, futile, very general and very limited, immensely large and very minute. Americans combine to give fetes, found seminaries, build churches, distribute books, and send missionaries to the antipodes. Hospitals, prisons, and schools take shape in this way. Finally, if you want to proclaim a truth or propagate some feeling by the encouragement of a great new undertaking . . . in the United States you are sure to find an association. (p. 513)

Just like in de Tocqueville's age, today we interact on a daily basis with a myriad of nonprofit organizations. Many of us were born in nonprofit hospitals; attended service in nonprofit churches, synagogues, or mosques; volunteered in local nonprofit soup kitchens or homeless shelters; adopted a puppy from the local nonprofit humane society; attended nonprofit schools, colleges, and universities; visited parents and relatives in nonprofit senior centers; and the list could go on and on. Nonprofit organizations, voluntary associations, and philanthropic giving are a central part of our lives.

Paradoxically, however, we are often only subconsciously aware of the nonprofit organizations' roles, in spite of their ubiquity. As a result, the common knowledge about the nonprofit sector and its multiple organizations is superficial at best and incorrect at worst. Common myths like "nonprofits cannot earn a profit," "nonprofits do not have paid staff and only use volunteers," and "nonprofits are small and unprofessional" harm the nonprofit sector and discourage individuals wanting to pursue meaningful careers in the nonprofit sector. Ironically, the notion that nonprofits are small, volunteer-based, and run by good-hearted amateurs is used to both praise and criticize nonprofit organizations. On the one hand, it seems to be expected that helping others should not come with any personal reward (whether professional or monetary). On the other hand, as any college student pursuing a degree in nonprofit studies can readily confirm, rolling eyes, skeptical looks, and worried inquiries about "how you can make a living" in the nonprofit sector are typical reactions to the mention of a degree in nonprofit studies.

This chapter aims to address some of this skepticism. It provides a broad understanding of both the nonprofit sector and the role of nonprofit professionals. Future nonprofit professionals should have a good understanding of the environment within which they will operate because:

1. **The nonprofit sector is rooted in a specific set of ethical values**. Nonprofit organizations and philanthropic institutions occupy a distinctive place in American society. This distinctiveness is rooted in the moral and ethical qualities that derive from nonprofit organizations' history and functions. As Thomas Jeavons (2010) has stated, nonprofit organizations are expected to demonstrate integrity, openness, accountability, service, and charity. Understanding the sector, its history and values, is crucial for a successful career in the nonprofit sector.

2. **Nonprofit organizations do not operate in a vacuum**. Leaders and managers must understand the sector as a whole because they will interact with other organizations that may compete for the same resources, may address the same issues and problems, and may advance alternative or contrasting solutions to those issues and problems.

3. **Nonprofit organizations address enormous social problems.** One organization cannot singlehandedly solve these problems, which require collaborations and partnerships both within and across sectors.

4. **The role of the nonprofit sector is often misunderstood.** One of the tasks of nonprofit leaders and managers is therefore to advocate for the sector and educate the public about the many roles and functions of nonprofit organizations.

Accordingly, this chapter will first describe the emergence of the nonprofit professional as a career option, then will define the nonprofit sector and the entities that are part of it, and finally provide an overview of the nonprofit sector today and historically.

A PROFESSIONAL FIELD

Leading and managing a nonprofit organization is a complex and daunting task. Nonprofit organizations operate in an increasingly intricate environment, which is regulated by state and federal laws, influenced by public policies, and shaped by local, national, and international economic, political, and social trends. The nonprofit sector therefore has to rely on an expert and professional leadership. **Expertise** and **professionalism** are needed to channel altruism and passion. "Helping others" and "making the world a better place" are strong motivating factors but risk being harmful if not informed by professional practice, understanding of issues and problems, and ability to adopt multiple perspectives.

As the operations of nonprofit organizations grew in complexity, **nonprofit education programs** developed to both inform practice and address broad theoretical questions on the nonprofit sector's nature and functions in American society (Mirabella, 2007; Shier & Handy, 2014). At the same time, a variety of organizations—commonly known as **infrastructure organizations**—has emerged, advocating for the sector (such as Independent Sector, the Council on Foundations, and the National Council of Nonprofits), as well as providing professional development (such as the Associations of Fundraising Professionals and the Young Nonprofit Professionals Network), management training (such as the Alliance for Nonprofit Management, BoardSource, and the Nonprofit Technology Network), and information resources (such as GuideStar, the National Center for Charitable Statistics, and the Foundation Center) (Abramson & McCarthy, 2012). The proliferation of nonprofit education programs and the multiplication of infrastructure organizations are both a symptom and a driving force of the nonprofit sector's professionalization.

The development of nonprofit education programs, however, suggests and presupposes a **uniqueness** of nonprofit leadership and management. In fact, the demand for and justification of these programs assume that managing a nonprofit organization differs from business management. On a foundational level, one of the central realities of nonprofit management and leadership as a profession is the pervasiveness of **change**. In fact, rapid and ongoing paradigm changes result in leaders' and managers' need to adapt to new political, social, and economic environments, as well as to evolving principles and practices of the profession. The role of the nonprofit professional has radically changed over the past decades, as the rapidly growing research body in the field informs practice and changes in the policy environment modify the framework within which nonprofit organizations work.

Nonprofit education programs need to address the challenges of a rapidly changing field and prepare nonprofit leaders for the twenty-first century (Weber & Witkowski, 2016). Lester Salamon (2012, pp. 20–39) has pointed to the changing context of nonprofit management and leadership and has identified six major challenges shaping the nature of nonprofit operations today.

1. **Fiscal challenge**. Federal and state funds (a major revenue source of the nonprofit sector) have been declining and changing in form with the shift toward **consumer-side subsidies** (in contrast to **producer-side subsidies** such as grants and contracts, consumer-side subsidies are tools of government action such as vouchers that allow

consumers to use them with a variety of service providers, thus forcing nonprofit organizations to compete with for-profit service providers). These changes in and reductions of public funding, coupled with private philanthropy's inability to compensate for the cuts, complicate the working of nonprofit organizations.

2. **Competition challenge**. Nonprofit organizations have been facing an increased competition of for-profit organizations (in particular in the fields of education, health care, and job training), which has resulted in the nonprofit sector losing market shares in some areas because of difficulties to access investment capital.

3. **Effectiveness challenge**. As a result of the trends described above, nonprofit organizations have been pressured to demonstrate effectiveness, which led to an increased emphasis on performance management and a centrality of managerial tools such as logic models, benchmarking, balanced scorecard, and blended values.

4. **Technology challenge**. Increased competition and the effectiveness demand contributed to the integration of technology into decision-making processes and program development. Technological innovations have disrupted approaches to the traditional areas of nonprofit management and leadership with social media revolutionizing the field of communication and marketing; the proliferation of human resource management software systems; new tools such as crowdfunding and online portals replacing costly and outdated approaches to fundraising; data collection and evaluation revolutionizing program development approaches; etc.

5. **Legitimacy challenge**. At the same time, however, the new centrality of performance management and business-like practices, as well as the competition with for-profits raised questions about the nonprofit sector's distinctiveness. With a nonprofit sector that in the public imagery is comprised of volunteer-based rather than professionally-run organizations, commentators have—for example—questioned the legitimacy of tax exemptions and of tax deductible donations.

6. **Human resource challenge**. The multiple demands and the challenges of leading a nonprofit organization have led to retention and talent acquisition problems. This challenge points to an intrinsic paradox. On the one hand, the nonprofit leadership deficit (Tierney, 2006; Landles-Cobb, Kramer, & Smith Milway, 2015) highlights the professional and career opportunities available in this sector. The proliferation of nonprofit education programs is a symptom of this demand for talent. On the other hand, this same proliferation of programs and certificates has transformed the field into a competitive one with the well-rounded professional (with managerial skills and a deep understanding of policy and legal issues) replacing the good-hearted and passionate individual as an ideal candidate.

Leading a nonprofit organization today, therefore, is radically different from leading a nonprofit organization in the even recent past. The reality of this changing environment is reflected in the proliferation of handbooks with multiple subsequent editions such as this volume following Weis and Long (2011) and Weis and Muller (2015), how-to guides, white papers, and best practices. As a result, curricula and syllabi in nonprofit education have radically evolved over the past years. Emblematically, the **Nonprofit Academic Centers Council** (NACC) refers to "salient" changes in its third edition of the curricular guidelines for nonprofit education, which include—among others—an emphasis on technology, a new centrality of global and international trends, and a growing relevance of social innovation and social enterprises (NACC, 2015, p. 3). Likewise, the **Nonprofit Leadership Alliance** (NLA) in a 2011 report concluded that its leadership competencies needed a combination of both interpretative and qualitative changes "to reflect the current context of nonprofit organizations" (p. 5). Indeed, in today's changing environment, no course syllabus could possibly remain the same for more than a couple of semesters.

From a broader perspective, it should be pointed out that leading and managing nonprofit organizations is more complex than managing a business or a public agency. The chapters of this textbook will describe in detail the distinctiveness of nonprofit leadership. Here it will suffice to point out some of the profession's distinctive features that are commonly identified in the literature (Renz, 2010; Worth, 2017).

1. **Mission centrality**: nonprofit managers need to integrate the values that underpin their organizations' missions in all operations. Strategic, financial, and operational decisions must constantly take into account the mission, thus making the means by which ends are achieved as important as the ends themselves.

2. **Financial structure**: nonprofit organizations commonly rely on a mix of financial streams that can include revenue sources as diverse as private charitable donations, grants from both public and philanthropic institutions, contracts with public agencies, and fees for services. These multiple financial sources come with different requirements and expectations regarding use of funds, performance measures, reporting, etc.

3. **Double bottom line**: unlike business leaders, nonprofit leaders must consider both a financial and a social bottom line. Financial survival must be coupled with the ability to reach the social goals identified in the mission.

4. **Unclear lines of accountability and ownership**: unlike businesses, a nonprofit organization does not have a clearly identifiable owner, as board of directors, staff, volunteers, beneficiaries, the broader public, and government can all legitimately claim to have a stake in the organization. As a result, nonprofit leaders are accountable to multiple stakeholders, thus often facing contrasting demands and expectations.

The distinctiveness of nonprofit leadership and management stems from the complexity of nonprofit organizations. The following sections of the chapter will shed light on the nature of the nonprofit sector, the organizational and legal characteristics of nonprofit organizations, the role and functions of mission-driven organizations, and the size and scope of the sector. This preliminary overview of the sector and its entities will provide students with a framework to understand the contextual challenges of managing and leading nonprofit organizations.

THE NONPROFIT SECTOR AND NONPROFIT ORGANIZATIONS

Nonprofit sector and **nonprofit organizations** (NPOs) are only apparently precise and unequivocal terms that aim to define the space between state, market, and family. They are highly debated among academics and practitioners because they define a sector by what it is not; we would not, for example, define lettuce as a "non-animal" (Lohmann, 1989). In the United States, the use of the term "nonprofit" has also been criticized because in a culture obsessed with success this term may be equated with failure (Salamon, 1996a, p. 9). In spite of criticism, however, the term "nonprofit" effectively communicates the central idea of the sector, that is, donations are not used for personal benefit but rather for public causes (Schaffer, 2016).

Outside the American context, a diverse vocabulary defines the field, influenced either by cultural traditions or disciplinary perspectives (Salamon & Anheier, 2006). While in Great Britain (and historically also in the United States) **charitable and voluntary sector** emphasizes service provisions to the needy and the lack of coercion and restraint in participation, in the French-speaking countries **social economy** points to the solidarity and mutuality that characterize these actions. Outside the Western world, **nongovernmental sector** stresses a confrontational relationship between state and voluntary associations. More broadly, **third sector** (emphasis on the separation from both market and state—and perhaps household) and **civil society** (looks beyond the organizational boundaries of the nonprofit sector) find respectively a decreasing and increasing usage. Alternative definitions like **nonprofit and voluntary sector** (indicating the presence of both tax-exempt organizations and small informal groups) (Frumkin, 2005) and the normative **commons** find also their place in the literature (Lohmann, 1992).

The term "nonprofit" is—by emphasizing legal issues related to corporations bound by a non-distribution constraint—a tax-based definition. It is a relatively recent classification, as it was only introduced during the reorganization of the U.S. tax code in the decade following the end of the Second World War (Hall, 2003). Nonprofit organizations are defined in the **Internal Revenue Code**, primarily in **Section 501**. All the organizations listed in Table 1.1 are nonprofit organizations in the sense that they are exempted from paying taxes on income. However, only 501(c)3 organizations qualify to receive **tax deductible donations**, that is, individuals donating to a 501(c)3 can deduct the value of the gift on their income tax return (thus the actual cost of the donation is reduced by the tax savings).

Table 1.1

IRS Nonprofit Organizations Tax Code Categories

Tax Code Number	Description of Organization and Activities
501(c)(1)	Corporations Organized under Act of Congress (Instrumentalities of the United States)
501(c)(2)	Title Holding Corporation For Exempt Organization (Holding title to property of an exempt organization)
501(c)(3)	Religious, Educational, Charitable, Scientific, Literary, Testing for Public Safety, to Foster National or International Amateur Sports Competition, or Prevention of Cruelty to Children or Animals Organizations
501(c)(4)	Civic Leagues, Social Welfare Organizations, and Local Associations of Employees
501(c)(5)	Labor, Agricultural, and Horticultural Organizations (Educational or instructive, the purpose being to improve conditions of work, and to improve products of efficiency)
501(c)(6)	Business Leagues, Chambers of Commerce, Real Estate Boards, etc. (Improvement of business conditions of one or more lines of business)
501(c)(7)	Social and Recreational Clubs
501(c)(8)	Fraternal Beneficiary Societies and Associations (Lodge providing for payment of life, sickness, accident or other benefits to members)
501(c)(9)	Voluntary Employees Beneficiary Associations (Providing for payment of life, sickness, accident, or other benefits to members)
501(c)(10)	Domestic Fraternal Societies and Associations (Lodge devoting its net earnings to charitable, fraternal, and other specified purposes. No life, sickness, or accident benefits to members)
501(c)(11)	Teachers' Retirement Fund Associations (Teachers' association for payment of retirement benefits)
501(c)(12)	Benevolent Life Insurance Associations, Mutual Ditch or Irrigation Companies, Mutual or Cooperative Telephone Companies, etc.
501(c)(13)	Cemetery Companies (Burials and incidental activities)
501(c)(14)	Credit Unions and Other Mutual Financial Organizations (Loans to members)
501(c)(15)	Mutual Insurance Companies or Associations (Providing insurance to members substantially at cost)
501(c)(16)	Cooperative Organizations to Finance Crop Operations (Financing crop operations in conjunction with activities of a marketing or purchasing association)
501(c)(17)	Supplemental Unemployment Benefit Trusts
501(c)(18)	Employee Funded Pension Trust (created before June 25, 1959)

Continued

501(c)(19)	Veterans' Organizations
501(c)(20)	Group Legal Services Plan Organizations
501(c)(21)	Black Lung Benefit Trusts (Funded by coal mine operators to satisfy their liability for disability or death due to black lung diseases)
501(c)(22)	Withdrawal Liability Payment Fund
501(c)(23)	Veterans' Organization (created before 1880) (To provide insurance and other benefits to veterans)
501(c)(25)	Title Holding Corporations or Trusts with Multiple Parent Corporations
501(c)(26)	State-Sponsored Organization Providing Health Coverage for High-Risk Individuals
501(c)(27)	State-Sponsored Workers' Compensation Reinsurance Organization
501(c)(28)	National Railroad Retirement Investment Trust
501(c)(29)	CO-OP health insurance issuers

Source: Based on IRS (2016).

It is advantageous for organizations, their staff, and board members to register with the IRS. The primary advantage of incorporation is that liability is confined to the organization and thus does not extend to those who manage or govern it. **Personal liability** means that "one or more managers of a nonprofit organization (its trustees, directors, and/or key employees) may be found *personally* liable for something done or not done while acting on behalf of the organization" (Hopkins, 2013, p. 7). By contrast, a possible disadvantage of incorporation is that the state grants the corporate status and requires in return compliance with certain reporting and disclosure requirements (Hopkins, 2013). Overall, in spite of concerns about governmental overreach voiced in some corners, these requirements are not extensive and guarantee organizations' transparency and accountability.

501(c)3 organizations are organizations that must benefit the interests of the broad public. In this sense they are social benefit (public serving) organizations. They generally fall into two broad classes: **public charities** (multiple sources of funding) and private foundations (one single major source of funding). 501(c)3 organizations can receive **tax-deductible donations** from individuals and corporations because of their public-serving function. The charitable contribution deduction was enacted in 1917 by Congress with the aim to ensure that the income tax would not discourage private giving, and is today primarily justified as a **subsidy** (that is, the deduction helps to support the provision of goods and services that most likely would not be sufficiently provided by the free market) (Colinvaux, Galle, & Steuerle, 2016/2012).

To qualify for the 501(c)3 status, organizations must pass an organizational test, an operational test, and a community conscience test (Anheier, 2014; Bennet, 2016; Hopkins, 2016/2011). It is necessary to pass all three tests to obtain and maintain the 501(c)3 status.

1. **Organizational test:** The IRS determines whether the organization is organized and operates for one or more of eight purposes: Religious, Educational, Charitable, Scientific, Literary, Testing for Public Safety, to Foster National or International Amateur Sports Competition, or Prevention of Cruelty to Children or Animals Organizations.

2. **Operational test:** The IRS determines whether the organization's operations are consistent with the purposes of the 501(c)3 category. Firstly, an organization's primary activities must fall within the purposes of section 501(c)3. Secondly, nonprofit organizations must comply with the **non-distribution constraint** (i.e., the prohibition to distribute its financial surplus to those who control the use of organizational assets). Lastly, organizations are not allowed to participate in political activities (that is, supporting political campaigns and lobbying). It is important to remember, however, that 501(c)3 organizations are allowed to engage in lobbying as long as these activities do not represent a substantial part of the organization's activities. (Depending on the organization's expenditures, the IRS allows up to 20% of total expenditures to be used for lobbying activities.)

3. **Community conscience test:** Organizations may not be granted the 501(c)3 status if their primary purpose is contrary to the community conscience. This test is more normative and was introduced by the IRS in the 1970s and supported by the Supreme Court with the aim to not grant the charitable status to organizations that, for example, discriminate on the base of race, religion, gender, or sexual orientation.

The 501(c)3 category also includes **private foundations** in addition to traditional public charities. Foundations (such as the Bill & Melinda Gates Foundation, the Ford Foundation, and the Silicon Valley Community Foundation) differ from public charities in that:

1. They often have a **single donor** (an individual or a family);

2. They exist in **perpetuity** because funds are placed in an **endowment** and only annual returns are donated;

3. Funds are not directly used for charitable purposes but rather donated to nonprofit organizations;

4. They are required to pay out (the **payout rate**) 5% of their endowment every year.

As Table 1.2 shows, while most foundations are independent, private foundations, other types of foundations exist that vary in terms of primary activity, financial base, and use of funds.

Table 1.2

Philanthropic Foundations, by Type, Activity, Financial Base, and Use of Funds

	Activity	Financial Base	Use of Funds	Number, as of 2013	Examples
Independent foundation	Grantmaking	Endowed	Grants to NPOs	79,616 (91%)	Bill & Melinda Gates Foundation; Ford Foundation
Operating foundation	Program administration	Endowed	Operation of internal programs	4,169 (5%)	Open Society Institute; Lilly Cares Foundation, Inc.
Corporate foundation	Grantmaking and public relations	Endowed or unendowed	Grants to NPOS	2,577 (3%)	Novartis Patient Assistance Foundation, Inc.; The Wal-Mart Foundation, Inc.
Community foundation	Grantmaking and fundraising	Building endowment	Grants to organizations in the community (depending on the definition of community)	780 (1%)	Silicon Valley Community Foundation; Greater Kansas City Community Foundation

Sources: Adapted from Frumkin (2006), p. 220; Data from Foundation Center

In addition to the legal definition and requirements of nonprofit organizations, Salamon and Anheier (1992) have proposed a structural/operational definition based on five key features that allow for cross-national comparisons. According to the Johns Hopkins Comparative Nonprofit Sector Project (CNP), nonprofit organizations share the following crucial commonalities encompassing different legal and cultural traditions.

1. **Organized**, institutionalized to some meaningful extent.

2. **Private**, institutionally separate from government.

3. **Non-profit-distributing**, not returning profits generated to their owners or directors.

4. **Self-governed**, equipped to control their own activities.

5. **Voluntary**, involving some meaningful degree of voluntary participation.

The last element deserves further explanation. While volunteers represent a major economic force, the professionalization of the nonprofit sector over the last three decades has increased the role and importance of paid staff. "Voluntary" refers therefore not exclusively to the voluntary provision of time, money, and expertise, but more broadly (and importantly) to the absence of coercion. Individuals, in other words, join (or contribute to) voluntarily and are equally free to leave (or stop contributing to) a nonprofit organization whenever they want.

In contrast to public charities, **501(c)4 organizations** are civic leagues and advocacy organizations that aim to primarily serve their members. 501(c)4 organizations do not have restrictions on lobbying and advocacy because they do not qualify for tax deductible donations. The distinction between lobbying and advocacy can be confusing. **Advocacy** is the process by which nonprofit organizations raise awareness about certain issues that affect the lives of their stakeholders and constituents. By contrast, **lobbying** refers to a form of advocacy that attempts to directly influence a specific piece of legislation (either by supporting or by opposing it). Examples of 501(c)4 organizations are the Sierra Club and the National Rifle Association (NRA).

Much of the discussions of the nonprofit sector are rooted in the notion that the nonprofit sector is somehow different or distinct from the other societal sectors. The **blurring of sectorial boundaries**, however, threaten this distinctiveness. Sectorial descriptions of society have traditionally placed the nonprofit sector next to the other sectors that form society, namely the public sector, the private (business) sector, and in some accounts the family. Scholars have pointed out how the nonprofit sector's professionalization and marketization have eroded some of the distinctive features of nonprofit organizations (Salamon, 1993; Eikenberry & Kluver, 2004; Galaskiewics & Colman, 2006). Nonprofit organizations increasingly rely on earned income and business practices and, at the same time, businesses tend to pay more attention than before to the social impact of their operations. Likewise, as the discussion of third-party government will detail, the distinction between nonprofit sector and government has never been as clear-cut as commonly imagined.

Nonetheless, the emphasis on "voluntary" and "non-distribution constraint" in the definitions of nonprofit organizations allows for a differentiation between nonprofit sector, market, and state. The sector's **non-coercive** (or voluntary) nature distinguishes it from the state and, by making choices available, situates it closer to the market. The **non-distribution constraint** draws a separation line between market and nonprofit sector, and situates the latter closer to the state. In addition to these two features, Frumkin (2005) suggests that the **unclear lines of ownership and accountability** establish a third differentiating criteria. In contrast both to government and business, the nonprofit sector "serves many masters"; although "private,"

NPOs have not clearly identifiable **stakeholders** (donors, governments, boards, public, or clients).

The concept of philanthropy provides an additional way to clarify the distinction between society's three, or four, sectors. The etymological root of the word **philanthropy** is the Greek *philanthrōpia* (love of mankind). It is typically juxtaposed to **charity**, which is meant to refer to gifts aiming to alleviate immediate needs whereas philanthropy is thought to address social problems at their root causes (Sealander, 2003; Gross, 2003; Carnegie, 1981/1889). More broadly philanthropy has been defined as "the voluntary action for the public good" and characterized by the giving of talents, time, and treasure (Payton & Moody, 2008, pp. 27–61). According to this broad definition, philanthropy encompasses both individual inclinations and an organizational infrastructure and can be considered more a *tradition* rather than a sector.

By centering the discussion on sectorial boundaries around philanthropy, the contrast between the sectors becomes more intuitive. While political as well as market exchanges focus on the medium (between giver and receiver), namely money and votes (**effective demand**), philanthropy focuses directly on the people who have needs (**affective demand**) (Schervish, 2005). The nonprofit sector is normatively different from both business and state because of the role of philanthropic activities. The characterizing features of NPOs (i.e., non-coercive nature, non-distribution constraint, and unclear lines of accountability) and the distinguishing role of philanthropy clearly set the nonprofit world outside the domains of both market and state. This separation is analytical rather than empirical and the growing literature on the blurring boundaries between nonprofit, for-profit, and public sectors—while raising concerns about the uniqueness and purity of an overly sanctified sector—does not diminish the need and importance of this analytical distinction.

The role of the family as a separated sector in a sectorial model of society is often debated. Analytically, political economy and political philosophy have considered the family as a distinctive unit (Smith, 1976/1759; Smith, 2003/1776; Hegel, 1988/1830). The rules that regulate modern state, market, and nonprofit sector are often in open contrast to family life. In fact, the "monopoly on violence" characterizes the **state** (Weber, 1946/1918), personal economic interests drive the **market**, and civil society emphasizes choice over the sometimes exclusive and limiting bonds of families (Gellner, 1996). **Families** represent a threat to the rule of law established by the state, limit economic development, and hinder the expansion of pluralistic associational life (Fukuyama, 1995; Banfield, 1958). While families play a vital role in all societies, the historical transition from traditional to modern societies also implies moving from a family's role as an all-encompassing dimension to one limited to the private sphere (Bellah, Madsen, Sullivan, Swidler, & Tipton, 2008/1985). While in a large part of the developing world the family still remains at the center of political, social, economic, and associational life (Diamond, 2008), in the Western context the separation between a public and private sphere suggests the restriction of the family domain and the consequent development of associational life as a product of a shifting balance of forces between social classes and between these classes and state (Habermas, 1991; Bellah et al., 2008/1985).

As this review shows, the concepts of nonprofit organization and nonprofit sector hide a complex reality behind apparently clear definitions. Nonprofit organizations are at the same time different from and similar to businesses and public agencies. Furthermore, as a report of the Kellogg Foundation (2003) aptly pointed out, the blurring of sectorial boundaries created shared responsibilities and new spaces for social innovation, thus bringing a "wave of new questions and fresh ideas that are challenging nonprofit sector leaders" (p. 3). The tension between the multiple impulses of the nonprofit sector, the evolving roles of nonprofit leaders, and the nonprofit sector's ethical and legal distinctiveness require a clarification of the roles and functions of nonprofit organizations and, more broadly, an understanding of why the nonprofit sector exists at all.

THE ROLE OF THE NONPROFIT SECTOR IN SOCIETY

Scholars have advanced multiple **theoretical frameworks** to explain the existence of non-profit organizations. In a multidisciplinary field such as nonprofit studies, these theoretical approaches take different disciplinary bends.

1. **History** focuses on philanthropic and voluntary traditions and emphasizes changing social, economic, cultural, and political dynamics' influence on the shape of the sector;

2. **Sociology** points to the social dynamics, social actors, and social relationships that associational life creates;

3. **Political science** highlights more specifically the relationship between the nonprofit sector and the state, either focusing on output dynamics and thus stressing the resid-ual character of the nonprofit sector (welfare theories) or focusing on inputs and thus describing the prerequisites of stable democratic regimes (civil society approaches);

4. **Economics** interprets the nonprofit sector in economic terms underplaying social and political dynamics.

Ultimately, notwithstanding these differences, all theories try to understand why as a soci-ety we rely on nonprofit organizations for the provision of certain services and goods, rather than expecting state or market to provide them. The crucial question does therefore not focus on the variation in emphasis of these disciplinary perspectives, but rather on whether these approaches are compatible or contradictory.

One major theoretical framework integrates political and economic theories under the umbrella of the **three failure theory**. The theory rests on the distinction between private and public benefits and the related concepts of **pure public goods** and **pure private goods**

("goods" refer to things, products, and services—even when intangible) (Anheier, 2014). Pure public goods are nonrival and nonexcludable, whereas pure private goods are distinguished by the contemporary absence of these two characteristics.

1. **Nonrival goods** are goods whose consumption by one consumer does not prevent simultaneous consumption by other consumers. An example of a rival good is food because if you eat a slice of pizza that same slice cannot be consumed by somebody else. By contrast, a museum is nonrival because admiring a painting does not consume it to the point that somebody else cannot look at it as well.

2. **Nonexcludability** refers to cases when it is impossible or costly to prevent people from consuming the goods. Food and a museum are good examples of excludable goods, as it is easy to set a price for them and exclude people from eating the slice of pizza or entering the museum if they are not willing to pay the established price. However, it is more complicated to exclude individuals from the consumption of clean air or from the protection guaranteed by the police force and national defense. These goods are examples of nonexcludable goods.

According to this approach, market and the government fail in providing certain types of goods, hence the nonprofit sector steps in (Steinberg, 2006). In turn, however, even the nonprofit sector fails in providing some goods, thus requiring the cooperation of the other two sectors.

Markets fail in providing public goods, hence justifying governmental and nonprofit provision. First, markets do not provide all types of goods for the simple reason that some goods are not profitable. We as customers are often not willing to pay for certain services and goods, which—as in the case of for example water and national defense—we consider a basic right that the government has to provide for. Second, in some cases the market fails because of **contract failure** (Hansmann, 1987). Contract failure refers to the fact that when the quantity and quality of the service cannot be verified, profit-driven organizations may take advantage of informational asymmetries. In fact, when we do not have the expertise to evaluate the quality of certain goods or services, or when we are not the direct beneficiaries of those services (e.g., the senior citizen center for our parents), we hesitate to rely on profit-oriented organizations that could exploit these situations to their advantage. While governments can address this problem by providing the needed information or regulating the sector, nonprofits address this lack of trust because, due to the non-distribution-constraint, they appear more trustworthy.

However, the government cannot fully address markets' shortcomings and fails in certain areas. In a democratic state, a natural tendency of politics is to satisfy the majority of the electorate, as 51% of the votes usually guarantees re-election. As a result, public policies are often aimed at the average voter, hence public good provision will reflect the preferences of a **median voter**. In heterogeneous countries, therefore, the nonprofit sector emerges because governmental provision does not satisfy in quality or quantity the expectations of **high demanders**; denominational education for example is provided to a good degree through the nonprofit sector (Douglas, 1987). Additionally, besides the demand for public goods, also social entrepreneurs are needed for the emergence of NPOs (**supply-side theories**). The nonprofit sector is a place that allows individuals with vision to create new organizations and projects; in other words, the impulses, vision, and energy of founders are as important as the demands for goods and services in explaining the emergence of nonprofit organizations.

The nonprofit sector addresses therefore the shortcomings of market and state. However, as Salamon (1987) has pointed out, the relationship between nonprofit sector and government has historically been one of cooperation rather than of confrontation. In fact, the U.S. welfare state has historically relied on nonprofit organizations, which it supports directly via grants and contracts and indirectly through tax exemptions and deductions. We should therefore speak of a pattern of **third-party government**, that is, the use of private (or non-federal governmental entities and thus also NPOs) to carry out governmental purposes. The government does not displace the nonprofit sector, and the cooperative relationship that exists between state and nonprofit sector emerges from the historical reality that nonprofit organizations fail in providing certain goods.

Just like market and state, the nonprofit sector fails in providing goods and services (**voluntary failure** or **interference theory**). Nonprofit organizations incur in three major failures.

1. **Particularism** refers to the tendency to focus on a particular population (for example an ethnic or religious group) with the resulting risk of duplicating services and under-providing some types of services.

2. **Paternalism** refers to the tendency to treat problems as we perceive them rather than to "listen" to the population we aim to serve.

3. **Amateurism** refers to the tendency to rely on good-hearted and passionate individuals who, however, may lack in expertise and professionalism.

Although the nonprofit sector has historically been the "preferred mechanism" for providing collective goods, market and state have stepped in to address its shortcomings.

The three-failure theory partially integrates economic and political theories. The leading **political theory** sketched in the late-1980s by James Douglas emphasizes the role of NPOs in heterogeneous nations. While public services or goods that are supported by the majority of the population are provided by public agencies, those goods that are more controversial or preferred by a minority are provided by NPOs. This approach, however, analyzes and evaluates the state and the nonprofit sector on the basis of the provision of certain goods and services. It is, in other words, an approach that focuses on outputs (the services provided). Scholars have started stressing the role of inputs, namely the dynamics that contribute to establish, maintain, and strengthen democracies (Clemens, 2006; Zimmer & Freise, 2008).

The interest in the dynamics that create democratic practices of governance led to the interest in civil society and social capital. Both concepts are controversial and hard to define. A full review cannot find a place in this chapter but it should suffice to say that, despite some disagreement, civil society and social capital focus on factors such as associational life, public sphere, social connectedness and trust, and civility in building and strengthening democratic societies. Broadly speaking, **civil society** refers to those practices and norms that help mediating between the different political, social, and economic interests of individuals, thus allowing them to participate in public affairs without losing sight of the common interest (Weber, 2013; Weber, 2015a). In practice, this translates into an attention to a space of society between state, market, and family where people associate voluntary for the common good (Anheier, 2004), with a focus on both the infrastructure of civil society, that is, associational life and nonprofit sector, and its normative underpinnings, namely civility (Edwards, 2014; Sievers, 2010; Shils, 1997).

Social capital describes the relationships between individuals that are created within associational life. Besides physical capital (objects like a hammer) and human capital (e.g., skills and education), social capital points to the importance of relationships based on **trust** and **reciprocity** at both the individual and group level. It refers to the benefits that derive from membership in social networks. At the individual level, social capital helps to explain the functioning of business transactions, as contracts could not work in the absence of an at least basic level of mutual trust (Coleman, 1988; Fukuyama, 1995). At a societal level, widespread social capital, even if unequally distributed, supports the working of democracy, as a healthy democratic state is rooted in the engagement of its citizens and thus could hardly fully function without networks of trust, social cohesion, and reciprocity (Putnam, 1993; Putnam, 2001). Civil society and social capital thus draw attention to the contributions of voluntary and nonprofit organizations to democracy.

By explaining the existence of the nonprofit sector, theoretical frameworks also provide us with a better understanding of the **roles and functions** of nonprofit organizations. By drawing on several leading theories, Peter Frumkin (2005) has developed a helpful matrix that allows us to identify key functions of nonprofit organizations. This matrix allows us to organize the multiple roles that are commonly identified in the literature (Salamon, 2012; Payton & Moody, 2008; Smith, 2016/1973) in basic categories. Some functions respond to an **instrumental rationale**, that is, nonprofit organizations are important instruments for the accomplishment of certain goals.

- ► **Service delivery function**: the nonprofit sector provides important services and in so doing responds to market and state failure. The service-provision function can differ in complexity (ranging from soup kitchens and homeless shelters to health centers and hospitals) and nature (ranging from human services to cultural centers and museums).
- ► **Social entrepreneurship function**: the nonprofit sector provides creative individuals with the means "to pursue their diverse and at times controversial visions" (Frumkin,

2005). While definitions of the social entrepreneur vary significantly (Anheier, 2014; Worth, 2017), emphasis is commonly placed on nonprofit organizations as viable tools for innovations and on the motivations of the founders/entrepreneurs. Muhammed Yunus, the founder of the **Grameen Bank** and pioneer of **microfinance**, is a good and celebrated example of social entrepreneurship.

By contrast, other roles follow an **expressive rationale,** that is, nonprofit organizations allow individuals (donors, volunteers, founders, staff) to express values, faith, and beliefs through work, volunteering, and philanthropy.

▶ **Civic and political engagement function**: the nonprofit sector provides individuals with multiple ways to participate in the political process. Nonprofit organizations build community and social capital (think of the myriad of small organizations that make up our community life), promote civic engagement, advocate for a variety of causes, and lobby for various legislative issues.

▶ **Values and faith function**: the nonprofit sector allows individuals to express values and commitments. Values and faith are in many cases the engines of nonprofit organizations (often more than particular demands or needs) because volunteering, donating, and working for a nonprofit organization often represent meaningful ways for individuals to create connections between work activities and deeply held beliefs.

As this brief review of theories shows, nonprofit organizations play multiple roles in our societies and have a major impact on our lives. Nonprofit organizations provide basic services such as food for the hungry and shelter for the homeless. They raise awareness and advocate for multiple specific causes such as drunk driving, gun violence, and sexual abuse. They represent laboratories of social innovation, as exemplified by the proliferation of microfinance institutions. They give voice to minorities as well as marginalized groups through organizations such as the National Association for the Advancement of Colored People (NAACP). They allow for opportunities of self-development such as in the case of the multiple youth and mentorship organizations that exist in our societies. They provide for safe spaces to express our beliefs and faith in the form of churches, mosques, and synagogues. These multiple roles of the nonprofit sector are deeply rooted in a long history of associational life in the United States, and it is to this history that we will turn in the next section.

THE NONPROFIT SECTOR'S LONG HISTORICAL ROOTS

The history of the nonprofit sector in the United States points to a complex mix of continuities and changes. America's **exceptionalism** is rooted in the historical role of voluntary and nonprofit organizations in U.S. society (Bell, 1989). This review cannot provide an exhaustive overview of this history and therefore primarily aims to provide a historical background to the trends toward professionalism and commercialization introduced in the earlier parts of this chapter. In so doing, this history will also provide a better understanding of the particular challenges of nonprofit leadership and management. The following section will highlight the appearance of charities in the colonial era, the development of associational life over the course of the nineteenth century, the emergence of scientific philanthropy at the turn of the twentieth century, and the trend toward professionalism and commercialism at the end of the twentieth century.

Voluntary action is an inherent aspect of American civic participation and a foundational element of American democratic engagement since the **colonial era**. In the colonial period, voluntary associations and charitable giving emerged only slowly, although settlers were not unfamiliar with them. Around the turn of the eighteenth century, the growth of trade, the integration of the colonies into the British commercial system, and renewed immigration disrupted the older form of community and forced Americans to rethink charitable models. In the decades prior to the Revolutionary War associational practices started to spread in commercial centers as well as in rural areas. Inspired by the Great Awakening, which gave politics a spiritual dimension and legitimized resistance to tyranny, these associations were effective in creating political unity during the conflict with Great Britain (Hall, 2006).

Over the course of the **nineteenth century**, Americans embraced the associational form. Having witnessed and relied on the strength of organizations in the years leading to the War of Independence, political elites were initially wary of the threats that associations could pose to the stability of the newly established Federation (Hall, 2006). Nonetheless, after the American Revolution, the tendency was favorable to associations and the Supreme Court's ruling in ***Dartmouth College v. Woodward*** (1819) started an American law of charity by protecting corporations from legislative interference (McGarvie, 2003). In this same period, **Alexis de Tocqueville** (2006/1835–40) chronicled Americans' reliance on associations to counterbalance the individualistic tendencies inherent to democratic societies, as numerous types of non-profit organizations including religious institutions, mutual aid societies, trust funds, and the first of the general purpose foundations emerged (Hammack & Anheier, 2013; McCarthy, 2005; Beito, 1999; Skocpol, 2004).

As observed by de Tocqueville, voluntary organizations became the seeds of emerging practices of **democratic governance**. Associational membership became a pathway to democratic citizenship by training citizenship skills and offering leadership opportunities, fostering cooperation across social classes, supporting civic virtues, and providing avenues of public discussion and political mobilization (Skocpol, 2004). The involvement in charitable organizations provided women with the means to participate in public affairs well before they won the right to vote (McCarthy, 2003; Goss, 2013). Associations thus served to counterbalance the growing influence of elites and the erosion of traditional communities and family ties, as well as to provide politically marginalized groups with avenues of participation in American political society.

The development of voluntary associations in the second half of the nineteenth century paralleled, and was possible because of, the expansion of the federal government. Improved navigation and transportation systems, as well as the U.S. postal service, favored the development of large **federated membership organizations** such as the American Temperance Society, the Free Masons, and the Young Men's Christian Association (Skocpol, 2004). In the same period, criticism of slavery became a major source of new philanthropic and associational endeavors and contributed to nationalize public life (Hall, 2006). **Immigration** waves also spurred the development of voluntary associations, both directly with the proliferation of ethnic-based organizations and indirectly with the emergence of societies that viewed the new immigrants as a threat to America (Kaufman, 2002).

During the decades around the **Civil War**, elites became increasingly involved in establishing charitable institutions. Reconstruction with its emphasis on volunteer workforce, the resistance of White Southerners through voluntary associations such as the Ku Klux Klan, and the creation of foundations addressing the economic and political repression of African Americans emphasized once again the new centrality of philanthropy and associations in American life (Hall, 2006). The creation of the **U.S. Sanitary Commission,** with its emphasis on science-based expertise, and the **U.S. Christian Commission,** with a focus on individual spirituality and relief of suffering, pinpoint the coexistence of two approaches to social problems, which are commonly identified with the notion of charity, rooted in Christian compassion, and philanthropy with its scientific approach to social issues (Gross, 2003; Hall, 2006).

The development of two competing traditions emphasizing scientific approaches and compassion characterized the turn of the twentieth century. The new modern philanthropic foundation brought these changes to the foreground by seeking solutions to societal problems through **scientific philanthropy**. Modern philanthropic foundations epitomized the transition from charity to philanthropy. Philanthropists such as **Andrew Carnegie** and **John D. Rockefeller, Sr.** preferred business-like approaches to "indiscriminate charity" (Carnegie, 1981/1889; Chernow, 2004; Nasaw, 2007). These new philanthropists viewed charity as an inefficient impulse to personal service and to acts of compassion, and—as a reaction—transferred rules and organizational models that had made their businesses successful to their newly established philanthropic foundations. These large general purpose foundations supported broad areas such as public health, medical standards, and higher education (Karl & Katz, 1981; Hammack, 1999). Additionally, these organizations increased their scope beyond the national level, thus pointing to a new internationalism of American elites (Weber, 2015b). The growth of foundations was paralleled by an increase of mass philanthropy for national causes and progressive era calls for state interventions in what appeared to be social problems' structural causes (Zunz, 2012).

Over the course of the **twentieth century**, we can observe the progressive diverging of the realities of a complex, modern society from the cherished tradition of volunteerism. The two world wars and the Great Depression required the central government to mobilize resources on a scale it had never done before. Still, the federal government nominally maintained America's traditional emphasis on voluntary action by framing the military draft during World War I as "service" to the nation (Kennedy, 1982). The new expanded role of the federal government was supported by the establishment of the **income tax**, which after World War II made the **tax exempt status** of charitable organizations significant for donors, leading to a growth in the number of recognized nonprofit organizations. Whereas before the war few nonprofit organizations filed with the Internal Revenue Service for recognition, after the war the number of nonprofits grew from an estimated 12,000 organizations in the 1940s to 600,000 by the 1970s (Hall, 2003). The growth of the nonprofit sector was related to the expansion of the U.S. welfare system, as this system relied upon nonprofit organizations to provide services (Hammack, 2005). Nonetheless, America remained in the public imaginary a **nation of joiners** (Schlesinger, 1944) and celebrates its voluntary associations in spite of the increasing complexity of life in a modern, industrialized society.

With the **Reagan Administration** the nonprofit sector faced new challenges as federal financial support for social services significantly decreased. The Reagan Administration's policies aimed at shifting the responsibilities of service provision from federal programs to the nonprofit sector but did not consider the reality of a sector that was largely supported financially by grants from and contracts with federal agencies. As a result, by cutting federal funds, these new public policies pressured nonprofit organizations to do more with fewer resources, and consequentially to seek alternative sources of financial support. By turning increasingly to fees and service charges, however, NPOs entered in competition with for-profit service providers. While the sector's growth in the 1980s testifies to its resilience, this expansion stemmed from an increasing **commercialization** (Salamon, 1993; Salamon, 1996b). This new reality drastically altered the outlook of the nonprofit sector with charity, altruism, and reliance on private philanthropy losing in centrality. As discussed at the beginning of this chapter, this trend toward commercialization continued over the past decades, thus challenging traditional views of the nonprofit sector and making the work of nonprofit leaders more sophisticated and complex.

The nonprofit sector's transformed nature also had an impact on the health of American democracy. In the 1980s and 1990s, the so-called **civic engagement debate** developed out of concerns with dropping voting rates, declining trust in governmental institutions, and decreasing membership in voluntary associations (Skocpol & Fiorina, 1999). A sector in which specialized, professionally-run organizations replaced large membership organizations could not fulfill anymore in the eyes of many the crucial task of developing leadership and citizenship skills (Skocpol, 2004; Goss, 2013). **Robert Putnam** rapidly became the face of the debate by painting a worrisome picture of America where "more Americans are bowling today than ever before, but bowling in organized leagues has plummeted in the last decade or so"

(Putnam, 1993, p. 70), thus making **bowling alone** the symbol of a society with eroding social links. While the civic engagement debate has lost centrality in public discourse and the emergence of protest movements as diverse as **Occupy Wall Street**, **Tea Party**, and **Black Lives Matter** seem to point to a new wave of engagement (Traub, 2011; Andersen, 2011), the professionalization and commercialization of the nonprofit sector might have channeled grassroots initiatives outside the nonprofit sector.

This history of voluntary and nonprofit organizations undermines traditional visions of the nonprofit sector. First, by increasingly relying on commercial revenues, competing with for-profits for government contracts, and moving toward new philanthropic models and social entrepreneurship, the internal balance of the nonprofit sector seems to be moving from the impulses of civic activism and voluntarism to those of commercialism and professionalism. These developments risk undermining the role of nonprofit organizations in supporting civil society, lead to shifts in mission and structure, and widen the distance between NPOs and their constituencies (Eikenberry & Kluver, 2004; Eikenberry, 2009; Hwang & Powell, 2009).

It will be important to the health of the nonprofit sector to maintain a balance between four different—at times contrasting—impulses that influence the working of nonprofit organizations (Salamon, 2012):

1. **Voluntarism** refers to a vision of the nonprofit sector that relies primarily on volunteers, is informal, often religiously motivated, supported primarily by charitable contributions, and with few or no ties to government;

2. **Professionalism** refers to a vision of the nonprofit sector centered on well trained experts, with a paid and professional staff, an emphasis on subject-matter knowledge, and a cooperative relationship with public agencies;

3. **Civic activism** refers to a vision of the nonprofit sector that views nonprofit organizations as the means to address the structural—social, economic, and political—inequalities that cause social problems, thus emphasizing advocacy and engagement over basic service provision;

4. **Commercialism** refers to a nonprofit sector that increasingly relies on earned income and fees for services, competes with for-profit service providers, and combines commercial and social goals.

Professionalism and commercialism should, however, not be exclusively seen as negative trends. In fact, these changes react to the awareness of a mismatch between (social, economic, and environmental) needs and (philanthropic and governmental) resources (Salamon, 2014). New models of philanthropy and social investment are needed to address the multiple social problems that characterize our society.

On a second level, the history of voluntary and nonprofit organizations is not one lacking **dark sides**, as organizations pursuing divisive, violent, exclusionary, and discriminatory goals abound. As we have seen in the discussion of the roles and functions of nonprofit organizations, individuals rely on voluntary associations to express deeply held beliefs, and these beliefs may be discriminatory, divisive, and inspired by hate. It should not be surprising therefore that the **Ku Klux Klan** was a "voluntary" association in spite of its hateful socio-political goals. Particularly during the 1920s, the Klan combined a rhetoric of hate and racist, violent, and exclusionary practices directed toward African Americans, Catholics, and immigrants with philanthropic and community-oriented endeavors aiming to strengthen a sense of belonging within group members (Moore, 1991). This perverse dynamic of inclusion and exclusion on the basis of race, religion, and ethnicity challenges common visions of the nonprofit sector.

The dark side of the nonprofit sector is not limited to organizations that promote bigotry and hate. In fact, as self-governing institutions, voluntary organizations have been historically able to set **exclusionary membership criteria** based on gender, race, and sexual orientation. It is against this background that we have to understand some of the provisions regulating the nonprofit sector, such as the **community conscience test** used by the IRS to grant the 501(c)3 status. It was for example only a controversial ruling by the Supreme Court in *Roberts v. United States Jaycees* (1984) that forced the United States Junior Chamber (a leadership training and civic organization, also known as the Jaycees) to admit women as regular members (Brody, 2006, p. 245; Rosenblum, 1998).

Both the existence of a "bad civil society" (Chambers & Kopstein, 2001) and the trends of professionalization and commercialization challenge common myths about the nonprofit sector. Nonprofit organizations have long roots in our history and their unique legal, cultural, and social role in society derives from this history. At the same time, the changing dynamics of our society have also modified the characteristics of the nonprofit sector. The challenging task of nonprofit leaders will be to negotiate between a **survival imperative** and **distinctiveness imperative**, that is, maintaining the nonprofit sector's normative distinctiveness while also relying on business approaches in order to guarantee the sector's financial survival (Salamon, 2012). Today, as we will see in the next section, the nonprofit sector is an economic powerhouse, a major employer, and as diverse as possibly imaginable by combining large organizations with billions of assets and small, informal organizations.

SIZE AND SCOPE OF THE NONPROFIT SECTOR

Mapping the nonprofit sector is not an easy task. Attempts to reliably measure the size and scope of the nonprofit sector started in 1977 with the Commission on Private Philanthropy and Public Needs (Filer Commission). Data on the nonprofit sector are limited because estimates are extrapolated from various sources that use different definitions, separating nonprofit organizations from other organizations in government statistics is complicated, and government data on employment exclude most organizations with less than four employees (Boris & Steuerle, 2006). While some attempts have been made to capture the full composition and structure of some regional nonprofit sectors (most notoriously the Indiana Nonprofit Project directed by Kirsten Grønbjerg), most scholars rely on data provided by the **National Center for Charitable Statistics (NCCS)**, which is the national repository of data on the nonprofit sector in the United States. These data are used by the **Urban Institute** to compile the annual *Nonprofit Sector in Brief*, which presents key information on the size and scope of the nonprofit sector.

The NCCS derives its data from information that tax-exempt nonprofit organizations file with the IRS. In reviewing these data, however, we must distinguish between **registered** and **reporting** nonprofit organizations. Most state laws require public charities that are incorporated to register either annually or periodically. This registration requirement serves to confirm and update contact information and—in most states—is required for nonprofit organizations that engage in soliciting donations. These latter state law requirements are commonly known as "charitable solicitation regulations," as fundraising activities are regulated by states. In addition, nonprofit organizations that are recognized as tax exempt are required to file an annual report, **Form 990**, with the IRS. However, approximately two-thirds of all organizations that register with the IRS do not file Form 990. Religious congregations, some other religious organizations, and organizations with less than $25,000 in gross receipts are not required to file Form 990. IRS statistics therefore exclude many small, informal (grassroots) organizations and as a result may underestimate the real dimension of the nonprofit sector by around 90% (Smith, 1997).

The 2015 edition of *The Nonprofit Sector in Brief*, published by the Urban Institute and based on NCCS data, reported **1.41 million nonprofit organizations** registered with the IRS. In 2013, approximately 950,000 organizations were classified as public charities, which thus composed over two thirds of all registered nonprofits (McKeever, 2015). This number includes all organizations classified under the 501(c)3 section, with the exclusion of private foundations. As Figure 1.1 shows, 501(c)3 public charities represent the lion's share of registered nonprofit organizations, and over the period from 2003 to 2013 they grew by 19.5% (McKeever, 2015). Together, 501(c)3 and 501(c)4 organizations compose 73% of all tax-exempt organizations.

The **2007–09 recession** had an impact on the nonprofit sector, although it also testified to its reliance. The recession led to both higher closure rates and a loss of revenue among organizations with revenues between $50,000 and $99,999. While overall during the recession period the number of charities with $50,000 or more in revenue did not substantially change, they

Figure 1.1

Overview of nonprofit organizations in the United States by number, as of 2013

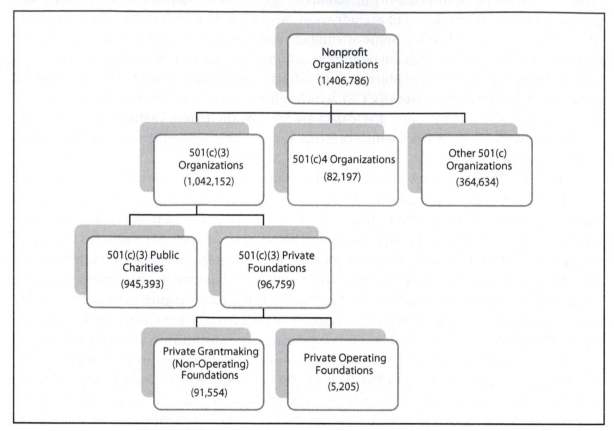

Source: Based on 2013 data from the National Center of Charitable Statistics (http://nccsweb.urban.org/PubApps/profile1.php?state=US)

faced the combined pressure of reduced government funding, declines in contributed revenue, and rising needs (Brown, McKeever, Dietz, Koulish, & Pollak, 2013). The largest closure rate was among international organizations, whereas closure rates of human service organizations significantly varied by size, with smaller organizations more likely to close than similar organizations in other subsectors and larger organizations less likely to close than other organizations at the same revenue level (Dietz, McKeever, Brown, Koulish, & Pollak, 2014).

The sheer number of public charities does not do justice to the great variations that exist within the U.S. charitable sector.

Figure 1.2

Number and Expenses of Reporting Public Charities as a Percentage of All Reporting Public Charities and Expenses, 2013

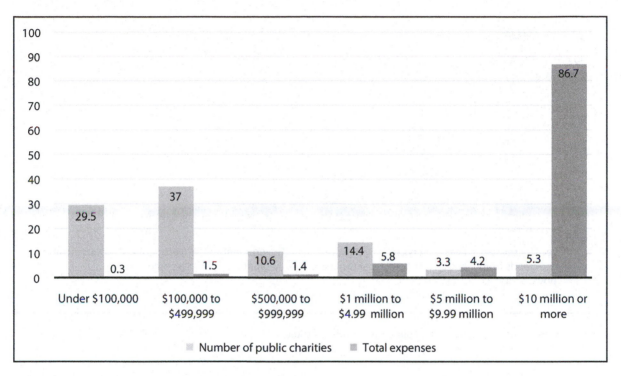

Source: McKeever, 2015. Copyright © 2015. Courtesy of the Urban Institute.

Figure 1.2 shows that three quarters of all public charities had less than $500,000 in expenses and accounted for less than 2% of all the expenditures of reporting public charities. By contrast, less than 5% of all public charities accounted for 86.7% of all expenditures. This disproportion points to a basic reality of the U.S. nonprofit sector, which is dominated in terms of revenues and expenditures by a few very large charities, whereas the majority of organizations are small.

The **revenue structure** of the nonprofit sector is much more diverse than commonly expected by the broader public. As anticipated in the previous sections of the chapter, the nonprofit sector as a whole does not substantially rely on private contributions. On the contrary, as Figure 1.3 shows, private contributions only account for 13.3% of all the revenues of reporting public charities.

Figure 1.3

Revenue Sources of Reporting Public Charities as Percentage, 2013 Data

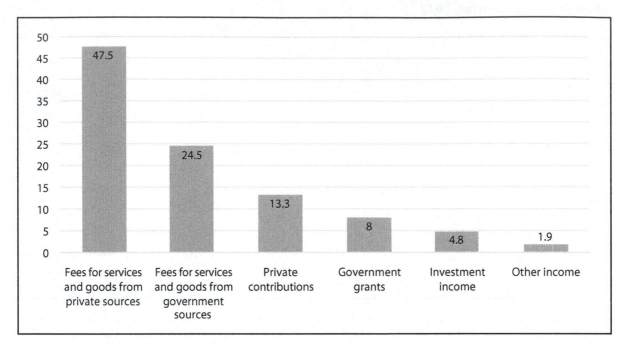

Source: McKeever, 2015. Copyright © 2015 Courtesy of the Urban Institute.

On average, the nonprofit sector primarily depends on fees for services (47.5%) and government contracts and grants (32.5%). The fact that one third of the revenues of the nonprofit sector comes from government sources points to the close cooperation between government and nonprofit sector in the United States. Revenue sources do, however, significantly vary across subsector. It should not be surprising that fees for services and commercial income play a crucial role in education-related organizations (think about universities' tuitions and apparel and gear) and health-related organizations, whereas government sources are more significant in human service organizations and private philanthropy is dominant in arts and culture organizations (Anheier, 2014).

The inner diversity of the nonprofit sector clearly emerges when we compare organizations by type. As organizations significantly differ across areas and fields, it is helpful to speak about **subsectors** of the nonprofit sector. Table 1.3 clearly shows how nonprofit organizations vary in terms of numbers, revenues, expenses, and assets across subsectors. Data on revenues, expenditures, and assets vividly picture the disproportion that exists across subsectors of the U.S. nonprofit sector.

Table 1.3

Number and Finances of Reporting Public Charities by Subsector, 2013

	Number	Percentage total	Dollar Total (Billions)			Percentage of Total		
			Revenues	Expenses	Assets	Revenues	Expenses	Assets
All public charities	293,103	100	1,734.10	1,623.8	3,225	100	100	100
Arts, culture, and humanities	29,136	9.9	33.6	30.2	110.7	1.9	1.9	3.4
Education	50,262	17.1	296.3	269.2	958.1	17.1	16.6	29.7
Higher education	2,050	0.7	188.1	174.6	617.7	10.8	10.8	19.2
Other education	48,212	16.4	108.2	94.6	340.3	6.2	5.8	10.6
Environment and animals	13,283	4.5	16.7	14.7	41.4	1	0.9	1.3
Health	37,732	12.9	1,025.30	975.8	1,392.80	59.1	60.10	43.2
Hospitals & primary care facilities	7,062	2.4	864	823.9	1,133.50	49.8	50.7	35.1
Other health care	30,670	10.5	161.3	151.9	259.3	9.3	9.4	8
Human services	104,002	35.5	214.2	206.9	331.5	12.4	12.7	10.3
International and foreign affairs	6,305	2.2	32.4	30.8	39.3	1.9	1.9	1.2
Public and social benefit	34,081	11.6	100.2	82.8	315.2	5.8	5.1	9.8
Religion-related	18,302	6.2	15.4	13.5	36	0.9	0.8	1.1

Source: McKeever, 2015. Copyright © 2015. Courtesy of the Urban Institute.

For example, while health-related organizations compose only 12.9% of reporting public charities, they account for 59.1% of revenues, 60.1% of expenditures, and 43.2% of assets. By contrast, human service organizations compose 35.5% of all organizations but account only for 12.4% of revenues, 12.7% of expenditures, and 10.3% of assets. The financial dominance of the health and education subsectors should not come as a surprise because it depends on the financial strength of hospitals and universities.

The nonprofit sector plays a large role in the U.S. economy. In 2013, the nonprofit sector contributed approximately $905.9 billion to the US economy in 2013, thus accounting for 5.4% of the country's gross domestic product (McKeever, 2015, p. 1). As Figure 1.4 shows, the nonprofit sector employed over 10 million workers in 2010, thus accounting for approximately 10% of U.S. total private **employment** and making the sector the third largest among U.S. industries. This means that one out of ten Americans works for a nonprofit organization.

Figure 1.4

Employment in the Nonprofit Sector vs. Selected Industries, 2010

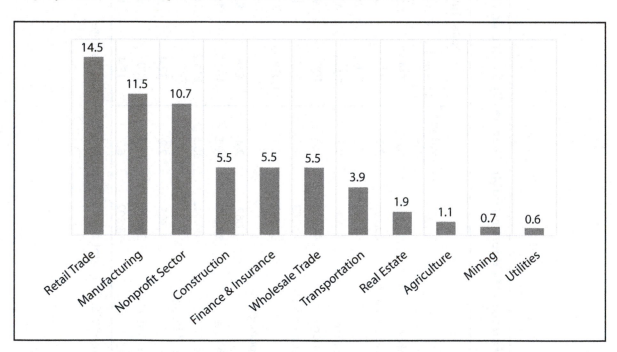

Source: Lester M. Salamon, S. Wojciech Sokolowski, and Stephanie L. Geller, "Holding the Fort: Nonprofit Employment During a Decade of Turmoil," *Nonprofit Economic Data Bulletin No. 39.* (Baltimore: Johns Hopkins Center for Civil Society Studies, January 2012). Available at: http://ccss.jhu.edu/publications-findings/?did=369.

Nonprofit jobs are, however, not equally distributed across subsectors, as the service fields of health care (57%), education (15%), and social assistance (13%) account for the vast majority of the sector's employment (Salamon, Sokolowski, & Geller, 2010). The sector is thus a major economic force and has fared well in comparison to both the public and the business sector over the past decade, thus showing its reliance in face of the economic recession.

The level of **private giving** is another sign of the economic strength of the nonprofit sector. Although, as we have seen, private contributions do not account for the majority of the nonprofit sector's revenues, a comparison of voting and giving data for the year 2012 shows that Americans are more likely to give than to vote (Goldberg, 2016). In 2015, private contributions totaled $373.25 billion, an increase of 4.1% from the previous year, and equal to 2.1% of the national gross domestic product (Giving USA, 2016). As Figure 1.5 shows, individuals were the largest contributor with 71%, followed by foundations with 16%, bequests with 9%, and corporations with 5%. Religion was by far the largest recipient category with 32% of all private contributions, followed by education with 15%, and human services with 12% (Giving USA, 2016).

Data on **volunteering** are a last measure often considered to assess the role of the nonprofit sector in American society. In 2015, 24.9% of Americans volunteered through or for an

Figure 1.5

Contributions by Source, as a Percentage

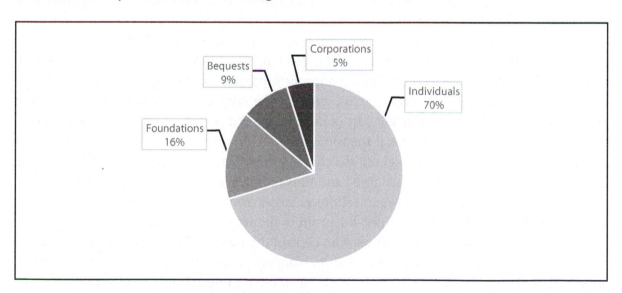

Source: Giving USA Foundation™. Copyright © 2015. Reprinted by permission.

organization at least once (U.S. Bureau of Labor Statistics, 2016). The data collected by the U.S. Bureau of Labor Statistics (2016) show that women on average volunteer at higher rates than men and that, by age, the 35- to 44-year-olds and 45- to 54-year-olds were the most likely to volunteer. Americans volunteer most frequently for religious organizations (33.1%), followed by educational or youth service related organizations (25.2%), and social or community service organizations (14.6%) (U.S. Bureau of Labor Statistics, 2016).

These data paint a very rich and complex picture of the nonprofit sector. The American nonprofit sector is extremely diverse not only in terms of type of organization but also in regard to finances. Huge differences in expenditures, revenues, and assets exist between the different organizations that form the sector. At the same time, the revenue structure dispels some common myths regarding the sector. Government sources are a significant form of support across organizational types. It should be pointed out that the government indirectly supports also those organizations that predominantly rely on donations, as donations to 501(c)3 organizations are tax deductible. Likewise, the central role of fees for services in the revenue structure of nonprofit organizations points to the reality of a sector that sharply contrasts with the common vision of a sector rooted in volunteering and philanthropy. Nonetheless, volunteering and philanthropy are still an important component of American tradition and identity, as the data discussed at the end of this chapter show.

SUMMARY

A common theme of this chapter is the professionalization of nonprofit work. Two related issues have been addressed in regard to the nonprofit professional. First, it is time to dismiss old and preconceived notions that view working in the nonprofit sector in terms of service and volunteering rather than professionalism. Working for a nonprofit organization is, today, a professional choice like many others. Nonprofit organizations employ paid staff and professionals with expertise in various areas, and—as the chapter has shown—mission-driven organizations represent a significant part of the U.S. economy. Second, while ideals of service, volunteering, and compassion are at the root of the sector, nonprofit professionals are, today, professionals. As discussed throughout the chapter, the reality of the nonprofit sector is much more complex than commonly imagined and thus requires expertise and professionalism.

The complexity of nonprofit organizations emerges from the difficulty to define them precisely. Nonprofit organizations are not-for-profit in the sense that they are not allowed to distribute a surplus among the individuals who control their assets. Rather, any surplus must be reinvested in the organization and its mission. Nonprofit organizations are, therefore, organizations that are private (as opposed to public agencies) and do not pay taxes on income. The sector thus includes organizations as diverse as soup kitchens and homeless shelters, the Red

Cross, the National Rifle Association (NRA), Harvard University, the Bill and Melinda Gates Foundation, World Vision International, and large hospital systems. The chapter introduced the 501(c) categories, the difference between tax exemption and tax deductibility, and the diverging concepts of charity and philanthropy.

The more theoretical discussion of the roles and functions of nonprofit organizations has addressed the foundational question of our profession. That is, why does the nonprofit sector exist in the first place? The chapter reviews political and economic theories, thus pointing to a variety of crucial roles nonprofit organizations play in our society. Nonprofit organizations provide crucial services, advocate for causes, are the means to express values and entrepreneurial forces, and symbolize pluralism. This variety of roles and functions can often coexist within one single organization, as a homeless shelter provides crucial services to the homeless but at the same time may raise awareness about the social causes of homelessness, provide individuals with the means to express their values and beliefs through work or volunteering, and offer entrepreneurial and innovative solutions through the structuring and development of its programs. These multiple roles add a layer of complexity to the work of nonprofit leaders and managers, who always have to wear multiple hats.

The brief review of the historical roots of the nonprofit sector in America stresses additional fundamental themes. Nonprofit organizations—or more correctly voluntary organizations—are an intrinsic part of the history and traditions of the United States. Americans have historically self-organized to solve social problems of all kinds. This long history explains the common narrative that views the nonprofit sector as rooted in volunteerism, service, and charity, although this vision does not correspond anymore to reality. At the same time, however, understanding and even welcoming the professionalization and commercialization of sector as a result of the Reagan Administration policies does not mean rejecting the ethical values that underpin the sector. The nonprofit sector is not like the business or the public sector, in spite of the blurring of sectorial lines and the increasing importance of contracts, fees, and earned income. The history of the nonprofit sector should teach any aspiring leader of the sector that, in order to maintain the legitimacy of the sector, professionalism and a willingness to serve should go hand in hand, even if this appears to be and indeed is a daunting task.

Lastly, the chapter has shown how the nonprofit sector is a major component of the U.S. economy. The number of organizations, revenues and expenditure, and nonprofit employment data paint the picture of a healthy and thriving sector that is growing in spite of the recession. The financial strength of the sector further shows that the nonprofit sector is not only a legitimate but also a logical career option for many students entering the job market. At the same time, however, in reviewing the size and scope of the nonprofit sector students should understand that working in the nonprofit sector can significantly differ depending on subsector. Revenue structure, size, and financial capabilities vary significantly across organizational type.

This chapter serves as a broad introduction to the nonprofit sector. As such, it provides students with foundational information on key concepts, roles and functions of nonprofit organizations, historical roots of the nonprofit sector, and size and scope of the sector. The following chapters of this volume—focusing on leadership, human resource management, program development, financial management, and risk management—rest on the broad framework laid out in this introductory chapter. While the remaining chapters focus primarily on the internal working of nonprofit organizations and the skills and competencies needed by nonprofit leaders and managers, this chapter's goal was to both dispel some of the common myths that surround the nonprofit sector and discuss some of the contextual factors that influence the work of nonprofit organizations. This chapter has addressed the Nonprofit Academic Centers Council (NACC) Undergraduate Curricular Guideline 2, Foundations of Civil Society, Voluntary Action and Philanthropy.

REFLECTION AND APPLICATION

1. What combination of soft skills, technical and managerial competencies, and policy and legal knowledge is in your opinion required to successfully lead a nonprofit organization?

_____

_____

_____

_____

_____

_____

2. Explain the differences between tax exemption and tax deduction. How does this difference relate to the limitations on lobbying that are imposed on 501(c)3 organizations?

_____

_____

_____

_____

_____

_____

_____

_____

_____

_____

3. The IRS treats all 501(c)3 organizations in the same way, thus equating (giving the same value to) for example a soup kitchen serving the poor and a symphony providing entertainment for the wealthy. Should we really treat this diverse universe of nonprofit organizations (soup kitchens, homeless shelters, museums, symphonies, hospitals, etc.) in the same way? Or should we rather establish clear priorities (a hierarchy of needs)? In other words, we could also ask, what are the "public purposes" of art and culture organizations that place them on the same level as human service organization? And, what is the public interest in fostering these organizations through tax exemptions?

_____

_____

_____

_____

_____

4. What is your opinion about the professionalization of the nonprofit sector? Does it really undermine the essence of a world we like to imagine as being rooted in altruism, notions of service and benevolence, and voluntarism? Or, is the professionalization trend to be welcomed? Professionals will help overcome the naiveté of "do-gooders," limit the amateurism of volunteers, and manage nonprofits like businesses (that is, efficiently in the common imaginary).

_____

_____

_____

_____

_____

5. Select five nonprofit organizations you are familiar with. After reviewing the differences between charity and philanthropy, explain why and how these organizations are involved in charitable or philanthropic activities.

_____

_____

_____

_____

_____

6. Select five nonprofit organizations you are familiar with. After reviewing the three failure theory, explain what type of failures these organizations address by providing services and goods.

    _____

    _____

    _____

    _____

    _____

    _____

    _____

7. Select five nonprofit organizations you are familiar with. Explain how these organizations fulfill different roles and functions in our society.

    _____

    _____

    _____

    _____

    _____

    _____

    _____

8. After reviewing the history of the U.S. nonprofit sector, discuss the key historical developments that have shaped today's nonprofit sector. What are the distinctive values that emerge from this history?

    _____

    _____

    _____

    _____

    _____

    _____

    _____

9. How does the reliance on different funding models influence the development of non-profit organizations in the different subsectors? And, is the selection of a particular funding model only a financial decision? Or, depending on subsector and role of the organization, does the funding model have implications on the organization's mission?

    _____

    _____

    _____

    _____

    _____

    _____

10. Consider the differences that exist between the various subsectors of the nonprofit sector. How does the work of an executive director differ across organizational types? Provide some examples.

    _____

    _____

    _____

    _____

    _____

    _____

11. Select an "infrastructure organization" and write a three-page report that provides information on the organization, explain what services the organization offers, and assess the organization.

REFERENCES

Abramson, A. J. & McCarthy, R. (2012). Infrastructure organizations. In L. M. Salamon (Ed.), *The state of non-profit America* (2nd ed.) (pp. 423-458). Washington: Brooking Institution Press.

Andersen, K. (2011, December 14). The protester. *Time*.

Anheier, H. K. (2004). The civil society diamond: The basics. In H. K. Anheier (ed.), *Civil society: Measurement, evaluation, policy* (pp. 14-42). Sterling: Earthscan.

Anheier, H. K. (2014). *Nonprofit organizations. Theory, management, policy* (2nd ed.). New York: Routledge.

Banfield, E. C. (1958). *The moral basis of a backward society*. New York: The Free Press.

Beito, D. (1999). *From mutual aid to the welfare state*. Chapel Hill: University of North Carolina Press.

Bell, D. (1989). American exceptionalism revisited: The role of civil society. *Public Interest*, *95*(Spring), 38–56.

Bellah, R., Madsen, R., Sullivan, W., Swidler, A., & Tipton, S. (2008/1985). *Habits of the heart. Individualism and commitment in American life*. Los Angeles: California University Press.

Bennet, J. C. (2016). The legal framework. In J. S. Ott & L. Dicke (Eds.), *Understanding nonprofit organizations* (3rd ed.) (pp. 33–42). Boulder: Westview Press.

Boris, E. T. & Steuerle, C. E. (2006). Scope and dimensions of the nonprofit sector. In W. W. Powell & R. Steinberg (Eds.), *The nonprofit sector. A research handbook* (2nd ed.) (pp. 66–88). New Haven: Yale University Press.

Brody, E. (2006). The legal framework for nonprofit organizations. In W. W. Powell & R. Steinberg (Eds.), *The nonprofit sector. A research handbook* (2nd ed.) (pp. 243–266). New Haven: Yale University Press.

Brown, M. S., McKeever, B. S., Dietz, N., Koulish, J., & Pollak, T. (2013). *The impact of the great recession on the number of charities*. Washington, D.C.: Urban Institute.

Carnegie, A. (1981/1889). Wealth. *The North American Review*, *266*(3), 60–64.

Chambers S. & Kopstein, J. (2001). Bad civil society. *Political Theory*, *29*(6), 837–865.

Chernow, R. (2004). *Titan: The life of John D. Rockefeller, Sr.* New York: Random.

Clemens, E. S. (2006). The constitution of citizens: Political theories of nonprofit organizations. In W. W. Powell & R. Steinberg (Eds.), *The nonprofit sector. A research handbook* (2nd ed.) (pp. 207–220). New Haven: Yale University Press.

Coleman, J. S. (1988). Social capital in the creation of human capital. *American Journal of Sociology*, *94* (Supplement: Organizations and institutions: Sociological and economic approaches to the analysis of social structure), S95–S120.

Colinvaux, R., Galle, B, & Steuerle, E. (2016/2012). Evaluating the charitable deduction and proposed reforms. In J. S. Ott & L. Dicke (Eds.), *Understanding nonprofit organizations* (3rd ed.) (pp. 59–69). Boulder: Westview Press.

de Tocqueville, A. (2006/1835-40). *Democracy in America*. New York: Harper Perennial.

Diamond, L. (2008). The rule of law versus the big man. *Journal of Democracy*, *19*(2), 138–149.

Dietz, N., McKeever, B. S., Brown, M. S., Koulish, J., & Pollak, T. (2014). *The impact of the great recession on the number of charities by subsector and revenue range.* Washington, D.C.: Urban Institute.

Douglas, J. (1987). Political theories of nonprofit organizations. In W. W. Powell (Ed.), *The nonprofit sector. A research handbook* (pp. 43–54). New Haven: Yale University Press.

Edwards, M. (2014). *Civil society* (3rd ed.). Malden: Polity Press.

Eikenberry, A. M. (2009). Refusing the market: A Democratic discourse for voluntary and nonprofit organizations. *Nonprofit and Voluntary Sector Quarterly, 38*(4), 582–596.

Eikenberry, A. M. & Kluver, J. D. (2004). The marketization of the nonprofit sector: Civil society at risk? *Public Administration Review, 64*(2), 132–140.

Frumkin, P. (2005). *On being nonprofit. A conceptual and policy primer.* Cambridge: Harvard University Press.

Frumkin, P. (2006). *Strategic giving. The art and science of philanthropy.* Chicago: Chicago University Press.

Fukuyama, F. (1995). *Trust: The social virtues and the creation of prosperity.* New York: Simon and Schuster.

Galaskiewics, J. & Colman, M. S. (2006). Collaboration between corporations and nonprofit organizations. In W. W. Powell & R. Steinberg (Eds.), *The nonprofit sector. A research handbook* (2nd ed.) (pp. 180–204). New Haven: Yale University Press.

Gellner, E. (1996). *Conditions of liberty. Civil society and its rivals.* New York: Penguin Books.

Giving USA. (2016). *The annual report on philanthropy for the year 2015.* Chicago: Giving USA Foundation.

Goldberg, E. (2016, June 21). More Americans give to charity than vote. *The Huffington Post.* Retrieved from http://www.huffingtonpost.com/entry/more-americans-give-to-charity-than-vote_us_576813d9e4b0853f8bf183d0

Goss, K. A. (2013). *The paradox of gender equality. How American women's groups gained and lost their public voice.* Ann Arbor: The University of Michigan Press.

Gross, R. A. (2003). Giving in America: From charity to philanthropy. In L. Friedman & M. Garvie (Eds.), *Charity, philanthropy, and civility in American history* (pp. 29–48). Cambridge: Cambridge University Press.

Habermas, J. (1991). *The structural transformation of the public sphere. An enquiry into a category of bourgeois society.* Cambridge: The MIT Press.

Hall, P. D. (2003). The welfare state and the careers of public and private institutions since 1945. In L. Friedman & M. Garvie (Eds.), *Charity, philanthropy, and civility in American history* (pp. 363–383). Cambridge: Cambridge University Press.

Hall, P. D. (2006). A historical view of philanthropy, voluntary associations, and nonprofit organizations in the United States, 1600–2000. In W. W. Powell & R. Steinberg (Eds.), *The nonprofit sector. A research handbook* (2nd ed.) (pp. 32–65). New Haven: Yale University Press.

Hammack, D. C. (1999). Foundations in the American polity. In E. C. Lagermann (Ed.), *Philanthropic foundations: New scholarship, new possibilities* (pp. 43–68). Bloomington: Indiana University Press.

Hammack, D. C. (2005). Donors, intermediaries, and beneficiaries: The changing moral dynamics of American nonprofit organizations. In D. H. Smith (Ed.), *Good intentions. Moral obstacles & opportunities* (pp. 183–203). Bloomington: Indiana University Press.

Hammack, D. C. & Anheier, H. K. (2013). *A versatile American institution. The changing ideals and realities of philanthropic foundations.* Washington DC: Brookings Institute Press.

Hansmann, H. (1987). Economic theories of nonprofit organizations. In W. W. Powell (Ed.), *The nonprofit sector. A research handbook* (pp. 27–42). New Haven: Yale University Press.

Hegel, G. W. F. (1988/1830). The moral life, or social ethics. In J. Goldstein & J. W. Boyer (Eds.), *Nineteenth century Europe. Liberalism and its critics* (pp. 126–154). Chicago: The University of Chicago Press.

Hopkins, B. R. (2016/2011). Organizational, operational, and related tests and doctrines. In J. S. Ott & L. Dicke (Eds.), *Understanding nonprofit organizations* (3rd ed.) (pp. 43–58). Boulder: Westview Press.

Hopkins, B. R. (2013). *Starting and managing a nonprofit organization. A legal guide* (6th ed.). Hoboken: Wiley.

Hwang, H. & Powell, W. W. (2009). The rationalization of charity: The influence of professionalism in the nonprofit sector. *Administrative Science Quarterly, 54*(2), 268–298.

Internal Revenue Service. (2016). *Tax-Exempt status for your organization*. Publication 557. (Rev. February 2016). U.S. Department of the Treasury.

Jeavons, T. H. (2010). Ethical nonprofit management. Core values and key practices. In D. O. Renz & Associates (Eds.), *The Jossey-Bass handbook of nonprofit leadership and management* (3rd ed.) (pp. 178–205). San Francisco: Jossey-Bass.

Karl, B. D. & Katz, S. N. (1981). The American private philanthropic foundation and the public sphere 1890–1930. *Minerva, 19*(2), 237–270.

Kaufman, J. (2002). *For the common good? American civic life and the golden age of fraternity*. New York: Oxford University Press.

W. K. Kellogg Foundation. (2003). *Blurred boundaries and muddled motives. A world of shifting social responsibilities*. Battle Creek: W. K. Kellogg Foundation.

Kennedy, D. (1982). *Over here: The first World War and American society*. Oxford: Oxford University Press.

Landles-Cobb, L., Kramer, K., & Smith Milway, K. (2015). The nonprofit leadership development deficit. *Stanford Innovation Review*. http://ssir.org/articles/entry/the_nonprofit_leadership_development_deficit

Lohmann, R. A. (1989). And lettuce is nonanimal: Toward a positive economics of voluntary action. *Nonprofit and Voluntary Sector Quarterly, 18*(4), 367–383.

Lohmann, R. A. (1992). The commons: A multidisciplinary approach to nonprofit organization, voluntary action, and philanthropy. *Nonprofit and Voluntary Sector Quarterly, 21*(3), 309–324.

McCarthy, K. D. (2003). Women and political culture. In L. Friedman & M. Garvie (Eds.), *Charity, philanthropy, and civility in American history* (pp. 179–198). Cambridge: Cambridge University Press.

McCarthy, K. D. (2005). *American creed. Philanthropy and the rise of civil society, 1700–1865*. Chicago: University of Chicago Press.

McGarvie, M. D. (2003). The Dartmouth College case and the legal design of civil society. In L. Friedman & M. Garvie (Eds.), *Charity, philanthropy, and civility in American history* (pp. 91–105). Cambridge: Cambridge University Press.

McKeever, B. S. (2015). *The nonprofit sector in brief 2015. Public charities, giving, and volunteering*. Washington, D.C.: Urban Institute.

Mirabella, R. (2007). University-Based educational programs in nonprofit management and philanthropic studies: A 10-year review and projections of future trends. *Nonprofit and Voluntary Sector Quarterly, 36*(4), 11–27.

Moore, L. J. (1991). *Citizen klansmen. The Ku Klux Klan in Indiana, 1921–1928.* Chapel Hill: The University of North Carolina Press.

Nasaw, D, (2007). *Andrew Carnegie.* New York: Penguin.

Nonprofit Academic Centers Council. (2015). *Curricular guidelines for graduate & undergraduate study in nonprofit leadership, the nonprofit sector and philanthropy* (Rev. ed.). Cleveland: NACC.

Nonprofit Leadership Alliance. (2011). *The skills the nonprofit sector requires of its managers and leaders. A preliminary report.* Kansas City: Nonprofit Leadership Alliance.

Payton, R. L. & Moody, M. P. (2008). *Understanding philanthropy. Its meaning and mission.* Indianapolis: Indiana University Press.

Putnam, R. D. (1993). *Making democracy work. Civic traditions in modern Italy.* Princeton: Princeton University Press.

Putnam, R. D. (1995). Bowling alone: America's declining social capital. *Journal of Democracy, 6*(1), 65–78.

Putnam, R. D. (2001). *Bowling alone: The collapse and revival of American community.* New York: Simon and Schuster.

Renz, D. O. (2010). The future of nonprofit management and leadership. In D. O. Renz & Associates (Eds.), *The Jossey-Bass handbook of nonprofit leadership and management* (3rd ed.) (pp. 794–804). San Francisco: Jossey-Bass.

Rosenblum, N. L. (1998). *Membership and morals. The personal uses of pluralism in America.* Princeton: Princeton University Press.

Salamon, L. M. (1987). Partners in public service: The scope and theory of government-nonprofit relations. In W. W. Powell (Ed.), *The nonprofit sector. A research handbook* (pp. 99–117). New Haven: Yale University Press.

Salamon, L. M. (1993). The marketization of welfare: Changing nonprofit and for-profit roles in the American welfare state. *The Social Service Review, 67*(1), 16–39.

Salamon, L. M. (1996a). Defining the nonprofit sector: The United States. In L. M. Salamon and H. K. Anheier (Eds.), *Working papers of the Johns Hopkins comparative nonprofit sector project* (no. 18). Baltimore: The Johns Hopkins Institute for Policy Studies.

Salamon, L. M. (1996b). The crisis of the nonprofit sector and the challenge of renewal. *National Civic Review, 85*(4), 3–15.

Salamon, L. M. (2012). The resilient sector: The future of nonprofit America. In L. M. Salamon (Ed.), *The state of nonprofit America* (2nd ed.) (pp. 3–86). Washington: Brooking Institution Press.

Salamon, L. M. (2014). The revolution on the frontiers of philanthropy: An introduction. In Salamon, L. M. (Ed.), *New frontiers of philanthropy* (pp. 3–87). New York: Oxford University Press.

Salamon, L. M. & Anheier, H. K. (1992). In search of the non-profit sector. I: The question of definitions. *Voluntas, 3*(2), 125–151.

Salamon, L. M. & Anheier, H. K. (2006). The nonprofit sector in comparative perspective. In W. W. Powell & R. Steinberg (Eds.), *The nonprofit sector. A research handbook* (2nd ed.) (pp. 89–116). New Haven: Yale University Press.

Salamon, L. M., Sokolowski, S. W., & Geller, S. L. (2010). Holding the fort: Nonprofit employment during a decade of turmoil. *Nonprofit Employment Bulletin no. 39.*

Schaffer, J. (2016, June 20). Can we stop arguing over "nonprofit"? *Nonprofit Quarterly*. Retrieved from https://nonprofitquarterly.org/2016/06/20/can-we-stop-arguing-over-nonprofit/

Schervish, P. G. (2005). The sense and sensibility of philanthropy as a moral citizenship of care. In D. H. Smith (Ed.), *Good intentions. Moral obstacles & opportunities* (pp. 149–165). Bloomington: Indiana University Press.

Schlesinger, A. M. (1944). Biography of a nation of joiners. *The American Historical Review, 50*(1), 1–25.

Sealander, J. (2003). Curing evil at their source: The arrival of scientific giving. In L. Friedman & M. Garvie (Eds.), *Charity, philanthropy, and civility in American history* (pp. 217–240). Cambridge: Cambridge University Press.

Shier, M. L. & F. Handy. (2014). Research trends in nonprofit graduate studies: A growing interdisciplinary field. *Nonprofit and Voluntary Sector Quarterly, 43*(5), 812–831.

Shils, E. (1997). Civility and civil society: Good manners between persons and concern for the common good in public affairs. In S. Grosby (Ed.), *The virtue of civility. Selected essays on liberalism, tradition, and civil society* (pp. 63–103). Indianapolis: Liberty Fund.

Sievers, B. R. (2010). *Civil society, philanthropy, and the fate of the commons.* Medford: Tufts University Press.

Skocpol, T. (2003). *Diminished democracy. From membership to management in American civic life.* Norman: University of Oklahoma Press.

Skocpol, T. & Fiorina, M. P. (1999). Making sense of the civic engagement debate. In T. Skocpol & M. P. Fiorina (Eds.), *Civic engagement in American democracy* (pp. 1–26). Washington: Brookings Institution Press.

Smith, A. (1976/1759). *The theory of moral sentiments.* D. D. Raphael & A. L. Macfie (Eds.). Indianapolis: Liberty Fund.

Smith, A. (2003/1776). *The wealth of nations.* E. Cannan (Ed.). New York: Bantam Classics.

Smith, D. H. (1997). The rest of the nonprofit sector: Grassroots associations as the dark matter ignored in prevailing "flat Earth" maps of the sector. *Nonprofit and Voluntary Sector Quarterly, 26*(2), 114–131.

Smith, D. H. (2016/1973). The impact of the voluntary sector on society. In J. S. Ott & L. Dicke (Eds.), *The nature of the nonprofit sector* (3rd ed.) (pp. 72–81). Boulder: Westview Press.

Steinberg, R. (2006). Economic theories of nonprofit organizations. In W. W. Powell & R. Steinberg (Eds.), *The nonprofit sector. A research handbook* (2nd ed.) (pp. 117–139). New Haven: Yale University Press.

Tierney, T. J. (2006). *The nonprofit sector's leadership deficit.* Boston: The Bridgespan Group, Inc.

Traub, J. (2011, December 30). Occupy everywhere. *Foreign Policy.*

U.S. Bureau of Labor Statistics. (2016). *Volunteering in the United States, 2015.* Washington, D.C.: U.S. Bureau of Labor Statistics.

Weber, M. (1946/1918). Politics as a vocation. In H. H. Gerth and C. W. Mills (Eds.), *From Max Weber: Essays in sociology* (pp. 77–128). New York: Oxford University Press.

Weber. P. (2013). Modernity, civil society, and sectarianism: The Muslim brotherhood and the takfir groups. *Voluntas, 24*(2), 509–527.

Weber, P. (2015a). The paradoxical modernity of civil society: the Weimar republic, democracy, and social homogeneity. *Voluntas, 26*(2), 629–648.

Weber, P. (2015b). The Pacifism of Andrew Carnegie and Edwin Ginn: The emerging of a philanthropic internationalism. *Global Society, 29*(4), 530–550.

Weber, P. & Witkowski, G. (2016). Philanthropic disruptions: Changing nonprofit education for an engaged society. *Journal of Public Affairs Education, 22*(1), 91–106.

Weis, R. M. & Long, R. F. (2011). *Leading and managing nonprofit organizations* (1st ed.). Peosta, IA: eddie bowers publishing co., inc.

Weis, R M. & Muller, S. M. (2015). *Leading and managing nonprofit organizations* (2nd ed.). Peosta, IA: eddie bowers publishing co., inc.

Worth, M. J. (2017). *Nonprofit management. Principles and practice* (4th ed.). Los Angeles: Sage.

Zimmer, A. & Freise, M. (2008). Bringing society back: Civil society, social capital, and third sector. In W. A. Maloney & J. W. van Deth (Eds.), *Civil society and governance in Europe: From national to international linkages* (pp. 19–44). Northampton: Edward Elgar Publishing.

Zunz, O. (2012). *Philanthropy in America: A history*. Princeton: Princeton University Press.

APPENDIX

JOURNALS, WEBSITES, AND OTHER ONLINE RESOURCES

The descriptions of the following resources are taken from the respective websites.

ACADEMIC JOURNALS

Voluntas: International Journal of Voluntary and Nonprofit Organizations (http://link.springer.com/journal/11266): *Voluntas* is the official journal of the International Society for Third-Sector Research (ISTR). Next to NVSQ, it is the major journal in the field of nonprofit studies and provides a central forum for worldwide research in the area between the state, market, and household sectors.

Nonprofit and Voluntary Sector Quarterly (NVSQ) (http://nvs.sagepub.com/): *NVSQ* is the official journal of the Association for Research on Nonprofit Organizations and Voluntary Action (ARNOVA). Next to *Voluntas,* it is the major journal in the field of nonprofit studies and provides cutting-edge research, discussion, and analysis of the field and leads its readers to understanding the impact the nonprofit sector has on society.

Journal of Civil Society (http://www.tandfonline.com/toc/rcis20/current#.V4j-nGgrKM8): The *Journal of Civil Society* provides a high profile, high impact outlet for world-class scholarship and debate on civil society, and serves as the authoritative source for research in an emerging field that lacks a central organ for dissemination.

Nonprofit Management and Leadership (http://onlinelibrary.wiley.com/journal/10.1002/(ISSN)1542-7854): The Nonprofit Management & Leadership is a quarterly peer-reviewed journal that publishes quality scholarship on all aspects of management and leadership important to nonprofit organizations and leaders.

Journal of Public Affairs Education (JPAE) (http://www.naspaa.org/initiatives/jpae/jpae.asp): *JPAE* is the journal of the Network of Schools of Public Policy, Affairs, and Administration (NASPAA). *JPAE* is dedicated to advancing teaching and learning in public affairs broadly defined, which includes the fields of policy analysis, public administration, public management, public policy, nonprofit administration, and their subfields.

Journal of Nonprofit Education and Leadership (JNEL) (http://js.sagamorepub.com/jnel/): The *JNEL* publishes quality manuscripts to disseminate the latest knowledge related to nonprofit education and leadership to help develop theory and practice. The Journal is endorsed by the Nonprofit Academic Centers Council (NACC),

Stanford Social Innovation Review (http://ssir.org/): The *Review* is a magazine and website that covers cross-sector solutions to global problems. SSIR is written for and by social change leaders in the nonprofit, business, and government sectors who view collaboration as key to solving environmental, social, and economic justice issues. It is published at the Stanford Center on Philanthropy and Civil Society at Stanford University.

TRADE JOURNALS

Chronicle of Philanthropy (http://www.philanthropy.com/): The *Chronicle,* published every other week, is a prime news source for people involved in the philanthropic enterprise. The website offers a summary of the contents of the current issue of the *Chronicle,* a list of forthcoming conferences and workshops, job opportunities in the non-profit world, and other information.

Nonprofit Times (http://www.nptimes.com/): Website of the popular monthly newspaper covering all aspects of nonprofit work, including volunteers.

Nonprofit Quarterly (http://www.nonprofitquarterly.org/): The website provides values-based management information and best practices. It also offers a free e-newsletter.

Philanthropy News Digest (http://philanthropynewsdigest.org/): A daily news service of the Foundation Center, *Philanthropy News Digest* (PND) is a compendium, in digest form, of philanthropy-related articles and features culled from print and electronic media outlets nationwide. It also offers a free e-newsletter.

Philanthropy Journal (https://www.philanthropyjournal.org/): An online daily newspaper, *Philanthropy Journal,* publishes state, national, and international news on fundraising, giving, managing, volunteering, innovation, and technology in the philanthropic community.

DATA AND INFORMATION ON THE NONPROFIT SECTOR

National Center of Charitable Statistics (NCCS) (http://nccs.urban.org/): The NCCS is the national repository of data on the nonprofit sector in the United States. The Center was established in 1982 and has been a project of the Center on Nonprofits and Philanthropy (CNP) at the Urban Institute since July 1996, when it was transferred from the research division of INDEPENDENT SECTOR.

Giving USA (http://givingusa.org/): *Giving USA: The Annual Report on Philanthropy* is the seminal publication reporting on the sources and uses of charitable giving in the United States. Its research, conducted by the Indiana University Lilly Family School of Philanthropy since 2000, estimates all giving to all charitable organizations across the United States.

The Johns Hopkins Comparative Nonprofit Sector Project (CNP) (http://www.jhu.edu/~ccss/): CNP is the largest systematic effort ever undertaken to analyze the scope, structure, financing, and role of the private nonprofit sector in countries around the world in order to enrich our understanding of this sector, and to provide a sounder basis for both public and private action toward it.

Volunteering in America (http://www.volunteeringinamerica.gov/): The website provides the most comprehensive look at volunteering and civic life in the 50 states and 51 cities across the country. Data includes volunteer rates and rankings, civic engagement trends, and analysis.

Urban Institute (http://www.urban.org): In the Nonprofit Almanac and the Almanac Briefs, Urban Institute publishes the most authoritative data on the size and scope of the nonprofit sector. See also the National Center of Charitable Statistics (NCCS).

Foundation Center (http://fdncenter.org/): The Foundation Center is the leading source of information about philanthropy worldwide—it maintains the most comprehensive database on U.S. and, increasingly, global grant-makers and their grants.

Internal Revenue Service (IRS) (http://www.irs.gov/): The IRS provides a variety of resources for organizations seeking exempt status as well as a codebook and downloadable list of registered nonprofits.

GuideStar (http://www.guidestar.org/): GuideStar gathers and disseminates information about every single IRS-registered nonprofit organization. The website provides easy access to the Form 990 of all registered NPOs.

Saguaro Seminar (http://www.hks.harvard.edu/programs/saguaro/): The Saguaro Seminar is an initiative of Professor Robert D. Putnam at John F. Kennedy School of Government at Harvard University focused on the study of "social capital" (the value of social networks) and community engagement.

VOLUNTEERS AND VOLUNTEERISM

Corporation for National and Community Service (http://www.nationalservice.gov/): CNCS is an independent federal agency, plays a vital role in supporting the American culture of citizenship, service, and responsibility, and is a leading grant-maker in support of service and volunteering.

National Conference on Citizenship (http://www.ncoc.net/index.php): NCoC is a congressionally chartered organization dedicated to strengthening civic life in America. It provides important reports on the civic health of the United States.

ServiceLeader.org (https://www.serviceleader.org): Serviceleader.org offers specialized resources for volunteers, volunteer managers, nonprofit leaders and staff, and instructors, faculty, and researchers.

Volunteers of America (https://www.voa.org/): Volunteers of America is one of the nation's largest and most comprehensive human services organizations, touching the lives of more than 2 million people each year in hundreds of communities across the United States.

SCHOLARLY AND NONPROFIT EDUCATION-RELATED ORGANIZATIONS

Association for Research on Nonprofit Organizations and Voluntary Action (ARNOVA) (http://www.arnova.org/): the major scholarly and professional association in the field of nonprofit studies.

The International Society for Third-Sector Research (ISTR) (http://www.istr.org/): ISTR is the major international association promoting research and education in the fields of civil society, philanthropy, and the nonprofit sector.

Nonprofit Leadership Alliance (NLA) (http://nonprofitleadershipalliance.org/): Formerly American Humanics, the NLA aims to strengthen the social sector with a talented and prepared workforce. It offers the Certified Nonprofit Professional (CNP) credential.

Nonprofit Academic Centers Council (NACC) (http://nonprofit-academic-centers-council.org/): NACC is a membership association comprised of academic centers or programs at accredited colleges and universities that are devoted to the study of the nonprofit/nongovernmental sector, philanthropy and voluntary action to advance education, research, and practice that increase the nonprofit sector's ability to enhance civic engagement, democracy, and human welfare.

ACCOUNTABILITY AND TRANSPARENCY

Charity Navigator (http://www.charitynavigator.org/): Charity Navigator is the nation's largest and most-utilized evaluator of charities.

Better Business Bureau Wise Giving Alliance (http://www.give.org/): The BBB Wise Giving Alliance produces reports about national charities, evaluating them against comprehensive Standards for Charity Accountability, and publishes a magazine, the *Wise Giving Guide*, three times a year.

Standards for Excellence Institute (https://standardsforexcellence.org/): The Standards for Excellence Institute is a national initiative established to promote the highest standards of ethics, effectiveness, and accountability in nonprofit governance, management, and operations, and to help all nonprofit organizations meet these high benchmarks.

ORGANIZATIONS ADVOCATING FOR THE NONPROFIT SECTOR AND ITS SUBSECTORS

Independent Sector (http://www.independentsector.org/): Independent Sector is the trade association for national nonprofit organizations. It is the leadership network for nonprofits, foundations, and corporations committed to advancing the common good and represent tens of thousands of organizations and individuals locally, nationally, and globally.

Council on Foundations (http://www.cof.org/): The Council is a membership organization providing a wide variety of services primarily for endowed, grant-making organizations throughout the United States and in foreign countries.

National Council of Nonprofits (https://www.councilofnonprofits.org/): The National Council of Nonprofits (Council of Nonprofits) is a resource and advocate for America's charitable nonprofits. Through a network of State Associations and 25,000-plus members it serves as a central coordinator and mobilizer to help nonprofits achieve greater collective impact in local communities across the country.

Kentucky Nonprofit Network (http://www.kynonprofits.org/): Kentucky Nonprofit Network is the Commonwealth's state association of nonprofit organizations. It aims to strengthen and advance the nonprofit sector through a unified public policy voice, education, technical assistance, networking opportunities, and sharing of best practices.

TECHNOLOGY AND BLOGS

Techsoup (http://www.techsoup.org/): TechSoup provides the nonprofit organizations and leaders with transformative technology solutions and skills they need to improve lives globally and locally. It provides both the digital platforms and in-person experiences that enable people to work together toward a more equitable world.

Blue Avocado (http://www.blueavocado.org/): Blue Avocado is the semi-monthly newsletter of American Nonprofits, a membership organization that provides practical financial information and support to U.S. 501(c)(3) nonprofit organizations, staff, stakeholders, and volunteers. It is created by and for community-based nonprofits.

Nonprofit with Balls (http://nonprofitwithballs.com/): "Nonprofit with Balls" is a blog by Vu Le, the Executive Director of Rainier Valley Corps, a nonprofit in Seattle with the mission of developing and supporting leaders of color to strengthen the capacity of communities-of-color-led nonprofits and foster collaboration between diverse communities to effect systemic change.

Indiegogo (https://www.indiegogo.com): Indiegogo is an international crowdfunding website that allows individuals to solicit donations for ideas, charities, and start-up projects. It aims to foster entrepreneurship.

Fundraise.com (https://www.fundraise.com/): Fundraise.com is a crowdfunding website that allows individuals to collect donations online.

COMMUNICATION

See3 (http://see3.com/home): See3 partners with nonprofits and social causes on a full range of digital services. It provides strategy, video, and Web services to nonprofits and social causes.

Spitfire Strategies (http://www.spitfirestrategies.com/): Spitfire Strategies assists nonprofit organizations with smart communications, winning campaigns, and learning opportunities.

Network for Good (http://www.networkforgood.com/): Network for Good is a hybrid organization—a nonprofit-owned for-profit. It offers a suite of fundraising software and services that help nonprofit organizations to raise money and reach more individual donors.

MANAGEMENT TRAINING

Don Kramer's Nonprofit Issues (http://www.nonprofitissues.com/): Nonprofit Issues is a national Web newsletter of "Nonprofit Law You Need To Know." Written for nonprofit officers and directors and their professional advisors, Nonprofit Issues provides clear, concise, and comprehensive coverage of real issues that affect nonprofits every day.

BoardSource (https://www.boardsource.org/eweb/): BoardSource is a national organization working to strengthen nonprofit board leadership. It offers a wide range of diagnostic tools, educational programs and resources, and consulting services to strengthen board performance.

Daring to Lead (http://daringtolead.org/): Daring to Lead 2011 is a national study produced in partnership by CompassPoint and the Meyer Foundation in which more than 3,000 executive directors participated. The website provides reports, current findings, and other opportunities to learn about the implications for nonprofit executives and boards, philanthropy, and capacity builders.

Nonprofit Good Practice Guide (http://www.npgoodpractice.org/): The Michigan Nonprofit Management Support Organization (MSO) Network, a collaborative of nine capacity building providers and other partner institutions from across the state, collectively manage and contribute to the Nonprofit Good Practice Guide to increase nonprofit organizational and financial stability, program quality, and growth.

Nonprofit Risk Management Center (https://www.nonprofitrisk.org/): The Center offers risk consulting services and assists clients in developing and improving their capacity to anticipate and manage risk.

LaPiana Consulting (http://lapiana.org/): LaPiana is a nonprofit consulting firm that aims to improve leadership and management practices throughout the sector for greater social impact.

Nonprofit Finance Fund (http://www.nonprofitfinancefund.org/): Nonprofit Finance Fund is a community development financial institution that supports mission-driven organizations through tailored investments, strategic advice, and accessible insights. It helps organizations connect money to mission effectively, and supports innovations such as growth capital campaigns, cross-sector economic recovery initiatives, and impact investing.

The Grantsmanship Center (https://www.tgci.com/): The Center offers training and publications to help organizations plan solid programs, write logical, compelling grant proposals, and create earned income opportunities.

Planned Giving Design Center (http://www.pgdc.com/): The primary mission of Planned Giving Design Center, LLC is to develop products and services for the charitable gift and estate planning industry that assist sothers in their efforts to increase philanthropy.

PROFESSIONAL DEVELOPMENT ORGANIZATIONS

Association of Fundraising Professionals (http://www.afpnet.org/): The AFP supports the development and growth of fundraising professionals and promotes high ethical standards in the fundraising profession, both nationally and internationally.

CFRE International: Certified Fund Raising Executive (http://www.cfre.org/): CFRE International is an independent nonprofit organization whose sole mission is dedicated to setting standards in philanthropy through a valid and reliable certification process for fundraising professionals.

Alliance for Nonprofit Management (https://www.allianceonline.org/): The Alliance is comprised of for-profit and nonprofit consultants, advisors and trainers, funders, academics, and thought-leaders supporting the capacity building efforts of nonprofits and other mission driven organizations.

Grant Professionals Association (http://www.grantprofessionals.org/): GPA is the first organization focused solely on the advancement of grantsmanship as a profession and the support of its practitioners.

Young Nonprofit Professionals Network (http://ynpn.org/): The YNPN aims to engage and support future nonprofit and community leaders through professional development, networking, and social opportunities designed for young people involved in the nonprofit community.

Independent Sector's NGen: Moving Nonprofit Leaders From Next to Now (http://www.independentsector.org/ngen): The program builds the capacity of nonprofit and philanthropic leaders age 40 and under to have significant impact on society's toughest challenges.

Net Impact (https://netimpact.org/): Net Impact is a leading nonprofit that empowers a new generation to use their careers to drive transformational change in the workplace and the world.

Emerging Practitioners in Philanthropy (EPIP) (http://www.epip.org/): EPIP is a national network of foundation professionals and social entrepreneurs who strive for excellence in the practice of philanthropy. It aims to develop emerging leaders committed to building a just, equitable, and sustainable society.

JOB SEARCH RESOURCES

Action Without Borders (http://www.idealist.org/): The website provides a collection of resources on diverse topics, including local and global volunteering, nonprofit careers, nonprofit management, and graduate school.

VolunteerMatch (http://www.volunteermatch.org/): The organization offers a variety of online services to support a community of nonprofit, volunteer, and business leaders committed to civic engagement.

The Bridgespan Group (http://www.bridgespan.org/Home.aspx): The Bridgespan Group is a nonprofit advisor and resource for mission-driven organizations and philanthropists. The website provides a searchable job database, as well as valuable resources for professional development.

Common Good Careers (http://commongoodcareers.org/): It is a nonprofit search firm to support hiring needs at every stage of organizational growth—in all functional areas and at all levels of seniority.

2

FOUNDATIONS OF LEADERSHIP, MANAGEMENT, CHARACTER, AND ETHICS

There has been a long-running discussion regarding the differences between managers and leaders (Gardner, 2010; Weis & Muller, 2015). In most cases, **managers** are considered to be individuals who direct, control, and organize tasks and people within organizations, whereas **leaders** may be considered individuals who inspire others to reach toward a vision and are willing to accept the risks involved in being at the forefront of reaching toward that vision. In an early work, Hitt (1988) combined the two labels to illustrate the need for individuals who have the knowledge and ability to organize as well as the ability to inspire individuals to realistic, yet challenging, heights, or **leader-managers**. The ability to function effectively in both roles is often a necessity in smaller organizations, like many in the nonprofit sector, that do not have the resources of a larger, diverse staff. Another possibility is when one individual accepts the "role" as leader and another individual the role of manager in the same organization, such as with presidents and vice presidents, or executive directors and assistant directors. And although leadership and management are not exactly the same, they overlap (Gardner, 2010) and a number of areas ahead focus on both leadership and/or management since both are necessary to the growth of nonprofit organizations.

MANAGING NONPROFIT ORGANIZATIONS

There are a number of areas that require effective management along with solid leadership. Management, as with leadership, has evolved over time from the conservative theories of Frederick Taylor that attempted to use scientific methods to make work more productive to Douglas McGregor's Theory X and Theory Y in which McGregor argues that individuals like responsibility and aspire to become self-directed and creative, all the way to Theory Z in which individuals seek long-term personal-advancement and achievement (Anheier, 2014). In 1954, Peter Drucker made a case for Managing by Objectives (MBO) in which goals were set and organizational members collectively worked toward those goals (Anheier, 2014). His concept worked for decades and still exists in some form in some places. This was followed by Deming (2000) who developed Total Quality Management, or TQM, in complete contrast to MBO in which the emphasis is on shared decision-making and individual/team responsibility. Management theories and models, just as with leadership theories and models, will continue changing, addressing old and new issues alike.

Over time, nonprofit organizations have had to become more **accountable** in order to be recognized as a respected and successful endeavor as well as for funding purposes. The public, including funding sources, need to know that nonprofits are ethically and legally effective (Worth, 2017). Both state and federal laws require nonprofits to be registered and follow specific reporting methods in order to operate. Nonprofits can and do **self-regulate**, at the same time charity watchdogs, such as the Better Business Bureau, among others, exist to confirm effectiveness. One essential way nonprofits self-regulate is through **performance measurements.** There are a number of ways of doing this, including examining financial ratios like comparing expenses directed for programs versus other organizational expenses. Another way is to use a **benchmark approach** comparing organizational outcomes with peer outcomes, and the **logic model** proposed by the United Way that links activities to outcomes which are measurable (Anheier, 2014; Worth, 2017). The logic model will be discussed further in Chapter 6 regarding the United Way's funding process. Like most management processes and policies, accountability always depends on the effectiveness of management/leadership at all levels of the organization.

Another area of significance is the **management of change** within organizations. Although change is inevitable, it can be difficult to leave what is comfortable for unfamiliar scenarios that might best serve the mission of the organization. Whether it is changing the accounting methodology or a new and different way of recruiting membership, change is often perceived as threatening to already established situations. Managing change within any organization calls for a high level of trust in leadership and governance that is capable of facilitating change with as little disruption as possible. It also requires patience and the ability to calculate and possibly alter the intended process if it could ultimately benefit the organization.

Leadership and management also seem to blend when we speak of **strategic planning and management.** Strategic planning refers to long-range planning with an emphasis on where the organization plans to go and how it intends to get there. Therefore, a strategic plan can provide guidelines on areas of location, programs, staff members, and outreach to mention several (Anheier, 2014; Worth, 2017). A strategic plan should always follow the mission, values, and vision of an organization and this is where an accepting, inviting, and democratic leader can be invaluable in bringing appropriate organizational and community members to the table to develop a long-range plan. Although long-range in nature, strategic plans like all plans must allow for some flexibility when unexpected circumstances occur.

Other important areas of management blending with leadership include major divisions such as the management of staff and volunteers as well as working effectively with governing boards (discussed in Chapter 3), development of marketing and public relations plans (discussed in Chapters 5 and 6) and the implementation of solid financial operations (discussed in Chapter 6).

As alluded to in the beginning of this chapter, **leadership** is about inspiring, motivating, guiding, directing, and influencing others to reach goals and to make a positive impact on the organization's mission. The mission is the most important resource for nonprofit organizations, from the focus on the public purpose it provides to the legal reason for IRS support (Brinckerhoff, 2009). The critical responsibility that leaders have to serve as stewards of the public missions of nonprofit organizations is a key reason that leadership needs to be seriously examined.

Leadership is frequently more art than science. While there are theories, principles, and approaches that can help improve effectiveness, leadership is the art of achieving goals and missions with and through groups of people. Whether by design or by circumstance, effective leadership is accomplished in many different ways. From individual actions to collaborative efforts and from carefully designed strategies to unplanned and spontaneous initiative leadership is about moving in a positive direction toward chosen goals. Leaders must consider a wide range of factors that impact every aspect of the context, the culture, and the people engaged in the process (Weis & Muller, 2015). This is particularly true in nonprofit organizations, where the purpose of the institution is to strive toward a public mission, and individuals at every level—administration, board, program staff, support staff, volunteers, organizational members, and constituents—have an opportunity to be a part of the endeavor. With approximately 12% of the workforce employed by nonprofit organizations and more than 50% of all individuals volunteering, it could be said that nonprofit organizations are the country's largest employer, therefore effective leadership is essential (Nonprofit Almanac, 2012).

Whether undertaken by individuals or groups, leadership in the nonprofit sector means strengthening individuals and communities by developing influence through collaborative and trusting relationships. Leading others involves skills, character, and a good moral compass that includes an accepted system of principles and ethics. Personal character implies traits and values that make each person who he or she is. Character is an essential ingredient in the formula for successful leadership, as is a personal system of ethics that helps an individual make effective moral decisions and commitments, and in so doing, inspire others to positive actions. This will be discussed in much more detail later in this chapter.

FUNDAMENTALS OF LEADERSHIP

REGARDING LEADERSHIP

Begin where you are
And do what you can.

Arthur Ashe
Tennis great and Philanthropist

Leadership opportunities in the nonprofit sector are diverse and exist in many different forms and at many different levels. Consider a Senior Citizen Center fitness director, a Substance Abuse Center education program coordinator, a Girl Scout field director, a Good Will Industries training supervisor, and an American Red Cross CPR trainer, among others. In all of these types of roles, leaders in one capacity or another are the essential individuals responsible for providing people with services and supporting those services once they are established. Consider the groups of staff and volunteers serving a Boys & Girls Club program committee, a Big Brothers/Big Sisters annual fundraising campaign, a Nature Center public education initiative, and a Coalition Against Sexual and Domestic Violence intervention education program, among others. Whether working in a positional leadership role or as a part of a group process, quality leadership provides the expertise, direction, guidance, support, inspiration, enthusiasm, and motivation needed to successfully pursue the mission. Regardless of the assigned role, the most effective leaders have the capacity to help a group arrive at a **shared vision** and the ability to contribute to the development and implementation of a quality plan of action to realize that vision (Kouzes & Posner, 1995; Collins, 2001). Nonprofit organizations need leaders who are excited about working in this cooperative and collaborative context, who inspire and motivate others to action, and who are eager to share leadership with others. If skills and character can be developed, as is the belief of the authors, then individuals can develop as leaders when they see needs that should be addressed and aspire to acquire characteristics and skills that are important in influencing others to assist with meeting those needs. Effective leaders understand that leadership is a journey that requires a commitment to continue learning and growing.

Effective leaders know that the ultimate success of their organizations is dependent on their followers, and therefore they work hard to **empower** others by providing them with training, support, and encouragement. By providing others with opportunities to lead and have influence themselves, a leader can provide perhaps the strongest base for success, a base of **empowerment** (Weis & Muller, 2015). Individuals who are empowered can operate confidently and competently, especially when they are encouraged to use their own initiative. In his book, *Developing the Leader Within*, John Maxwell writes, "The one who influences others to lead others is a leader without limitations." (2001, p. 141) Investing in building the capacity of others to lead, and trusting them to do so, is the mark of a true leader. One key piece of evidence that a person has become a successful leader is found when leadership is fully extended to others.

One essential aspect of empowering individuals is the function of **delegation**, or providing individuals with opportunities to share in responsibilities and authority. Out of both necessity and trust, leaders and managers realize they must share responsibilities and authority in order for the organization to succeed. Effective leaders monitor the progress of individuals who have been delegated responsibilities and make adjustments when necessary; a process referred to as **responsible delegation**.

WHAT IS A LEADER?

A leader is concerned with the purpose, vision, and direction of the organization. Worth (2009) describes leadership as interactive and based on the relationships among those serving the organization's mission. By contrast, Worth describes management as generally concerned with the ongoing operation of the organization and the effective implementation of policies, procedures, rules, and processes of organizations. Considering this distinction, the authors support the framing that a leader is someone who inspires others to engage their character, purpose, and passion in a collective effort to pursue the mission that brought them together around the vision of an organization (Weis & Muller, 2015; Weis & Muller, 2014; Weis & Gantt, 2009).

Leadership surfaces in a wide variety of ways in the day-to-day work of nonprofit organizations. At any given time, a leader needs to be able to call on a wide range of skills, capacities, and commitments in response to the needs of the organization, the staff and volunteers, and the constituents it seeks to support. A leader may provide guidance for individuals to meet their goals as a part of the mission of the organization. For example, a leader in a performing arts setting can offer suggestions on various classes that individuals could consider in order to develop competencies in the arts. Once a person becomes involved in a program, a leader can offer directions and instructions on how to learn and perform in a particular artistic area. For instance, a dancer might be directed in various movements or exercise techniques. Leaders recognize an opportunity or a need that should be addressed and are willing to accept the responsibility and risks involved in leading and influencing others to meet certain challenges.

What are some characteristics necessary for successful leadership? Because of the increasing complexity of operations and programs in nonprofit organizations and the mission focus of their contributions to the public good, it is particularly important that leaders demonstrate the following (Weis & Muller, 2015):

▶ **Commitment.** The focus of a nonprofit organization is on the purpose or public good mission of the organization. The mission becomes a beacon of light for the public and members of the organization toward which all activities and energies are directed. In other words, all activities are directed toward the perceived organizational purpose. Leaders of nonprofit organizations must have a strong belief in the purpose of their organization and must inspire and guide others to the realization of that purpose.

▶ **Concern.** Leaders of nonprofit organizations must have a genuine interest in the well-being of the people in their community. Members of nonprofit organizations describe effective leaders as individuals who express a real interest in their lives and demonstrate that interest through programs and other actions.

▶ **Competence.** Nonprofit leaders must have competence in human relations and in technical and conceptual skills in order to provide effective programs and services as well as the support for these programs and services.

▶ **Flexibility.** Because of the complexity and difficulty of tasks involved, nonprofit leaders must be able to coordinate a number of different tasks, often at the same time. They must be able to develop and utilize a variety of resources, coordinate and sometimes initiate change.

▶ **Determination**. Staff and volunteer members are faced with a number of hurdles on a daily basis. By focusing on the mission of the organization, staff members and volunteers need to work together to overcome whatever obstacles develop in working to fulfill that mission.

▶ **Integrity.** Establishing a tradition of trust and responsibility encourages confidence from members of the community that is important for successful practices and programs.

▶ **Communication**. Understanding what the community needs in relation to the organization's mission and communicating the organization's intentions to the community is essential for the realization of goals and their mission. The purpose and intent of the organization must be continually monitored and communicated with the community.

▶ **Motivation**. It is important that nonprofit leaders understand the nature of human motivation. Understanding motivational concepts can lead to the establishment of a **motivational environment**. Staff, board, volunteer, and organizational members clearly expect something for their participation and performance, and an effective environment can provide positive reinforcement for all of these groups. This is particularly true of volunteers. All the stakeholders involved in the work of nonprofit organizations expect more than good management skills and commitment to the mission, they expect leadership. Sessoms and Stevenson (1981) write about the range of what is expected of nonprofit leaders today, "Constituents expect (nonprofit) CEOs to articulate clearly and persuasively the organization's mission, beliefs, values, and culture. Both the process and the substance should galvanize widespread commitment towards those ends." (p. 3) Chait and his coauthors (2005) go on to report that these leaders are expected to inspire and guide the organization by:

▶ Shaping agendas, not imposing priorities.
▶ Allocating attention, not dictating results.
▶ Defining problems, not mandating solutions.

The question is often asked, **"How do individuals become leaders?"** Shivers (1980) suggests that people move into leadership roles by one of the following methods:

▶ **Appointment.** Individuals often attain leadership roles through an appointment based on their level of skills and knowledge. This type of appointment is usually officially sanctioned by the organization.
▶ **Election.** In some cases, nonprofit leaders are selected through some sort of elective process. Elected leaders are generally people who are valued, respected, and capable of fulfilling the requirements of the position. Those who elect them have confidence in their abilities to take on the leadership role.
▶ **Emergence.** Emergent leaders become leaders when there is a void in the leadership position, and these individuals have the experience and motivation to fill a particular role.
▶ **Charisma.** Sometimes individuals are so well-liked and respected that they are selected by group members to be a leader. These people lead with intangible qualities and a demeanor that are desired by other group members. These individuals tend to be persuasive and influential in a likable way.

Each of these ways of moving into leadership roles can be found in the nonprofit sector. Demonstrating skills and knowledge that prove effective and result in increased support, respect, and appreciation by others involved in an organization combine to identify potential leaders.

> *If your actions inspire others to dream more,*
> *learn more, do more and become more,*
> *you are a leader.*
>
> **John Quincy Adams**

LEADERSHIP AND POWER

A correlation exists between successful leadership and the use of power to get things accomplished. Some people perceive power as a negative thing, but when it is equated with the positive influence involved in leading nonprofit organizations it becomes one of the most desirable aspects of leadership. Nonprofit leaders who understand this correlation and strategically use the right type of power in the appropriate situation can improve their effectiveness. Power can come from several different sources as illustrated by Stojkovic, Kalinich, & Klofas (2007), who describe the following types of power: **reward, coercive, legitimate, referent, and expert**. A discussion of the use of each type of power in the broad context of the nonprofit sector follows:

▶ **Reward Power.** Reward power means a person believes that they are going to get some type of reward if they do what they are being asked to do. Being in a position of offering a reward for desirable behavior can be very effective. Rewards can take the form of tangibles or intangibles, from pay to days off, from improved work conditions to access to additional program budget support, from a pat on the back to public recognition, and so on.

▶ **Coercive Power.** Coercive power means that a person believes that there will be a form of loss for not doing what they are being asked to do. Leaders can and should incorporate the threat of such loss to get some things done effectively. This power can be particularly important in enforcing practices that have to do with safety and health or in dealing with areas of member or client confidentiality, among other sensitive program and service delivery issues. Coercion can take the form of loss of position, control, funding, and access. This power, however, is sometimes misused, resulting in hostility, distrust, and turmoil.

▶ **Legitimate Power.** Legitimate power means that a person believes that what they are being asked to do is based on a foundation of power assigned to a position or office of the person providing the direction. The importance of influencing others from an official position should not be underestimated. The authority that goes along with a position is particularly important in hierarchical organizations where there are pronounced superior-subordinate relationships. Regardless of the organizational structure, people depend on the legitimate power of those with whom they work in order to value and follow the directions being given.

▶ **Referent Power.** Referent power is when a person has an attraction somehow to the person giving the direction. Individuals sometimes arrive at a position of leadership based on their level of energy and desirability as perceived by others. These individuals lead through the strength of their personality and usually develop a loyal following.

▶ **Expert Power.** Expert power is when a person believes that another person has so much expertise in an area that they believe what they are being told and follow the directions given based on this belief. Individuals who have significant knowledge and skills in particular areas are often influential, and their advice and counsel are highly sought after by other members of the organization.

These powers can influence behavior when used individually or collectively. Nonprofit leaders who understand and use these powers effectively have a greater potential for making a positive difference in people's lives.

> *The key to successful leadership today*
> *is influence, not authority.*
>
> **Kenneth Blanchard**

LEADERS AND FOLLOWERS

Leaders must aspire to develop certain characteristics and competencies in order to be effective. Good leaders also understand that the base of their support is from their followers; without followers there could be no leaders. As a matter of fact, some of the best training for leadership is to follow others. Individuals learn from modeling the behavior of successful leaders and also learn, in some cases, what not to do in particular situations from observing unsuccessful leadership practices. To be a good leader, it is important to understand the benefits of cultivating an active **leader-follower** approach to leadership. Hollander (2009) defines this approach as inclusive leadership that involves an essential leader-follower relationship that requires building a two-way flow of influence between the two. He refers to the benefits of upward influence and makes the case that a two-way operation of leadership and followership must involve the four "Rs" of inclusive leadership: **Respect, Recognition, Responsiveness, and Responsibility** in both directions.

Understanding the many reasons that people may identify their role in an endeavor as one of follower may also help a leader develop productive, quality relationships. Individuals become followers in certain situations because their needs are being fulfilled. Sometimes it is easier for an individual to be a follower; it takes less time and energy. At other times it is a matter of comfort with the current leadership, and at still others it may have something to do with comfort and previous experiences. Being aware of the different reasons that individuals become followers should help in making a leader more responsive and effective.

LEADERSHIP DEVELOPMENT

Former White House Fellow Thomas Cronin wrote that leadership cannot be taught, as such, but that individuals can learn in their own minds the strengths and limitations of leadership (Wren, 1995). An integrated approach to developing leadership that incorporates study, modeling, sharing, and practice in intentional and strategic ways is the best way to develop as a leader. *There are typically four ways to develop as a leader*: (1) examining theories and models, (2) assessing the lives of past leaders, (3) mentoring with effective leaders, and (4) engaging in experiential activities (Weis & Muller, 2015). **Examining leadership theories, studies, and models** provides a theoretical and academic foundation for learning about leadership. **Assessing the actual lives of leaders** can provide understanding and inspiration for self-development. Another process, **mentoring**, allows current leaders opportunities to pass on their knowledge of leading to the next generation. Finally, **experiential education,** a field experience that combines projects with specific learning objectives, provides individuals with opportunities to perform meaningful service while developing knowledge, skills, and character are all important for effective leadership (Weis & Muller, 2014). These aspects of leadership development will be discussed in the next four sections.

LEADERSHIP THEORIES AND MODELS

The literature on leadership is rich, diverse, and continuing to evolve. Some leadership theories maintain importance because they have withstood the test of time and are worthy of consideration. Others gained importance as they have demonstrated their usefulness in practice, become integrated with other theories, and supported effective response to changing dynamics in the need for leadership across context, culture, and regions of the globe. Emerging leadership theories and frameworks add to the understanding and continuing development of effective practice. Some of the foundational theories are presented here, followed by a discussion of evolving and emerging thinking about leadership and management.

Classical Organizational Theory

Frederick Taylor (1967) suggested that natural work, completing tasks in a natural manner, was uneconomical and inefficient; he stated that organizations needed to plan, organize, direct, and control in order to be successful. Taylor determined that there was only one right way to complete a task and any other way was inefficient. Dividing tasks up into different processes, and training an individual for each part of the task seemed much more efficient to Taylor than having one individual complete an entire task alone. As the employee became more skilled at a particular task, according to Taylor, the more efficient production became overall. A great deal of the traditional organizational framework for nonprofit organizations was informed by this theory. Whether this theory is based more in the context of management or leadership is certainly debatable, though a case could be made that both are involved.

Great Man Theory

Eugene E. Jennings (1960) developed the Great Man Theory based on the idea that leaders develop in relation to the situations and the times with which they are confronted. According to Jennings, past leaders such as George Washington, John F. Kennedy, and Martin Luther King developed their platform for leadership and power because of specific circumstances they were passionate about and were successful in their response. In the nonprofit sector there are a number of individuals throughout history who have recognized various needs in the community and have gone about initiating an organization of people to respond to those needs. Clara Barton recognized a need to respond to casualties of war and natural disasters, and she developed the American Red Cross. Juliette Gordon Low thought young girls should have an opportunity to expend their energies in productive and character developing ways and founded the Girl Scouts of America. Sir Robert Baden-Powell believed these same kinds of opportunities should exist for boys and started a scouting program in England that eventually led to the Boy Scouts of America, founded in this country by William D. Boyce.

When we consider some of the enormously complex situations that have occurred throughout history and the number of leaders who have risen to the occasion, one of these categories of the great man theory appears to be at work. The nonprofit sector has its share of founders and current leaders who illustrate this theory in practice.

The Trait Theory

The trait theory (Northouse, 2010) attempts to identify and explain what traits might be helpful for individuals to be leaders. The great man theory of leadership provided the stimulus for this theory and a number of studies indicate that certain characteristics correlate with successful leaders. Traits that are considered important for effective leadership include:

- **Intelligence.** Able to think critically and creatively.
- **Desire for Achievement.** Need to achieve goals and willing to work tirelessly toward that end.
- **Decisiveness.** Thoroughly study the situation then carefully weigh the pros and cons in making a decision.
- **Maturity.** Trusted and counted on for their experience, knowledge, and responsibility.
- **Confidence.** Gives a sense of quiet strength without appearing overbearing or flashy.

> ▸ **Ability to Work with Others.** Work cooperatively with others and provide support, encouragement, and inspiration.
> ▸ **Initiative.** Initiating tasks and activities from an inner sense of what is necessary and appropriate, rather than from an outside source.
> ▸ **Flexibility.** Able to adapt to new trends, issues, activities, and individuals readily and effectively.

Traits are present in other theories and useful in many leadership styles and models. For example, the above traits are clearly woven into the six practices of high-impact nonprofits and their leaders identified by Crutchfield and McLeod Grant in their book *Forces for Good* (2008).

Situational Theory

Situational theory (Bass, 2008) is based on the idea that the leader takes into account different aspects of a situation prior to deciding on a leadership approach. A good leader will consider a number of variables, such as the skills and abilities of the group members and the kind of task involved, before deciding upon a particular approach. Additional variables, such as social, political, cultural, and financial considerations, may also be figured into the decision-making process.

Depending on the circumstances, a leader may decide to take a highly disciplined, authoritative style of leadership, if this approach seems appropriate for the group in the context of the tasks at hand. Or in a different situation, the leader may take a more democratic approach to leadership and invite input from group members before making a decision on how to reach goals. According to the theory, the best approach is the one that works best for a particular situation, and effective leaders are consistently successful at selecting which approach works best for any given situation. The situational framing has great utility in the nonprofit context with its many diverse stakeholders and potential for changing circumstances where flexibility and responsiveness are valued (Weis & Muller, 2015).

Humanistic Theory

The humanistic theory's underlying assumption is that all individuals naturally seek responsibility and that external stimulus affects behavior, rather than personality traits or internal motivation. Humanistic theorists are interested in developing organizations that are structured to motivate individuals to seek responsibility and to realize their full potentials (Nevid & Rathus, 2005). As individuals realize their full potential, they will invariably assist the organization in realizing its goals.

The humanistic leader's purpose, therefore, is to develop organizations that provide guidance, support, and encouragement for individuals to reach their full potential and to acquire expertise in various areas of importance. As individuals mature in the levels of expertise, the leader will provide less guidance but continue with support and encouragement (Weis & Muller, 2015).

Excellence Theory

Appearing in the literature in the 1970s, the excellence theory was articulated further and brought to the forefront of leadership concepts in the next decade by the works of Peters and Waterman (1982). According to the theory, an organization can excel only when individuals aspire to individual and organizational excellence. The theory pulls from the transactional/transformational model of leadership, in which leaders and followers motivate each other to reach higher and higher levels of quality in service and products.

In this concept, a leader works actively with followers to complete tasks and reach goals. One way to do this is to incorporate a process referred to as **managing by walking around** (MBWA). This process can lead to a strong rapport between leaders and followers; it can ensure more effective communication, and it can assist in addressing problems before they become significant. If enacted effectively, it can build camaraderie and even increase morale for leaders and followers. The cooperative nature of many volunteer-based nonprofit programs and organizations frequently promote and benefit from this theory's framework (Weis & Muller, 2015).

The Principle Theory

Character traits, such as honesty and patience, have often been mentioned as essential aspects of good leadership. Stephen Covey (1989) took this concept in a specific direction in the 1980s and 1990s with his idea that effective living and leadership could only be achieved if individuals integrated principles character into all aspects of their lives. The principles Covey selected were based in all the major religions and include *integrity, fairness, honesty, service, human dignity, excellence,* and *potential*, among others. Covey believed people could develop and maintain these principles by processes he referred to as *habits*. He referred to habits as purposeful systems that involve knowledge, skills, and desires, and once formed and practiced would be difficult to let go.

Incorporating habits based on principles, Covey thought people would be able to take charge of their lives; they would set goals and priorities based on what is truly important and act accordingly. This process would encourage all parties involved in situations to feel as if they are winning. It would also encourage leaders to listen and understand individual input from group members, provide a way to enhance collaborative creativity and energy, and give some direction on keeping that energy fresh.

Jim Kouzes offers a Foreword to the *Jossey-Bass Reader on Nonprofit and Public Leadership* (Perry, 2010) in which, after providing a long list of world leaders across the ages, he asks "what do these people have in common?" Kouzes writes, ". . . the list is populated by people with strong beliefs about matters of principle. They all have, or had, unwavering commitment to a clear set of values. They all are, or were, passionate about their causes. The lesson from this simple exercise is unmistakable. People admire most those who believe strongly in something, and who are willing to stand up for their beliefs. If anyone is ever to become a leader whom others would willingly follow, one certain prerequisite is that they must be someone of principle."

The Lewin, Lippin, and White Studies

A number of studies were conducted by Lewin, Lippin, and White in the 1930s that involved young boys who were members of a hobby club (1939). The boys took part in a number of activities involving different kinds of crafts, and the studies examined the effectiveness of various leadership styles. The styles that were identified are explained below:

- ► **Democratic Leadership Style.** Members in this group are asked for their input on goals, processes, and even the individuals they may wish to work with. An attempt is made to treat individuals fairly and equally.
- ► **Authoritarian Leadership Style.** During this type of leadership, the leader directs group members toward the goals of the organization, the processes involved to reach those goals, and the individuals with whom members would work. The leader often maintains a distance from the group and can appear to be aloof, but not hostile.
- ► **Laissez Faire Leadership Style.** There is very little guidance or direction involved with laissez faire style of leadership. Although the leader may provide some of the supplies and materials, he or she does not provide guidance and support. There is also little monitoring or feedback provided by the group leader.

Comparisons were made among the different styles of leadership, and it was determined that members in the authoritarian-led group were more hostile and aggressive than the members of the democratic group. Members reported positive feelings toward the democratic and laissez faire leaders when compared with the authoritative leader. The Lewin, Lippitt, and White studies have been considered groundbreaking research into understanding the nature of leadership, and the results have been the foundation for training, teaching, and further research. Their findings also provide support to the emerging thinking about more collaborative approaches to leadership reported in the previous section.

The Ohio State Studies

The Bureau of Business Research at Ohio State University initiated a series of studies on leadership in 1945 (Stogdill & Coons, 1957). A group of researchers involved with these studies developed an instrument referred to as the Leader Behavior Description Questionnaire. The instrument was designed to assess a leader's conduct in a number of different work settings, including the armed forces, manufacturing, civil service, and education. Two important areas of leadership behavior were identified as a result of the studies, *initiating structure*, and *consideration*.

1. **Initiating Structure.** The way in which the leader determines group goals, group structure, and role expectations.

2. **Consideration.** The relationship that develops between the leader and group members regarding their ideas and feelings. This consideration may be weak or strong depending on the level of trust and respect that exists between the group leader and group members.

University researchers Halpin and Weiner conducted a study in which 83.2% of a leader's behavior was determined by combining these two factors (Stogdill & Coons, 1957). Prior to this, it was thought that leaders were either task-oriented or people-oriented, but the results of the Ohio State Studies indicated both factors should be considered when examining leadership styles and models.

Figure 2.1 demonstrates the different combinations of the factors of *consideration* and *initiating structure*. *Initiating structure* has been designated as task orientation and *consideration* has been designated as human relations orientation. Each of the four quadrants represents a possible leadership style. For instance, a leader with a high human relations orientation and a high task orientation would be interested in doing a good job while at the same time establishing good relationships with employees. This study did not suggest which of the styles was most effective, just that the styles occurred under certain circumstances.

Figure 2.1

A Leadership-Style Model Portraying the Ohio State Studies Dimensions

		Task Orientation	
		Low	High
Human Relations Orientation	High	High human relations orientation and low task orientation	High human relations orientation and high task orientation
	Low	Low human relations orientation and low task orientation	Low human relations orientation and high task orientation

© Kendall Hunt Publishing Co.

The New Managerial Grid

Robert R. Blake and Jane S. Mouton (1978) developed another leadership style model, the New Managerial Grid, in the 1950s. This model includes two dimensions: concern for production and concern for people. Concern for production might include completing organizational tasks and meeting various quotas. Concern for people would include developing effective employee benefits packages and activities to enhance employee morale.

These two variables are placed along two axes (Figure 2.2). Concern for production is positioned along the horizontal axis, and concern for people is placed along the vertical axis. A high concern is represented by the number 9 and a low concern by the number 1. Blake and Mouton identified five different leadership styles using this grid.

- ► **1,1 Impoverished Management.** This individual has little interest in getting work done and little interest in developing relationships. This leader essentially manages in name only.
- ► **1,9 Country Club Management.** With a high concern for relationships but little concern for accomplishing tasks, this person would spend his or her time effecting positive relationships with others.

Figure 2.2

Managerial Grid

HIGH

	1	2	3	4	5	6	7	8	9	
9	Country Club Management								Team Management	
8										
7										
6										
5					Organization Man Management					
4										
3										
2										
1	Impoverished Management								Authority Obedience	
LOW	**1**	**2**	**3**	**4**	**5**	**6**	**7**	**8**	**9**	**HIGH**

© Kendall Hunt Publishing Co.

- ▶ **9,1 Authority-Obedience**. This individual would have a strong interest in completing tasks but little interest in the ideas or feelings of employees. This individual usually uses a leadership position within the organization to control others and to get the job done.
- ▶ **5,5 Organization-Man Management**. This person tries to take a middle-of-the-road approach to leadership, often compromising both production and employee needs.
- ▶ **9,9 Team Management**. This individual attempts to reach organizational goals through trusting and effective relationships with employees. Creating a sense of interdependence and commitment to organizational goals can do this.

Blake and Moulton suggest that the first four styles listed are ineffective. A leader can only be effective by concentrating on a high level of achievement and by developing trusting and respectful relationships with employees. Again, the study provides additional support for the emerging thinking about leadership as a group process of shared vision and action presented earlier.

Transactional/Transformational Leadership

Burns (1978) incorporated the social exchange theory developed by Hollander (2009) to advance the concept of transactional/transformational leadership in the 1970s. Burns used the exchange theory as a foundation, stating, "Leadership occurs when one person takes the initiative in making contact with others for the purpose of an exchange of valued things. The exchange could be economical, political, or psychological in nature" (p. 156). Burns thought that leadership involved mutually shared influences as perceived by followers.

Transactional Leadership. This type of leadership involves the exchange of something of value between the leader and someone who may be thought of as a follower. For instance, a leader may exchange a salary for an employee's time and expertise in a particular area. In a nonprofit setting, individuals often exchange money for the opportunity to participate in a program, to develop a skill, to learn something, or experience something else of significance (Weis & Muller, 2015).

At one level, a transaction may seem like a practical and effective exchange process, but it can also have a negative connotation if more meaningful processes are not present. Exchanges that do not involve other meaningful processes can lead to a carrot and stick mentality where individuals are rewarded if they provide the right exchange, but might be punished if the exchange is inadequate. This process could lead to a wage mentality in a work environment where individuals compete solely for the highest salaries at the expense of feeling proud of accomplishing something worthwhile. The process of treating people according to their productivity can also lead to a negative environment of hostility between employees and between leaders and employees.

Transformational Leadership. Burns suggested that individuals could motivate each other toward higher levels of job satisfaction and wrote that transformational leadership occurs "when one or more persons engage with others in such a way that leaders and followers raise one another to higher levels of motivation and morality" (1978, p. 20). Authors Peters and Waterman (1982) proposed that leadership is a system of transforming individuals and organizations to pursue excellence. Using the transformational model, a leader would empower employees and inspire them to work together to achieve greater heights.

Transformational leadership assumes that individuals need commitment and self-fulfillment, which might actually enhance personal productivity. It is a leadership process that is based on fairness and trust and as Burns wrote, "Transformational leadership is elevating" (1978, p. 455). This type of experience "can take place in many aspects of our personal, professional, and moral lives. These transformations can be physical, intellectual, aesthetic, psychological, social, civic, ecological, transcendental, moral, spiritual, and holistic" (Rost, 1993, p. 126). With this process, individuals are important in and of themselves and are encouraged to pursue a more visionary approach to productivity. As Peters and Waterman (1982) noted, individuals will commit a great deal of themselves to efforts they deem worthwhile.

Tri-Dimensional Leader Effectiveness Model

Hersey and Blanchard (1977) incorporated elements of the Ohio State Studies (human relations orientation and task orientation), in developing a situational leadership theory called the **tri-dimensional leader effectiveness model.** This model is based on the idea that leadership style should be determined based on three variables: (1) the demands of a particular situation or tasks, (2) the type of supervision needed or relationship, and (3) the level of maturity of the individual. A mature individual is described as someone who sets high goals, accepts responsibility for attaining those goals, and has the knowledge and skills to realize those goals. Leadership styles, then, would vary according to the maturity levels of group members (Figure 2.3).

Four different leadership styles are suggested: telling (S1), selling (S2), participating (S3), and delegating (S4). The telling quadrant involves a high task and low relationship orientation. Selling involves a high task and a high relationship orientation. Participating includes a high relationship with a low task orientation, and delegating involves a low relationship with a low task orientation. As an individual progresses in their level of responsibility, knowledge, and skills, they would move from a low level of maturity to a higher level, resulting in a leader changing styles accordingly (Weis & Muller, 2015).

An example of how this process might work would be an employee who is relatively new to an organization and who has not had a great deal of practice in using skills relevant for a particular project. A leader using this concept might adopt an S1 or S2 style of leadership while the individual is developing competence and confidence. As both competence and confidence

Figure 2.3

Tri-Dimensional Leader Effectiveness Model

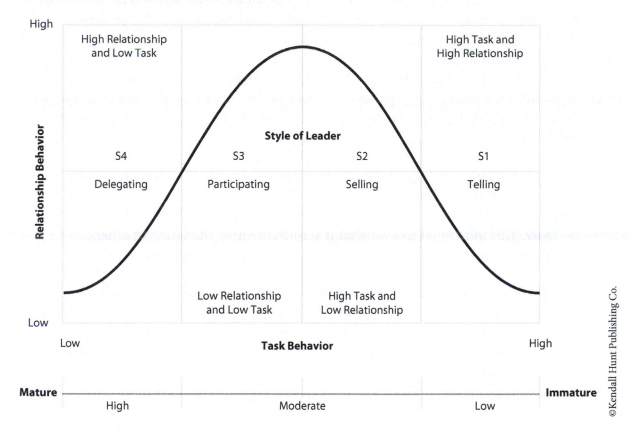

are enhanced, the leader might assume an S3 or S4 position, encouraging the employee to take more initiative while still monitoring his or her progress.

An employee who reaches a high level of maturity in one project may not reach the same level under different circumstances, and it is important for a leader to adjust leadership styles accordingly. The bell-shaped curve running through the quadrants is a continuum, and a leader can go back and forth on this continuum, depending on the circumstances and the maturity level of the employees. The model is particularly relevant as a guide to leading and guiding people on an ongoing basis, where context and experience may influence the need for regular supervision. As a matter of fact, the **Tri-Dimensional** model is an *ideal supervisor tool* when used with good leadership, ergo a wonderful example of the concept of "leader-manager." This finds real relevance in the staff and volunteer work of nonprofit organizations.

Hitt's Model of Leadership

Hitt (1988) proposed a simple model of leadership in which a leader would create a vision for an organization and then develop a plan of action to reach that vision. The process of leadership, then, would be in creating a desirable vision and developing an effective plan for people to follow to achieve success.

Hitt suggested that the leader must both create a vision and develop an effective plan to follow in order to motivate others, and he refers to these qualities as dreaming and doing. In the two-dimensional model below (Figure 2.4), Hitt designates the four possible types of leadership styles:

- ▸ **Victim.** This person has little vision or initiative and often complains about unfair practices within the organization.
- ▸ **Dreamer.** The dreamer has a lot of vision but few implementation skills.
- ▸ **Doer.** This individual will work hard at implementing the vision of others.
- ▸ **Leader-Manager.** This person is high on vision as well as implementation.

The victim is someone with little motivation and vision and remains happy regarding almost everything within an organization. The dreamer is an individual who has high goals but little ability to reach those goals. The doer will work diligently to reach the goals of others. The leader is someone who can help create an exciting and worthwhile shared vision and can motivate group members toward a plan of action to reach goals.

Figure 2.4

The Nature of Leadership

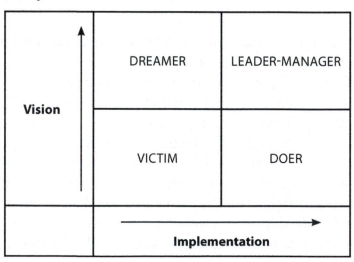

Collaborative Leadership

Collaborative leadership involves people coming together to build trust, cooperation, and communication as they work toward a shared vision and common goals. This is a contemporary style of leadership that continues to evolve. When it emerged in the early 1990s it was described as what was happening when a leader brought people together in a synergistic mode to develop leadership in groups who are working together to make decisions and solve problems. More recent framings of the style shift the focus from the actions of an individual leader to the collective efforts of the members of the group. Archer and Cameron (2009) write about the strategic use of collaboration with the focus on capitalizing on the mutual responsibilities and benefits within the group and the resulting interdependence that strengths the partnerships formed among the group members. They write about success being based, to a great extent, on the attention given to deciding when to collaborate and when not to collaborate. This style of leadership emphasizes sharing ideas and listening, understanding, and supporting the group in acting on the input of those involved. Collaborative leaders are empowering leaders who bring people together for discussion and reflection; then they encourage individuals to accept responsibilities and take actions, depending on situations and levels of professional expertise (Weis & Muller, 2015).

In their book, *The Flight of the Buffalo,* Belasco and Stayer (1993) developed an interesting model of collaborative leadership based on analogies to geese. Belasco and Stayer describe the way geese communicate with each other and change leadership positions in flight when one becomes tired or the situation changes in some other way. Accordingly, in the discussion presented by the authors, effective communication and trust is encouraged as is the sharing of leadership. Individuals are encouraged to accept positions of leadership at opportune times, when their personal strengths and capacities are most appropriate and when others need support and encouragement when their strengths and capacities are challenged or wane. This sharing of leadership responsibilities results in a strong commitment to the goals of the group. Like the smooth transitions observed as the flight of geese seem to shift roles with ease and without significant communications, a quality team of people shift roles and responsibilities naturally as the needs of the group change as work unfolds.

Comprehensive Approach to Leadership

For a leader to be effective, it is essential to be aware of important variables associated with a particular project or activity. A flexible and responsive approach to leadership requires consideration of factors such as the particular situation, group members, and the leader are important in the selection of a leadership style and are depicted in Figure 2.5. These three factors are interrelated and are discussed in detail next.

Figure 2.5

A Comprehensive Approach to Leadership

The Leader's Style		
LEADER	**SITUATION**	**GROUP MEMBERS**
• Knowledge, skills, and abilities • Need disposition • Experience • Style flexibility • Source of power	• External forces • Group goals • Methods/processes • Type of environment	• Knowledge, skills, and abilities • Need disposition • Experience • Task-relevant maturity

Situation. The term *situation* has to do with the task at hand and the process involved in accomplishing the task. Consideration needs to be given to:

▶ **External Forces.** External forces are those forces that individuals have little or no control over, such as weather conditions, political conditions, cultural preferences, customs, and traditions. Knowledge of these circumstances can help in the selection of a leadership style.

▶ **Group Goals.** Having a clear understanding of organizational goals can be helpful in selecting a leadership style and determining the process for reaching those goals.

▶ **Methods and Procedures.** There are a number of different methods that a leader can choose from to achieve results. For instance, programs can take the form of leagues, special events, seminars, classes, or workshops. Different situations call for different approaches.

▶ **Type of Environment.** Environments can be more or less stable, depending on circumstances. A more stable environment calls for a more task-oriented leadership style, whereas a less stable environment might call for a more people-oriented style.

Group Members. Understanding the background and qualifications of each member of the group is essential in selecting a style of leadership. A number of factors should be considered.

▶ **Knowledge, Skills, and Abilities.** A leader must have an understanding of individual areas and levels of expertise in order to match this expertise with specific, correlating tasks.

▶ **Needs Disposition.** Group members are each motivated differently, so a leader must have knowledge of individual interests, needs, and desires prior to developing a plan of supervision.

▶ **Experience.** Members of a group who have had a broad range of experience might require a less direct approach than members with minimal experience.

► **Task-Relevant Maturity.** Individuals who have proven to be responsible and/or high achievers may require less supervision than individuals with less task-relevant maturity.

The Leader. The leader is the key in pulling all of the elements together for the success of programs and organizations. Some of the factors important in the development of a successful leadership style are detailed below:

► **Knowledge, Skills, and Abilities.** Being aware of one's own strengths and weaknesses is important when selecting a leadership style.
► **Needs Disposition.** The leader's own interests, needs, and desires are significant factors, since a leader operates according to his or her own motivational factors and comfort levels.
► **Experience.** The leader who has had previous experience working with group members can use this experience in making decisions in the future.
► **Style Flexibility.** The degree to which a leader can adapt to different leadership styles should also be a factor in selecting a style of supervising.
► **Source of power.** The ability of a leader to incorporate sources of power (covered previously in this chapter) is important in selecting leadership style. A leader who is charismatic may need to take a more relaxed style, while an individual who is comfortable with a legitimate or authoritative style may be more directive in supervising others.

Being able to evaluate each of these areas effectively—the situation, group members, and the leader—provides the leader with valuable information in selecting the best leadership style and therefore might even be considered a common-sense type of leadership model. Many effective approaches to nonprofit leadership seem to naturally incorporate deliberate consideration of such factors in framing a response or action plan.

Servant Leadership

Robert K. Greenleaf is credited with a theory of leadership in which an individual begins with a natural feeling of wanting to serve others first. This individual then makes a conscious decision to develop as a leader. According to Greenleaf, a servant-leader's passion is to make sure that people's needs are being served and they are growing stronger and more competent and confident as the servant-leader works to empower them. A servant-leader works for his or her people and does everything possible to help them accomplish their goals and be successful. A good servant leader places the well-being of others above him/herself and often directs credit for successes to others (Weis & Muller, 2014).

Invitational Leadership

In the book *Becoming an Invitational Leader,* Purkey & Stegel (2003) develop a holistic and dynamic model of leadership suggesting that leaders need to *invite* their colleagues and others to participate in more effective relationships. They suggest leaders practice four specific guiding principles when *inviting* others to become involved in more successful processes and activities; these are *respect, trust, optimism,* and *intentionality.*

One way to show *respect* toward others is to treat them with appreciation and care. This is important on a day-to-day basis and particularly important in times of crisis. By *trusting* others we are expressing the idea that we value their abilities as well as their integrity, and yes there is vulnerability in trusting relationships but this leads to much greater strength in the long run. *Optimists* tend to expect the best from the human spirit and believe that each individual can and should strive toward their full potential. Optimists often make good leaders. *Intentionality* is the key component of invitational leadership concept because such leaders focus on being respectful, trustworthy, and optimistic, which encourages individuals to be the very best they can be and to grow stronger together (Weis & Muller, 2014).

Leadership Theory and Concept Development

In her book *Finding Our Way: Leadership for an Uncertain Time* (2005), Margaret Wheatley states that she believes organizations should grow and adapt organically with little structure; that there should be a freer flow of communication throughout so that more individuals will be open to creating ideas and solving problems.

Quinn (2000) combines models from leaders around the world in developing his philosophy for "*How Ordinary People Can Accomplish Extraordinary Results,*" which is part of the title of his book, *Change the World.* In this book, Quinn smartly describes how community change only begins when we look within and begin by evaluating, understanding, and transforming ourselves in the shape similar to those who have come before us such as Gandhi, Martin Luther King, Jr., and Jesus. Then he offers a detailed way in which these individual changes can lead to entire community transformations for the better.

Bill George in *Authentic Leadership* (2003) seems to combine elements from Covey's principle driven leadership theories, and Wheatley's relationship driven leadership theories and focuses on these themes regardless of the fact that he was working in financial organizations with billions of dollars of holdings. The value of his organization went up substantially under his direction while concentrating on people and principles and seemingly letting financial development become a by-product of these two other interacting processes.

Another emerging leadership theorist, Stewart Friedman (2008), placed leadership into a total package of work, home, community, and self with his book *Total Leadership*, which guides individuals to focus on what is most important in their lives in each of these areas and to organize their lives and activities around what's important. This is somewhat similar to Stephen Covey's *7 Habits of Highly Effective People*, which also asks the question what is most important in one's life and are you living your life around your principles?

Author and theorist Peter Block begins his book *Community: The Structure of Belonging* (2008) by reflecting on Robert Putnam's claim in his book *Bowling Alone* that community health, educational achievement, economic strength, and community well-being in general was dependent on the quality of relationships and the cohesion that exists among citizens. With that said he discusses how whole communities can overcome old and negative stereotypes and develop strategies for transformation by incorporating individuals from all backgrounds into a theme of restoration and pride. This transformation takes place by convening individuals from all walks of life and by listening to what they have to offer and learning about where they want to go together, a concept so different from managing and directing individuals toward predetermined goals. By identifying and using existing neighborhood assets, Block says we can create citizen activist movements that help form a welcoming and positive environment for growth, now and in the future.

Another author on leadership development, Simon Sinek, *Leaders Eat Last* (2014), seeks to blend concepts such as collaborative leadership, invitational leadership, and servant leadership into an eclectic concept in which leaders are much like parents, protecting and treating employees as family members while encouraging and empowering each member to provide input and to work effectively together.

One way to keep up with emerging leadership theorists is by following the continuing series of *Jossey–Bass Reader on Nonprofit and Public Leadership,* edited by James Perry. These publications contain a number of the more current experts and their theories for leaders in the nonprofit and public sector. Another great way to look at a thorough history of leadership as well as some helpful studies on the field is by obtaining a copy of *The Bass Handbook of Leadership: Theory, Research, and Managerial Applications, 4th Edition* by Bernard Bass with Ruth Bass, a Free Press publication (2008).

Since nonprofit organizations are taking on more and more concerns in more communities than ever before, they deserve the best leadership and management that's possible. It is incumbent on any leader that is providing services and leading others in these efforts to be as sharp and capable as those found in any other sector of our society.

THE CONNECTION BETWEEN LEADERSHIP, CHARACTER, AND ETHICS

Too often, leadership models fail to include the importance of character and ethics in the overall scheme of leading and influencing others. Aristotle identified *ethos* as a central element in understanding how one person influences another. He contended that our perception of another person is based heavily on our perception of that individual's virtues, wisdom, and good will (Kennedy, 1991). **Character** includes the beliefs, traits, and values that distinguish one person from another. This involves being true to a standard or standards that a person has set to govern his or her life. **Ethics** is a system of moral principles and values and moral duty and obligation; it not only deals with what people believe about how they should act, but what they *should* believe (Jeavons, 2010). Leaders must have the kind of character it takes to represent the organization effectively and the type of ethical system that allows them to lead with a strong moral compass. An examination of a leadership model that includes character at the center will be followed by review of a concept for maintaining ethical standards in nonprofit organizations (Weis & Muller, 2014).

The Integrated Leadership and Character Model

The Integrated Leadership and Character Model (Figure 2.6) focuses on the importance of character in leadership (Weis & Muller, 2014). The model identifies critical skills and knowledge areas and illustrates the central function of personal character. According to the model:

- ▶ To be successful, organizations must have leaders with traits and values (personal character), shared purpose and passion that are important to the overall development of the organization.
- ▶ Leaders must also possess or develop an effective level of conceptual, technical, and human relation skills.
- ▶ The interaction and effectiveness of these three skill areas is dependent on the personal character, purpose, and passion of individual leaders within the organization.

To develop and implement effective programs in a nonprofit organization, a leader must have an idea of what individuals need and want (conceptual skills); skills in planning and implementing programs (technical skills); and be able to inform and motivate staff members to implement programs and know how to encourage constituents to participate in the programs (human relations skills). The more determined an individual is to make a program work and the more trusted the leader (personal character), the more likely the program is to succeed.

This same concept can be effectively applied to any process or procedure being undertaken in a nonprofit organization. For instance, in developing and implementing a budget, leaders must have an understanding and a vision of financial matters. They need to be knowledgeable and skilled in developing the technical aspects of the budget and the budgeting process, along with being able to communicate budgetary procedures effectively to others. Personal character is also critical in making certain all of the skill areas are working effectively and that the processes are moving along smoothly.

Figure 2.6

Integrated Leadership and Character Model

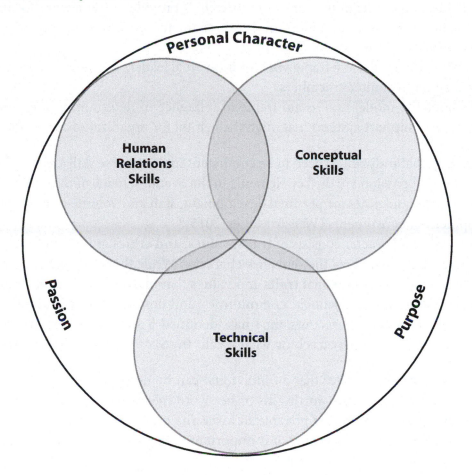

PERSONAL CHARACTER	Includes traits, values, and ethics which make each person unique
Conceptual Skills	Identify the critical thinking side of a person and include: vision, planning, decision making, and problem solving
Technical Skills	Identify a person's specific expertise and include: program development, marketing, budgeting, management of time and technology
Human Relations Skills	Identify a person's ability to interact effectively with others and include motivation, conflict management, teamwork, and intercultural sensitivity

© Roger M. Weis and Vernon W. Gantt

There are three important **implications** to consider in the context of this model:

► Consider the model in the context of oneself. It provides a framework for individuals to go by to assess and develop their own character and skills for any given circumstance being addressed.

► Consider the model as a framework for individual leaders to use in selecting and training staff and volunteer members.

► Consider the model as a useful frame of reference in determining the types of programs and support systems that might be helpful for organizational members.

Recognizing that individuals need to be competent in these three skill areas and that character, purpose, and passion are the key elements in the overall scheme of things provides nonprofit leaders with guidelines for personal development, staff and volunteer development, and the development of constituents (Weis & Muller, 2015).

In realizing that character consists of **traits, values, and ethics**, it is important to examine these attributes to discover how they enhance character. While there might not be total agreement on the specific list of **personal traits** and **values** that make up character, a nonpartisan, nonsectarian coalition of 454 schools, communities, and nonprofit organizations, **Character Counts!** (http://www.charactercounts.org/) has identified a short list. This group works to advance character education by teaching what it calls the **Six Pillars of Character:**

1. **Trustworthiness** implies that an individual can be depended upon. When a person is considered to be trustworthy, his or her word means something. He or she can be expected to do everything possible to assist the organization and the individuals in the organization in succeeding. It is important to be able to work alongside people we believe in and that we can trust.

2. **Respect** includes valuing the contributions, the differences, and the feelings of others. It is only possible to value someone else's ideas and feelings through a genuine effort of understanding. Understanding means making an attempt to gather as much information as possible regarding another person in order to empathize and collaborate with that person.

3. **Responsibility** means accepting a degree of ownership for all areas of an organization and accepting strong ownership for particular areas of an organization. Accepting responsibility is important for the overall health and success of an organization. Leaders of good character do not waste time blaming others, but rather work cooperatively to ensure success.

4. **Fairness** involves full consideration of all information to assure that all parties in a situation are listened to and dealt with without favoritism. Being fair is not always

popular or necessarily expedient, but it is always just and equal. Fairness is a trait that, when perceived, brings with it the trust and loyalty of others.

5. **Caring** for others is essential in a nonprofit organization and includes compassion and concern for others. Members of nonprofit organizations report that good leaders are those who care about their needs, concerns, and feelings. Members are not so concerned about the behind-the-scenes activities of organizations, but they are concerned about leaders who exhibit a genuine interest in their well-being.

6. **Citizenship** means taking an active and thoughtful interest in the community. Leaders of nonprofit organizations have an opportunity to incorporate their position to make things happen in the community. They also have the opportunity, and perhaps obligation, to involve staff, volunteers, and members in community action, when appropriate.

Organizations such as the YMCA, Big Brothers/Big Sisters, and Girls, Inc., often have other traits and values they associate with character, and these traits and values might differ from individual to individual or from culture to culture. The important consideration is that character is critical to effective leadership, especially in the nonprofit sector. Greater attention should be given to the role character plays in leadership, regardless of context. Doing the right thing for the right reasons as opposed to doing what works is the subject of the next section, ethics.

The Role of Ethics in Nonprofit Leadership

REGARDING ETHICS

*"We are discussing no small matter,
but how we ought to live."*

SOCRATES,
AS REPORTED BY PLATO IN THE REPUBLIC (CA. 390 B.C.)

Staff members, volunteers, and constituents often look to positional leaders to set the standards for moral thought and behavior in the nonprofit sector. Nonprofit organizations benefit when they have an established ethical culture to guide their work toward their public good mission. It needs to include key ethical *obligations* that the organization believes must be embraced and pursued. Jeavons (2010) suggests five such obligations necessary for developing an **ethical culture**: *integrity*, *openness*, *accountability*, *service*, and *charity*.

Integrity implies that the organization and individuals within the organization can be depended upon to do what they have stated they intend to do. In other words, their deeds match their words. Integrity is critical for establishing trust within the organization and between the organization and the community. Integrity can be demonstrated in a number of different ways. Organizational literature such as promotional brochures, fundraising materials, and other reports should match actual situations. In other words, documents should never be embellished for organizational gain. If actual performance in an area does not match the degree to which it is billed, then mistrust develops between the organization and its constituents and other members of the community.

Another way integrity can be demonstrated is to have leaders who represent the values and mission of the institution effectively. In other words, trustworthiness can and should be demonstrated on a daily basis. In 2001, the American Red Cross generated hundreds of millions of dollars to assist the victims of the terrorist attacks of September 11th. When it is was revealed that a small portion of the money contributed would go elsewhere, the public was outraged and the organization quickly reverted to its original plan and worked hard to rebuild the public trust that may have been lost with the incident. Some donors may have been lost or slow to return as a result. Nonprofit leaders have an obligation to be as honest as possible with the public as well as with their own staff members. Attempts to disguise facts or offer misleading information can create dramatic results often with far-reaching consequences (Weis & Muller, 2015).

Openness might not accurately qualify as a moral value, but for organizations operating in the public sphere, maintaining openness to public observation and scrutiny is certainly virtuous and even practical. For organizations that provide public services or advocacy and have impact on community life, operating in secrecy would arouse skepticism regarding motivation. Part of this skepticism is historical in nature, since a small number of service organizations from time to time have operated with ulterior motives. The most successful nonprofit organizations operate effectively and welcome inquiries regarding any area of their operation.

Organizations that are concerned with maintaining a culture of interest and excitement realize that maintaining a climate of trust is essential to this interest and excitement and that operating openly is the best way to develop trust. Another reason to maintain openness is that many nonprofit organizations began as volunteer associations with a rich, populist, democratic background, and maintaining openness and democratic ways helps to ensure that tradition. Maintaining openness in decision-making, programs, financial matters, and other issues relevant to the overall operation of an organization is key to maintaining the trust of the community. Transparent and open communications are essential to maintaining integrity for nonprofit organizations (Weis and Muller, 2015).

Accountability means that not only should organizations maintain an openness regarding all operations, but they must also be able to explain and be accountable for their activities. Nonprofit organizations often solicit tax-deductible contributions, or at least receive a tax-exempt status, and with that they have an obligation to perform public service as effectively and as efficiently as possible. These tax benefits are contractual in nature, which obligates organizations both ethically and legally to perform according to promise and to be evaluated accordingly.

By accepting the privilege of tax-exempt status or the opportunity to solicit tax-deductible contributions, organizations accept the responsibility to be evaluated not only by their constituents but also by the public at large. This also obligates organizations to pursue the stated mission and purpose of the institution and to be accountable to the membership in working toward that end. The need for accountability has motivated more and more states to pass laws mandating financial disclosures and regulating fundraising activities for nonprofit organizations. Additionally, watch-dog groups such as the National Charities Information Bureau and the Better Business Bureau's section on nonprofit organizations are taking a closer look at organizational finances and other operations. Nonprofit leaders have an obligation to ensure that the organization and all individuals within the organization are accountable to their constituents, their board members, and to the broader public (Weis & Muller, 2015).

Service is similar to accountability in the sense that nonprofit organizations exist, and are granted special privileges, because of their commitment to serve the public, or at least to the membership. The social contract they receive, which provides them with special privileges, obligates them to work toward a mission of public good; the membership dues, program fees, special event money, contributions, volunteer time, and other resources these organizations receive also obligate them ethically toward service.

This service ethic must also be manifested in the leaders of nonprofit organizations, who can certainly work toward their own advancement, but, without sacrificing personal well-being, they must always place the cause of the organization and the well-being of the people the organization is serving uppermost in their priorities. The idea of leaders seeing themselves as servants for the cause of the organization and for their constituents is critical in focusing others within the organization on the needs of the members. Nonprofit organizations are by nature altruistic, and it is therefore necessary for the leaders of these organizations to operate with a philosophy of selflessness and service (Weis & Muller, 2015).

Charity is one of the most important ethical obligations of all, since the word charity comes from the Latin *caritas*, which means more than giving to those in need (Jeavons, 2006). Originally, the translation of the word charity was love, but not romantic love. Rather, it meant the kind of love a person shows for a neighbor in need. It also meant to be caring, putting the welfare of others above one's own, and sharing one's resources with others out of a sense of concern and social obligation rather than a sense of pity.

From an organizational standpoint, an ethical obligation to the principle of charity is derived in part from reciprocity. In other words, nonprofit organizations benefit from the generosity of others and are therefore obliged to express generosity themselves. The motivation of the supporters of many of these organizations comes from the idea that the organization is committed to caring for others. Additionally, individual service recipients often indicate that they believe that they will receive more personable and more caring service from private, nonprofit organizations than from public entities. The leaders of these organizations must be selected for their character traits that include a caring and respectful nature. Leaders often set the tone for all operations within the organization and a caring and giving person will influence the way the organization operates.

The elements of character, ethics, and purpose, among others, are central to the notion of effective leadership for the good of others. The Integrated Leadership and Character Model offers a straightforward framing of how these elements can be thoughtfully and intentionally woven into a more holistic approach to bring the full range of human emotions, commitments, and skills to the responsibilities of leadership (Weis & Muller, 2014; Weis & Gantt, 2009).

LEADERS THROUGH THE AGES

Assessing the lives of effective leaders provides understanding and inspiration for leadership development. Following are brief profiles of leaders across eras, regions, and perspectives that offer a range of experiences for considering and exploring leadership in action:

Lao-Tzu was a Chinese sage who lived in sixth century B.C. and described leadership as providing a service in a selfless manner. According to Lao-Tzu, a leader should place the well-being of others above oneself and accordingly, these acts of selflessness would actually enhance oneself. He compared an enlightened leader to water that "cleanses and refreshes all creatures without judgment" (Wren, 1995). A leader is yielding, like water, and if a leader does not push forward too severely, group members will not resent or resist being led. He thought leadership should be a nourishing experience and that leaders should be humble and direct credit for successes to others. He imagined leaders as facilitators who would lead with as little direction as possible.

Lao-Tzu also compared the process of leadership to being a midwife, in which the leader is merely facilitating another person's process. The leader needs to be reminded that it is basically someone else's process and that the leader should guide the process with as little intrusion as possible. If the leader trusts the other person in the process, according to Lao-Tzu, that person will also trust the guidance of the leader (Weis & Muller, 2015). Just as a midwife assists at someone else's birth, a leader should facilitate what is happening, rather than what he or she thinks should be happening. If the leader must take the lead from time to time, the leadership should be such that the group member is assisted, yet still feels a sense of autonomy.

Plato lived between 428–347 B.C. and was a student of Socrates. He founded the Academy in 387 B.C., and this was the first permanent institution in Western civilization completely devoted to education and research. Plato often expressed disappointment in the excesses of liberty and democracy and, writing in his *Republic*, suggested these excesses often led to tyranny and anarchy. He thought wise philosophers, selected for their love of philosophy and knowledge, should lead the state. These philosopher-kings should rule the state based on their natural inclinations and should set themselves apart from their followers in order to rule more objectively with their intellect.

Plato thought these philosopher-kings would be discovered as individuals who naturally wished to study philosophy and who would also exhibit leadership qualities. These individuals would be intelligent, noble, gracious, courageous, and temperate, and they would therefore appear different from the rest of the citizenry (Weis & Muller, 2015). These philosophers would be able to focus on the eternal nature of truth and justice without varying from generation to generation and without being led astray by corruption.

Aristotle (384–322 B.C.) was the gifted student of Plato, yet he disagreed with his teacher and mentor regarding the selection of philosopher-kings as leaders of the state. Aristotle believed all citizens should have an opportunity to govern and to be governed. He believed that all men should experience being governed in order to be more effective as leaders themselves. Aristotle thought all men should be treated equally by the state and that all men should have an equal chance to govern. These were concepts he believed to be essential in order for the state to survive. Anything else would lead to anarchy and revolution and the demise of the state.

Aristotle stated that it was impossible for any single class or group of citizens to assume a place of superiority over another. According to Aristotle, it was the charge of the state, therefore, to provide education that would allow each person to learn to be a good citizen, to learn obedience, and at the same time to learn to command (Weis & Muller, 2015). Obeying and commanding were both honorable in themselves, as long as the intentions and the end results were good. It could be said that Aristotle was one of the first philosophers leaning toward democratic governance.

Niccolo Machiavelli (1469–1572) was trained as a humanist and served as a diplomat for Florence prior to being exiled. While in exile, he wrote his infamous *The Prince*, which addresses the idea of gaining and maintaining individual power by any means. Although *The Prince* describes the importance of individual power, his other famous work, the *Discourses*, describes the important aspects of a republic. In *The Prince*, Machiavelli suggests that individuals should be merciful, gracious, upright, and religious, whenever possible, but should revert to trickery and deceitfulness whenever it is necessary to gain power and to maintain authority.

Machiavelli postulated that individuals who used cunning measures when necessary to reach their goals accomplished more and would win over individuals who incorporated honesty in their dealings. He believed that men were generally dishonest by nature, and therefore a leader should not keep his (or her) word when it becomes advantageous to do otherwise. According to Machiavelli, whenever a leader succeeds in establishing and maintaining authority, regardless of the means of accomplishment, the leader will be judged honorable and be approved by all (Weis & Muller, 2015). Although this philosophy was timely for Machiavelli's day, its treatise resonates to present time and *The Prince* remains a classic in the study of leadership.

Thomas Jefferson (1743–1827) was a brilliant statesman, scientist, architect, inventor, educator, and public servant (Koch & Peden, 1993). Jefferson was the author of the Declaration of Independence, the founder of the University of Virginia, and the third president of the country. He was born into a Virginia family of means; his father was a wealthy plantation owner, and his mother was of distinguished English and Scottish pedigree. He took advantage of the opportunity for a formal education and eventually earned a law degree from William and Mary College in 1762.

Jefferson's interest in politics led him to become an accomplished statesman. His Southern aristocratic background and culture generally served him well, and he incorporated his vast knowledge and statesmanlike abilities to move the country toward the birth of its independence from England. This same culture, however, led to a contradiction for the man who wrote, "We hold these truths to be self-evident, that all men are created equal, that they are endowed by their Creator with certain unalienable Rights, that among these are Life, Liberty, and the pursuit of Happiness" in the Declaration of Independence. At the same time, he bought, sold, and owned slaves, and did so even later when he became president (Weis & Muller, 2015). In spite of this contradiction, Jefferson continues to be revered as one of the greatest leaders of the country and a champion of democratic ways.

Harriett Tubman (1820–1913) was born into a slave family on the Eastern Shore section of Maryland on a plantation owned by Edward Broadas (Petry, 1955). Growing up, Tubman learned what it meant to be a slave and was taught to say, "Yes, Missus," "No, Missus," to white women and "Yes, Mas'r," "No, Mas'r," to white men (Petry, 1955, p. 21). At nighttime she would sometimes hear the hoof-beats of horses as slave owners would ride up and down the dirt roads looking for runaways. Runaways would sometimes be brought back shackled in chains and beaten, or worse, *sold south*, a term that meant a slave was sold to a plantation in the deep South (Petry, p. 9). As a young girl, Tubman worked in the fields of the plantation, often from dusk to dawn, but when hard times came to the plantation, she was sometimes hired out to other families for cleaning, weaving, watching trap lines, and caring for their children.

Tubman later married a freed slave named John and was allowed to live in his cabin with him. But Tubman feared being sold South, and she plotted running away to the North. When John refused to accompany her, she left anyway. On her escape north, she was befriended and supported by people along the way. This assistance came to be known as the Underground Railroad, but it was little more than a loosely organized group of people who offered hiding and food. She soon found herself a free person in Pennsylvania, but missed her family and friends and made the dangerous journey back and forth to Maryland numerous times, always guiding a group of slaves North with her. Later in life, Tubman became a scout and a spy for the North, but she is remembered most as a conductor for the Underground Railroad. In later years, she had a difficult time financially and even sold produce door-to-door. In 1913, she died penniless, but free (Weis & Muller, 2015).

Clara Barton was born on Christmas Day in 1821 in an unpretentious farmhouse in Oxford, Massachusetts (Boylston, 1955). Barton was a shy student as a youngster but was something of a tomboy and relished the idea of jumping on a wild colt and racing across the Massachusetts countryside. It was during her early years that her younger brother David was injured in a fall, and she was asked to assist in his care. Barton was a natural nurse and completely took over the care of her brother until he was well. Later, she became a teacher, winning the admiration of her students for her caring ways and her ability to keep up with them in recreational pursuits. After teaching for a number of years, Barton left to work in the U.S. Patent Office in Washington, D.C. While she was there, war broke out between the states, and Barton accepted a nursing position and was able to go to the battlefront, where most of the casualties were. As a nurse, Barton saved countless lives, often working from daybreak until long past dusk (Weis & Muller, 2015).

Following the war, President Lincoln recruited Barton to assist in locating 22,000 missing soldiers, which she did for four long years. Afterward, tired and ill from her efforts, she sailed to Europe to recuperate. While in Europe, Barton learned of the International Red Cross, an organization designed to provide relief for people during a time of war. Upon returning from Europe, she began forming the American version of the IRC. In no time at all, Barton's organization was providing relief services for flood and fire victims, and in 1882 President Arthur appointed her as the first president of the National Red Cross, which later came to be known as the American Red Cross (Weis & Muller, 2015). Her desire to help others has changed the lives of millions, and in so doing helped to change the shape of an entire nation.

Geronimo (1829–1909) was born in the mountains of Arizona into a Bedonkohes Apache family (Debo, 1976). As a young man, Geronimo was very athletic. He played games that prepared him for a rigorous adult life, which often involved raiding the enemies of his people and then fleeing to the mountains for weeks at a time. He was considered stronger and wiser than his years and was admitted into the council of warriors for his skill and knowledge in battles at the early age of seventeen. He experienced a great personal tragedy a little later in life, when his entire family—mother, wife, and three children—were slain by the members of the

Mexican Army. From that day forward, he vowed never to be killed by a Mexican bullet, and he managed to live to be over eighty and died of natural causes.

Geronimo became one of the most feared Indians ever and could ride a horse, handle a lance, and shoot a rifle better than anyone. Once with Geronimo at the lead, he and 18 Apache warriors were able to confront and deter the forces of 5,000 U.S. Troopers. Since there was no formal leadership structure with the Apache Indians, Geronimo led by example and was admired by his fellow warriors for his independence, integrity, courage, determination, and ruthlessness. He was often very persuasive and led through this skill as well as by being trusted by the other Indians. He was a highly spiritual man, and his sense of honor and courage had been observed in battle on numerous occasions. They earned him the respect of friend and foe alike (Weis & Muller, 2015). Although Geronimo had been lied to many times by his enemies, he never broke his own code of honor. In fact, it could be said that the Apache culture itself was the style of leadership adopted by Geronimo.

George A. Custer was a West Point graduate who served as a general and became a true hero in the Civil War (Utley, 1988). As one of the leaders for the Michigan Wolverines, he and his troops defeated the Confederate cavalry General Jeb Stuart at Gettysburg and defended the Union Army from attack by General Pickett and over 12,000 Confederate infantrymen. He and his troops also dogged General Robert E. Lee in his final retreat and eventually forced Lee to surrender. He was described by his superiors as a warrior who fought with audacity, courage, and an unparalleled fury and a focus on winning. He was revered by most and considered to be one of the greatest military leaders of his time. In fact, had it not been for a place in Montana named Little Big Horn, Custer could very well have become President Custer.

Following the Civil War, millions of Americans moved West in search of cheap land and encountered nearly 200,000 Indians, many of whom were determined to defend their territory. The dashing Civil War hero, Custer was sent along by his government to protect the pioneering Americans. Custer and the U.S. Army adopted a tactic referred to as total war, which meant that all Indians were viewed as dangerous and were to be attacked wherever and whenever possible. He again became a national hero for the successes of this tactic and planned his next attack against the Indians at Little Big Horn. But Little Big Horn was to be his undoing, and Custer and all of the men in his unit were killed by an enemy enraged by past brutalities. Brimming with confidence from his successes, he had tragically underestimated the spirit and experience of his enemy, and overestimated his own ability and the will of his troops (Weis & Muller, 2015).

Mohandas Gandhi (1869–1948) was educated in law but devoted his entire life to helping the disadvantaged. He worked to bring an end to discrimination against the lower orders of India, known as the untouchables, he helped establish Hindu-Muslim unity, and he was instrumental in securing independence for his native India from Great Britain. But it was not so much the issues he was involved in but the method he used that brought him fame and the honorable title of Mahatma, which meant Great Soul. His use of passive resistance to organize his countrymen in the wake of overwhelming British odds is legendary. He believed that passive resistance should only be used for just causes, and individuals espousing passive resistance must be willing to suffer to the end for those causes.

For Gandhi, evil was only to be overcome by good, anger by love, and untruth by truth, and always through peaceful means. He believed that only the courageous could be passive resisters and that, in the long run, both the individuals involved in resistance and the individuals who were being resisted benefited from the process. Gandhi thought that men of integrity would disregard unjust commands from leaders, even if it meant putting their lives in jeopardy, and that in defying death they freed themselves from fear (Weis & Muller, 2015). He believed there was no one in the world so bad that they could not be converted by love. His example of practiced non-violence inspired millions of people to emulate his example for decades.

Helen Keller was born in the small town of Tuscumbia, Alabama, in 1904 and had a pretty normal childhood until she reached the age of nineteen months, when she developed a fever that left her blind, deaf, and unable to speak. Because this left Keller with limited opportunities for effective communication, she became something of a behavior problem. Her parents were encouraged to take her to Dr. Alexander Graham Bell, a prominent teacher of the deaf and inventor of the telephone. Dr. Bell recommended that Keller receive schooling from Anne Sullivan, who had become nearly blind herself and had overcome many obstacles to become a teacher of the blind, the deaf, and the mute. Under Sullivan's care, Keller began to read and write by using braille and became calmer as she grew in her communication skills. By the age of seven, Keller had mastered four alphabets: the manual one for the deaf, the square pencil script, raised letters, and braille dots.

Eventually, Keller wrote her own story about growing up with so many complications and the story became a book, *The Story of My Life* (2005), which was printed in 50 different languages. Keller went on to encourage thousands of others with similar afflictions and was deeply involved in what was then a new organization, the American Foundation for the Blind. She also wrote *Teacher*, a tribute to her teacher and mentor, Anne Sullivan (Weis & Muller, 2015). Keller, with the unparalleled assistance of Sullivan, had overcome incredible obstacles to become a source of inspiration for millions of people worldwide.

Cesar Chavez grew up in the small town of Gila Bend, Arizona, where his father and grandfather were local business and landowners (Levy, 1975). The depression of 1929 left the Chavez family nearly penniless, however, and they had to leave their home and begin a life of crop picking. The conditions in the labor camps where the Chavez family had to live were horrible; there was no heat, sanitation system, running water, or electricity. The school system where Chavez and his brother and sister attended was racist, and children were punished if they spoke Spanish during school hours. Outside of school their life consisted of picking walnuts, cherries, cotton, potatoes, apricots, melons, and grapes for meager wages and for labor contractors who often cheated the growers regarding the weight of their daily production (Weis & Muller, 2015).

Following a stint in the United States Navy during World War II, Chavez began working for the Community Service Organization. His job was to register people to vote, and he learned about power, organizing agencies, and organizing sit-ins. Later, Chavez's determination and personal involvement was critical in organizing the National Farm Workers Association to work for better wages and conditions for crop pickers. He successfully incorporated nonviolent strategies, such as boycotts and picketing, against the powerful California Growers Association, represented by the Teamsters Union and the AFL-CIO. When the Teamsters began physically attacking NFWA members, Chavez adopted the Hindu concept of fasting, which encouraged other NFWA members to commit to his nonviolent movement, and the NFWA was eventually victorious in its fight for fairness with the growers in California (Weis & Muller, 2015). Like Ghandi before him, Chavez put his beliefs and his life on the line again and again in support of the culture and people he loved.

Dr. Martin Luther King, Jr. was born on January 15, 1929, in Atlanta, Georgia, the son of a minister (Frady, 2002). Dr. King became the pastor of the Dexter Avenue Baptist Church in Montgomery, Alabama, when he was 25 years old in 1954. Educated at Morehouse College and Crozer Theological Seminary, he completed his doctoral studies in 1955 at Boston University. As injustice toward African Americans gained increasing attention across the country, Dr. King sought ways of helping move toward civil rights. His learning journey included being inspired by Mahatma Gandhi's success with nonviolent activism. Dr. King was inspired by a 1959 visit to Gandhi's birthplace in India that he returned to claim that "nonviolent resistance was the most potent weapon available to oppressed people in their struggle for justice and human dignity."

Dr. King inspired and informed the Civil Rights Movement in the United States with his leadership. From his organizing role in the 1955 Montgomery Bus Boycott after Rosa Parks refused to give up her seat to a white man to his 1963 "I Have A Dream" speech during the march on Washington, Dr. King was the guiding force and inspiration for a generation of people from all walks of life and across all races in pursuit of civil rights for all Americans. His list of accomplishments is long and the impact he had on the country and the world beyond measure. His leadership was recognized with the Nobel Peace Prize in 1964. He was martyred by an assassin's bullet on April 4, 1968, in Memphis, Tennessee (Weis & Muller, 2015). The night before he had expressed the commitment of his life to the cause of social justice when he responded to a reported bomb threat with what became known as the "I Have Been To The Mountain Top" speech (Montefiore, 2005). He said,

And then I got to Memphis. And some began to say the threats, or talk about the threats that were out. What would happen to me from some of our sick white brothers? Well, I don't know what will happen now. We've got some difficult days ahead. But it doesn't matter with me now. Because I've been to the mountaintop. And I don't mind. Like anybody, I would like to live a long life. Longevity has its place. But I'm not concerned about that now. I just want to do God's will. And He's allowed me to go up to the mountain. And I've looked over. And I've seen the promised land. I may not get there with you. But I want you to know tonight, that we, as a people, will get to the promised land. And I'm happy, tonight. I'm not worried about anything. I'm not fearing any man. Mine eyes have seen the glory of the coming of the Lord (p. 155).

William Henry "Bill" Gates III was born in Seattle, Washington, in 1955 to a prominent and philanthropic family (Rogak, 2012). As a teenager, he attended an exclusive preparatory school that purchased a block of computers. Gates took an almost immediate interest in programming the system. He and several classmates were once banned from the computers for a summer because they had developed a way to work the operating system to provide free computer time. Gates was so proficient at programming and operating computers he was hired by Computer Center Corporation (CCC) and eventually was also hired by his preparatory school to write the school's computer program to schedule students in classes. This passion for computer technology grew until he formed his own software company, Microsoft, which quickly became the most proficient and profitable software company in the world.

Following decades as CEO and chief software architect, he stepped down as chair of Microsoft in 2000 while still holding more stock in the company than anyone else. Gates realized his status as one of the richest individuals in the world provided him with a platform to help others. He and his wife Melinda formed the largest charitable foundation in the world, the Bill and Melinda Gates Foundation. Most of the foundation money goes to socially-economically oppressed regions around the world addressing needs such as poor health, lack of education, and unemployment. Eventually, the couple plan to give 95% of their wealth away through the foundation (Rogak, 2012).

Blake Mycoskie was visiting friends in Argentina when he met a young American lady who was volunteering her time with an organization that collected shoes in the USA then gave them away for free to disadvantaged children in Argentina. Mycoskie was taken aback by the presence of blisters, sores, and infections on their young feet from being barefoot, unable to afford even one pair of shoes (Mycoskie, 2011). This left a profound impact on Mycoskie. He noticed that many folks in Argentina wore a style referred to as *alpargata,* and so he thought if he could make a similar shoe, sell it world-wide, and give a pair to an impoverished child for each pair of shoes sold, he could make a profitable living while addressing a huge social/health need.

In the beginning, the shoes were referred to as Shoes for <u>Tomorrow</u> then shortened to **TOMS** in order to fit on the tag. Hence the name of the shoe company is not even closely related to the name of the inventor, Blake Mycoskie. Business started slowly, selling only a few shoes a day, but once the media became aware of what Mycoskie was doing and patrons began to really appreciate the casual shoe style and the purpose of TOMS, a few pairs turned into thousands a day. Tying a for-profit with a social mission was a new model, one that many people didn't believe would be sustainable. In fact, after developing, selling, and giving away millions and millions of models over the past decade this just might be one of the best models for success on so many levels ever conceived.

These individuals represent a wide range of philosophies regarding leadership and provide insight for a variety of approaches. Aspiring nonprofit leaders should assess these approaches and their experiences when developing a philosophy of leadership.

USING MENTORING TO DEVELOP LEADERS

U.S. tennis great Althea Gibson once said, "No matter what accomplishments you make, somebody helped you." This statement is a starting point for discussing **mentoring**—people helping people. Some of the more positive terms associated with the term mentoring include *counselor, consultant, expert, referee, advocate, motivator, coach, guide,* and *teacher.* Applebaum, Ritchie, and Shapiro (1994) point out that there is a close relationship between mentoring and leadership, but the defining characteristics are elusive. Mentoring provides opportunities for seasoned leaders to counsel and guide aspiring leaders in the nuances of successful organizational processes. Nonprofit organizations that support mentoring activities can benefit immensely from the results. Perhaps mentoring is best understood in terms of the relationship that exists, or should exist, between or among organizational members. For effective mentoring to occur in an organization, four desirable qualities must exist: **caring, sharing, correcting,** and **connecting** (Gantt, 1987):

1. **Caring** involves a genuine concern for the well-being of others. For true mentoring to occur, the individual being mentored should feel that the mentor is highly concerned for his or her growth as a person and a leader. Successful mentors accept individuals for themselves, but recognize their potential and will work with them to achieve high results.

2. **Sharing** suggests helping a person to become knowledgeable in any and all areas relevant to the successful operation of the organization. This might also include the sharing of information that could help an individual avoid making mistakes. While learning from mistakes is important, it can also be detrimental if those mistakes are significant. Sharing some information can be risky, and the information could be used

against the mentor, or in some other harmful way, so the mentoring process should be undertaken carefully.

3. **Correcting** implies that a mentor should be able and willing to point out mistakes, misperceptions, and incorrect assumptions. Since correcting is sometimes associated with criticizing, *it must be handled carefully*. The way in which situations are addressed may be just as important as the subject matter addressed, and an employee being mentored should feel that the mentor is addressing a specific situation for the benefit of the organization and the development of the employee. Correcting is about helping a person change, not about punishing someone for making a mistake.

4. **Connecting** means having an active level of consideration for whom a mentee needs to know or meet in order to be successful in the organization and which activities an employee should be involved in for professional growth.

When all four of these qualities exist in an organization, learning can best occur. When learning occurs, the employee is actively developing, and the organization benefits from this development, as do all of those served by the organization. According to Applebaum, et al. (1994), there is a positive correlation between mentoring and career commitment and a negative correlation between mentoring and dissatisfaction on the job. Everyone benefits from successful mentoring.

Mentoring is a highly important companion to leadership. A leader must be able and willing to provide mentoring to aspiring leaders for the sake of their development and for the continued growth of the organization.

DEVELOPING LEADERS THROUGH EXPERIENTIAL EDUCATION

Another way of developing leaders is by providing individuals with activities that offer the opportunity for skill and character development through an experiential learning process. This might take the form of an internship, co-op, or service learning. **Service learning** is one such concept; it is a field experience that combines community service with reflection and various learning objectives (Weis & Gantt, 2009) and it has gained a lot of ground over the past two decades. It is a way in which individuals can perform meaningful service to the community while incorporating theoretical constructs that can include skill and/or character development. It is a process that combines community service with personal growth, learning, and civic responsibility. Individuals learn and develop by using newly acquired knowledge and skills in actual community situations. This helps them develop a sense of caring and responsibility for others, while learning through real-world applications of the principles and skills being studied.

One example of a service learning application is found in a college class that is learning about financial resource development in nonprofit organizations. Once the students have completed a thorough study of the processes of fundraising, they partner with local nonprofit organizations to participate in the annual fundraising campaign. Using classroom time, the students work in groups to select fundraising methods, coordinate scheduling to complement the set of methods to be used, and launch the campaign. Working closely with the nonprofit partner, the student groups complete the fundraising and turn in the money raised. Then, the students return to the classroom and conduct a thorough evaluation of the experience, complete written reports of the findings, and spend time reflecting on what they learned from the process. The students provide a copy of the written report to the nonprofit partner. As a result, everyone involved benefits from the service learning project, including the students, the nonprofit partners, and the beneficiaries of the organization's programs and services (Weis & Muller, 2015).

Research on the effects of service learning indicates a number of positive benefits for the participants, several of which are included below (Caskey, 1991):

1. **Capacity for Action.** Makes a difference, meets real needs.

2. **Self-worth.** Identify, moral development, humane values.

3. **Citizenship.** Connections to leadership for community.

4. **Academic Development.** Increased relevance, challenge to think critically.

5. **Career Development.** Increases understanding of the world of work, as well as providing a familiarity with and knowledge of specific job skills.

6. **Social Development.** Enhancing interpersonal skills.

The many benefits derived from service learning can be very useful in developing skill areas as well as character attributes important in leadership development. Introducing service learning projects into a community, an organization, or educational institution can produce the following kinds of benefits beyond those to the individual participants (Caskey, 1991):

- ▶ Educational Institutions
  - ▶ **Engaged Learners.** Motivated, responsible for own learning.
  - ▶ **Collegiality.** Staff, participants, community working together as partners.
  - ▶ **Educational Excellence.** Enhanced climate, enriched curriculum, performance-based evaluation.
- ▶ Community and Organizations
  - ▶ **Valuable Service.** Unmet needs addressed, often uniquely.
  - ▶ **Citizenship.** Participants become active stakeholders, now and in future.

Research shows the positive impacts of quality service learning programs on all those involved. Most studies regarding service learning have been conducted in an academic setting. One such study involved 24,000 K–12 grade students participating in the Learn & Serve America program in Florida. In this study, Grade Point Averages improved for most of the students, attendance improved, and disciplinary referrals declined during the program period (Follman & Muldoon, 1997).

A study at Murray State University compared students in a service learning experimental group with a control group that was not involved in service projects and found the students in the experimental group felt a stronger sense of achieving something important in their lives as well as a stronger sense that they had made a positive contribution to the community. They reported a belief that what they did made a difference for the population they served and for the community, as well as for themselves (Weis, 1998).

Service learning is like a laboratory in which character and skills relevant to effective leadership can develop under supervision, while important needs in the community can be addressed. It is a very appropriate leadership development strategy to present at the close of this chapter, because the basic nature of service as a teaching and learning technique is deeply woven into the fabric of the nonprofit sector. The sector was founded on the basic notion that people can organize a voluntary response to any opportunity or challenge that faces them. It is a basic motivation to serve that drives the continuing growth and improvement of the sector. Collaborating in building the response and ensuring that the life in their community improves as a result is central to leadership for the public good. Leadership at all levels and of all types are found in the nonprofit sector, effectively combining the two elements of leadership and service. Greenleaf (2002) brings these two elements together in the **servant leadership concept**, in which the great leader is a servant first. Greenleaf writes that whether leader or follower, those who work together to make the world a better place are always searching, listening, and expecting the goal to be accomplished. They are optimists committed to a shared vision in which the world is better for them having been involved and in service. He believes that people will "freely respond only to individuals who are chosen as leaders because they are proven and trusted as servants" (p. 24).

SUMMARY

Leadership and management in the nonprofit sector means strengthening individuals and communities by developing influence through managerial processes as well as collaborative and trusting relationships. Quality leader-managers play a wide range of roles in helping others reach higher and higher goals. They provide what is needed in each situation, from inspiration and motivation to guidance and facilitation. They both direct others to action and empower others to lead, depending on what is best for the circumstances at hand. A combination of characteristics and criteria is necessary for successful leadership. Leaders become leaders by a number of methods including appointment, election, emergence, and charisma. It is suggested that there are several ways that leaders might influence the behavior of others including the use of personal power, referent power, legitimate power, expert power, reward power, and coercive power. To be a good leader, it is important to understand some of the reasons that individuals follow others. The ultimate success of an individual leader is often evident when they empower others to lead.

The authors stated there are four main ways to *develop* as leaders: (1) examining theories and models, (2) assessing the lives of past leaders, (3) mentoring with effective leaders, and (4) engaging in experiential activities (Weis & Muller, 2015). For a better understanding of the concept of leadership through theories and models, the authors have incorporated a framework of classic theories, beginning with the Classic Organizational Theory that is based on a scientific approach to getting things done all the way up to more modern, less structured concepts of leadership.

Too often, leadership models fail to include the importance of character and ethics in the overall scheme of leading and influencing others. The Integrated Leadership and Character Model was developed to discuss the importance of character in leadership. The model emphasizes the importance of three interrelated skill-areas—conceptual, technical, and human relations—and the significance personal character, purpose, and passion has in the effectiveness of these three areas. Personal character is made up of traits and values, including trustworthiness, respect, fairness, caring, and citizenship. Putting values to work is the role of ethics, and it is suggested that an ethical culture can be created in a nonprofit organization by emphasizing five ethical obligations: integrity, openness, accountability, service, and charity.

A second way of developing leadership is through the study of leaders past. Studying leaders such as Lao-Tzu, Thomas Jefferson, Harriett Tubman, Clara Barton, Dr. Martin Luther King, Bill Gates, and a number of others can provide insight for a variety of leaderhip approaches.

Being a part of a mentoring plan can encourage aspiring leaders through qualities of caring, sharing, correcting, and connecting. Finally, experiential education/service learning, a field experience that combines community service with various learning objectives, provides individuals with opportunities to practice skills and develop character while addressing important needs in the community.

Leaders and those concerned about improving leadership practice should review the many resources available. It is reasonable to expect that the importance of the subject will continue to advance the commitment to improved understanding and practice for the nonprofit sector and society at-large.

This chapter addresses in part competencies encouraged by the Nonprofit Academic Centers Council (NACC) such as ethics, values, management, and leadership.

REFLECTION AND APPLICATION

1. Drawing on the leadership theories, models, and studies presented in the chapter, write a description of your personal approach to leadership.

    _____

    _____

    _____

    _____

    _____

    _____

2. List characteristics necessary for successful leadership today.

    _____

    _____

    _____

    _____

    _____

3. How do individuals become leaders?

    _____

    _____

    _____

    _____

4. Define the five types of power used in leadership:

    _____

    _____

    _____

    _____

    _____

    _____

5. Select someone who has influenced your life and identify and describe the leadership theory that best aligns with how they lead.

_____

_____

_____

_____

_____

6. Using the Integrated Leadership and Character Model, describe your Personal Character using traits, values, and ethics that you believe make you unique. Then, list the strongest skill you have in each category. Finally, list the skill in each category that you want to improve.

_____

_____

_____

_____

_____

7. Describe the five ethical obligations that an organization must embrace and pursue in developing an ethical culture.

_____

_____

_____

_____

_____

8. What are the positive benefits of service learning to the individual and to the community organization in which the service occurs?

_____

_____

_____

_____

_____

REFERENCES

Anheier, H. K. (2014). *Nonprofit organizations: Theory, management, policy.* New York: Routledge Publishing.

Applebaum, S. H., Ritchie, S., & Shapiro, B. T. (1994). Mentoring revisited: An organizational behaviour constuct. *International Journal of Career Management.*

Archer D., & Cameron, A. (2009). *Collaborative leadership: How to succeed in an interconnected world.* Oxford: Elsevier Ltd.

Bass, B. M. (2008). *The Bass handbook of leadership: Theory, research, and managerial applications* (4th ed.) New York: Free Press.

Belasco, J. A., & Stayer, R. C. (1993). *Flight of the buffalo.* New York: Warner.

Blake, R. R., & Mouton, J. S. (1978). *The new managerial grid.* Houston: Gulf.

Block, P. (2008). *Community: The structure of belonging.* San Francisco, CA: Berrett-Koehler Publishing.

Boylston, H. D. (1955). *Clara Barton: Founder of the American Red Cross.* New York: Random House.

Brinckerhoff, P. C. (2009). *Mission-based management: Leading your not-for-profit* (3rd ed.). Hoboken, NJ: John Wiley & Sons, Inc.

Burns, J. M. (1978). *Leadership.* New York: Harper and Row.

Caskey, F. (1991). Model learner outcomes for service learning. *Minnesota Department of Education.*

Chait, R. P., Ryan, W. P., & Taylor, B. E. (2005) *Governance as leadership.* Hoboken, NJ: John Wiley & Sons, Inc.

Collins, J. (2001). *Good to great.* New York: Harper Collins Publishing, Inc.

Covey, Stephen R. (1989). *The seven habits of highly effective people.* New York: Simon and Schuster.

Crutchfield, L. R. & McLeod Grant, H. (2008). *Forces for good: The six practices of high-impact nonprofits.* San Francisco, CA: Jossey-Bass.

Debo, A. (1976). *Geronimo: The man, his time, his place.* Norman: University of Oklahoma Press.

Deming, W. E. (2000). *The new economics for industry, government and education* (2nd ed.) Cambridge, Mass., MIT Press, 2000

Follman, J., & Muldoon, K. (1997). Florida learn & serve 1995–96: What were the outcomes? *National Association of Secondary School Principals Bulletin.*

Frady, M. (2002). *Martin Luther King, Jr.* New York: Penguin Group.

Friedman, Stewart. (2008). *Total leadership.* Boston, MA: Harvard Business Press.

Gantt, V. W. (1987). Beneficial mentoring is for everyone: a reaction paper. Paper presented at the November 1987 National Communications Association Convention, Chicago.

Gardner, J. W. (2010). The tasks of leadership. In the *Jossey-Bass reader on nonprofit and public leadership.* J. Perry (Ed.). San Francisco: Jossey-Bass.

George, B. (2003). *Authentic Leadership: Rediscovering the secrets to creating lasting value.* John Wiley and Sons Publishers.

Greenleaf, R. K. (2002). *Servant leadership: A journey into the nature of legitimate power and greatness* (3rd ed.). Mahwah, NJ: Paulist Press.

Hersey, P., & Blanchard, K. (1977). *Management of organizational behavior—utilizing human resources* (3rd ed.). Englewood Cliffs, NJ: Prentice-Hall.

Hitt, W. D. (1988). *The leader manager: Guidelines for action.* Columbus, OH: Battelle Press.

Hollander, E. P. (2009). *Inclusive leadership: The essential leader-follower relationship.* New York: Routledge, Taylor & Francis Group.

Jeavons, T. H. (2006). When management is the message: relating values to management practice in nonprofit organizations. *Nonprofit Management and Leadership.*

Jeavons, T. H. (2010). Ethical nonprofit management: Core values and key practices. In *The Jossey-Bass handbook of nonprofit leadership and management.* D. Renz and Associates (Ed.). San Francisco: Jossey-Bass.

Jennings, E. E. (1960). *Anatomy of leadership,* New York: Harper.

Keller, H., Shattuck, R., Herrman, D., & Sullivan, A. (2005). *The story of my life.* New York: Bantam Books.

Kennedy, G. A. (1991). *Aristotle on rhetoric: A theory of civic discourse.* Oxford University Press.

Koch, A., & Peden, P. (1993). *The life and selected writings of Thomas Jefferson.* New York: Random House.

Kouzes, J., & Posner, B. (1995). *The leadership challenge: How to keep getting extraordinary things done in organizations.* San Francisco: Jossey-Bass.

Levy, J. E. (1975). *Cesar Chavez: Autobiography of La Causa.* New York: W.W. Norton and Company, Inc.

Lewin, K., Lippitt, R., and White, R. K. (1939, May). Patterns of aggressive behavior in experimentally created social climates. *Journal of Social Psychology.*

Maxwell, J. C. (2001). *Developing the leader within you.* Thomas Nelson, Inc.

Montefiore, S. S. (2005). *Speeches that changed the world: The stories and transcripts of the moments that made history.* London: Quercus Publishing.

Mycoskie, B. (2011). *Start Something That Matters.* New York: Random House Publishers.

National Center for Charitable Statistics. (2008). *Nonprofit almanac.* Urban Institute.

Nevid, J. S., & Rathus, S. A. (2005). *Psychology and the challenges of life: Adjustment in the new millennium.* Hoboken, NJ: John Wiley & Sons.

Nonprofit Almanac, 2012.

Northouse, P. G. (2010). *Leadership: Theory and practice* (5th ed.). Thousand Oaks, CA: Sage Publications.

Perry, J. L. (Ed.) (2010). *Jossey-Bass reader on nonprofit and public leadership.* San Francisco, CA: Jossey-Bass.

Peters, T. J., & Waterman, R. H. (1982). *In search of excellence.* New York: Harper and Row.

Petry, A. (1955). *Harriett Tubman.* New York: Thomas Y. Crowell Company.

Purkey, W. & Stegel, B. (2003). *Becoming an Invitational Leader: A New Approach to Professional and Personal Success.* Humanics Trade Group Publication. Atlanta, GA.

Quinn, R. E. (2000). *Change the world: How ordinary people can accomplish extraordinary results.* San Francisco, CA: John Wiley & Sons, Inc.

Rogak, L. (2012). *Impatient optimist: Bill Gates in his own words.* Evanston, IL: Agate Publishing.

Rost, J. C. (1993). *Leadership for the twenty-first century.* Westport, CT: Praeger.

Seagal, S., & Horne, D. (1997). *Human dynamics: A new framework for understanding people and realizing the potential in our organizations.* Waltham, MA: Human Dynamics International.

Sessoms, H. D., & Stevenson, J. L. (1981). *Leadership and group dynamics in recreation services.* Boston: Allyn and Bacon.

Shivers, J. S. (1980). *Recreational leadership: Group dynamics and interpersonal behavior.* Princeton, NJ: Princeton Books.

Sinek, S. (2014). *Leaders eat last.* New York, NY: Penguin Group.

Stogdill, R., & Coons, A. (1957). *Leader behavior's description and measurement.* Columbus, OH: Bureau of Business Research, Ohio State University.

Stojkovic, S., Kalinich, D., & Klofas, J. (2007). *Criminal justice organizations: Administration and management.* Belmont, CA: Wadsworth Publishing Company.

Taylor, F. W. (1967). *The principles of scientific management.* New York: W. W. Norton and Company, Inc.

Utley, R. M. (1988). *Cavalier in buckskin.* Norman: University of Oklahoma Press.

Weis, R. (1998). *Service learning training manual for faculty K–16.* Murray, KY: American Humanics, Murray State University.

Weis, R., & Gantt, V. (2009). *Leading with character, purpose, & passion.* Dubuque, IA: Kendall Hunt Publishing, Inc.

Weis, R., & Muller, S. (2014). *Leading with character, purpose and passion* (2nd ed.). Dubuque, IA: Kendall Hunt Publishing Company.

Weis, R., & Muller, S. (2015). *Leading and managing nonprofit organizations* (2nd ed.). Peosta, IA: eddie bowers publishing company, inc.

Wheatley, M. J. (2005). *Finding our way: Leadership for an uncertain time.* San Francisco, CA: Berrett-Koehleer Publishers, Inc.

Worth, M. J. (2009). *Nonprofit management: Principles and practices.* Thousand Oaks, CA: Sage Publications, Inc.

Worth, M. J. (2017). *Nonprofit management: Principles and practice* (4th ed.). Thousand Oaks, CA: Sage Publications, Inc.

Wren, J. T. (1995). *The leader's companion.* New York: The Free Press.

STAFF, BOARD, AND VOLUNTEERS: LEADING EFFECTIVELY

Many people look at nonprofit organizations and see small for-profit organizations and try to suggest that nonprofits need to be organized and run in the same way as for-profit organizations. While these organizations share many qualities and characteristics and despite globalization and the eroding of traditional boundaries between the operation of for-profits and non-government organizations (NGOs), there remains significant differences between these two worlds. What is successful in one environment will not automatically succeed in the other. What is good for General Motors may not be good for the American Red Cross. As economist Milton Friedman famously said, "The social responsibility of business is to increase its profit." When dealing with products and/or services that are difficult or impossible to monetize, placing them beyond the realm of the private sector, nonprofit organizations step in to offer these for the lowest economic strata of society where the rewards lie in enriching people's lives, not their bank accounts (Agarwal & Siddique, 2011).

Much, if not most, of the products or services delivered by the for-profit organization is created through advertising and marketing. In the nonprofit world, most, if not all, of the services delivered result from an individual or community need. The very assumptions about why organizations exist and the core values are very different. For-profit organizations exist, first and foremost, to make a profit. They are profitable or they cease to exist. Nonprofit organizations exist to help people. They help people or they no longer exist. With funding for all organizations becoming a major issue, nonprofits are being pressured to provide evidence of their impact. Failure to document that services provided have helped people and made a positive impact will lead to a redirection of precious funds toward programs that are able to make their case and demonstrate effectiveness (Agarwal & Siddique, 2011).

While this characterization is very brief and simplified, it is necessary to set the stage for viewing the similarities that matter and the differences that are significant when it comes to staff, board, and volunteer fundamentals (Weis & Muller, 2015).

Organizations, regardless of classification, depend on the successful integration of three key components: people, resources, and a service or product. No matter how important or needed the product or service of an organization, the absence of appropriate resources or qualified and motivated people will cause the organization to struggle and ultimately fail. It might help to visualize an organization as a stool sitting on three legs (one for people, a second for resources, and a third for the product or service). The seat represents the organization's mission or reason for being. If one leg is missing, weak, or flawed, the seat of the stool will be adversely affected. Ultimately, it will fail to support its share of the weight of the mission. A successful nonprofit organization, like any organization, must have three strong legs for its stool to fulfill its purpose.

Within the people component of nonprofit organizations exists three major components: the **staff**, **board,** and **volunteers**. If any group is ineffective, not as effective as required, or not willing to live up to its potential, the entire organization is placed at risk. To ensure that each of these categories of personnel are effective, it is essential that each individual understands what the organization does or doesn't stand for. When each person knows the organization's mission statement, it is more likely that they will make decisions that align with the organization's core values and mission. The mission should be embedded into the core values and culture of the organization. Doing this will strengthen the collective sense of purpose and help everyone move forward in a unified direction and will encourage each person to work with a passion for the desired outcome. Word and Norton in their report on nonprofit culture note that their study examining engagement and satisfaction among 2,615 nonprofit employees showed that those with a higher level of mission attachment were also more likely to respond that they were satisfied, engaged with their work, and intended to remain with an organization (Word & Norton, 2013). These findings demonstrate the importance of helping your team feel like they're not just at a job, but on a mission. The excitement to keep the vision alive will impact the vibrancy of your organization, and naturally, its interactions with supporters.

People fall into general categories when it comes to the types of interactions they desire when engaging others, desire for working conditions, and their reactions to very stressful situations. There are many tools that help leaders understand the general categories and support their work with this wide variety of people. One of those tools is the **Personal Profile Preview**™ (Resources Unlimited, 2010). The research by the developers of the Personal Profile shows that people fall into four general interaction styles, with all four styles interacting to produce a highly predictive tool for what happens when people interact at work, at home, or at play. The following is a review of the four general styles:

▶ **Dominance.** People who emphasize this style like to solve problems and get immediate results, question current methods, enjoy independence and varied tasks.

▶ **Influence.** People who emphasize this style enjoy persuading and influencing others, are highly verbal and open to expressing feelings, prefer to work with others.

► **Steadiness.** People who emphasize this style prefer a stable and organized work climate, usually are patient and listen well, enjoy working in groups more than directing others.

► **Conscientiousness.** People who emphasize this style want to achieve high personal standards, carefully weigh all sides of an issue, are diplomatic, desire clearly defined expectations with no surprises.

It is possible that the greatest risk of all is to offer unsolicited suggestions as to how others can best do their jobs. It often seems easy to give advice to others. The advice frequently does not work well when applied to real-world situations. The best way to view suggestions from others is to consider the suggestion as a choice rather than as the answer. There is a line in the 2002 movie *Solaris* when the lead character is trying to determine if his true love is real or a figment of his imagination. He is told by a space station veteran that "There are no answers, only choices."

This chapter explores the role of leadership in human resource development, examines each group of people involved in nonprofit organizations—staff, board, volunteers (their role and how to recruit the best people and develop them); makes suggestions as to how best to assure the success of each group (how to integrate the roles of each group and how to evaluate each group); and examines the central role of communication skills needed by leaders to help ensure a solid, effective stool (through evaluation and re-direction).

THE ROLE OF ORGANIZATIONAL LEADERSHIP

The Chief Executive Officer (CEO), who typically carries the title of Executive Director (ED) in a nonprofit organization is often thought of as the person who actually runs the organization. The ED does have many significant responsibilities that come along with the title as would be expected of a chief executive officer. The roles of the Executive Director are as follows:

1. Staff management:
    a. The ED hires and oversees the training of staff members.
    b. The ED motivates, supervises, and evaluates staff members.

2. Development and Management of Programs and Policies:
    a. The ED works with staff to develop policies to guide the work of the organization.
    b. The ED works with the staff to develop and implement programs that will fulfill the organization's mission.

3. Staff liaison to the Board of Directors:
    a. The ED keeps the board informed as to all significant activities of the organization.

    b. The ED attends board meetings and keeps the lines of communication between the board and staff open.

    c. The ED reports significant messages from the board to the staff.

Responsibilities that are shared between the Board and the Executive Director:

1. Strategic planning:

    a. The ED and board work together to develop a strategic plan that will guide the efforts of the organization.

    b. The ED and board work together to update the strategic plan on a regularly scheduled basis (should be no greater than 5 years).

2. Fundraising:

    a. The ED and board work together to establish fundraising goals.

    b. The ED and board work together to establish plans for fundraising activities.

3. Evaluation of the organization:

    a. The ED and board work together to evaluate the overall financial health of the organization.

    b. The ED and board work together to review the overall mission and programming alignment of the organization.

    c. The ED and board work together to conduct a general evaluation of the organization.

As the main onsite leader, the ED plays a key role in selecting, developing, and leading people in the organization. He or she often becomes the face of the organization, setting the tone for the way business will be conducted, so it is essential that this person be someone of high character. Remember, leadership is much more a matter of character than of certain qualities (Weis & Gantt, 2002). Leadership qualities are critical for success, but leadership qualities alone are not sufficient nor do they guarantee success. Character is a significant component of leadership. In the nonprofit sector, anyone with good character and a desire to help others can become a true leader. Martin Luther King, Jr. put it this way, "Everyone can be great because anyone can serve. You don't have to have a college degree to serve. You don't even have to make your subject and your verb agree to serve. . . . You only need a heart full of grace. A soul generated by love. . . ." (National School and Community Corps, 1998). However, not everyone who serves effectively can lead a nonprofit organization. What are those extra qualities required of the ED that are essential for the success of the nonprofit organization?

Research shows that certain skills, strategies, and attributes help define what those individuals who have been identified as successful leaders possess that sets them apart from those who have failed in their attempts at leading. A review of those leadership characteristics was provided in Chapter 2. In the context of identifying those special individuals who tend to succeed at leading nonprofit organizations, a more appropriate word for leader might be mentor. The concept of a mentor goes beyond leading from afar, it denotes leading on a personal level with a commitment to the individual being led. Being a good leader, someone with whom people enjoy working, should be the goal of every ED. How can an ED successfully mentor large groups of people within the organization, the board, the clients, the staff, and the volunteers all fall within this context of leading through mentorship? There are six key qualities that, if expressed, will help the ED serve as a mentor to many rather than a few.

The ED should strive to be:

1. **A person who works to ensure a feeling of inclusion**—The good mentor/leader treats people fairly but not necessarily the same. The inclusive ED seeks feedback, not just accepts it graciously, and encourages innovation and creativity as long as it is true to the organization's mission. An ED should want all staff, volunteers, and board members to be engaged and feel as though they are an important part of the business or mission of the organization. People do not feel included or think they have a voice (being heard) in an organization by accident. A feeling of inclusion is produced for staff, clients, volunteers, and board members by thoughtful action, by taking effort to plan and review continuously. Inclusion is felt when there is an environment of trust and respect where every effort is made to treat people fairly and the processes occur in a transparent manner.

2. **A person with a sense of mission**—Every organization needs to do something well and provide something of value to the community it serves. The ED should set the agenda and establish the culture for the organization, and identifying what it will be known for in the community. This might be a service such as hot meals, on time by Meals on Wheels; or it might be an attitude or emotion such as compassion and caring from Hospice. The ED must be a good business person, known for running a tight ship, as someone who inspires staff and volunteers to pursue the mission. Organizational skills are crucial for leaders, but there must be a touch of humanity and compassion along with these organizational skills. People want to work with and for someone who goes about doing the right thing in an effort to achieve the mission.

3. **A desire to learn and promote learning**—The freedom to make mistakes is a powerful freedom. The ED who allows, even encourages, staff and volunteers to test innovations and advance their creative ideas, while learning from the mistakes that might occur is often an effective mentor/leader. To stop learning is to stop growing and to eventually die professionally and intellectually. The ED must also be willing to learn in

order to encourage learning by others, as people get the most powerful message from a person's actions. New ideas and technology are not just for full-time employees, they are for everyone, even the volunteers. True learning cannot be forced, it is best when learning new skills is encouraged for all and rewarded regularly.

4. **A coach, counselor, mentor**—The very best EDs are the ones who **help** staff, volunteers, and board members become the best they can be. It takes less time to help a person grow than it does to correct errors, smooth over hurt feelings, or repair damaged relationships. In the long run, an ED must view coaching, counseling, and mentoring as *investment time*, not lost time. When the ED cannot do this personally, he or she can show an interest in the process and acknowledge that the process is occurring. A little praise and acknowledgment from the ED goes a long way toward increasing a sense of satisfaction among staff.

5. **A person who helps everyone position for advancement**—The greatest mistake a human being can make in dealing with another is to try to hold a person back, slow career development, or be jealous of someone who jumps past him or her in their career path. Helping others succeed in a wide variety of ways is a leader's reward. If every person in an organization is prepared to advance and is committed to helping others advance, the organization will have a great pool of qualified and motivated people to draw upon for its future efforts. If only select people are prepared or supported in their advancements, while others are ignored or discouraged, the organization suffers. The pool of available talent to draw upon will be reduced each time someone is denied an opportunity. Individuals might not be ready to advance when they are needed. Also if there is no clear career path for advancement within the organization, the best people will find another alternative where their talents can be applied and recognized. They will find a way to succeed in spite of the lack of effort to help them prosper within the current organization.

6. **A person who personally learns from mistakes**—The best way to demonstrate that an organization values learning from mistakes is for the ED to be seen learning from his or her mistakes in an open and honest way. Leaders should admit mistakes, talk about what was learned, and encourage others to talk about what they have learned from their mistakes. This is a sign of strength and a willingness to learn and grow as a leader and a person.

In addition, the ED should be capable to handling and resolving conflict. In the mentoring process, it is essential to handle adversity with grace and refrain from taking criticism personally. An effective mentor/leader will be skilled in actively receiving input and listening to the viewpoints of others. He or she will collaborate with others and keep a sense of perspective (Moran, 2008).

MANAGEMENT DUTIES REQUIRED OF THE EXECUTIVE DIRECTOR

Financial Management

An executive director should have some experience with finance, including hands-on knowledge of basic cash flow management and bookkeeping skills. Financial controls should be put in place to manage day-to-day operations. These processes should account for the systematic documentation of every dollar raised and spent by the organization. It is essential that the ED understands how to generate and analyze basic financial documents such as balance sheets and reports on the organization's assets and liabilities for any given moment in time.

An organization's assets might include cash, accounts receivable, equipment, real estate holdings, and intangible resources that have value, such as a curriculum or copyright. Liabilities include cash owed, payroll, rent or mortgage, transportation, and supplies. A Statement of Activities is a statement of profit and loss, which compares funding sources with program and administrative expenses, and other operating costs. Unlike the balance sheet's financial snapshot, the statement of activities reports on a specific time frame (e.g., quarterly) and shows whether the nonprofit is financially solvent or not for that time period. The executive director is also responsible for working with the board of directors and other financial officers of the organization to develop the annual budget.

The ED is also responsible for approving day-to-day expenditures within the authority delegated to him or her by the Board. He or she oversees the organization's bookkeeping and accounting procedures, making sure that sound financial practices are followed. The ED administers funds according to the approved budget and monitors monthly cash flow of the organization by regularly meeting with the chief financial officer (CFO). The ED regularly provides the Board with complete reports on the revenues and expenditure of the organization. These reports might be prepared by the CFO or someone in accounting.

Community Relations/Advocacy

A very important role of the ED is to communicate with stakeholders, to keep them informed of the initiatives being conducted by the organization. The contact will also help the ED identify changes in the community served by the organization. This is important because these changes might influence service delivery plans. The ED should be invested in relationship building within the community as well as within the specific population that the nonprofit is serving. Promoting awareness of the organization to the outside community is crucial to recruiting potential donors and volunteers. Additionally, the target population must feel genuinely supported and connected with the staff, vision, and mission of the organization. The ED is responsible for fostering this connection and is, essentially, the face of the nonprofit organization. The ED must present him or herself as a spokesperson that both listens and communicates with good intention and thoughtfulness. He or she must also be present, at least periodically, when the staff implement programs or activities designed to benefit the target population.

The ED should use the information gained through community interactions and organizational programming to promote increased awareness of relevant issues within the community. Assessment of program impact is essential. This cannot be done without the assistance of those being served. The nonprofits rely on feedback from those being served to determine whether programs and activities have been successful. Many times this involves talking to community members and getting their feedback verbally.

Maintaining good working relationships with community groups, community leaders, potential and current funders, politicians, and other nonprofit organizations all helps the nonprofit organization achieve its goals.

Fundraising

Working with the board of directors and the director of development, the executive director is responsible for developing and implementing a plan for raising the funds needed to cover the proposed annual budget. The process of developing a fundraising plan involves examining the organization's history to identify previous funding sources. The recent past provides the single best indicator of the immediate future fundraising success. The plan for raising funds should outline steps for acquiring funds from each potential source or donor.

Suggested steps for creating a fundraising plan:

1. Review the foundation's funding from previous years to determine whether the organization is eligible for continued financial support from each of the various funders.

2. Conduct research on potential foundations for compatibility with the organization in regard to mission alignment, common outcome orientations, and organizational life cycle looking for new sources of funding.

3. Construct profiles on potential donors including foundation priorities that might align with the specific funder, contact information, proposal due dates, submission instructions, and funding range (maximum awards).

4. Create a matrix to determine the probability of receiving grants from each of the identified foundations. Criteria for the matrix might include compatibility with the mission, foundation's funding priorities, whether or not the organization had previous funding, funding of comparable organizations in the geographic area, and type of relationship with the potential funder.

5. Many people determine how much the proposal is worth in terms of effort by multiplying the probability of funding by the dollar amount of request. If the proposal is not worth the time, it can be eliminated. Focus on those proposals with the most potential for success.

The ED should participate in fundraising activities as appropriate. This will depend upon his or her fundraising experience, the type of activities the organization is undertaking, and the experience of the board members, as well as the extent of the development staff of the nonprofit organization.

Strategic Planning

The ED works with the board to develop a strategic plan. The function of the strategic plan is to provide a vision for where the organization will be in the short-term future as well as the long-term, usually a 5-year projection. This plan sets a course for action that helps an organization reach its goals and evaluate progress along the way. A well thought-out plan will identify goals, target dates for completion, and assign person(s) or committees to be responsible for achieving each goal by specified dates. Goals should be written in such a way that they are measureable. It is important to know whether or not a goal has been attained. If there is a plan in place, when a new ED is hired, it is usually reviewed, revised, and then implemented. This is the case because changes in the ED position typically are accompanied by a need for modifications in the strategic direction.

Developing the Strategic Plan

- ► Be inclusive; provide opportunities for all stakeholders to provide input into identifying the goals. Solicit information from those who will be responsible for implementing the plan.
- ► Set long-term goals with action steps to be accomplished along the way. The action steps should be very realistic and logically lead to accomplishing the goal.
- ► Identify measurable, achievable goals. It is good to set aspirational goals, but by and large goals need to be realistic and within the capabilities of your staff.

Implementation of the Strategic Plan

Once the plan is developed, it is the responsibility of the ED to put it into action.

- ► Make sure each staff member knows his or her assigned task(s) and associated due dates. If tasks are complex or involve large projects, consider creating Gantt charts to keep everyone on schedule.
- ► For significant tasks, incorporate them into most staff members' job descriptions and include the items on their evaluations to help monitor progress.
- ► Circulate the plan among staff in a format that is easy to read and encourages implementation.

Hiring, Managing, and Retaining Staff

In the nonprofit sector, it is the quality of the people that makes or breaks the organization. Without good people, the most needed service cannot be delivered in an efficient way for maximum effect. A great vision can also be thwarted by an ineffective board. The ED plays a key role in staff recruitment, management, and retention. It is essential that the ED develop skills in writing effective job descriptions, managing effectively, and keeping his or her staff on task and dedicated to the mission.

The ED can help guide each staff member's efforts by providing a detailed job description for his or her position. By providing a task-specific description of the position's major duties and responsibilities, a job description can also provide supervisors guidance during the orientation of new staff members. The description also stipulates the boundaries of each person's responsibilities and provides a framework for developing a performance plan.

An *effective job description* will contain these essential elements: An **overview**, which provides a brief history of the position. When advertising, the description might include when the organization was founded, the mission, and a list of the organization's programs. **Responsibilities**, which describe, in detail, each of the duties the person in the position will be responsible for performing. **Qualifications**, which includes a list of all the minimum requirements that applicants must possess to be considered for the position. Typically, this includes a set of preferred skills, knowledge, experiences, or credentials. **Application Instructions**, which includes directions on submitting the application. Provide the name of the hiring manager and an e-mail address or human resources website for submitting applications. Specify those materials that must be included for consideration (e.g., cover letter, resume, references) and the deadline for applying. Additional information that might be provided in a job description includes a description of the work environment, any travel requirements, title of the person(s) to whom the employee will report, terms of employment (e.g., short-term, contract, or full-time), salary and benefits, and the hours or work schedule.

Complete **job descriptions** to be used for internal purposes, rather than for hiring, must exist for every paid position in the organization. All internal job descriptions should consist of **seven components:** *position title, purpose of the position, credential requirements, to whom does the position report, responsibilities of the position, specific duties of the position, and evaluation timetable along with the criteria for that evaluation.*

A visionary ED can be undermined by a staff unwilling or unable to keep pace with the changing nature of the dynamics within their community. A committed and dedicated staff can be frustrated and rendered impotent by an ED who will not allow them to do their job. It is easy to identify all of the things that can go wrong. The task is to identify how all these very different and capable human resources can be melded together to produce a useful, dynamic, vision-driven nonprofit organization that can make a difference in the lives of people who need its services.

The **staff** of any organization, collectively, has more to do with the ultimate success of the organization than does the designated leader. While the vision of the organization and direction is the responsibility of the positional leader or ED, it is essentially the day-to-day function of any organization that determines its success. The key to day-to-day accomplishment is the quality of the work of the paid staff. What constitutes a quality staff member? The staff member must be capable of performing each aspect of the job description of the position for which he or she was hired.

The **seven most critical issues** with respect to staffing an organization are: *recruitment, selection, hiring, training, evaluation, termination, and retention* (Weis & Muller, 2015):

▶ **Recruitment**

Positioning the organization to be seen as a desirable place to work is essential to successful recruiting. If the organization's image in the community is positive, it is much easier to attract a better pool of potential employees. Positive activities produce positive perceptions by the community and potential employees. There are several steps in the recruiting process.

First, the best source for finding the right person for the position is through the people who know the organization and what is required for the position—other staff, board members, satisfied clients, and financial supporters. The one danger here is that some of these people will recommend people based on their personal relationship with the person rather than what is in the best interest of the organization. Therefore, it is important to be cautious, but do not reject this type of recommendation without thoroughly considering the qualifications of the recommended candidate.

Second, network with other nonprofit professionals and ask for suggestions they might have regarding possible candidates and other people in the industry to contact for recommendations. Often, a person who is not right for one organization or position is perfect for another similar organization. Networking can extend beyond the immediate community to surrounding communities and can include contacts within for-profit organizations and government departments. At times, highly qualified people want a change of scenery and will trade the for-profit or government positions for one in the nonprofit world.

Third, advertise in organization publications—newsletters, job listings, journals, and online job markets. Use local newspapers, radio, and social media to get the word out.

Fourth, prospect and recruit from the whole community. Read the newspaper, listen to the radio, watch television, and view social media for new companies coming to the community. Watch the performance of volunteers in other organizations when you have that opportunity. A good volunteer for one organization could become a great paid staff member for another organization. Many nonprofit professionals started their careers as dedicated volunteers.

► **Selection**

Most application processes require the applicants to submit a **letter of interest**, a **resume**, and a set of three to five **references**. To select the candidates to be interviewed, compare each candidate's application materials to the requirements listed in the **job description**. Rank candidates by how well their qualifications fit the job description. Screen the top few candidates to determine if you would like to conduct a phone interview with them. Before a selection can be made, **three criteria** must be clearly determined and reflected in the job description: what training/education is required, what level of experience is required, and what personal qualities are required

Phone Interviews: Prepare a set of open-ended questions that are specific to the position. The purpose of the phone interview is to discuss a wide range of the required competencies and experiences identified in the job description with the goal of developing a baseline knowledge of each candidate's strengths and weaknesses in regard to whether he or she would be a good fit for the position. Select a pre-determined number of candidates from these phone interviews to continue the process with in-person interviews, usually three or four individuals.

In-Person Interviews: The in-person interview takes your relationship to another level with each candidate. You should have an interview itinerary to include each person or committee that the candidate will meet with and any familiarization tours that will be provided. This process provides both you and the candidate an opportunity to go into more detail about the nuances of the position. It also enables both parties to clarify anything about the job description, compensation, benefits or terms of employment. In-person job interviews should last at a minimum of 45 minutes for lower-level positions and significantly longer for more senior-level positions. A hiring manager and perhaps additional representatives from the organization who would be working with the candidate should serve as the screening committee at this stage.

Follow-up Interviews: Once the screening committee has had time to review the results from all of the in-person interviews the pool should be narrowed to the one or two candidates you are most interested in. To help you make your final decision, a follow-up interview with each finalist is a common method used to assist with the decision. At this point, it is imperative that you gauge each candidate's continued desire for the position. By this time, candidates have become more familiar with your organization; have met those individuals with whom they would be working with on a day-to-day basis; and have been informed about the details such as benefits and compensation. It is not uncommon for some candidates to withdraw from a search, which makes your decision process a bit simpler if you were down to two candidates. If both candidates remain interested, conducting this additional interview provides an opportunity to clarify any questions by either party. At this point, for most positions it is time to make a hiring decision, although it is not unusual for a senior candidate to have two or three more meetings prior to a hiring decision being made.

If none of the applicants meet the requirements, continue the search. It is never a good idea to fill the position with an unqualified candidate just because there is pressure to get someone on the job quickly. It is much better to cover the work of the vacant position with temporary staff assignments until a well-qualified person is found.

All necessary background checks should be completed prior to an official offer of employment is made, including everything required by law. Depending upon the services to be performed, states often require criminal background checks on all employees coming into contact with children. Background checks also involve a careful check of references, which can be a significant factor in making the right choice and reducing **risks**.

The general process of **risk management** is discussed in detail in **Chapter 7**. Selecting the wrong person can be very costly to an organization, resulting in the delays of termination and conducting another search. Risk reduction is a critical consideration. No organization wants to risk exposing its clients to potential physical harm, and no organization wants to chance being accused of unfair or biased hiring practices, as just two of the potential risks encountered in the hiring process. Every applicant deserves full and fair consideration, but the organization must also protect its clients and itself.

Checking social media: The trend for hiring managers to spend time checking out job candidate's digital footprint began around 2010 according to Erin Nunn, assistant director of experiential learning at Case Western Reserve University's Career Center. This trend is on a rapidly upward trajectory as evidenced by a survey of approximately 2,200 hiring and human resource managers conducted in 2015. The survey was done for an organization called *CareerBuilder*, a global human resource and recruitment company that is located in Chicago, Illinois. The survey revealed that 60% of employers use social networking sites to research job applicants in 2016, a jump from 52% in 2015, 43% in 2014, and 39% in 2013.

The survey results showed that 49% of hiring managers that used social media for the purpose of screening job applicants found information that caused them to eliminate candidates from consideration, including:

- ▶ Photographs that were provocative or inappropriate, 46%
- ▶ Evidence of the candidate drinking excessively or taking drugs, 43%
- ▶ Posts where they had bad-mouthed prior company/employees, 31%
- ▶ Evidence of poor communication skills, 29%
- ▶ Discriminatory behavior related to race, religion, gender, etc., 33%

On the positive side of the results, approximately one third of the hiring managers found evidence influencing them toward hiring an applicant, including:

- ▶ Applicant's information supported the specific job qualifications, 44%
- ▶ Applicant seemed to be a good fit with company culture, 43%
- ▶ Applicant's site portrayed a professional image, 44%

▶ Applicant demonstrated superior communication skills, 36%
▶ Applicant was well-rounded, 40%

Maybe the most startling statistic of all is that 41% of hiring managers surveyed by Career-Builder in 2016 reported that they are less likely to interview job candidates if they are unable to find information about that person online, which is a 6% increase from the 2015 data (CareerBuilder, 2016). The importance of social media cannot be overstated for either the hiring managers or the potential employee.

▶ **Hiring**

The best indication of future behavior is past behavior. Construct the interview to determine **three** things: *are the credentials accurate, will the person fit with others in the organization, and does the person's work experience predict success in the position being filled*.

The more care taken at the hiring stage, the more likely the new employee will become a permanent employee. Mistakes made by not being careful here tend to turn into bigger problems as time goes on. Firing someone is never easy, so it is much better to hire well and avoid the need to terminate due to a poor hire.

▶ **Training**

Organizational training should be considered an investment as well as an expense. It is best practice to hire for attitude and train for skills. The time and money involved with new and continuing staff training are essential investments that help ensure that the organization will continue to deliver effective service.

Training new staff in the organization's way helps everyone understand and adjust to the changes that will occur when a new person joins the team. Training must be presented to employees in such a way as to enhance productivity and to meet any legal requirements.

The employees must find training useful for it to ultimately be worthwhile.

When training is built into a mentoring process, it often becomes more effective and relevant. Training inside the mentoring process tends to be delivered when and where it is needed, not on an arbitrary time schedule that meets the needs of the trainer. It can be very comforting for a new employee to have an experienced employee assigned as a mentor to help them feel welcomed and navigate the new organizational culture.

▶ **Evaluation**

In the ideal situation, evaluation should be an ongoing **process**. When evaluation is treated as an event rather than a **process**, problems tend to be magnified. Even if a person is given a six-month probationary period, he or she should not have to wait six months to learn about performance issues. **Evaluation** is the comparison of expectations to actual performance. Assessment should occur regularly with feedback to the employee being provided to help ensure that expectations are being met.

With a well-written job description and daily interaction about expectations and observed performance, evaluation becomes simplified. If problems arise that are not covered by the job description, they must be addressed immediately and agreement reached as to how each issue will be addressed.

► **Termination**

Anyone associated with an organization can be asked to leave. While an organization leader is well advised to work to get the best out of everyone—staff, board members, and other volunteers—some people are just not a good fit for specific organizations. The central reason for termination is that day-to-day performance is not matching the expectations of the position. When a person is asked to leave due to another reason, such as they cannot get along with others, it can reflect very badly on a leader's ability to mentor and monitor staff or volunteers. Effective leaders must find a way to help all personnel contribute to the mission. When that is done, everyone benefits. The payoff is worth the effort of quality leading, mentoring, monitoring, and evaluation.

In most situations all employees can be terminated for any reason if there is no contradicting employment agreement. However, everyone from paid staff to volunteer should know that if there is a problem, every effort should be made and sufficient time spent to correct those problems. No person should ever be surprised with a notice of termination, regardless of the seriousness of the reason.

If termination is necessary for someone who has an employment agreement with an organization, there are **three justifications** for ending an employment: **incompetence; violating agency rules; and violating local, state, or federal laws**. A person who cannot perform the required task after due training and coaching can be dismissed. A person who violates agency rules, such as leaving young children unattended in a dangerous location, may be dismissed. A person who breaks the law, for instance traffics in drugs or firearms, may be dismissed. And in each case, it is advisable to leave a **"paper trail"** of documents detailing the situations which might lead to dismissal and to share those documents with appropriate board members.

In today's poor economic conditions, a **fourth justification** for termination bears mentioning. When an organization is facing financial issues and must down-size in order to remain solvent, employees may be terminated without cause. The terms of the employment contract should include these conditions and the terms of notice required by the organization to the employee. Most organizations will provide an ample period of notice so that the employee can seek alternative employment.

▶ **Retention**

Efforts made to retain effective staff are never wasted. The key is to give people meaningful work to do, appreciate them for what they add to the success of the organization, and reward them for a job well done. Retention is also an issue for board members and volunteers.

The relationship an ED establishes with each staff member, board member, and each volunteer is critical to the success of the organization's mission. Since human beings are so adaptable and resilient, the importance of relationship is often downplayed. Naisbitt and Aburdene (1985) report research that points to the central importance of relationships to job satisfaction. They report 10 qualities that people want in their work—for-profit or nonprofit. Notice that high pay, good benefits, and job security are not in the top 10, while they are in the top 15. Here is what research suggests that people want from their work and workplace:

- ▶ to work with people who treat them with respect
- ▶ interesting work
- ▶ recognition for good work
- ▶ a chance to develop skills
- ▶ to work for people who listen if they have ideas about how to do things better
- ▶ a chance to think for themselves rather than just carry out instructions
- ▶ seeing the end result of their work
- ▶ working for efficient supervisors/managers
- ▶ a job/task that is not too easy
- ▶ to think they are well informed about what is going on (pp. 85–86)

While the order of these qualities could vary among staff and volunteers, all 10 represent what people want to see if they are to consider their work rewarding and meaningful. Collectively these workplace qualities create a culture that employees must function within on a daily basis. Frances Frei and Anne Morriss write in their book, *Uncommon Service: How to Win by Putting Customers at the Core of Your Business* (2012), "Culture guides discretionary behavior and it picks up where the employee handbook leaves off. Culture tells us how to respond to an unprecedented service request. It tells us whether to risk telling our bosses about our new ideas, and whether to surface or hide problems. Employees make hundreds of decisions on their own every day, and culture is our guide. Culture tells us what to do when the CEO isn't in the room, which is of course most of the time." As you can see, workplace culture, established by the qualities and characteristics of day-to-day operations, influence employees' behavior, for better or worse.

Rich and coauthors were also interested in the workplace. These researchers examined the relationship between employee engagement and job performance. Their study demonstrated that employees who were engaged not only invested their energy into executing their major performance tasks, but also tended to be helpful, courteous, and involved in organizational matters (Rich, Lepine, & Crawford, 2010).

Can a person do well without these workplace qualities? Certainly! The better question is what organization would want to be known for providing its staff the kind of environment where these qualities are absent? In fact, Levering and Moskowitz (2003) write in the January 7th issue of *Fortune* that the 100 best companies to work for are expanding and increasing benefits, in spite of difficult economic times. The leadership of these organizations understands the importance of investing in building happy and satisfied employees.

What is the proper way to establish an **appropriate relationship** with others in the work environment? An appropriate relationship is open, honest, caring, and genuine. Appropriate relationships are professional. They are two-way, joint ventures in which both parties must want to participate and see rewards from participation. Openness includes the opportunity to talk freely, expressing feelings and ideas. Honesty requires that each person be willing to discuss difficult issues and share views even when different, but this must be done with compassion and sensitivity. Caring is best shown by attentive listening to another and especially listening to how a person feels, not just what the person thinks. Being genuine is shown by actually living the other three, and this is best shown by taking time to learn about and from another, admitting mistakes, enjoying common good times, and sharing times of sadness or disappointment. A healthy working relationship requires frequent and focused effort to prosper and grow.

How does a person know if a work relationship is decaying? While each relationship will have its own unique qualities and characteristics, signs of decay might cause anyone to stop and take stock of the relationship so that a discussion can occur to address the current problems. If a relationship appears to be changing, it is a good practice to ask yourself these questions: Is the change a natural and maturing progression? Is it really the relationship that is changing? Is the change comfortable or uncomfortable for either party?

Here is a list of signs of a decaying relationship. Remember, these signs can be adapted and applied to any relationship—personal or professional:

- ► Shorter encounters
- ► Increasing physical distance between parties
- ► Increasing time between interactions
- ► Less personal information exchanged
- ► Less relationship talk
- ► Fewer favors given and/or asked for
- ► More negative evaluations and absolutistic statements and fewer positive superlatives
- ► Less nonverbal immediacy—less eye contact, colder vocal tone
- ► Increasing concern for self rather than for the other person or the relationship
- ► Less compromise due to increasing win–lose orientation

▶ More individual activities rather than mutual activities

▶ Return to more formal language and formal etiquette instead of comfortable, informal language and action

If work relationships are sound and appropriate, an organization will prosper. If staff relationships are neglected or ignored, an organization will suffer. This is also true for board and volunteer relationships (Weis & Muller, 2015).

BOARD OF DIRECTORS

A board of directors, board of trustees, or administrative committee, hereafter referred to as the **board,** is common in the governance of nonprofit and for-profit organizations. Great resources on board development are provided by Board Source and can be found online at www.boardsource.org. The board serves to monitor organizational operations, set and adjust policies, and assure the financial support for the programs and personnel of the organization. The board is responsible for:

1. Legal oversight:
   a. The board approves the direction, mission, and vision of the organization and ensures that the organization operates in accordance with the regulations pertaining to its tax-exempt status.
   b. The board ensures legal and ethical integrity.
   c. The board is responsible for legally protecting the organization's assets.

2. Management oversight:
   a. The board is responsible for selecting the Executive Director and overseeing his or her performance.
   b. The board is responsible for writing the position description for the Executive Director position and modifying his or her duties as needed.
   c. The board manages the performance of all other employees indirectly through their evaluation of the Executive Director. They have the power to hire and fire the Executive Director as needed.

3. Financial oversight:
   a. The board sets and approves an annual budget.
   b. The board ensures that there are adequate financial resources. They might conduct fundraising activities in some instances or oversee these activities.
   c. The board reviews the results of financial audits and makes adjustments to budgets as needed.

4. Program oversight:

    a. The board makes sure that the programs in place are appropriate to further the mission of the organization.

    b. New programs and initiatives need to be approved by the board for consistency with the mission and to ensure availability of adequate funding.

    c. Program elimination is typically also approved by the board as are other major operational changes proposed by staff and recommended for approval by the Executive Director.

Since board members work without pay, they are considered volunteers. They are, in fact, key volunteers or stakeholders. Their role is important, but not more important than any other group in the agency—staff or other volunteers. They, in fact, need to be examined for inclusion on the organization's team in the same way as would be done in recruiting and selecting staff and other volunteers.

All boards have four primary roles: (1) legal and fiduciary responsibilities; (2) represent an interested community constituency; (3) monitor agency operations; and (4) assist in fundraising. It is useful to examine each of these four broad roles.

Legal and fiduciary responsibilities include attending to local, state, and federal laws which impact the operation of the organization. Board members must also guard against misuse of the assets of the organization. If something goes wrong in either area, a board member cannot claim ignorance as a defense. The law assumes the individuals will exercise due diligence when making decisions with legal or financial stewardship implications. In legal terminology, all board members have the ***duty of care*** (due care), which is usually defined as the "care that an ordinarily prudent person would exercise in a like position and under similar circumstances" (*Black's Law Dictionary*, 1990, p. 499).

Representational responsibilities include acting in the best interest of all who receive benefit from the organization. Each board member should give **voice** to one or more of the groups or viewpoints served by the organization. In addition to a particular expertise (financial, legal, visioning, advocacy, etc.) that a board member brings to the group, members should represent and give voice to those served. Great care must be taken to make sure the board members can represent the skills necessary for a board to do its job well. Every board should have some members who have strong financial backgrounds, others who have knowledge of the laws governing nonprofits, others with strong programming experience, others with fundraising skills, while all should have strong ties to the community and a genuine interest in the organization's success. A board member should never receive personal benefit from their board membership. This is a part of a board members' ***duty of loyalty***, which is the legal standard of fairness (Gill, 2006). Said in another way, a board member must be true to the interests of the organization when making decisions that affect the organization.

Monitoring duties include assuring that the organization is effectively and efficiently run. This is part of the board member's *duty of care* in terms of each member's legal duty to be faithful to the organization's mission (Gill, 2006). The board is responsible for hiring and firing the chief executive officer/ED. It is also the responsibility of the board to periodically evaluate the ED's performance and provide constructive feedback. If changes need to be made, the board must clearly spell out what action is expected and within what time frame. The board must follow-up on the action plan and timetable for suggested improvements.

Financial support responsibility does not mean board members must personally fund the organization. However, it is good practice to recruit board members if they have already demonstrated their belief in the mission of the organization by offering some financial support. Their most important role, aside from making sure the organization adheres to local, state, and federal legal requirements and remains solvent, is to attract potential donors. In other words, the board must set an example for the community and help those responsible for fundraising make contact with community members who are capable of making meaningful contributions. They must also support and speak for the organization's mission in such a way as to generate a positive image for the organization among potential donors.

Another way of describing the key roles of board members is presented in *Governance as Leadership* (Chait, Ryan, & Taylor, 2005) in which the terms fiduciary, strategic, and generative are used. The case is made that the organization will be more successful when the board has time to work with all three roles and to look for the interconnections among them. The case for viewing nonprofit governance within a much broader context is made by Cornforth in *Nonprofit Governance: Innovative Perspectives and Approaches*. He states that the governance of the nonprofit organization includes a framework of responsibilities, requirements, and accountabilities that include regulatory, auditing, and reporting to key stakeholder functions. He goes on to remind readers that managers, advisory boards, and others within the organization also participate in the governance of the organization (Cornforth & Brown, 2014). All of this is noted within the dramatically changing external context for nonprofit organizations.

The delivery of public goods and services has shifted significantly since the 1980s to the present day. During the 1980s and 1990s there were a series of reforms that involved the movement of private sector management practices into the public sector, which changed the relationship between public and nonprofit organizations. Next there was a separation of the role of public authorities as the purchasers of services as being the responsible entity for providing public services. This introduced competition among service providers by having private and nonprofits compete for public service contracts.

Finally, the government strengthened control via target setting, standards, audits, and inspections. All of which increased competition, but blurred the lines between nonprofit and for-profits even more. Therefore, today's nonprofit boards have expanded responsibilities that include ensuring that the organization remains compliant with the ever-expanding legal requirements in a system where more organizations are competing for fewer dollars (Cornforth & Brown, 2014).

Fiduciary or financial responsibilities remain as the core of the traditional role of board members. It has historically consumed the majority of the time board members give to the organization, from fundraising to financial oversight. The expectations of financial stewardship weigh heavily on most board members and, therefore, get a great deal of attention. Legal compliance and financial health dominate most board meeting agendas. With all of the changes occurring in the government regulations, it becomes imperative that some board members with this area of expertise are selected to serve.

Board members also need to have the opportunity to contribute to the **strategic** development of the organization's pursuit of its mission. Time needs to be available for the board to contribute to the alignment of programs and services with the mission, to help make sure that constituent needs are being most effectively met. This can involve such things as strategic discussions about program evaluation results with staff, giving board members a chance to have input to future directions.

Finally, board members need the opportunity to participate in periodic **generative** discussions about the future. These exchanges involve stepping back from the daily operation of the organization and its delivery of programs and services to think together about the mission and the ways in which the organization can become more effective in achieving it. Generative thinking is a process that helps every board member share their wisdom, inspiration, and most creative ideas about the core issues and how they can most effectively be addressed. Such discussions are often the source of new thinking about the future and creative strategies that might impact the way the organization pursues its vision of that future. Attention must be paid to providing board members with a balanced experience that includes sufficient time on the fiduciary, strategic, and generative roles in order to make sure that the organization is healthy and effective today as well as into the future.

The members of the board represent various groups and constituents from the community. As new members rotate on and off the board, balance in representation must be maintained. Therefore, there should be a staggered rotation of board members that has a strategic aspect associated with it. This would include a strategy where those with a specific expertise would not all rotate off during the same cycle. The most common model is a three-year rotation system with one third of the membership replaced each year, for an established board. If a new organization is selecting its first board, one third would serve one year, one third for two years, and one third for three years. This helps keep a board from becoming stagnant and unproductive.

Board members are assigned specific roles as officers or committee members as a way of organizing the work and guiding participation. Most often there are four board officers as follows: **President/Chair, Vice President, Secretary, and Treasurer**. The duties of each office are the same as it would be for any organization. Specific or special responsibilities may be added due to the nature or mission of the organization. Officers should be eligible for re-election, but there should be some reasonable term limits or rotation of members through these offices, although this is not always practical. For example, the skills of the person who serves as Treasurer or Secretary may not be shared by all members of the board. Whatever system is selected, a board does not need to be taken hostage by one or a few members and controlled for satisfaction of their egos over the best interest of the agency. A dominating board leader can destroy the effectiveness of an agency (Weis & Muller, 2015).

The **President/Chair** is responsible for running meetings, assuring that board members receive the information to discharge their duties, appointing committees as prescribed in the organizations governing documents, presiding over executive committee meetings, speaking for the organization as appropriate, and leading the annual review of the Executive Director.

The President/Chair is also responsible for assuring that the board stays on task and runs efficiently. As part of this duty he or she must manage conflict among board members. Gill offers advice on the sensitive task in his book, *Governing for Results: A Director's Guide to Good Governance* (2006). The following techniques might be useful for a board chair faced with conflict among the members:

▶ Acknowledge the value and importance of divergent views in informing decision-making.

▶ Practice and encourage good listening skills, understanding, and respect.

▶ Clarify the ground rules for all discussions: what is said remains confidential; everyone has a chance to express an opinion; participants must listen in order to understand; the entire group "owns" the issue and the solutions; the focus should remain on the issue rather than on personalities.

▶ Help the parties define the issues. State what you believe is the issue. Seek agreement from both parties on a clear definition of the issue. Name the problem or issue.

▶ Seek agreement on the objectives, outcomes, or decisions sought by placing this issue on the board agenda. (Why should the board address this issue?)

▶ Help the disputants identify and expand points of agreement.

▶ Assist the disputants in determining why the issue is of importance to them.

▶ Ask the disputants to verbalize the issue from the other person's point of view.

▶ Paraphrase the disputant's main points of agreement and sticking points until there is consensus on what is agreed or disagreed upon.

► Encourage both parties and other board members to offer new insights. Try to reach a compromise.

► Check with both parties to see if they are okay with the compromise.

► If no compromise can be reached, table the item to allow time for cooling off and/or additional information to be sought to provide new insights for potential solutions (Gill).

The **Vice President/Vice Chair** assumes the duties of the President when he or she is unable to discharge those duties. The Vice President serves on committees as appointed by the President and represents the organization at public meetings when appropriate. This person is often the next one to serve as President of the board, which allows a person to prepare for the position of President with proper orientation and training. This succession process is often employed to ensure a smooth transition of leadership.

The principle function of the **Secretary** of the board is to maintain accurate minutes of all board meetings. This is critical since in legal terms a board speaks through its minutes, which are maintained over time to record all significant decisions, recommendations, and actions. These minutes must be prepared in a timely fashion and distributed to all board members and other stakeholders. Taking attendance for all meetings is also the duty of this officer. The safe-keeping of all official board records and documents is also the responsibility of the Secretary.

The **Treasurer** monitors the financial business of the agency to assure that sound and accepted accounting procedures are followed and that annual, external audits are conducted and reported to the board. The Treasurer must keep in touch with day-to-day fiscal activities of the organization, working closely with the staff that is managing these processes. The Treasurer must make sure that all legal and governmental regulations are observed with respect to payroll and other financial obligations of the organization.

An effective board is organized into committees to divide the workload and assure proper monitoring of organizational operations (*BoardSource*, 2012). The number and size of committees varies by the size and scope of the organization, the number of board members, and the nature of the work to be done. In one respect, committees keep an eye on the big picture for the organization, doing work that complements and supports the work of the staff. It is a serious mistake for the board or its committees to become involved in micromanaging the organization and interfering with the work of the staff. At the same time, the board must be interested in and aware of the day-to-day activities of the agency.

A board can rely on a committee to do its work as long as the following requirements are met (Berman, 2010):

► the purpose, powers, procedures, and limitations of the committee are clearly defined in the organization's bylaws and in formal board actions

► the committee maintains and distributes minutes of its meetings and other records appropriate to its assignment

▶ the committee regularly reports its work to the board through established channels

▶ the membership of the committee is appropriate to the assignment

▶ the committee is meeting and addressing matters appropriate to its assignment

The typical board committees include:

▶ **Executive Committee**—This committee usually consists of the officers of the board. It can be expanded to include the chairpersons of standing committees or anyone else the board designates. Size of the executive committee is always an issue. An executive committee of more than seven would be considered large and potentially difficult to assemble for important functions. This committee makes recommendations for board action. It only has authority as authorized by the entire board. The board President serves as chair of the executive committee and calls necessary meetings between the regular meetings of the full board. The ED should be an ex-officio member of this and all other board sub-committees.

▶ **Budget & Finance Committee**— This committee works with the ED to prepare and monitor the annual budget of the organization. The Treasurer serves on the committee and frequently serves as chairperson. If necessary, the committee recommends adjustments in the budget throughout the year to stay on track for good financial health. He or she also oversees fundraising and provides liaison with external funding sources such as the United Way. In some cases, the committee also plans capital campaigns, usually with the help of a consultant, and planned-giving programs to benefit the organization and its loyal supporters. In other cases, a subcommittee might be established to oversee fundraising in general or specific fundraising activities like capital campaigns and planned giving programs.

▶ **Strategic Planning Committee**—This committee should be an ongoing committee and not just one that functions every five years or in times of crisis. This is the vision monitoring and adjustment committee. They should not be distracted by day-to-day issues. They must always be looking to the horizon to recommend needed change in strategy or direction. They must watch for community changes, need for program modification, trends in funding, facility needs, personnel issues, opportunities for expansion and growth of the agency mission, and board issues. They engage the whole board in strategic and generative discussions to help inform the long-range plans and the ongoing strategies, goals, and activities that help prepare for that future.

▶ **Program Committee**—This committee monitors the programs of the organization for effectiveness and recommends changes and updates after appropriate consultation with clients and community representatives and reviewing evaluation activity conducted by the staff. Membership should include the ED and appropriate program staff along with one or two board members to serve as liaison with the full board. They should prepare a calendar of activities for each year. This can be distributed to board members, clients, media, or any interested person.

▶ **Facilities or Property Management Committee**—This committee keeps track of needed repairs and renovations of the organization's real estate holdings. They plan for long-term funding of maintenance and improvements, working with the Budget and Finance Committee and whole board to prepare for those costs. They need to assure that all facilities meet or exceed local codes and that all risks associated with the facilities are addressed in a timely fashion. This group should monitor the inventory of equipment and facilities and periodically review the insurance coverage for all property.

▶ **Human Resource Committee**—This committee is charged with developing appropriate written personnel policy for board approval. Policies, practices, and procedures typically include affirmative action compliance, conditions of employment, probationary period, job descriptions and classifications, performance review criteria, working conditions and hours, benefits, vacations, expense reimbursement, promotion options, training and conference attendance requirements, leave policies—family, illness, military service, termination of employment, and severance pay. The committee must also ensure that meaningful and timely evaluation of all staff and volunteers occurs on a regular basis. A critical function of this committee is to assure the benefits and compensation package for all positions is competitive with similar organizations. Additionally, this committee must ensure that appropriate training exists for all employees, volunteers, and board members.

▶ **Marketing and Advertising Committee**—This is a year-round functioning committee charged with the promotion and marketing of all organization programs and services by working in support of the ED and appropriate staff. It ensures that all activities are exposed to the community by using appropriate newspaper, radio, television, and social media to tell the story of the organization through press releases, flyers, and the annual report. This committee works in conjunction with local civic organizations, such as the local Chamber of Commerce, to increase the visibility of the organization in the community.

▶ **Legal Issues Committee**—This committee monitors all issues related to legal requirements, risk management, and insurance. The use of external specialists, including legal counsel and insurance agents, can be recommended by this committee if the situation warrants.

▶ **Board Recruitment and Recognition Committee**—This committee constantly searches the community for potential board members who could make a positive contribution to the mission and vision of the organization. This group devises strategies for recruiting desirable board members. The committee also prepares a process for current member evaluation and recognition. It prepares a slate of officers for annual elections and recommends term limits and rotation of board members through appropriate board positions. It formulates and recommends to the board policies and actions for filling expiring terms of officers and other members. Members should be sensitive to the representational charge of the board.

▶ **Activities or Special Events Committee**—This committee might not exist in every organization, since its work may be handled by staff and volunteers. It can be the source of input and/or support for a wide range of activities that are important in the life of the organization, including such things as an annual banquet to honor clients and volunteers, public relations events to promote new programs, or any other event outside the work of other committees.

Boards may have fewer or more committees or specialized committees to meet the challenges of their work of running the organization. The number and size of committees is largely determined by the overall size and complexity of the organization. Too many committees can get in the way of organizational effectiveness. Committees of more than nine people can become unwieldy and ineffective. In short, a board needs the committees required to make it effective, not a long list of committees in order to look as important as other agencies.

VOLUNTEERS

Volunteers are critical to most nonprofit organizations. **Volunteers** can save an organization or they can be the cause of death of it. The key to volunteer success lies in how clearly the organization defines the role of each volunteer, and evaluates and rewards each volunteer. Notice the use of "each" in the preceding statement. While it is always important to understand that each person is an individual with unique qualities, needs, drives, abilities, interests, and skills, it is critical when working with volunteers. It is essential to remember that board members are key volunteers.

Why do people volunteer to work for no pay? The answer is, they never do! While it is true that people who volunteer do not expect to receive money for their efforts, they do expect to get something for their experience. Basically, volunteers are drawn to an organization because they see a need that they would like to help fill and the organization provides a mechanism for them to do so; or they feel a need to be involved. These altruistic motives help organizations fill positions without having to hire full-time staff. Worth (2009) reports that volunteers come to an organization and stay over time because they have:

▶ a desire to serve the organization's mission
▶ positive relationships with other volunteers
▶ a rewarding experience with the work of the organization
▶ learned new skills

Just like quality paid staff management practices, volunteers want clear expectations for their work with the organization and the amount of time involved. Volunteer job descriptions can help provide this information. Volunteers also need quality supervision to help ensure that their contributions of time are most effectively utilized. However, most nonprofit organization leaders find it more difficult to terminate a volunteer or board member than to terminate a paid staff member. Since this tends to be true, great care must be taken when selecting volunteers and matching them to tasks within the organization. Three broad categories of volunteer management must receive special attention: **planning, recruitment,** and **integration** (Weis & Muller, 2015).

Planning is certainly the first step in the process of meaningful use of volunteers for any nonprofit organization. While planning comes first, it must also be viewed as a continuous process for the life of the organization. The initial stage in planning is assessment of needs, asking:

- ▶ What positions can be filled by volunteers?
- ▶ How many are needed?
- ▶ How much supervision or oversight is required?
- ▶ How will the time required for oversight impact staff time constraints?
- ▶ Is the use of a volunteer of real value or just a way to hold down the number of paid staff members?

Once the assessment is complete, the results must be discussed with all staff, not just those who are most directly affected. A common mistake is to assume that only those most directly affected by an organizational change need to know what is happening. In truth, if organizational leaders only share information with people who are directly affected by a decision, those not included might think that information is being hidden, which gives rise to mistrust and feeds the negative rumor mill. With the assessment results discussed openly and honestly, the organization can secure staff consensus. The time spent during this stage is time well spent. If the staff does not agree with or understand the need for volunteers, it is a waste of time to look for them. If they are a part of the decision, they will more actively support and engage volunteers as a resource to the organization.

The final stage in the planning step requires great care. Clear and thorough **job descriptions** for each volunteer position are paramount to the meaningful utilization of any volunteer. All job descriptions should include position title, reporting line, how the position fits into the organizational pattern, essentials duties, training requirements/plans, expected time contribution, value to the organization, and benefits to the volunteer.

Recruitment is almost as important as planning. In addition to organizational needs, leaders need to consider the motivation of people who volunteer. People seek to volunteer for the same reasons that everyone seeks to be a part of any group or relationship. Humans have four impulses that cause them to seek the companionship of other humans: to receive stimulation, share experiences, assert oneself, and for the increased enjoyment of certain activities.

People are attracted to each other much as a volunteer is attracted to an organization. Volunteers are attracted to nonprofit organizations because of:

- ▶ **Reward or punishment**—The volunteer gets something from the relationship. The person might feel good about what they do for the organization or its clients. On the other hand, the volunteer might be compelled by guilt or some motive, which is a form of punishment for the person. In either case, the volunteer is getting a return on their investment.
- ▶ **Proximity**—The opportunity to engage an organization is close to the volunteer and easily accessed or an organization is distant enough to remove the volunteer from some undesirable condition or influence.
- ▶ **Similarity or dissimilarity**—Volunteers might turn to an organization because they see themselves and the organization traveling the same road, wanting the same things in terms of helping people. On the other hand, they could see the organization doing something they have never done and they want to try. It might also be that they see the organization going in the opposite direction to the one they have personally chosen.
- ▶ **Physical attractiveness**—The organization might be the place to be. It might be the one that all the best people choose to engage. It might be the community golden child. Volunteers might conclude that association with such an organization will improve their community standing or make them attractive to other organizations.

Whatever a volunteer's motives, the organization can benefit or suffer. The organization that chooses to engage volunteers must have volunteers who have motives that blend with and support its mission. The most effective volunteers are driven by service to the organization and not by service to themselves.

In addition, due diligence must be taken in selecting volunteers, as with staff, in order to reduce and manage any **risk** to the organization. General guidelines for **risk management** are discussed in some detail in **Chapter 7**.

Integration is the third consideration in the effective utilization of volunteers. The organization can have a great plan for the use of volunteers and recruit only people with motives that support the mission and still fail to retain the best or make optimal use of each person if the organization does not properly integrate the volunteers with its programs and paid staff. Just as with paid staff, volunteers must have meaningful work; appropriate recognition; helpful feedback as to the effectiveness of their contribution to the mission; regular opportunities for input based on their experience and wisdom; and the chance to expand their skills, if they so desire. The more thoroughly integrated volunteers become with the flow of the organization, the more likely they are to have a positive impact on the mission (Herman, 2005).

COMMUNICATION

Quality communication is central to effective leadership. Time invested in understanding and developing communication skills will improve the work of leaders and managers working at all levels in nonprofit organizations. With the mix of paid staff, board members, and volunteers, it can be challenging work. The quality of the relationships that are developed across an organization is the secret to the success of its team of staff and volunteers; and the key to successful relationship building is communication. A leading author on the subject of people helping families get along puts it this way, "Once a human being has arrived on this earth, communication is the largest single factor determining what kinds of relationships she or he makes with others and what happens to each in the world. How we manage survival, how we develop intimacy, how productive we are, how we connect with our own divinity—all depend largely on our communication skills" (Satir, 1988, p. xi). A brief review of the foundations of effective communication sets the stage for understanding quality practices in leading nonprofit organizations.

The reason it is so difficult to achieve effective communication is that too many people assume that success is as simple as creating clear and understandable messages. This is often referred to as the **conduit model**. The conduit model assumes that communication is the simple passage of messages from a sender to a receiver through a channel (or conduit). The **conduit model** is source oriented (Bokeno, 2002). Sometimes the idea of feedback is added as a way of checking with the sender to verify if the receiver clearly and correctly received and understood the message. Even when consideration of interaction or feedback is added, it is easy to see why people mistakenly oversimplify communication and reduce it to the sending and receiving of messages. If someone misunderstands, is it the sender's or receiver's fault? The fault most often lies in the search for simple answers to difficult questions. Bokeno (2002) posits that the conduit model of communication, which predominates in most organizations, is theoretically inappropriate, dysfunctional and ineffective for generating creative communication such as dialogue.

Anne Lane examined dialogue as a normative, aspirational construct in her thesis, Pragmatic Two-Way Communication: A Practitioner Perspective on Dialogue in Public Relations (2014). Lane states that it is acknowledged within the public relations literature that the implementation of dialogue in practice is very difficult, or even impossible. When studied, interactions among practitioners undertaking two-way communication generally displays characteristics very different from those that characterize an ideal dialogue. The observed two-way communication served to provide the individuals with a practical means of moving between their personal expectations, those of the organization, and the stakeholders. These practical two-way communications provided people with a way to carry out their work with stakeholders and organizations, but failed to achieve the outcomes hoped for when envisioning communication between these individuals using the ideal method of communication, dialogue.

Effective communication is all about understanding meaning. It is not just about sending clear messages. Satir (1988) offers a practical definition of communication which works as well in the workplace as it does in a family setting. She contends that communication evolves from "the ways people use to work out meaning with one another" (p. 4).

In order to be an effective communicator, it is necessary to understand the nature of interacting with others, to alter or adjust messages to achieve meaning, and that bridges must be built between and among individuals because of differences resulting from variables such as experience, culture, education, area of expertise.

The kind of communication which makes an organization really succeed comes from genuine dialogue; it is a learned art. All humans have a natural desire to understand and be understood. The most helpful way to learn to communicate more effectively is to observe and study individuals who are effective with this art form. Ask questions, try different styles, and ask more questions to become a better communicator.

There are **four communication truths** that can help prepare an individual for daily interaction with people from a wide range of backgrounds, experiences, and cultures. Taking these truths into consideration helps improve the effectiveness of leaders and supervisors working with staff, board, and volunteers in nonprofit organizations (Weis & Muller, 2015).

1. **Understanding must precede any agreement.** Understanding is required if an agreement between two people is to result. Agreement implies that both people are clear on each other's assumptions, values, and positions.

2. **Agreement without understanding is usually meaningless.** In order for two people to agree, they must be talking about the same issue, idea, emotion, or relationship. To say they agree is without any substance unless they are talking about the same issues, idea, emotion, or relationship.

3. **Genuine disagreement is not possible without understanding why or how they disagree.** For disagreement to be genuine, it must be based on a clear understanding of the issue at hand—their positions, why they take these positions, and the implication of these positions for the relationship between the two people. Unless these conditions are met, genuine disagreement is not possible. It is not based in substance but is fueled by assumptions which might or might not be accurate. Understanding of another does not require agreement, but it does require a clear and accurate comprehension of the other person's position.

4. **Disagreement without understanding is almost always meaningless.** Just like statement number two, there is no meaning or substance to a disagreement based on potentially inaccurate or unclear information. If there is clear understanding, there can be genuine disagreement. If there is no understanding, there can only be shouting, anger, assertion, name calling, or, worst of all, violence.

Deetz and Stevenson (1986) describe **five assumptions about communication** that can help a person determine what can be done to modify and build useful communication skills for any workplace:

1. Communication skills are learned.

2. Interpersonal skill needs to be modified over time and situation.

3. Personal, situational, and relationship needs determine the usefulness of various skills.

4. Individuals can exert considerable control over their communication behavior and skill development.

5. Self-esteem and healthy relationships require successful skill development or each person will enjoy only very limited personal and professional accomplishment. (p. 3)

Whether preparing a personal development plan for one employee or a board training program for that critical leadership group, these assumptions will help inform the design and delivery of the program.

In addition to such things as training and development, another factor in successful communication that must be considered is the **interaction environment**. When one person talks with another person, they use words that have specific meaning to them. Those meanings have evolved along with the person. The point is that the meaning of words is in the people who speak and use them, not in a dictionary. There are two factors affecting the interaction environment: the **cultural environment** and the **physical environment**.

1. The **cultural environment** consists of the behaviors, attitudes, and values that are shared by enough people to exert an influence on the messages we create. A person can begin to deduce the prevailing cultural factors by observing patterns of work, relationship styles, attitudes toward self-fulfillment, and messages sent by the mass media.

2. The **physical environment** consists of the natural and human constructions that frame our conversations and relationships. These frames include a person's idea of what constitutes appropriate formality, warmth, privacy, familiarity, constraint, and distance.

Tools for groups to use, such as the Ladder of Inference in Senge's *The Fifth Discipline Fieldbook* (1994), can promote the practice of checking with each other to ask for the meaning and the reasons behind it in clarifying and improving understanding. It is through such group processes that everyone learns to communicate more effectively together while becoming more familiar with those attributes that each person brings to the interaction environment. When this happens, communication improves and the human resources of the organization become more effective in pursuit of the mission.

What are the essential communication skills and how does a leader use each one? There are **six** skills that are important for anyone working in nonprofit organizations: **listening, conflict management, decision-making, team building, coaching/counseling, and sensitivity to differences.**

Listening

Aside from our physical ability to hear sounds, perception is the most important variable in determining if a person is an effective listener. Frequently, the mistake is made in equating hearing and listening. If one person hears someone speaking to them, they believe that they are listening. That may or may not be true. If a person does not respond as expected, does this mean that they are not listening? What is the difference between listening and hearing? Simply put, hearing is using the human senses to receive sensory data and store it in the brain. In its basic form, it is not listening. Listening, unlike hearing, which is a natural phenomenon, is a **learned skill.** It involves selecting, testing, and adding meaning to the sensory data that is being received. Any person can listen more effectively by understanding and acting on the following information (Weis & Muller, 2015):

- ► Effective, active listening is a difficult skill that practice and training can improve.
- ► There is no relationship between intelligence and listening skill. Highly intelligent people are often very poor listeners, because they jump to conclusions rather than hearing all that is being said.
- ► Listening is an active process. It requires a person's participation and involvement. Good listeners often notice a sense of fatigue after an intense listening experience.
- ► Personality plays an important role in how well a person listens. The more other-focused a person, generally, the better their listening skills.
- ► Effective listening requires the whole body. Proper eye contact and body posture facilitate effective, active listening.
- ► Feelings are often as important as the words being spoken. People must look for the underlying feelings in any message. These feelings are often the *real* message that is being delivered via body language rather than verbally.

The practice of **active listening** can help improve communication. It involves listening for more than the apparent meaning of the words and includes listening for the feelings and emotions behind words or messages. There are **four** main **qualities of an active listener:**

1. Physical proximity or closeness

2. Appropriate, direct eye contact

3. An open mind

4. A demand for clarity as demonstrated by a willingness to ask questions to get clear meaning and to uncover underlying emotions and feelings

Conflict Management

Conflict is a naturally occurring phenomenon in all societies. Hocker and Wilmot (1985) define **conflict** as "an expressed struggle between at least two interdependent parties who perceive incompatible goals, scarce rewards, and interference from the other party in achieving their goals" (23). Conflicts are one of the major stressors individuals face in the workplace (Hahn, 2000). Conflicts in the workplace are on the rise as diversity and the associated differences in personal values increases (Dijkstra, Beersma, & Cornelissen, 2012). As stress rises in society, conflict follows, and the workplace both reflects the results and provides a perfect place in which to address the negative impacts it has on people. Nonprofit organizations are a great place to manage conflict because they are more flexible and self-determined than the government and business sectors and the majority of the staff and all of the volunteers are involved by their own personal choices (Maravelas, 2005). While many people try to avoid conflict, it can produce the following **positive rewards** that can help improve the nonprofit organization's efforts to develop human resources:

1. Conflict can produce a greater understanding by the people in disagreement and clarify their relationship.

2. Conflict can focus and clarify the similarities and differences between the people in disagreement.

3. Successful conflict management can help the people in disagreement discover better methods for dealing with future conflicts.

4. Conflict can expose areas where communication can actually be improved and strengthened.

The best way to look at the true value of conflict is to ponder the African proverb, "Smooth seas do not make skillful sailors." People must be tested and trained on the seas of conflict in order to learn how to deal with it effectively. Experience working with conflict is the best way to improve the capacity to manage it.

Nonprofit organizations often operated in a context of limited resources. Most definitions of conflict include reference to the inability to share limited resources as a common source of disagreement. This source of conflict occurs frequently in nonprofit organizations. Another recurrent source of conflict in an organization with very diverse staff and volunteer groups with different experiences and backgrounds, comes from communication rules violations. Communication rules define required, preferred, and prohibited behaviors. The severity of the conflict often generates from the costs or rewards of rule violations. Understanding the communication rules of others helps to reduce conflicts over violations of rules. This can be even more pronounced when the diversity includes different roles, relationships, experience, and education that can often be found between staff and volunteers in nonprofit organizations.

A conflict is not just a momentary disagreement, it is a situation in where one or both individuals or groups perceive a threat, whether or not that threat is real. With conflicts involving perceptions of threats to well-being, these feelings remain an issue until we resolve them (Segal & Smith, 2016). Resolving conflicts can be challenging because perceptions of each situation are influenced by every individual's life experiences, culture, values, and beliefs. Remember that some of the most important information exchanged during conflicts and disagreements is communicated nonverbally. This communication, also called body language, is conveyed by emotionally driven facial expressions, posture, and gestures in addition to one's pace, tone, and intensity of voice.

Writers often suggest that conflict resolution should be a goal. In reality, conflict is rarely resolved. One conflict leaves a residue that is built upon through future conflicts. If that residue is basically negative, the subsequent conflicts start in a hole and tend to become more negative than the issue warrants. People typically choose from five options when they are faced with a conflict: **avoiding, accommodating, competing, compromising, or collaborating** (Borisoff &Victor, 1998). While each has its place and each has its advantages, the first four usually lead to more conflict or at least some unhappiness.

> ▶ **Avoiding** can be an appropriate approach to conflict if there is risk of harm. Otherwise, conflicts which are avoided tend to simply grow larger. Avoiding conflict does not solve anything and typically produces little satisfaction for any of the people involved since nothing is resolved. The main residual of avoiding conflict is to continue to avoid conflict even if it causes more harm.
>
> ▶ **Accommodating** can be very appropriate when the issue of the conflict is more important to one person than the other. If two co-workers are disagreeing over the best way to advertise a new program and one is insistent on the need for radio advertising while the other thinks social media advertising is enough, the one can accommodate the other by supporting social media. It does not matter and if there is enough money in the budget to manage the social media sites, the costs of fighting may be too high. Accommodating involves one person giving in to the other. If a person uses this approach too often, it may lead to others taking advantage by cutting that person out of discussions where the issue might matter a great deal, expecting that they are always going to accommodate.

▶ **Competing** is a common approach to conflict management in the United States and is a favorite of most men. The objective is to win on the issue in question and have the other person lose. This approach can be effectively employed when there is a clear-cut solution with profound impact on an organization or when critical information for decision-making is not fully available to all those involved. If there is no real justification for the competing approach, the result can be stifled ideas, weaker solutions, hurt feelings, damaged relationships, and little teamwork. In fact, since competing is so dominant in the U.S. culture, it is rarely justified between co-workers. The main reason for its ineffectiveness is that it tends to promote compliance with power more than promoting open communication and effective conflict management. It can undermine efforts to build the positive relationships necessary for organizational success.

▶ **Compromising** involves all those involved giving some ground in order to move beyond the conflict. This approach is very appropriate when there is no clear-cut answer to an issue and no one has cause to impose a solution on the others involved in the conflict. The worst effect of compromise is that everyone might leave the conflict with some dissatisfaction, which can dampen the enthusiasm for the results achieved by the compromise.

▶ **Collaborating** promotes discussing all perspectives in the creation of a solution, which can make every party's satisfaction maximized. It focuses on issues, not positions. All the other approaches invite participants to adopt a position and stick to it. Collaboration, by its nature, invites all parties to look to the potential outcome and determine an outcome that will benefit everyone. This approach usually requires more time and effort but has the potential to produce high degrees of satisfaction and more creative solutions. It also creates a residual of success, which in turn encourages those involved in a collaborative effort to have less fear of future conflict because there is a pattern of success to build upon. Collaborating is the most desirable approach in most situations.

There are **three skill sets** to help people **focus on a win-win prospective** that is central to the collaborating approach. These three tend to open a path to cooperation more than competition:

▶ See the disagreement from the point of view of the other person
▶ Actively listen to the other person, try to hear their emotions and their meanings
▶ Seek mutual problem solving with principled negotiation

Decision-Making

Decisions can be easy to make but difficult to live with over time. People often forget that decisions are best made using a process that considers not only the final decision but the consequences of that decision. Research has produced and encouraged some useful models that help people remember the nature of the decision-making process.

Tuckman (1965) introduced a very useful four-stage description of the typical process used by small groups when they initially come together or are assigned a task: **forming, storming, norming, and performing.** The model has great usefulness for nonprofit organizations that are continually creating and reforming groups.

▶ **Forming**—Another word to describe this stage is confusion. Group members frequently have very different ideas as to why the group was put together and what it is supposed to accomplish even when all have received the same written or oral instructions concerning the purpose for the formation of the group. There are many questions at this stage. What are we doing here? Why are we here? What do they really want? Are we going to have any real power? Can we select our own leader? Why am I here? Why are you here? When do we have to present our report? Who is going to prepare it? There is little attention paid to process or protocol during this stage. Members often test the tolerance of each other and the appointed or emergent leader. At the other extreme there may be a great dependence on the leader and no one will participate until encouraged or forced to do so. This is particularly true when there is a high level of anxiety or suspicion among group members.

▶ **Storming**—Another word for this stage is uncertainty. While clarity of purpose and task direction improves, people have difficulty working together at this stage because they are positioning for power, influence, and recognition. Power struggles might appear, as well as alliances or factions. Relationship and emotional issues tend to take center stage. A clear focus on the task at hand is very important if the group is to continue to mature and begin to move toward a meaningful outcome. The leader might need to suggest compromise or encourage members to look for win–win solutions to resolve their conflicts.

▶ **Norming**—The one word to describe this stage is stability. Work is now directed toward the goal(s) agreed to by the group. Decisions are made within the context of guidelines and processes understood and accepted by the members. Some decisions are made by the group as a whole while others are delegated to teams within the total group. The group might now take time for some fun or social outings to build quality relationships. Respect replaces uncertainty and suspicion. The uncertainties that still remain will usually be focused on the task and not on relationship or emotional issues. These uncertainties are understood as a natural part of group process and viewed as challenges that can be overcome.

▶ **Performing**—The word for this stage is productivity. The group has now answered most of the questions that arose in the first stage (forming). They now know why they are doing what they are doing. The group shares a vision of the desired outcome and is able to act without supervision in completing its assigned task. When disagreements occur, they are now handled within an understood process and managed according to accepted guidelines. The group finishes its task.

The time spent in each stage is not the most important factor. The stages must follow the natural progression needed by each unique group. The style of leadership employed by the appointed or emergent leader will largely determine how quickly and how well the group proceeds through the stages to become an effective, performing group. The more quickly a group can move to the performing stage the better, if they have satisfied all the behavioral obstacles inherent in the preceding stages.

One time-honored tool for groups is the **reflective thinking agenda** promoted by the American educational reformer, John Dewey, in the early 1900s. The **five-step agenda**, when applied thoughtfully, can ensure higher quality decisions:

1. Clearly describe the problem

2. Analyze what is causing the problem

3. Establish criteria for solving the problem

4. Brainstorm solutions that match the criteria

5. Pick the solution or solutions that best fit the criteria

The decision-making approach promotes groups working together to understand the situation and develop a shared and supported response. It is a traditional way that nonprofit organizations make decisions, while also promoting quality relationships and effective communications.

Elizabeth Dole, former president of the American Red Cross, demonstrated her understanding of effective decision-making when she outlined the steps for making and selling decisions. She observed, "What you always do before you make a decision is consult. The best public policy is made when you are listening to people who are going to be impacted. Then, once policy is determined, you call on them to help you sell it." Her insight about public policy is just as applicable to any decision made by any nonprofit organization, at any level, with respect to any issue.

Team Building

The old expression "two heads are better than one" could easily be changed in the twenty-first century to "teamwork is the best approach." A very good website for resources on teamwork can be found at www.teambuildinginc.com. In addition to articles on important variables, there are links to other sources, a bookstore, team building exercises, assessment tools, and more. A great deal of information is known about teamwork. It seems obvious that working together improves productivity, discourages less productive activity, gives everyone an opportunity to get some of the glory, and provides encouragement and protection when someone makes a mistake or is simply discouraged.

It is common for leaders promoting teamwork to remind group members that "There is no 'I' in team." This does not mean there is no room for individual achievement since most of what a team is able to accomplish is magnified if all individuals are striving for what Senge (1990) calls **personal mastery**. As individuals work to be the best they can be, everyone they work with is made better. "Organizations learn only through individuals who learn" (p. 139). Personal mastery is not achieved at the expense of other team members; it is achieved at the expense of personal effort.

Several concepts relate directly to successful team building, team success, or teamwork. Excellent resources to support team building can be found at www.teambuildinginc.com, including Zoglio's (1993) *Seven Keys to Building Great Work Teams*. These keys are commitment, contribution, communication, cooperation, conflict management, change management, and connections.

1. **Commitment**—In order for a group to become a team, the team members must understand what they are doing and why they are doing it. To achieve commitment, people need to work together to develop a mission for the team, a vision, and value statements which fit with the mission and still reflect the individual nature of the group. The members need the experience of developing their measures of success and the opportunity to celebrate their accomplishments.

2. **Contribution**—Everyone must contribute to the team effort, but it is not necessary that they all contribute in the same way or the same amount. All team members need strong technical and interpersonal skills and must be willing to learn new skills or improve current skills for the benefit of the team effort. Balanced contributions are more easily obtained when each member thinks he or she has been included, has confidence, and is empowered. A person can be included by being allowed to talk and being asked to provide input if he or she seems reluctant. A team member's confidence can be enhanced through encouragement and coaching and by keeping past successes in front of the group. Empowerment comes from appropriate training, sufficient resources, showing respect, and involving members in decisions that affect the team (not informing them after a decision is made).

3. **Communication**—In order for a team to succeed, the most important factor is the freedom to communicate openly and honestly. Members must be able to ask for help without feeling inferior; offer ideas that might appear to be off the wall without being laughed at; think out loud without being scolded for not considering the feelings of

others; and risk making a mistake without being ridiculed. Trust must be built and maintained above all else. To improve communication, emphasize the importance of listening actively; using language with sensitivity; giving and receiving feedback with consideration for others; showing trust, and efficiently using meeting time. If some team members need training in interpersonal skills, provide it as enhancement not as punishment.

4. **Cooperation**—Very few programs or projects can be successful unless there is a sense of interconnectedness. From for-profit to nonprofit organizations, the information age relies on people sharing information and working together to meet goals and achieving organizational missions. Cooperation is very highly valued in the nonprofit sector. An effective leader can stimulate cooperation by demonstrating and rewarding behaviors that facilitate cooperation among staff and volunteers. These behaviors include doing work accurately, doing it on time, keeping in touch with others who need to share information, being creative enough to be willing to do something a new way and promoting healthy, open, trusting relationships.

5. **Conflict Management**—Conflict happens, it is natural and inevitable. Conflict can be good! If conflict is well managed, it can, in fact, stimulate creativity and keep teams and individuals from becoming stale. If conflict is not well managed, future conflicts will be more intense or avoided all together, neither of which is ultimately constructive for those individuals involved or the organization as a whole. Leaders can help team members reduce the damaging effects of conflict by teaching members to manage rather than avoid conflict and provide them the skills needed to produce more constructive outcomes.

6. **Change Management**—For-profit organizations thrive and survive on the basis of their ability to stay out front in their area of business. They must stay ahead of the competition to continue to do well. Nonprofit organizations that best satisfy community and individual needs learn to act rather than react. Change happens! The best way to survive change is not to try to avoid it and hold on to the past, but to manage it and grow as a result of the process. Leaders can help team members manage change by modeling a positive attitude toward change and by continually supporting their team efforts to manage change with resources and encouragement. If leaders want team members to believe that change is truly expected and desired, freedom to make a mistake or fail during the change effort is critical.

7. **Connections**—It is important for any team to take a systems view of its own work and consider how these efforts are connected to the mission of the organization, the work of other teams in the organization, and the issues and concerns of its own team members. The operative word here is *networking*. Two critical connections must be mon-

itored continually: the connection to mission and the connection to feedback from constituents. Leaders can support these connections by helping to keep communication lines open to all levels of the organization and its clients. If people are rewarded and recognized for helping each other, they will tend to continue to this practice.

Alexander Graham Bell put it this way, "Great discoveries and achievements invariably involve the cooperation of many minds." If this is true for great discoveries, how much more can people accomplish with respect to ordinary challenges and opportunities if they are approached with many minds rather than in isolation. Henry Ford described the value of teamwork and cooperation this way, "Coming together is a beginning, staying together is progress, working together is success."

COACHING/COUNSELING

People frequently know they need to learn new skills to survive in their work but often do not know how to go about identifying the specific skills required and finding the time to learn them. Many people simply need a little assistance with the learning process whether it involves providing instruction, setting deadlines, or offering time to study. Helping individuals triumph at work helps any organization succeed at its mission. If a person is unwilling or unable to do what is necessary for an organization to fulfill its mission, that person should be *freed* to find another job. If, however, a person is willing and able to improve, an organization should protect its investment and help improve the person's skills.

Skill improvement or enhancement can be achieved through the use of organizational training programs. When a person needs substantial help that can be provided by outside vendors or through national affiliate organizations and professional associations, the local organization should invest in its people and cover the cost of the training whenever possible.

When the improvement or enhancement needed can be addressed by local staff, it should be conducted at the local level. This assumes that someone is capable of helping the employee(s) in need. This might be a coaching/counseling task or a formal teaching situation. One of the most powerful coaching and counseling tools is **mentoring**. Mentoring is a process that occurs within the context of a relationship. To be successful, a mentoring relationship is best built from a base of genuine dialogue (Bokeno & Gantt, 2000). Genuine dialogue is characterized by open interaction, a problem-solution mind-set, an effort to generate new ideas (not just to choose the best from the past), and a joint-venture thought process. Mentoring is characterized by **caring, sharing, correcting,** and **connecting** (Gantt, 1997). This was discussed in-depth in Chapter 2.

Mentoring is **not** a program to be implemented, an initiative to be started, or an assignment to be discharged. Mentoring only works well when people have a trusting relationship where they can share without fear of punishment or sabotage, where refinement or correction can occur without defensiveness, and where genuine attempts are made to provide appropriate access to networks which will lead to advancement, development, or improvement. Other-centered communication is the basic building block of mentoring relationships. This simply means that both people in a mentoring relationship use communication skills and techniques designed to understand others rather than techniques or strategies intended to promote self-interest.

There are a lot of things that a mentor should do to help someone develop. Mentors should collaborate, not tell the other person what to do. Mentors should seek to construct solutions by working together, not by recycling past solutions that seem to fit the situation in question. Mentors should engage in critical reflection by thinking out loud and risking mistakes by openly discussing concerns, problems, and issues, not by trying to make new problems fit old solutions or using past analysis as a standard for new solutions. Mentors fully and openly participate in dialogue; they do not sit back and wait until they are obviously needed. Mentors give voice to their protégé (Bokeno & Bokeno, 1998).

George Bernard Shaw provides a nice illustration of mentoring in his play "Getting Married." He writes, "I am not a teacher, only a fellow traveler of whom you asked the way. I pointed ahead—ahead of myself, as well as you." Thus mentoring, coaching and counseling, in their best form, becomes a joint venture between two people growing with help from each other.

If a person does not respond well to mentoring, the best way to proceed is to clearly define what behavior(s) is/are deficient; explain why change needs to occur; stipulate the consequences of a failure to change or improve; detail a plan for the person to demonstrate progress; and specify any appropriate rewards for achieving agreed-upon goals. If change does not occur, change personnel!

Sensitivity to Difference

Diversity on all levels of life is a resource upon which to capitalize in order to enrich the relationships, generate creative thinking, and promote new ways of working together. To use an agricultural metaphor, hybrid vigor has unlimited potential when the members of the group are increasingly diverse. Many factors combine to promote this growing diversity, including changing demographics, accelerating communication, globalization, and multiculturalism, to name just a few. To capitalize on the potential of diverse groups, it is important to understand others in all of their human conditions. William Schutz's theory of interpersonal needs (1966) identifies **three basic needs** all humans share:

► The need for **inclusion** can be satisfied by joining a civic club, church, fraternity, or sorority; deciding to marry; attending a family reunion. What a person **wants** from others is **acceptance**. What a person **expresses** to others is **interest**.

▶ The need for **control** manifests itself in the choices made in interactions with others. It is shown in attempts to influence others, positions of authority taken, or choices made that involve others. What a person **wants** from others is **guidance**. What a person **expresses** to others is **leadership**.

▶ The need for **affection** is defined as caring and respect for others. A person receives care and respect from others when care and respect for another is shown. What a person **wants** from others is **closeness**. What a person **expresses** to others is **liking**.

How each person behaves or shows these needs is influenced by age, gender, nationality, race, ethnicity, religion, etc.

Very often a person's failure to be sensitive to others who are different can be traced to one or more of the following misconceptions about communication in relationships. Any one of these **false assumptions** can limit the formation of a successful relationship with a person who is different because of age, ability, culture, education, ethnicity, experience, race, or sexual orientation. A person is asking for difficulty in any relationship when he or she assumes any of these (Weis & Muller, 2015):

▶ **Communication in a relationship is consistent**. Just as people change over time so does the need for different communication skills and different sensitivities with respect to others. The journey from the first meeting to working together occasionally, to working together regularly, to a deep, genuine friendship requires very different skills. Communication can vary significantly!

▶ **Communication has simple meaning**. Any interaction with another person is never simple, even if it is with someone well known. How much more complicated can interaction become if it is someone only known through work. Psychologists established many years ago that human brains react to sensory stimulation in three domains: the affective or feeling domain, the cognitive or intellectual domain, and the behavioral or action domain. Interactions with another person are based on predictions that are based on psychological data that comes from how one **feels** about the person, the situation, self, past interactions, or potential for future interactions. Interactions with another person are also based on our intellectual abilities or what the person **thinks** they know, can understand, or can explain. Finally, interactions with another are based on personally established rules for what is right and wrong or appropriate and inappropriate. Communication is very complex!

▶ **Communicators are independent**. Every person is connected to each and every person he or she has ever met, talked with, worked with, dated, and so on. No relationship is ever truly ended except by death of one or both of the parties. Every communicator is influenced by others and influences others. Communication is dependent on many factors!

▶ **Communication behaviors have obvious causation**. Nothing is ever obvious. Some things might appear to be obvious. It is human nature to try to explain everything that is observed. If someone smiles, most people want to know why. If someone yells, most people think they must be angry. Since there are many explanations for the smile or the yell, it is very dangerous to assume the reason for any communication behavior is obvious. There is nothing wrong with speculating and trying to think of causes. The error is not in speculating; it is in being convinced that we *know* the *correct* cause. Communication is very complicated!

▶ **Communication interactions have a final point**. Interactions might have a temporary end or pause but not a final point. With every interaction, there is a residual, something left over, something unfinished, and something to build on for the future. If there were a true final point to interactions, everyone would have to start all relationships and interactions from the beginning each time there was a new contact. All interactions are built on previous interactions. Communication is continuous!

Sensitivity to diversity is not just the politically correct thing to do; it is necessary for success in nonprofit organizations that seek to engage and serve their communities. The arrogance of one race, one generation, one nation, or one group of people claiming to have the best answers to all the important human questions is not only very narrow and limiting, it can lead to the ineffectiveness or death of any organization. Diversity challenges assumptions, opens minds, and unlocks potential to solve problems. Being sensitive to what others bring to the relationship enriches everyone's life.

Valuing diversity in teams of staff and volunteers comes from knowing and appreciating individuals for what they are bringing to the group. The best way to achieve unity is to create a culture in your organization that appreciates diversity. A diverse organization adequately represents the community that it is in. It is not about setting targets or trying to be all things to all people. The diversity must have a natural or realistic feel to it rather than one achieved through artificial targets. With this in mind, what can be achieved in terms of making everyone feel welcome, in particular consider how your volunteer team could have a mix in terms of:

▶ age
▶ socio-economic status
▶ employment status
▶ religion
▶ education level
▶ ethnicity
▶ gender
▶ race
▶ sexual orientation

- ► political affiliation
- ► marital status
- ► disability

If a diverse group is unified, it is capitalizing on its diversity with everyone adding their distinctive perspective—way of thinking and way of acting—to each and every challenge faced. Being sensitive to differences is essential for success in groups. Going beyond sensitivity and valuing what each person brings to the group capitalizes both on each member as individual assets and on what the group does differently for having them as members.

A FINAL THOUGHT

This deep exploration of communication skills illustrates how important these are in all aspects of nonprofit organization leadership, human resource development, and program and service delivery. Without effective communication, nonprofit organizations would fail to accomplish their missions. It is essential that nonprofit leaders commit to working on quality communications throughout the organization on a continuous basis.

SUMMARY

Effective leadership does not occur by accident. All organizations survive or perish based on their use of three key components: people, resources, and service or product. The people component of an organization is at the heart of successful leadership. Character is the variable that separates the effective leader from the ineffective one.

The Executive Director (ED) must be a person of high character, effective in managing the staff, the board, and the volunteers. In each group clear expectations are essential. Meaningful work is required. Regular and appropriate feedback is indispensable where reward for a job well done is appreciated.

The glue that holds the work of everyone together and makes the organization successful and effective is communication. The goal of all interactions should be to first understand and then to be understood. In order to do that, an organizational leader must develop, refine, and hone skills in attentive listening, fair conflict management, meaningful decision-making, cooperative team building, compassionate coaching, counseling and mentoring, authentic sensitivity, and cultural competency.

This chapter addressed, in part, the Nonprofit Academic Centers Council (NACC) Competency Requirements of Communication Skills, Personal Attributes, Board/Committee Development, Human Resources Development and Supervision, and General Nonprofit Management.

REFLECTION AND APPLICATION

1. Make a list of the responsibilities of the Executive Director of a nonprofit organization:

   _____

   _____

   _____

   _____

2. What are the major responsibilities of the Board of Directors of nonprofit organizations?

   _____

   _____

   _____

   _____

   _____

3. What responsibilities are shared between the Executive Director and the Board of Directors of nonprofit organizations?

   _____

   _____

   _____

   _____

4. Describe what nonprofit board members do for the organization and be prepared to discuss how each role and responsibility helps accomplish the mission:

   _____

   _____

   _____

   _____

5. What can an ED do to integrate volunteers into the work of a nonprofit organization?

_____

_____

_____

_____

_____

6. Which is the most important board committee and what is its role?

_____

_____

_____

_____

_____

7. In what ways can conflict produce positive rewards for a group?

_____

_____

_____

_____

_____

8. How do people typically respond to conflict? How might you work to resolve issues-based conflict?

_____

_____

_____

9. What are the most effective approaches to building teams in nonprofit organizations?

_____

_____

_____

_____

_____

REFERENCES

Agarwal, S., & Siddique, A. (2011). Why do NGOs exist, and where are they headed? *Fair Observer Newsletter*, July 17, 2011.

Bermann, H. (2010). *Making a difference: The management and governance of nonprofit organizations* (2nd ed.). CCE Publications.

Black's Law Dictionary (6th ed.) (1990). St. Paul, MN: West Publishing.

BoardSource. Retrieved from http://www.boardsource.org

BoardSource. (2012). *The nonprofit board answer book: A practical guide for board members and chief executives* (3rd ed.). San Francisco, CA: Jossey-Bass.

Bokeno, R. M. (2002). Communicating other/wise: A paradigm for empowered practice. *Reason in Practice: The Journal of Philosophy of Management, 1*(2), 11–23.

Bokeno, R. M., & Bokeno, J. K. (1998). The cultivation of participative change: Managerial development influences on employee communication practice. *Compendium of winning papers from the IABC Reseach Foundation 1997–1998, 37–67.*

Bokeno, R. M., & Gantt, V. W. (2000). Dialogic mentoring: Core relationships for organizational learning. *Management Communication Quarterly, 14*(2), 237–270.

Borisoff, D., & Victor, D. A. (1998). *Conflict management: A communication skills approach* (2nd ed.). Boston: Allyn and Bacon.

CareerBuilder. (2016). http://www.careerbuilder.com/share/aboutus/pressreleasesdetail.aspx?sd=5%2F14%2F2015&id=pr893&ed=12%2F31%2F2015

Chait, R. P., Ryan, W. P., & Taylor, B. E. (2005). *Governance as leadership.* Hoboken, NJ: John Wiley & Sons, Inc.

Cornforth, C., & Brown, W. (2014). *Nonprofit governance: Innovative perspectives and approaches.* New York, NY: Routledge.

Deetz, S. A., & Stevenson, S. L. (1986). *Managing interpersonal communication.* New York: Harper & Row.

Dijkstra, M., Beersma, B., & Cornelissen, R. (2012). The emergence of the activity reduces conflict associated strain (ARCAS) model: A test of a conditional mediation model of workplace conflict and employee strain. *Journal of Occupational Health Psychology, 17*(3):365–75.

Frei, F., & Morriss, A. (2012). *Uncommon service: How to win by putting customers at the core of your business.* Harvard Business Review Press.

Gantt, V. W. (1997). Beneficial mentoring is for everyone: A reaction paper. Paper presented at the National Communication Association Convention, Chicago.

Gill, M. (2006). *Governing for results: A director's guide to good governance.* Trafford Publishing Co., UK.

Hahn, S. (2000). The effects of locus of control on daily exposure, coping and reactivity to work interpersonal stressors: A diary study. *Personality and Individual Differences, 29,* 729–748.

Herman, R. D., & Associates. (2005). *The Jossey-Bass handbook of nonprofit leadership and management* (2nd ed.). San Francisco: Jossey-Bass.

Hocker, J. L., & Wilmot, W. W. (1985). *Interpersonal conflict* (2nd ed.). Dubuque, IA: William C. Brown.

Lane, A. (2014). *Pragmatic two-way communication: A practitioner perspective on dialogue in public relations.* Queensland University of Technology Business School. Queensland University of Technology.

Levering, R., & Moskowitz, M. (January 7, 2003). How companies satisfy workers. *Fortune.*

Maravelas, A. (2005). *How to reduce workplace conflict and stress.* Franklin Lakes, NJ: Career Press.

Moran, B. (2008). Twelve attributes of great nonprofit leaders. Leawood, KS: The Moran Company LLC.

Naisbitt, J., & Aburdene, P. (1985). *Re-Inventing the corporation.* New York: Warner Books.

National School and Community Corps. (1998). *Dr. Martin Luther King, Jr. day of service packet.* Free Library of Philadelphia.

Resources Unlimited. (2010). DiSC Personal Profile System. Inscape Publishing.

Rich, B., Lepine, J., and Crawford, E. (2010). Job engagement: antecedents and effects on job performance. *Academy of Management Journal, 53*(3), 617–635.

Satir, V. M. (1988). *The new peoplemaking.* Palo Alto, CA: Science and Behavior Books.

Schutz, W. (1966). *The interpersonal underworld.* Palo Alto, CA: Science and Behavior Books.

Segal, J., & Smith, M. (2016). *Conflict resolution skills: Building the skills that can turn conflicts into opportunities.* Helpguide.org.

Senge, P. M. (1990). *The fifth discipline: The art and practice of the learning organization.* New York: Doubleday.

Senge, P. M. (1994). *The fifth discipline fieldbook.* New York: Doubleday.

Tuckman, B. W. (1965). Developmental sequence in small groups. *Psychological Bulletin,* 63, 384–399.

Weis, R. M., & Gantt, V. W. (2002). *Leadership & program development in nonprofit organizations.* Peosta, IA: eddie bowers publishing company, inc.

Weis, R., & Muller, S. (2015). *Leading and managing nonprofit organizations* (2nd ed.). Peosta, IA: eddie bowers publishing company, inc.

Word, J., & Norton, L. (2013). Engaging the nonprofit workforce: Mission, management and emotion. Opportunity Knocks.org.

Worth, M. J. (2009). *Nonprofit management: Principles and practices.* Thousand Oaks, CA: Sage Publications, Inc.

Zoglio, S. W. (1993). 7 keys to building great workteams. (path: www.teambuildinginc.com, select: "Articles"; scroll down and select: "7 Keys to Building Great Workteams.")

4

HUMAN DEVELOPMENT, COMPETENCIES, ISSUES, AND TRENDS

Individuals go through an incredible range of developmental changes and situations throughout their lifetime, and it is critical that nonprofit leaders/managers understand the nature of human development and various other issues in planning programs that enhance people's lives.

Understanding human development provides leaders with a foundation of knowledge about what most individuals are facing in terms of developmental stages and how best to address these stages with supportive programs. Knowing, for instance, that adolescents between the ages of 12 and 17 are searching for a positive identity is important in structuring programs that would help them find a sense of self-worth, self-knowledge, and some direction. Similarly, being aware of important issues and trends allows nonprofit leaders to structure programs that address specific individual, family, and community situations.

The first section of Chapter 4, Human Development, provides the reader with insight into the ways that people develop including specific areas of competency development. The section, Issues and Trends, presents information on important issues and trends that are developing within the nonprofit sector. All three sections are intended to provide guidance for setting priorities in program planning.

HUMAN DEVELOPMENT

The highest goal of any youth, human service, or nonprofit leader is to develop programs that enhance people's lives and to provide supportive relationships for members/clients. With that in mind, it is essential to understand the nature of human development as each individual progresses through their various life stages.

The changes that occur between birth and death contribute to an amazing odyssey, and the saying "change is the only constant" is particularly true as individuals pass from one of life's many stages to another. Young children, for instance, often view their parents' commands as pronouncements to be accepted as what is right, but within a few years they begin to believe their parents are not always right. During adolescence, a young person might begin to think his or her parents are rarely correct; this often changes yet again into an appreciation of the parents' viewpoints later in adolescence or early adulthood. Mark Twain once wrote, "When I was a boy of 14, my father was so ignorant I could hardly stand to have the old man around. But when I got to be 21, I was astonished at how much *he* had learned in 7 years" (Shapiro, 2006, p. 782). Physical changes are not the only growth occurring as we age; health, attitudes, beliefs, values, and behavior are continually evolving from one experience to another and from one time of our life to another (Weis & Muller, 2015).

Most experts believe developmental changes occur as a result of the interaction of genetic and environmental influences. The term **maturation** is most often used to describe the unfolding of the genetic plan, such as the appearance of baby teeth, facial hair in boys, and the oncoming of menstruation in adolescent girls. The maturation process is determined by internal signals. The concept of **learning**, however, involves changes that occur as a result of interactions with the environment. Learning has been defined by various educational psychologists in many different ways, which give the term slightly varied meanings. Learning has been described as a quantitative increase in knowledge, as an action involving memorizing facts, mastering skills, and remembering methods that can be retained and used as needed in various situations. Learning has also been viewed as making sense out of something or abstracting meaning from unorganized information, relating parts of the information to one another and to the actual world, interpreting or understanding reality, demonstrating a comprehension of the world by reinterpreting information (Behlol & Dad, 2010).

Development involves the interaction of genetic and environmental influences. With this in mind, it is easy to understand the responsibility and opportunities nonprofit leaders have in shaping human development as the programs and services they provide through their organizations influence the lives of so many.

Development does not happen in isolation, but occurs in the **context** of various circumstances and situations. One of the most important contexts is the **family**, which has tremendous influence on individual development. Most young people spend a tremendous amount of time in the presence of their family members, therefore being influenced by their beliefs, experiences, and practices. Nonprofits play an important role in providing families services in times of need. Other important contexts for healthy development include **school** and **community experiences**. These groups influence the development of individuals in much the same way as families, by providing social norms, cultural context, and a sense of belonging to the person. This influence is so important that to some degree, individuals are products of their school systems and neighborhoods.

The **media** also plays a significant role in the process of human development. People are greatly influenced by what they watch on TV, experience at the movie theaters, and view on social media sites. Taken together, these sources of information frequently provide the lens through which individuals filter their view of the world. This in turn influences the choices that they make, the behaviors that they choose, and the people that they select to associate with. As a young person matures, he or she eventually begins to think about a career. All of their previous life experiences influence their decisions. The decision regarding a career path is critical in a person's development since most people's days are centered on their jobs, **career paths** provide an important context for individual growth.

Culture also has a great deal to do with who we are and who we become. A child growing up in China will have different experiences and values than a child who grows up in the United States of America. Children in rural settings often have different challenges and activities than those growing up in urban environments. In complex societies, groups exist within every community that differ from the majority in one or more areas such as beliefs, attitudes, behaviors, values, or traditions. These **subcultures** or smaller communities can also have a legitimate and profound effect on individual development, depending upon the extent of the groups' isolation from the mainstream community and the degree of separation between their practices and beliefs.

Considering the contextual nature of human development, nonprofit leaders have a tremendous opportunity to enhance areas of family structure and support, individual growth, and community development. Nonprofit organizations can help communities come together and utilize resources more efficiently for the benefit of all of those living within the community.

DEVELOPMENTAL THEORIES

Theories explaining human development are important because they help us to explain various processes and stages of human nature, and they assist us in predicting what might come next. They also help us develop the kinds of programs necessary to address individual needs in various life stages and situations. Good theories are testable, can enhance understanding, and they can help us make accurate predictions about items of interest. There are a number of developmental theories worthy of consideration (Kaplan, 1998).

Freud's Psychoanalytic Theory

Sigmund Freud postulated that there were three levels of awareness: the **conscious**, which consists of immediate awareness; the **preconscious**, which consists of memories that can readily become conscious; and the **unconscious,** which is beyond normal awareness and which sometimes manifests itself in dreams and inadvertent actions or words. Freud argued that behavior and actions could sometimes be caused by memories that had been stored and forgotten in the unconscious.

Freud (1923) used three constructs to explain the workings of the mind: the **id**, the **ego**, and the **superego**. The id is the construct that controls wishes and desires. It wants what it wants when it wants it and expects instant gratification. The ego interacts with reality and satisfies the needs of the id in a socially acceptable manner. The ego grows in importance as a child develops. The superego is similar to the conscious. It contains principles and compares behavior with the **ego ideal**, which is what individuals think they should be. The ego ideal tries to maintain a balance between the desires of the id, the constrictions of the ego, and the restraints of the superego (Kaplan, 1998).

Anxiety can develop between the desires of the id and the restrictions of the ego that may lead to the ego creating **defense mechanisms** to protect itself. These mechanisms take the form of behavior designed to relieve stress and create emotional peace.

Early experiences, particularly those between parents and children, were considered to be very important by Freud, who thought bad experiences in childhood left irreversible impressions on children. More contemporary experts believe that subsequent positive experiences can ease the trauma of these earlier negative experiences.

Although some of Freud's other theories, such as the **Psychosexual Theory,** are not as respected by modern theorists, his overall impact on psychological theory and the study of human behavior is unmistakable, as is evidenced by the fact that his theories are still used by developmental psychologists in understanding human nature.

Erikson's Psychosocial Theory

A proponent of many of Freud's theories, Erik Erikson has had a strong influence on the study of human development. Erikson developed a theory that holds that individuals pass through eight different stages of life. At each stage, each individual encounters the possibility of a crisis. If the crisis at each stage is handled relatively well, a positive outcome occurs, and the person develops into a healthy individual. Few people advance through Erikson's eight stages with an entirely positive outcome, but a mostly positive outcome is critical for healthy development. Passing through one stage successfully makes the next stage easier, and so on (Weis & Muller, 2015).

> ▶ **Trust versus Mistrust.** When caregivers and others support infants by expressing love and protection, a child emerges from infancy with a sense of trust for people and for their surroundings. Children may become distrustful if caregivers are perceived as angry and stressed. Infants who develop a sense of trust will feel more comfortable in their environment and will be more likely to develop positive attitudes toward life.

▶ **Autonomy versus Doubt.** Young children between the ages of two and three begin exploring their world by practicing new physical skills. When this exploration process is encouraged and supported by caregivers, the toddlers develop a sense of autonomy. If, on the other hand, this exploration process is discouraged, a child might begin to question his or her abilities. It is important that caregivers reward and encourage youngsters to explore and practice new skills.

▶ **Initiative versus Guilt.** When children around the age of four are encouraged to develop plans and to carry out these plans, they begin to develop a sense of initiative and often become self-starters. When plans are not encouraged and actions are often discouraged, a child might feel a sense of guilt and develop a lack of assertiveness.

▶ **Industry versus Inferiority.** Children between the ages of six and eleven who are rewarded for developing skills in such areas as reading, math, and socialization begin to develop a sense of industry and feel that their efforts are worthwhile. Children who feel that their efforts are not appreciated or who are compared unfavorably with other children could very well develop a sense of inferiority.

▶ **Identity versus Role Confusion.** Adolescents involved in healthy experiences who receive encouraging feedback for their actions usually begin to understand who they are and develop a positive self-image. Self-knowledge and a positive self-image provide adolescents with a sense of security and confidence. Adolescents who have less self-knowledge might begin to feel confused regarding their identity and could engage in negative behavior in an effort to be noticed.

▶ **Intimacy versus Isolation.** Young adults who have entered into positive activities and who have developed a strong identity are often ready to share themselves in relationships that require commitment and sacrifice, such as a healthy marriage or close friendships. Individuals who are unable to form close relationships might become isolated and lonely or even despairing.

▶ **Generativity versus Self-Absorption.** Middle-aged adults who invest in the future through children, grandchildren, and/or community involvement generally experience a sense of fulfillment and gratification. Adults who concentrate on the acquisition of material possessions and physical well-being might fail to develop a similar sense of gratification.

▶ **Ego Integrity versus Despair.** Older adults who look back on their lives with a sense of accomplishment and gratification develop a sense that their lives have had meaning. Individuals who realize they have missed too many opportunities and made a number of significant mistakes might experience depression or despair.

According to Erikson, the resolution of each stage depends on the interaction between individuals and their culture, their relationships, and the historical context in which they lived.

The development of identity, for instance, could be very different for someone growing up in Hollywood compared to a child's development in Afghanistan. In a similar sense, the development of industry for someone growing up in the industrial age would vary significantly from someone growing up in the twenty-first century. Erikson's theories have been difficult to test, but they are easy to understand, and they provide an excellent foundation for the general concerns at each stage of life.

Piaget's Theory of Cognitive Development

Jean Piaget spent his entire adult life studying the cognitive growth processes of children and determined that development occurs as people assimilate and organize their lives in relation to their environment. Development, according to Piaget, is defined by four principal factors: **maturation, experience, social transmission,** and the **process of equilibration.** Maturation involves the gradual unfolding of each person's genetic plan for life. Experience includes the interaction of the child with his or her environment. The traditions, customs, and information that parents and others pass on to the child make up social transmission or education. The process of equilibrium occurs when children try to balance what they have learned with what they have experienced. When a disequilibrium occurs between what one has learned versus what has been experienced, one develops abilities to deal with situations differently and in a mature and sophisticated manner.

Piaget created the term **functional invariants** to refer to the processes that individuals use to adjust to situations throughout their lives (Bjorklund, 1995). He defined the two most important processes as **organization** and **adaptation.** Organization refers to structuring knowledge in a way that makes knowledge helpful, and adaptation means being able to use knowledge to adapt to the environment and to survive. Essentially, as the environment changes, individuals must change to meet environmental demands.

For Piaget, maturation was the result of experience, and he believed experiential educational processes were more important than formal education. Piaget's theories have been criticized because they were not tested in a controlled environment, but his theories include the most complete description of cognitive development from infancy to adulthood and have been very influential within developmental psychology.

Behavior Theory

Behaviorists believe that behavior is determined in part by environmental influences and that when the environment changes, behavioral change will follow. For instance, when a neutral experience, such as seeing someone in a white lab coat, is paired with pain, such as getting a shot with a needle, then the neutral experience might become associated with the negative feeling. Repeatedly pairing the neutral experience with the negative experience until a similar response is elicited from both is referred to as **classical conditioning**. The sight of the needle prior to the conditioning process might have caused concern and is therefore referred to as an **unconditional stimulus**, and a response to the needle, such as grimacing, prior to the conditioning is referred to as an **unconditional response**. A **conditional stimulus**, then, is the pairing of the neutral stimulus with the negative stimulus, and the **conditional response** would be the individual's concern about the person in the white lab coat.

This kind of conditional process might help us to understand some emotional responses. For instance, if a newly married stepfather begins to berate and criticize his new stepson, the stepson might begin to associate stress and anger with the sight of the stepfather, whom he might have previously trusted and been happy to be around. **Operant conditioning**, in which a behavior is either reinforced or punished following its occurrence, is also important in understanding human development. With operant conditioning, if a behavior is reinforced with a positive response, it will continue and possibly increase in occurrence; if the behavior is followed by a negative response, it will decrease in occurrence.

The behavioral view has been criticized by some theorists who believe it is too mechanical and fails to include conscious thought and subjective experiences in the overall scheme of things, but it can be helpful in understanding some behavior and successful in modifying behavior in a number of situations.

Social Cognitive Theory

Social theorist Albert Bandura postulated that individuals learn by watching and imitating others and learn from examining the consequences of what they are observing. For example, a person who watches someone else pick up a hot pan and then flinch in pain does not need to replicate the event to understand that the hot pan is dangerous. Bandura organized his theory into a four-step process. First, an individual must concentrate on the model. The model must be retained in memory. Next, the stored information must be used in an attempt to replicate the action in the model. For example, a person watching a baseball player at bat might try to duplicate a certain swing. Finally, motivation in the form of reinforcement must occur in order for the person to learn the behavior and use the behavior again and again in the future.

According to social theorists, behavior is divided into two processes: learning and performing. Learning can occur through observation and other activities, but performance depends partly on what Bandura calls **self-efficacy**, or the belief one has about his or her ability to do something in a particular situation (Schunk, 1996). When individuals believe a task is within their capabilities, they will attempt to do it; when they doubt their abilities with various tasks, they are more likely to avoid those activities. The Social Cognitive Theory is helpful in understanding behaviors that are learned and imitated from others.

Ecological Theory

Urie Bronfenbrenner (1979) formulated the Ecological Theory in order to expand the viewpoint that human development is contextual in nature, involving families, communities, culture, and even historical periods. According to Bronfenbrenner, individuals are influenced by four different environmental systems: the **micro-system**, the **meso-system**, the **exo-system**, and the **macro-system**. The microsystem includes an individual's immediate experiences, such as a child's experiences at home with the family. As the child develops, additional settings emerge and the mesosystem involves the child in two or more settings such as a day care center or school. This entry of a child into a new setting invariably has an effect on other major settings. For instance, a child's attendance at day care will have some effect on family activities at home.

The exo-system describes settings the child is not actively involved in, but that have an effect on the child and/or the family, such as the actions of the local school superintendent or a sibling's involvement with the local theater group. Although the child is not directly involved with these activities, the activities may have a direct effect on the child. For example, the sibling's involvement in theater may affect the opportunities the child has to play and interact with his or her sibling. It might also affect the amount of time the parents have to spend with the child, since they might have to spend time transporting the sibling to and from theater practice and participating in related activities.

Finally, the macro-system includes the ideology or belief system inherent in the social institutions as well as the ethnic, cultural, religious, political, and economic processes of the country in which the child resides. These differing ideologies can have a profound influence on the development of a child. For instance, the increased percentage of single parent families, the changes in the welfare system, and the increased numbers of disappearing dads, separately and/or together, could have a significant effect on a child's life.

An advantage of this theory is that it provides us with the idea that individuals are always moving between one system and another, and back again. This information allows us the opportunity to assist in the transactions from system to system. The interaction an individual has with each of these systems has a profound effect on his or her life.

DEVELOPMENTAL COMPETENCIES

Edginton and Edginton (1994) subscribe to five basic areas of importance for the development of youth (as adapted from Pittman, 1991), and these include:

► **Health/physical competence.** Youth need to have good health and to maintain knowledge, attitudes, and behaviors to ensure good health for the future. This includes exercising, maintaining a healthy diet, and being aware of nutritional requirements.

▶ **Personal/social competence.** It is important that youth develop several good *intrapersonal skills*. They need the ability to understand and deal with personal emotions and to maintain-self discipline; they need to develop effective *interpersonal skills*, including the ability to work with others, to develop friendships, and to understand and empathize with others; they need *coping skills* and the ability to adapt and assume responsibility; and they need *judgment skills*, for making good decisions and solving problems.

▶ **Cognitive/creative competence.** Youth need to have a broad base of knowledge and the ability to appreciate and participate in creative expression, good oral and written *language skills*, problem solving and *analytical skills,* and an interest in learning and achieving.

▶ **Vocational competence.** It is important that youth develop an understanding and awareness of vocational and avocational opportunities. It is also important for youth to grasp the function and value of work and leisure time and for them to learn how to prepare for both.

▶ **Citizenship competencies (ethics and preparation).** Youth need to understand their nation's history and values and develop a sense of personal responsibility for community and national enhancement.

As young people move toward these competencies they develop a sense of self-confidence and self-efficacy and feel good about being themselves. Although Pittman focused on youth and competencies, it is easy to see that individuals develop competencies throughout their lives. Leaders of nonprofit organizations need to understand and incorporate these developmental competencies and other developmental theories into goal setting, program planning, and other relevant aspects of organizational operations when appropriate (Weis & Muller, 2015).

Understanding situations that people might face throughout their lives is equally important and will be discussed in the section on issues and trends.

HUMAN DEVELOPMENT MOVEMENT

Within the nonprofit world, a movement to switch toward an alternative approach for helping people began during the 1970s and picked up momentum in the 1990s. The human development concept was initially developed by Mahbub ul Haq, an economist. While at the World Bank in the 1970s, and later as minister of finance in Pakistan, Dr. Haq worked to convince others that existing measures of human progress used by organizations such as the United Nations and the World Health Organization did not account for the true purpose of development, which is to improve people's lives. More specifically, he believed that the Gross Domestic Product, which was used to measure prosperity in countries, failed to adequately measure the well-being of the people living within those countries. As his view became more widely accepted, the Human Development movement began to gain momentum. There was a shift toward a process of expanding people's choices, enhancing their capabilities, and providing them more freedoms. The goal was to increase the quality of life for more people, to increase the standard of living among people, and to increase the level of participation of people in the decision-making processes regarding those issues that would impact their day-to-day lives.

The **Inequality Human Development Index** (HDI) was adopted as a way to measure prosperity instead of using the GDP. The HDI aggregates health, education, and income. It does not take into account gender, equity, or sustainability. The HDI is currently used as a way of measuring progress in the human development movement by the United Nations. Rather than focus on economic growth, the shift called for looking more at social justice as a way of understanding and measuring progress across the globe.

Amartya Sen, who won the Nobel Memorial Prize for Economic Science in 1998 for his Social Choice Theory, joined the Human Development movement in the 1990s, working with Dr Haq. As an economist, Sen posits that "a strict equation cannot be drawn between primary social goods and well-being because the former cannot always be converted into the latter" (Sen, 1992, p. 232). He believes that welfare economics portrays poverty narrowly, limiting this definition to a lack of income. This narrow concept of poverty does not shed very much light on the reasons why people are often deprived of their well-being. This restricted view of poverty also fails to tell the extent or the kind of deprivation that people suffer. Sen states that the real extent of deprivation might be underestimated if income is the only place that we focus our attention (Sen, 1992, p. 113).

In several countries, the Human Development Index has become an official government statistic; its annual publication initiates serious political debate and renews efforts at every level to improve lives (Measure of America, 2016).

The group, Measure of America, has developed a modified HDI called the American HD Index. This modified index measures the same basic dimensions as the standard index, but it uses alternative indicators to best reveal the U.S. context and to make the best use of available data. The American Human Development Index demonstrates the well-being for all Americans in a single measure, disaggregated by state and congressional district, as well as by race, gender, and ethnicity. The data used to determine the index are provided by official U.S. government sources such as the U.S. Census Bureau and the Centers for Disease Control and Prevention (Measure of America, 2016).

Advancing human development requires, above all else, expanding the opportunities people have to live in healthy environments, maintain a healthy lifestyle, receive high quality medical care, and to attain the high standards of physical and mental health. Life expectancy is the data used to measure this variable within the A-HDI. The second variable is access to knowledge. This is a significant determinant of long-term well-being and is vital in the pursuit of self-determination, individual freedom, and self-sufficiency. Education is essential for people to be informed and capable of deciding what to do and who to become. The third, and final, variable in the A-HDI index is income. Everyone understands the importance of money in our society. Without money, a person cannot eat or would not have a place to live. Money to maintain food, shelter, security, and to pay for education and healthcare is a necessity for a person's well-being. These three variables are used together to calculate the American HDI (Measure of America, 2016).

The Human Development movement was picking up steam as other related changes were occurring in the nonprofit environment. As the economy slowed and turned toward a worldwide recession, available funds for nonprofit efforts became harder to acquire. Communities began to demand greater accountability for funds directed to any organization. This era of accountability coupled with an increasing awareness of drastic inequalities in the distribution of goods and services across the globe, forced nonprofits to think about the process of doing business a little bit differently.

Today, the focus is on impact. We have been made aware that it is not about what a nonprofit organization does, or how many people are provided their services, or how long they have been providing these services, or even how far their service area reaches. It is about the positive change that is achieved and whether or not it is sustainable. Communities now expect a lasting impact. The bar has indeed been raised.

How have nonprofits attempted to meet this challenge? Many have banded together to form coalitions with other nonprofits to increase the likelihood of making an impact on their communities. Nonprofit organizations achieve impact through dedication and rigorous attention to high standards.

> *"Creating lasting change requires a collective response. Being committed to partnering with purpose means future efforts will not only be aligned, but they'll be much more strategic and better able to take on the complexities of our community's challenges."*
>
> **Brian Gallagher**
> President and CEO, United Way Worldwide

ISSUES AND TRENDS

The world is changing rapidly, due in large part to technology and the rapid movement of information. The changes influencing the nonprofit world can be seen in the news, on social media, or wherever humans are discussing the quality of life anywhere in our society. Whether we are at school, work, attending a party, a religious service, a political function, sporting event, or other social function, we hear about quality of life because people enjoy talking about the human condition.

In the section above, the Human Development movement was described. This movement, along with increasing pressures for fiscal accountability and attempts at social justice have moved nonprofit organizations more toward a collective mindset. As nonprofit organizations form coalitions or join an existing coalition, the trend is to strive for a larger impact. We will provide an example of how a typical coalition positions the collective group of nonprofit organizations to better contribute to making that impact, then we will review the statistics on the various social parameters to see whether this movement has the human condition trending in a positive direction.

The Alliance for Strong Families and Communities is one example of a coalition or group of nonprofit organizations working together to make an impact. This organization has a vision of a healthy society and strong communities for all children, adults, and families. The leaders of the organization conducted a literature review and identified a series of commitments that each member organization will dedicate itself toward fulfilling. These commitments include leading with vision; governing for the future; executing on mission; partnering with purpose; investing in capacity; measuring that matters; co-creating with community; innovating with enterprise; engaging all voices; advancing equity. This is an excellent example because their list of commitments, derived from a review of the literature, captures each of the trends within the nonprofit sector (Alliance for Strong Families and Communities, 2015).

Leading with vision—The importance of a nonprofit organization having a realistic vision statement cannot be overstated in the current environment of accountability. Gone are the days where lofty proclamations and unmeasurable goals filled pretty brochures. In today's nonprofit environment, vision statements must align with goals, which need to be measured and achieved for funding to continue. The trend is for vision to be much more focused. For organizations, this requires a review of all business and service practices. Leaders need to update or eliminate practices to ensure that they remain current. This also involves identifying new opportunities and responding to change with creative solutions.

Partnering with purpose—Rather than competing with similar nonprofit organizations and duplicating services, partnering provides opportunities to build consensus around the issues, solutions, and potential success metrics. The partner organizations share interest and responsibility in creating solutions; and they are all accountable for the impact achieved. They do this by clearly defining each organization's role in delivering products and services as well as in collecting and sharing data. It is essential that these organizations have continuous communication and function, to some extent, as one large organization, the coalition.

Investing in Capacity—Nonprofit organizations that invest in capacity develop and use their budgets as a means of guiding organizational policy and strategy. This is different from the traditional method, where budgets restricted activities. Funds are allocated to capitalize on potential opportunities. The trend is to use unrestricted funds to upgrade systems and functions that support resource generation and performance, such as technology, professional development activities, modernizing physical spaces, improving marketing strategies, and resource development.

Measuring that Matters—Nonprofit organizations create a culture of performance assessment in all levels of the organizations. Each staff member is able to see how their efforts contribute to the execution of the mission because data are collected, monitored, and reported to stakeholders. For this to be meaningful, it is essential that nonprofits align measurements with strategies used. They work with the communities that they serve to identify and track the outcomes that will result in the impact that they seek.

Co-creating with Community—Nonprofit organizations know that the communities which they serve are constantly changing. Therefore, they continuously seek opportunities for outreach and engagement, gather data, and synthesize information. Nonprofits use these data to inform decision-making, enhance current strategies, and improve their operations. By working together, nonprofits are better able to mobilize around emerging challenges. By analyzing their collective data they are better able to understand their communities' histories, cultures, strengths, and issues and are able to use that information to inform their efforts.

Innovating with Enterprise—Nonprofit leaders today engage in generative thinking and discussions. They attempt to identify new, creative solutions to existing challenges by looking at emerging opportunities as well as potential risks. The trend is to recruit and hire as diverse a staff as possible. The idea is to gather together a group of individuals with different backgrounds who will challenge one another and traditional thinking in an effort to generate new ideas and connections and actively discourage doing things the same old way, especially if those ways do not result in the impact that is desired.

Engaging all Voices—Nonprofits leaders encourage those with viewpoints that are unrepresented or underrepresented in most community settings to speak and be heard; as well as for others to listen. These leaders create a wide variety of channels through which all people, including staff, can provide feedback to the decision-makers that eventually shapes the pathways taken by the organization and community. The trend for shared governance continues and has expanded from the organizational level into the community, where the voices of those being served are as important as those providing the services.

Advancing Equity—The trend is away from exerting efforts to advance equity separately from programs or services. Organizations have found that is much more impactful to embed their social justice orientation within all of their efforts. Therefore, nonprofits now seek to achieve systems change to avoid having advantage and disadvantage distributed on the basis of any demographic characteristic. In so doing, real equity might be achieved, which is an example of the impact that programs are seeking.

As you can see from the above example from the Alliance for Strong Families and Communities (2015), the business of running a nonprofit has change dramatically over the past decade. The shift in focus is toward creating a greater, more lasting impact upon communities, by working together more collectively, and being held accountable for our efforts. Now, let us review the trends within the various human service issues to see whether the nonprofit industry has made progress in improving quality of life as measured by these individual data points.

Households, Families, Children, and Youth

Households can be distinguished from **families** in that a household is considered to be a residential and economic unit, whereas families imply a construct of meanings and relationships (Osmond & Thorne, 1993; Rapp, 1982). The U.S. Census Bureau defines households as taking one of three basic forms: **family**, **non-family**, and **single-person** household. Family households are considered to be two or more persons living together who are related through marriage, birth, or adoption. The most common type of family household is a married couple with or without children. Non-family households consist of two or more unrelated individuals who are residing in the same living area. Single-person households are made up of those individuals who live alone in a residential unit (Weis & Muller, 2015).

U.S. households continue to change in important areas. For instance, the number of households is still growing, but at a much slower rate, and there were approximately 124.6 million households in the year 2015. Another important change is the average size of a household which has gotten smaller and smaller over the last 50 years and in 2015 represented an approximate average of 2.54 individuals per household. Two trends that might work to counteract this are the growing number of adult children who are living with their parents, and the growing number of elderly mothers and fathers who reside with their children. There are more single-parent families, childless married couples, and people living alone than ever before, and no household arrangement can be classified as typical. A noteworthy trend is the percentage of households headed by married couples, which has declined significantly over the decades to under 46% in 2016, according to a PEW research study (2016).

Not only has marriage decreased and the wide variety of living arrangements increased since the early 1960s, but so too has the fluidity of the family as a unit. Regardless of how one defines their family, the stability of that unit is less than it was in years past. Non-marital cohabitation and divorce, remarriage, and non-marital recoupling all create family structures that tend to be fluid. In the past, a child born to a married couple was very likely to grow up in a home with those two parents. This is much less likely to happen today. Children and their living arrangements change with each alteration in their parents' relationships. The Pew Research Center's, *Parenting in America* reported on a study that revealed that over a three-year period, 31% of children under the age of 6 years had experienced a major change in their family structure due to parental divorce, separation, marriage, cohabitation, or death. It seems that change is now the norm (Pew Research Center, 2015).

As with households, families have also changed in some important ways. For instance, there is a greater variety of family circumstances than ever before. **Traditional families**, in which there is a working father, children under the age of 18, and a mother who is not in the work force, have diminished in number. Social forces, such as high divorce rates, an increased number of women in the work force, and declining fertility rates, have added to the growing variety of family situations.

Some of these social forces have also added to the numbers of **single-parent families**, at least 90% of which exist with a woman as the head of the household. In spite of the fact that teenage pregnancies have declined in recent years, teen parents lead a significant percentage of single-parent families. Although a number of children from single-parent families become successful adults, children from single-parent families have comparatively poorer academic achievement and are more likely to drop out of school. They are more likely to be poor, to marry early, and are more likely to divorce. They are also more likely to become involved in criminal activity, including the use of illegal drugs. Since there is a strong correlation between single parenting and living in poverty, it is difficult to separate the effects of these two factors. In many single-parent families, the father is absent, and there is minimal interaction or financial support, if any. In families with **absentee dads**, the children are at much greater risk of dropping out of school, getting in trouble in school, and having poor grades.

When a parent cannot or will not take responsibility for a child, a **skip-generation** family often develops in which a grandparent becomes the primary caregiver. This can become emotionally and financially difficult for grandparents, who might have to raise two generations of children but be unable to receive public assistance because they often do not have legal custody of their grandchildren. A large number of skip-generation families have the mother living there as well, but not as the head of the household. Family court judges and social workers often link drug and alcohol abuse to the skip-generation phenomenon.

Children staying at home longer and aging parents living longer due to advanced health technologies indicate there will be more **multi-generational** families in which the parent or parents are wedged between at least one child at home and their own frail and elderly parents. This is also sometimes referred to as the **sandwich generation** and has become more intense since families are smaller and the burden of caregiving falls on fewer siblings. Fortunately, more and more corporations are providing elder care assistance to their employees (Hewitt Associates, 2004).

Approximately half of all marriages end in **divorce** and that percentage has plateaued and even declined in recent years. The median duration of marriage before a divorce is about seven years, and over half of all divorces involve children who will experience a permanent disruption. Many divorces involve tremendous emotional, psychological, and financial upheaval for everyone involved. A large number of divorced fathers will let this upheaval become a reason for them to become completely absent from the lives of their children. Fortunately, divorce is expected to continue to decline since it is viewed with less favor as its disruptive and damaging impacts, especially on children, are increasingly recognized. There is also an increased disenchantment with the single lifestyle and a continuing fear of sexually transmitted diseases. One fifth of all married couples with children make up **step-families**, in which at least one child under the age of 18 is involved. Step-families often have their own special dynamics and provide unique challenges for parenting and developing relationships. Most step-children live with their biological mothers and step-fathers.

Amongst all the negative news about families, there might be some reason for optimism. According to the Pew Research Center (2015), "While parents today are far less likely to be married than they were in the past, they are more likely to be older and to have more education." More educated mothers is due, in part, to older mothers. The age when women are first giving birth has increased across all major race and ethnic groups. Despite the increase across all groups, substantial variation exists across these groups. The average age for giving birth the first time among Whites is now at 27 years old. The average age at first birth among Blacks and Hispanics is lower, at 24 years. The prevalence of teen pregnancies brings down the average among Black women. Only 5% of births among Whites occurs in women under the age of 20, this number is 11% for Black and 10% for Hispanic women. White women are waiting longer to get pregnant with 45% of births for White women occurring after the age of 30, while only 31% of Black and 36% of Hispanic women wait until the age of 30 to give birth for the first time.

These delayed birth statistics align with the fact that mothers today are far better educated than they were in the past. While in 1960 just 18% of mothers with infants at home had any college experience, today that share stands at 67%. This trend is driven in large part by dramatic increases in educational attainment for all women. While about half (49%) of women ages 15 to 44 in 1960 lacked a high school diploma, today the largest share of women (61%) has at least some college experience, and just 19% lack a high school diploma.

Another demographic with significant implications is the growing number of senior citizens over the age of 85, which has increased at a rate three times that of the general population. These citizens seek to live independently, but the frailty that comes with old age catches up with them, and **elder care**, in which seniors require assistance to remain somewhat independent, is a growing consideration. Many of these citizens are cared for at home, but the main caregiver often works a full-time job and caregiving can be difficult for the caregiver as well as for the recipient. Although nursing home care is a consideration, only a small percentage of seniors ever live in a nursing home. Adult home-care programs, foster-care, daycare programs, Meals on Wheels, and telephone reassurance are just some of the programs that provide seniors with the support necessary to remain in their homes.

Most experts agree that the care-giving and educational preparation for children from birth to age 18 in the United States is too often inadequate. Youth face other challenges as well, such as alienation, loneliness, social depravity, and a lack of connectedness. Low-income families, in particular, face hardships that include inadequate health care, crime and drugs, lack of successful role models, financial hardships, and a sense of hopelessness. An incredible

20% of all children in the United States live in **poverty**, which is often due to parental job loss or underemployment and to the increase of children living in single-parent families. These families, usually with a female at the head, have a poverty rate of approximately five times the poverty rate of married-couple families.

In order to escape poverty and low income, most mothers work out of economic necessity, and the lack of affordable and effective **day care** for children under the age of six has become a serious social problem. Many studies, including a study involving Head Start enrollees and a control group, concluded that the children involved with Head Start were more likely to become high school graduates, enroll in college, or be employed. And they were less likely to become involved in crime or be on welfare by the age of 19 (Eitzen, Stanley, Zinn, & Eitzen, 2009).

Each year, tens of thousands of infants die before they reach the age of one. The infant mortality rate for the United States is one of the highest among the industrialized nations, and the main reason for this is **low birth weight**, often a result of inadequate prenatal care. A significant portion of these children will end up with permanent disabilities. Many other children will have chronic and disabling conditions as a result of being born **HIV positive** or as a result of **cocaine exposure.** Spiraling health care costs make it difficult for many families to receive proper care, let alone incorporate preventive measures. Another health concern is the immunization process for preventable diseases. Although the vast majority of children are immunized against measles, mumps, and rubella, there are still a significant number of children who are not, particularly in urban areas. For instance, there are still tens of thousands of measles cases reported each year, which in severe cases can result in death. In spite of numerous diseases and other conditions, the number one cause of death among children is **accidents**, which can also result in permanent disabilities.

Another serious health concern for children is the lack of **proper nutrition**, which is closely associated with poverty. This can lead to several health issues such as iron-deficiency anemia. Proper nutrition for low-income pregnant women, new mothers, and infants is critical. This is often provided by a program for Women, Infants, and Children known as **WIC**, which was created to do just that. But WIC is seriously under-funded and cannot meet the needs of all of those who meet the criteria for assistance. Incredible as it may seem, **hunger** is another serious problem for children: between five and six million children will go hungry nearly every day, and that number increased throughout the 2000s. The rate of hunger is closely related to childhood poverty.

Another area of risk for children is the area of **education**, in which American students often lag behind students in developed and developing countries, particularly in math and science. A significant percentage of students fail to graduate from high school, or they graduate without the knowledge and skills necessary for acquiring and keeping a job. There is a strong correlation between dropping out of school and crime and poverty. Factors associated with **dropouts** include being poor, belonging to an ethnic or racial minority, having limited English proficiency, and being a child from a single-parent family. Though often interrelated, any one of these factors can create challenges in school.

Each year, about one million teen girls become **pregnant**, and a significant number of these will conceive again in one to two years. These young mothers are overwhelmed with responsibilities and are unlikely to finish high school and are more likely to face a life of economic hardship and dependency. Statistically, the children of teen mothers are less likely to finish high school and are more likely to achieve lower levels of education, become involved with crime and drugs, and to become teen parents as well.

Nearly one million children are considered **discarded**, which means they live in foster homes, detention centers, hospitals, and mental health centers. These living arrangements are necessary for a number of reasons, including family breakup, homelessness, child abuse, and alcohol or drug abuse. Teenagers are going through a rapidly changing period of life and require constant support. **Suicide** is the second leading cause of death among adolescents. Additionally, there are over a million **runaways** living on the streets or in less than desirable shelters, and tens of thousands of youth are classified as **lost**, **injured**, or **missing**. In a country that prides itself on its diversity, about half of all teenagers have witnessed racist acts, and a significant portion of teens report having been the victims of bias.

Although most families are healthy, functional units, researchers sometimes consider families to be the most violent social group, next to the police and the military. **Child abuse** is too often the result of this family violence. Child abuse is an act carried out with the intent of injury or acts of omission that place children in danger. The incidents of child reported abuse increased in the 1980s, 1990s, and 2000s. **Neglect** is another type of abuse directed toward children. Neglect includes inadequate feeding of children, poor sanitary conditions, or leaving children in a potentially dangerous setting.

Health and Education

Americans are living longer than anytime in history with **life expectancies** ranging from the early 60s to high 70s, depending on race and gender. On the average, men die younger than women do, and African Americans die younger than Caucasians, primarily due to cancer, heart attack, and strokes. **Heart disease** still causes more deaths than any other disease, with **cancer** coming in second as a cause of death. One of the reasons that life expectancy rates are so high is that **infant mortality** rates have been reduced so significantly from the beginning of the century. Despite the overall reductions in infant mortality, poor and rural communities maintain higher infant mortality than urban settings, and life expectancy is lower for racial and ethnic minorities. This is often attributed to living in poor communities with inadequate medical care.

Acquired Immune Deficiency Syndrome (AIDS) is caused by the **HIV** virus which damages the body's immune system and leaves the body more susceptible to infections and cancer. AIDS is spread through sexual contact, needles or syringes shared by drug abusers, infected blood or blood products; it is also passed from pregnant women to their offspring. People who are at high risk for contracting AIDS include those who practice unprotected sex with infected partners and drug abusers who share needles. AIDS has also spread among groups not previously thought of as high risk, such as crack smokers, women, and teenagers. AIDS has also increased in rural communities, where residents are often ill-equipped to handle the disease medically or socially. African Americans and Hispanics are disproportionately affected by AIDS, and the estimates of those infected ranges from the hundreds of thousands to several million. **Sexually Transmitted Diseases (STDs)** such as syphilis, gonorrhea, and pelvic inflammatory disease (PID) remain serious health threats and can cause a great deal of suffering and even death.

Another disease, **tuberculosis**, was once the leading cause of death in the United States, but it has been in decline for decades. Unfortunately, it is making a comeback in major cities, and drug addicts, the homeless, and people with AIDs are especially susceptible to it. Airborne bacteria spread tuberculosis, which has led some cities to forcibly hospitalize patients and test schoolchildren. In the future, viral conditions that are not curable with conventional therapies are predicted to be on the rise as are bacterial infections that have become resistant to commonly used antibiotics.

It has been suggested that as many as one in four American workers suffer from **stress-related** illnesses or **anxiety disorders**, and **depression** is thought to affect a similar number of individuals. Increasing competition, advanced technology, work-family issues, and job uncertainties are just a few of the variables contributing to these conditions. Electronic monitors that count the number of keystrokes made by some computer operators and electronic surveillance of telephone conversations are also causing increasing stress in the workplace. Medical experts generally agree that workers who are under electronic surveillance suffer higher levels of stress-related medical problems such as fatigue, ulcers, depression, and even heart disease.

Millions of Americans are addicted to **drugs** and millions more suffer from **alcoholism** or **alcohol dependence**. An estimated 5–10% of the population have experimented with marijuana, the most popular illegal drug (Caplow, Hicks, & Wattenberg, 2001; Drug Enforcement Administration, 2007). Millions of Americans also use or experiment with cocaine, heroine, hallucinogens, and inhalants. Illegal drug use seems to have peaked in the 70s and 80s and has leveled off since. Factors contributing to drug abuse and addiction include boredom, social and work pressures, and medical needs. In moderation, alcohol is considered to be relatively safe, but when abused it is the leading cause of accidents and accounts for about half of all traffic-related deaths. Criminals, prior to committing a criminal act, often use alcohol or drugs. There is a strong correlation between abusing alcohol and the overall suicide rate, and it is a big factor in drowning. Consumed in large quantities over long periods of time, alcohol almost always results in serious health consequences.

Although **tobacco** smoking has been on the decline for years, millions of Americans still use tobacco and there has been a disturbing, steady usage by women, young people, teens, pre-teens, and minorities. Additionally, there has been a movement on the part of tobacco companies to market tobacco overseas, which increases health and financial problems in other countries that result in global consequences for all of us. **Second-hand smoke** also causes significant health problems and deaths from cancer and heart disease for thousands of individuals each year. Premature deaths as a result of smoking are possibly the most preventable kind in the United States, and the cessation of tobacco use results in almost immediate health benefits for individuals of all ages.

Alternative health care methods, such as holistic medicine and self-help groups, have grown in popularity in the United States. Some of these techniques include biofeedback, acupuncture, chiropractic medicine, meditation, yoga, massage, hypnosis, and homeopathic medicine. Many experts define health in terms of mind and body balance or harmony.

Health care is one of the most complicated, highly political and emotionally charged issues our nation is facing. Health care costs represent a significant percentage of the gross national product (GNP) and are rising steadily. While most people look to job-related insurance to cover the majority of their health costs, insurance costs reflect the increased rise in health care costs, and a significant portion of the population simply do not have insurance coverage. While health care costs are spiraling upward, the availability of services (**health care delivery**) has declined, particularly in rural and poor sections of the country; although the Health Care Reform bill of 2010 was intended to change both of these aspects of health care along with a number of others. The need for long-term care is increasing as Americans become older on the average. **Medicare** is the governmental health care program that assists senior citizens with these costs and others and **Medicaid** was implemented to address the health care needs of the poor. The level of support from Medicare and Medicaid varies depending on circumstances and current policy. Free clinics for the working poor, volunteer nursing visitations, and programs to help individuals save on medical costs are just a few of the ways nonprofit organizations are addressing needs that are not now or in the foreseeable future addressed through health insurance, Medicare, or Medicaid.

Education will remain one of the highest priorities on the national agenda, and the correlation between excellence in education and quality of life has been proven again and again. For decades, **educational reforms** have been taking place in school systems around the nation. The most recent wave of reforms includes the concept of **school-based management**, in which there is a transfer of decision-making power from a centralized authority to instructors, parents, and administrators of the schools. These decisions range from developing the curriculum to deciding how a school will spend its money. With reform in mind, many school systems are also incorporating **service learning** into the curriculum. Service learning combines community service with specific learning objectives, reflection, and helping others. This has proven to be an invaluable pedagogy for teaching values and character and for bridging the gap between theory and practice. Other school districts have adopted an option of a **choice** for parents as to which school their children will attend. This concept is designed to develop competition among schools and to stimulate curricula and facilities improvement. Still other educational systems have adopted **year-round school** programs in an effort to expand educational opportunities and provide additional support systems for students and parents the entire year. Having met with some opposition initially, this program continues to gain favor because of its flexibility and continuity of academics and extra-curricular activities.

A number of studies indicate that high quality early-childhood education programs make a significant difference for at-risk youth, and more and more experts are stressing the importance of early-childhood education. **Preschool** has been integrated into many educational systems, and the majority of all three- and four-year-olds take part in some form of early childhood education. The federal preschool program, **Head Start,** has helped millions of children since its creation in 1965 and is regarded as one of the government's most successful programs. Enrollment in both elementary and secondary schools has steadily increased, and more opportunities will develop for after-school activities. **Home schooling** continues to be on the rise as some parents contend that public schools have poor academic standards, poor discipline, and crowded conditions. Post secondary enrollment has been up and down so far in this decade, particularly among 18–24-year-olds, and the average age of college students continues to rise.

The American way of life is still highly valued by many worldwide. Consequently, immigration has led to a **mosaic classroom** in which a significant number of students have limited English proficiency. This generally makes instruction much more challenging, and the combination of language and cultural differences sometimes leads to clashes in the school system. Even when **bilingual-education** programs are introduced, it takes about seven years for a non-native student to reach national norms on standardized tests. **English-as-a-Second-Language (ESL)** has also been expanded, and many non-English speaking students have been mainstreamed into regular classrooms with ESL-trained instructors. A major concern remains regarding the educational underachievement among minority racial and ethnic groups. The situation is critical, since approximately one in three elementary and secondary school children are minorities. Clearly, there are numerous opportunities for nonprofit organizations to step in and assist in developing foundations for academic achievement.

About one in four students **drop out** each year, and that number is often higher in urban centers and a number of studies identify a correlation with difficulties in school and family problems (Walsh, 2006). The consequences of high dropout rates are costly for individuals and for society. Jobs require higher skill levels than ever before, unemployment rates are twice as high for high school dropouts as for graduates, and dropouts are more likely to become involved in crime and taking or selling drugs. Dropouts are also more likely to come from a single-parent family, live in a household that is considered at the poverty level, and be at home alone more than three hours a day. Having limited skills in English and/or coming from a home where the parents are dropouts adds to the potential of dropping out. The nation's number of **illiterates** is in the millions and illiteracy is increasing at an alarming rate. Millions of Americans are classified as **functionally illiterate**, which means they are able to read at a fourth grade level; there are even more people referred to as **marginally illiterate**, who read at the eighth grade level. This is frustrating and demeaning for individuals; it costs them billions of dollars in unrealized earnings and costs the country billions of dollars in welfare and unemployment compensation each year. There are also a disproportionate number of African American and Hispanic children living in poverty who also have trouble reading.

The ratio of computers to students in the classroom has moved ahead at a rapid pace and **technology** has made **distance learning** and **online learning** established pedagogical methods. **Global classrooms** in which students search the Internet for information and interact with individuals online could help develop technical expertise, cultural understanding, and knowledge.

Population and Aging

The American population has nearly quadrupled in the past century, and the number of people in the country has exceeded 270 million (Weis & Muller, 2015). The combination of falling death rates due to **medical advances,** massive **immigration**, and **increased birth rates** has led to significant population growth, although population has declined somewhat in percentage of growth over the last several decades. The 1990 Immigration Act led to significant increases in immigration, and medical advances have made it easier for women to become pregnant and for individuals to have longer, healthier life spans on average. Approximately 600,000 individuals immigrate to the United States each year and an estimated 200,000 to 1,000,000 people enter the country illegally on an annual basis (Caplow et al., 2001). As a matter of fact, it has been reported that 485,000 undocumented Mexican immigrants crossed into the U.S. in 2004 (Bailey, 2006). This influx of immigrants creates a number of cultural, educational, vocational, and financial challenges as new citizens prepare for a life sometimes far different from that in their native land.

Fertility rates have increased due to a number of factors, including the increased number of women bearing children in their middle to late thirties, the increased number of female immigrants who have higher fertility rates than native-born Americans, and an increased number of unplanned and too often unwanted births. Minority birth rates exceed that of the population in general.

About a third of the current population was born between the years 1946 and 1964. These individuals are usually referred to as **baby boomers**, since many were conceived following the end of World War II, when people were putting their lives and families back together. Over the past century, the proportion of children and adolescents in the population has decreased as the proportion of older Americans has increased. As people live longer on the average and the proportion of births decreases, the average age of Americans will increase. The percentage of people 75 years old and older has increased and the proportion of **centenarians** increased more than any other age group in the last two decades of the past century. This trend will create tremendous challenges and opportunities for the social security system, health care, families, and certainly for nonprofit organizations.

Social Security is a major source of income for most seniors, and in many cases it is the only source of senior citizens' income. But Social Security is coming under increased pressure by the growing number of applicants, and people in certain occupations, such as agriculture, who are often exempt from the Social Security program. Additionally, women who have worked as homemakers receive no credit for their work, and a woman who is widowed might not receive benefits until she is 60, unless she has a child under 16 or a disabled child, or unless she herself is disabled.

Although the majority of older people are in good health, the elderly are more affected by poor health than any other group. Both physical and mental conditions affect older people, and **Alzheimer's disease** is the leading cause of dementia in old age afflicting millions of senior citizens. Older people usually have more contact with physicians than any other age group. Their prescription drug cost represents the largest out-of-pocket health-care expense for the majority of the elderly and their medical expenses are three times greater than those of middle-aged adults, yet their incomes are significantly lower (Eitzen et al., 2009). When senior citizens need to be institutionalized, an affluent minority receives **therapeutic care**, an approach that focuses on meeting the needs of patients and providing for their treatment. On the other hand, homes with welfare recipients tend to provide **custodial care**, which too often focuses on meeting the needs of the institution, rather than those of the patients.

The majority of the elderly are not institutionalized, and since senior citizens are living longer, family members will spend longer periods of **elder-caregiving.** Because there are fewer siblings in families than in decades past, caretaker responsibilities will fall to a very few individuals, usually daughters or daughters-in-law. Although most of the elderly benefit from family caretakers, there can also be an increased likelihood of **elder abuse.** Abuse can take a number of different forms. Physical abuse involves individuals being slapped, hit, or restrained. Psychological abuse includes verbal assaults or threats. Drug abuse may occur when seniors are encouraged to over-medicate. Material abuse includes theft or misuse of money. A violation of rights occurs when an elderly person is forced into a nursing home against his or her will. Abuse may occur more often when the caretaker is overwhelmed physically, emotionally, or financially.

Poverty, Housing, and Homelessness

A family of four is considered to be living in **poverty** if their pre-tax income is approximately $20,650 per year (U.S. Department of Health and Human Services, 2007), which includes about 15% of all families. A study by the U.S. Bureau of the Census found that families living in poverty were twice as likely to divorce as families not in poverty; thus poverty can be a significant factor in the break-up of some families (Eitzen et al., 2009). The picture is even bleaker for single-parent families, who often have to get by on the income from one parent when child support is not available for whatever reason.

The number of children living in poverty has more than doubled in the past several decades with approximately fourteen million children living at the poverty level. Child poverty has been reduced by other industrialized nations, but the United States has failed significantly in this regard. Poverty can affect health, physical, and intellectual development and a number of social conditions, and there is a growing number of children living in **extreme poverty**, in which the family lives at half or less of the official poverty level. Extreme poverty can put a child at serious risk of malnutrition or some other threat. It is estimated that as many as one in five children live in poverty.

Individuals between the age of 19 and 24 are more likely to live in poverty than older individuals, and families with the head of the household under the age of 30 are more likely to live in poverty than families with older heads of households. Two out of three adults living in poverty are likely to be women. Poverty rates for minorities are disproportionately high compared to Caucasians, but the overall number of Caucasians living in poverty is still higher. Immigrants have a higher rate of poverty than do native-born individuals, and a larger percentage of rural families live in poverty than do people living in cities. With fewer business and commerce centers, it is difficult to move out of poverty.

The poverty rates for senior citizens over the age of 65 has improved significantly over the past several decades as America has done a better job of retraining and supporting the older generation. However, there is a higher percentage of the elderly living just above the poverty level than those that are non-elderly. Senior citizens are therefore over-represented among the **near poor**. In spite of all of the improvements, the United States is still in the lower tier of success stories with poverty among senior citizens.

With more than forty million people in the United States living in poverty and another thirty million or so living just above the poverty level, more effort needs to go into eliminating poverty. Welfare reform, school breakfast programs, school reforms that include family resource centers, Head Start, the United Way's Success by Six program, job- and business-related investment initiatives, and other public and private assistance programs have made a marked impact on poverty. Still, America lags behind most of the other industrialized nations, and until national policies are changed to address poverty genuinely and effectively, the non-profit sector must make additional efforts to address the needs of the poor.

Most Americans cannot afford to purchase a home because of the often-required down payment (approximately 20%) and/or high mortgage payments that go along with **home ownership**. Individuals and families who own their home often develop a greater sense of personal and community pride and benefit financially from home equity and tax incentives. Some individuals are able to purchase a home only with the aid of governmental, private, or nonprofit programs that assist with the down payment, interest rates, or construction costs. A significant number, about one third of all Americans, are **shelter poor**, which means they spend so much of their income on home ownership that paying for necessities like food, clothing, and utilities is difficult.

Poor families must often live in **public housing**, which is often substandard and inadequate, and housing for poor minorities, the elderly, and households with females at the head is twice the average of substandard housing in general. Nearly a fourth of all **rural poor** live in substandard housing, and even though the cost of rural housing is less than for urban housing, the income of rural families is typically lower.

Incidents in which senior citizens share their homes with unrelated people, referred to as **shared housing**, for the purpose of rent, companionship, assistance with daily living, and/or security, has increased and will continue to do so in the future. The government's definition of disability now includes the de-institutionalized mentally disabled, as well as some classifications of drug addicts and alcoholics, and public housing for the **disabled** has increased significantly. Advocacy groups often make a point of working for fair housing for the disabled, the homeless, and the very poor. These efforts often run counter to the unwritten policies of housing managers who prefer residents with more options for paying rent.

Homeless families have increased in number and will probably continue to do so in the future. About one third of all homeless families include children. Homelessness might come about through a variety of causes, including low-paying jobs, terminations and lay-offs, domestic problems, alcohol and drug addictions, old age, and disabilities to mention several. There can be a number of solutions that involve shelters, job training and retraining, support, and sobriety programs.

The World of Work and Technology

Changes continue to take place at a dizzying pace as a mostly **information-based** economy replaces an industrialized one, and technology becomes more and more integrated into the way we conduct business and our personal lives as well. Businesses and organizations that are designed to incorporate information resources and electronic networks into their operating procedures can be responsive to changing customer demands and will have a decided edge over less enlightened organizations.

Individuals with specialized skills are in greater demand to work in information-based organizations. People who are innovative in developmental and problem solving areas will continue to be sought after by organizations. Individuals with critical skills and innovative character will find the highest paying jobs in all areas of work.

One of the benefits of enhanced technology has been that organizations have developed **flexible working environments** for employees who are unable to work a nine-to-five schedule, or are unable to work at a corporate headquarters. This flexible workplace also includes **job sharing**, in which several people share the same position. Working a **compressed work week**, working forty hours in less than five days, has become more popular and seems to enhance morale and efficiency, while reducing absenteeism. **Telecommuting** via computers from home provides individuals flexibility and provides opportunities for productivity and collaboration they might not have otherwise.

Changing demographics have made **managing diversity** a critical concern for organizational leaders. The rising number of women, minorities, and senior citizens in the workplace has made it a mosaic of different cultures and has led to a need for programs designed to empower and enhance a culturally diverse work force. These types of programs are important and demand for them will continue to grow.

As an increasing number of mothers come into the workplace, there is a growing need for more high quality, yet affordable, preschool, before school, and after school **child care** programs. A significant number of parents believe that present-day affordable child care is often inadequate in staffing and content, therefore the demand for better child care will continue to grow. Organizations that recognize and address this need should be in great demand.

Employees can experience a sense of **alienation** when working conditions become such that individuals feel separated from others, from themselves, and even from the work they do, if there is a lack of satisfaction and personal accomplishment. Additional factors, such as the transition to an information-based economy, inadequate child care, increased responsibilities, ambiguous job descriptions, and lack of security, have taken their toll on many employees who report significant **stress** and **fatigue** at the business site.

Unemployed workers whose skills are obsolete can be **trained** or **retrained** by companies who find themselves in partnerships with educational institutions more and more. Transitional approaches such as **school-to-work** initiatives can be critical for the millions of individuals for whom high school is the end of their formal educational experience. A number of programs including **cooperative education**, **monitored work experiences,** and **vocational education** are sometimes necessary for establishing important connections for this transition.

A wired world, where machine-to-machine communications became faster and less expensive, developed when telephone transmission was converted from analog to **digital** and **fiber-optic** phone lines were installed, became a wireless world as WiFi and other wireless technologies emerged. The investment, transfer, and distribution of finances occur more and more frequently through **electronic mediums** as do the design, production, installation, and sale of goods and services. The slowdown for brick and mortar retailers is evident as online retailers prosper.

Computers continue to become smaller and less expensive while providing more and more functions. The trend is toward more wearable technology such as watches and glasses in addition to medical devices that monitor bodily functions. **Artificial intelligence processes** provide support for human problem-solving processes, rather than mimic them and continue to assist in analyzing complex data such as with space travel and medical diagnostic procedures. **Wireless phone service** has become the preferred communication process worldwide, with texting, tweeting, and snapchatting all replacing conversations on the phone to a large degree. This **multimedia technology** interconnects different technologies for use in business, entertainment, and home.

Interactive design procedures have become a multibillion dollar business by making it possible to create **manufactured materials** for health care, agricultural, and other technologies that have completely revolutionized various problem-solving processes. Knowledge of and skills in technology are critical for success in nearly all aspects of work and many aspects of home as well. A schism already exists between the information-rich, those with access to electronic technology, and the information-poor, whose access is difficult at best. The Human Development Movement has as one of its priorities the establishment of **information utilities** to ensure equal access by everyone.

Crime

Crime, particularly violent crime among teenagers, has gone down and now begun to rise again. According to Annest (2013), between 1992 and 2011, the violent crime rate for the United States continually fell. However, the rate of violence ticked upward in 2012. The FBI reported that law enforcement agencies on average reported an increase of 1.2% in the number of violent crimes reported during 2012 when compared to the number reported for 2011. The crimes in this category include murder, forcible rape, robbery, and aggravated assault. This is not good news and the trend reflects civil unrest between communities and the police as well as continued challenges among minority youth (Annest, 2013). The increase in mass shootings will also inflate those statistics and cause the numbers to trend in a negative manner.

Young people need role models and guidelines for values and behavior. This might be particularly true for teenagers who are attempting to understand the world around them and their role and purpose in the world. When these guidelines are not available through the family structure, individuals sometimes look elsewhere and **gangs** too often take the place of the absent family. Gangs provide security and a sense of belonging and are most often driven by drug sales as a means of financial stability. Gangs represent all ethnic and racial groups and recruit both male and female members.

Hate crimes related to race, religion, sexual orientation, and ethnicity, and organizations that support one group's beliefs and values over another have continued to flourish in spite of the great strides that have been made in equal opportunities and cultural diversity. With the trend toward increased terrorism, the responsive hate crimes also appear to be trending upward. Deloughery and coauthors examined the relationship between terrorism and hate crimes. These authors report that hate crimes tend to follow terrorist attacks that target symbols of core American values and those perpetrated by groups with a religious motivation tend to be followed by sizeable increases in hate crimes targeting minorities during the week following the attack. Hate crimes remained elevated for about a month, with the retaliatory attacks not being limited to any confined or immediate geographic area where the terrorists perpetrated their initial attack (Deloughery, King, Asal, & Rethemeyer, 2012).

Family violence, also called **domestic violence,** remains a constant reminder for the need for nonprofits to become involved in delivering family enrichment, support, and intervention programs. Domestic violence can be one of the cruelest types of violence, since the individuals causing pain are those who are supposed to protect, support, and love the victim. This type of violence can take the form of **child abuse, spousal abuse,** or violence against **elderly** relatives. In a 2011 National Crime Victims Survey, 22.4% of children indicated that they had witnessed an act of violence in their homes, schools, or communities within the previous year, while 3.4% reported that they had indirect exposure to violence. Of those children who were surveyed, 39.2% claimed to have witnessed an act of violence and 10.1% stated they were indirectly exposed to violence at some point during their life (NCVRW Resource Guide, 2015, p. 19).

The murder rate is 5 per 100,000 people in the United States, which is twice the rate for Canada, but only one third the rate for Mexico; and is much lower than other countries such as Venezuela reporting in at 49 and Honduras at 67 per 100,000 people. **Homicide** is a part of both large cities and mid-sized cities, with a rate of violent crime known to law enforcement within large metropolitan areas for 2012 reported at 409.4 per 100,000 persons; in smaller cities outside the larger metropolitan areas this drops to 380.4 per 100,000 persons, and for more rural counties it drops even further to 177.0 per 100,000 persons (NCVRW Resource Guide, 2015).

Gang-related crime continues to be a factor in almost all cities regardless of size. **Gun control** remains a volatile issue with individuals and groups taking a strong stance on both sides. State and local gun control bills are constantly being challenged and changed, and the issue will continue to remain volatile in the future. A disproportionate number of young African American men between the ages of 16 and 24 become the victims of crimes involving hand guns. Homicide is the number one cause of death in this age group.

The production, transfer, and sale of **illegal drugs** is a crime, and there is a significant correlation between dealing in drugs and other criminal activities. Drug trafficking and sales have emerged as huge businesses involving tens of billions of dollars in revenue annually and often including high-powered weaponry in the battle for control. There has been some shift away from some drugs, such as **cocaine** toward prescription drug abuse and the use of more domestic drugs that can be made cheaply in home labs with easily available products.

Some states have legalized **marijuana,** hoping to decriminalize possession and capitalize on the ability to tax the sale of it. This has brought few of the sought after benefits and several unintended consequences. As the debate over whether other states should legalize marijuana continues, the **heroin epidemic** has taken center stage in many communities across the country. The abuse of and addiction to opioids including heroin, morphine, and prescription pain relievers is a serious problem that affects the health, social, and economic welfare of everyone involved. In 2012, estimates were that 2.1 million people in the United States suffered from abusing prescription opioid pain relievers and an estimated 467,000 were addicted to heroin. The number addicted to heroin continues to rise sharply. Prescriptions for opioids (e.g., hydrocodone, oxycodone) increased from around 76 million in 1991 to nearly 207 million in 2013, predominantly here in the United States (Volkow, 2014).

A get-tough policy on crime as a way of **punishment** and **deterrence** by the United States has led to seriously overcrowded jails. America has a high incarceration rate compared to most countries, with a disproportionate number of those prisoners being African American men. Nearly one fourth of all Black men between the ages of 20–29 are incarcerated or under some form of supervision from the criminal justice system, as compared to 1 out of every 16 White men and 1 out of every 10 Hispanic men (Weis & Muller, 2015).

Over four million people are being supervised in some way by the criminal justice system, and the cost for corrections is often the largest financial item in a state's budget. Alternatives to prison can be effective and less costly and include **halfway houses**, **community service programs**, **revised sentencing policies**, increased **electronic monitoring**, and a fairer system of **matching the punishment to the crime**.

Environmental Issues

Some environmental concerns such as earthquakes and tornadoes are natural occurrences and beyond human control, but others like water and air quality are very much a by-product of mankind and human interaction, with national and often global consequences.

The **biosphere** is made up of the surface of our planet and surrounding atmosphere. Together they provide the air, land, water, and energy necessary for life. The **ecosystem** is the mechanism that supplies human beings with the essentials to sustain life and involves plants, animals, and microorganisms interacting with each other and the physical environment. These ecosystems are being disturbed by a number of forces. The tremendous growth in human population (approximately seven billion people) takes a tremendous toll on the supply of food, energy, and minerals. The concentration of so many people in urban areas makes it difficult for the air, water, and land to handle waste and other toxic elements. Finally, some environmental problems are the result of modern technology and its uses.

Pollutants are a major cause of various health hazards and are an example of how humanity is fouling up the world. Specific examples of mankind's polluting the environment include **chemical pollution**, in which toxic chemicals are released into the air, water, and land during the development of chemical products; **solid waste pollution**, which includes the disposal of billions of tons of glass, plastics, textiles, and other materials each year; **water pollution**, involving contaminants, sewage, and oil spills that pour into rivers, lakes, and oceans; **radiation pollution**, which occurs through x-rays, nuclear fallout from weapons testing, and nuclear accidents; and, **air pollution**, which is caused primarily by automobile emissions and industrial plants.

The burning of fossil fuels and the destruction of tropical forests contribute to the **greenhouse effect**, in which harmful gases, such as carbon dioxide, nitrous oxide, chloro-fluorocarbons, and methane accumulate and act much like the glass roof in a greenhouse. When sunlight reaches the earth's surface, this roof traps heat radiating from the ground and causes a warming of the earth, the melting of the polar ice cap, and other significant changes in climate. Although still theoretical, the greenhouse effect is supported by the fact that sea level has risen gradually of late, indicating that the earth is at a warm point in comparison to where it has been in the past 100 years.

Trends in Philanthropy

Americans are among the most giving people in the world. The majority of contributions received by nonprofit organizations are donated by individuals. Giving USA 2016 estimated that giving by individuals amounted to $373.25 billion in 2015. The report notes that Americans truly want to make a difference, and that people are electing to support those causes that matter to them. These record setting numbers show that Americans are embracing philanthropy at a higher level than ever before (Giving USA Foundation, 2016).

Approximately 50% of all American adults formally **volunteer** in a nonprofit organization each year. Nearly half of teenagers volunteer to provide service, usually through their school, church, synagogue, or mosque. Nearly 40% of senior citizens volunteer their time and an almost larger percentage are willing but have not been asked. Of those who volunteer, the majority take part on a regular basis, monthly or more often. This translates into more than ninety million individuals volunteering approximately twenty billion hours of service each year (Independent Sector, 2002).

There is a correlation between being asked to volunteer and volunteering and a correlation between those who attend some kind of religious service and volunteering. Women are more likely to volunteer than men, and there is a correlation between volunteering and contributing financially to an organization.

People with certain values and attitudes, such as those who want to help the less fortunate, those who gain personal satisfaction from giving and volunteering, and those who want to increase opportunities for others, are more likely to contribute financially to a nonprofit organization. Approximately 90% of all American households **contribute to charities** each year with an average household gift of over $1,000. Individuals who volunteer and contribute generally give more than those who just contribute financially (Weis & Muller, 2015). A higher percentage of adults who become involved with volunteering and giving in their youth are more likely to continue that pattern later on than those who do not. Individuals who attend religious services on a regular basis give twice as much as those who do not.

People who worry about the economy give about half as much as those who are not worried about the economy in general (Independent Sector, 2002). During and immediately after the recession, which started in 2008, many donors carefully directed their donations to ensure that there was adequate assistance for issues that they perceived as pressing needs. This caused a shift in giving in terms of where charitable dollars were headed. This shifting appears to have stabilized with the share of total giving that was donated to each type of recipient looking very similar from 2014 to 2015 (Giving USA Foundation, 2016).

Religious organizations generally receive the greatest dollar amount in gifts, although donations to religious organizations have been decreasing steadily as American society becomes more secular. Historically, education receives the second largest amount of donations, followed by human services, health, arts, culture, humanities, and public/society benefit groups. Americans have demonstrated a willingness to work together in addressing problems in their communities and nonprofit organizations need to tap into this spirit by implementing innovative volunteer programs and creative financial development plans.

AMERICAN CHARITABLE CONTRIBUTIONS BY INDUSTRY FOR 2015 AS REPORTED BY GIVING USA: 2015

Religion—$119.30 billion
Education—$57.48 billion
Human Services—$45.21 billion
Foundations—$42.26 billion
Health—$29.81 billion
Public–Society Benefit—$26.95 billion
Arts/Culture/Humanities—$17.07 billion
International Affairs—$15.75 billion
Environment/Animals—$10.68 billion

Trends in philanthropy are hard to explain and even more difficult to predict. Current events, political changes, and economic swings all influence the way that people choose to give, or not. The year 2015 saw a rise in giving to every sector except foundations. This might be due to some of the negative publicity being generated politically with the Clinton Foundation and the Chan/Zuckerberg announcement. Negative news regarding misuse of donated dollars will tend to make individual donors look elsewhere for organizations worthy of entrusting the care and use of their money intended for the common good (Callahan, 2016).

Big donors will continue to contribute to politicians in an effort to sway electoral outcomes. Millions of dollars are spent attempting to increase or decrease voter turnout among subgroups of the voting population. The 2016 election demonstrated that the very wealthy are becoming more polarized in their views on many of the major issues.

Experts predict major changes in funding for education over the next few years as donors move away from debates over choice and accountability and focus on student learning. While funders, both large and small, have poured millions into higher education in the hopes of preparing young people for future employment through education or workforce development projects, very little money has gone toward helping entrepreneurs (Adeniji, 2015). That is expected to change in 2016 as donations to foster entrepreneurship on campus and a growing effort to help low-income women and minorities start businesses as a path to economic security.

SUMMARY

The goal of most nonprofit organizations is to enhance the quality of life in communities, and understanding human development is important for effective program planning. Organizational leaders must understand that human development is contextual in nature, meaning that development occurs in the context of various circumstances and situations, and leaders must understand developmental theories as well. Developmental theories provide information on how individuals pass through various processes and stages and provide a foundation to develop approaches that will assist individuals in addressing life situations.

Nonprofit leaders must incorporate their knowledge of human development with their awareness of issues and trends that individuals and communities are facing and will face in the future. Educational concerns, such as illiteracy and technology in the classroom, and health problems, such as AIDS, STDs, drugs, and alcohol, and the complexity of the health care system are staggering issues. A growing population and aging continue to present challenges and opportunities for nonprofit leaders. Children, individuals, and families are often devastated by poverty, housing costs, and homelessness that can and must be addressed effectively. Technology and other changes taking place in the workplace are occurring at a dizzying pace, leaving some employees stressed and feeling disenfranchised. Although aspects of crime have ebbed and waned over the last several decades, the family structure and support are too often diminished, creating opportunities for criminal behavior and leaving a huge gap for nonprofit organizations to fill. Environmental systems have suffered the consequences of human greed and thoughtlessness and will continue to require a special area of attention.

Throughout time, societies have been faced with challenging situations. There are no quick fixes to the numerous problems and situations that confront families, children, and individuals daily. Nonprofit organizations have a unique opportunity and responsibility to work with educational institutions and governmental agencies to address the needs of all citizens through programs.

This chapter addressed, in part, the Nonprofit Academic Centers Council Competency Requirements of Youth and Adult Development and Philanthropy.

REFLECTION AND APPLICATION

1. Why is it important to understand human development and the context for nonprofit activity?

   _____

   _____

   _____

   _____

2. Which developmental theories do you believe might impact the way that nonprofits deliver their services, and why?

   _____

   _____

   _____

   _____

   _____

3. What is the major influence of the Human Development Movement on the day-to-day operations of nonprofit organizations?

   _____

   _____

   _____

   _____

   _____

4. Which of Erikson's stages can you identify with, and why?

   _____

   _____

   _____

   _____

5. Describe a situation in which you have incorporated the Social Cognitive Theory.

_____

_____

_____

_____

_____

_____

_____

6. Which issue or trend is most important to you as a future nonprofit employee, and why? How do you believe this trend should be addressed by nonprofits?

_____

_____

_____

_____

_____

_____

7. Using Erikson's Psychosocial Theory as the foundation, develop an idea for a program directed toward individuals in a specific stage of development.

_____

_____

_____

_____

_____

_____

_____

_____

_____

REFERENCES

Adeniji, A. (2015). A growing niche in alumni giving: Nurturing entrepreneurs on campus. *Inside Philanthropy.* Retrieved from http://www.insidephilanthropy.com/home/2015/7/1/a-growing-niche-in-alumni-giving-nurturing-entrepreneurs-on.html

Alliance for Strong Families and Communities. (2015). Retrieved from http://alliance1.org/commitments/about Accessed June 13, 2016

Annest, J. (July 2013). *Homicide rates among persons aged 10–24 years—United States, 1981–2010,* Centers for Disease Control and Prevention, MMWR, 62(27), 545–548.

Bailey. A border war. *Washington Post Weekly Edition* (October 23–29, 2006).

Behlol, M., & Dad, H. (2010). Concept of learning. *International Journal of Psychological Studies, 2*(2), pp. 231–239.

Bjorklund, D. F. (1995). *Children's thinking: developmental function and individual differences* (2nd ed.). Pacific Grove, CA: Brooks/Cole.

Bronfenbrenner, U. (1979). *The ecology of human development.* Cambridge, MA: Harvard University Press.

Callahan, D. (2016). Philanthropy forecast, 2016: Trends and funders to watch. *Inside Philanthropy.* Retrieved from http://www.insidephilanthropy.com/home/2016/1/6/philanthropy-forecast-2016-trends-and-funders-to-watch.html

Caplow. T., Hicks, L., & Wattenberg, B. (2001). *The first measured century: An illustrated guide to trends in America, 1900–2000.* Washington, D.C.: The AEI Press.

Deloughery, K., King, R., Asal, V., & Rethemeyer, R. (2012). *Analysis of factors related to hate crime and terrorism.* Final report to the national consortium for the study of terrorism and responses to terrorism. College Park, MD: START.

Drug Enforcement Administration. (2007). Retrieved from http://www.drugsense.org/html/modules.php?name=wodclock.

Edginton, S. R., & Edginton, C. R. (1994). *Youth programs: Promoting quality services.* Champaign, IL: Sagamore Publishing.

Eitzen, D. S., Zinn, M. B., & Eitzen K. S. (2009). *Social problems.* Upper Saddle River, NJ; Pearson Publishing.

Freud, S. (1923). *The ego and the id.* New York: Norton.

Giving USA Foundation. (2016, June 13). Giving USA: 2015 was America's most-generous year ever. River, NJ: Pearson Publishing. Retrieved from http://givingusa.org/giving-usa-2016/ Accessed on June 15, 2016

Hewitt Associates. (2004). *Worklife benefits provided by major U.S. employers, 2003–2004.* Lincolnshire, IL; Hewitt Associates.

Independent Sector. (2001). *The new nonprofit almanac.* Washington, D.C.

Kaplan, P. S. (1998). *The human odyssey: Life span development.* Pacific Grove, CA: Brooks/Cole Publishing Company.

Measure of America. (2016). *About human development.* Social Science Research Council. Retrieved from http://www.measureofamerica.org/human-development/

Mills, C. W. (1959). *The sociological imagination*. New York: Oxford University Press.

NCVRW Resource Guide. (2015). *Engaging communities, empowering victims: Statistical overviews*. Retrieved from https://www.ncjrs.gov/ovc_archives/ncvrw/2015/pdf/StatisticalOverviews.pdf

Osmond, M. W., & Thorne, B. (1993). Feminist Theories. Sourcebook of Family Theories and Methods, 591–625. Pew Research Center (2015). *Parenting in America*. Pew Research Center, Washington, DC. Retrieved from http://www.pewsocialtrends.org/2015/12/17/parenting-in-america/

Pittman, K. J. (1991). *Promoting youth development: Strengthening the role of youth serving and community organizations*. New York: Center for Development and Policy Research.

Schunk, D. H. (1996). Goal and self-evaluative influences during children's cognitive skill learning. American Educational Research Journal, 33, 359-382.

Sen, A. (1992). *Inequality reexamined*. Oxford: Oxford University Press.

Shapiro, F. R. (2006). *The Yale Book of Quotations*. Yale University Press, New Haven.

U.S. Department of Health and Human Services. (2007). *HHS poverty guidelines*. Washington, DC: Author. Retrieved from http//aspe.hhs.gov/poverty/07 poverty.htm

Volkow, N. (2014, May 14). America's addiction to opioids: Heroin and prescription drug abuse. NIH: National Institute on Drug Abuse. Retrieved from https://www.drugabuse.gov/about-nida/legislative-activities/testimony-to-congress/2016/americas-addiction-to-opioids-heroin-prescription-drug-abuse

Walsh, F. (2006). *Strengthening family resilience* (2nd ed.). New York: Guilford Press.

Weis, R., & Muller, S. (2015). *Leading and managing nonprofit organizations* (2nd ed.). Peosta, IA: eddie bowers publishing company, inc.

PROGRAM DEVELOPMENT, MARKETING, AND PROMOTION

Programs developed by organizational leaders and managers are the means by which organizations achieve many of their objectives and goals as they work to fulfill their mission. In addition to exploring program development in Chapter 5, we will also take a look at some classic approaches to marketing, promoting, and evaluating programs in organizations and discuss ways to improve customer service.

Most experts and authors agree that program development and measurement are critical for success in the nonprofit world (Kerzner, 2009; Cobb, 2012) and generally concentrate on planning, inputs, and outcomes in various ways.

Although our primary program methodology is the Customer-Centered/Benefits Approach developed by the authors in past editions of this text (Weis & Muller, 2015; Weis & Gantt, 2009), measuring program outcomes in determining a program's effectiveness has gained broad acceptance since the 1990s primarily through the efforts of the United Way of America; therefore we will also incorporate concepts from United Way's Program Outcome Model which follows "inputs all the way to outcomes" (Worth, 2017) and helps determine if a program is reaching its potential as well as Balanced Scorecard which measures various data from several perspectives and Paton's Dashboard (2003) which simply asks two questions: (1) Does the program achieve the intended results, and (2) is the organization well run?

A CUSTOMER-CENTERED/BENEFITS APPROACH TO PROGRAM DEVELOPMENT

Programs communicate to customers what the organization is trying to accomplish. A **customer-centered/benefits** approach to developing programs implies that leaders strive to develop programs that not only meet the needs of their customers, but often exceed them and provide customers with some form of positive outcome or benefit. This approach to program development communicates a quality organization with quality staff members. Quality programs must be carefully planned, implemented, and evaluated. Programs of all kinds can be developed for organizational members as long as they fall under the umbrella of the overall purpose of the organization (Weis & Muller, 2015).

Staff and volunteer members who are responsible for developing programs should meet certain **criteria** that include (1) believing in and being committed to the purpose of the organization; (2) being knowledgeable and skilled in program development; and, (3) being aware of the situations, needs, and desires of the constituents of the organization (Weis & Muller, 2015). Programs should meet the needs of the organization's constituents in the context of the organizational mission or purpose.

In addition to meeting certain criteria, it is important that leaders in nonprofit organizations commit to developing programs of the highest quality. More and more citizens are relying on nonprofit organizations to provide services to assist them in reaching their goals or in times of need, and these individuals deserve program services of the highest possible quality (Weis & Muller, 2015).

Quality. Once the need for a program is established, it is time to turn attention to establishing programs of the highest quality. **Quality programs** are those programs that *meet or exceed* the standards and expectations set for program activities (Russell & Jamieson, 2008). They are programs of excellence that focus on the needs of the customers and make them feel as if they are valued members of the organization; such programs also provide members with a positive outcome or benefit (Edginton & Edginton, 1994). *Meeting and exceeding* the expectations of the members of an organization is the hallmark of a competent, caring, and dedicated staff with the knowledge and skills to develop exceptional programs. Programs that meet or exceed expectations are rare, and customers take note when their expectations are exceeded (Weis & Long, 2011).

Developing programs that meet and exceed customer expectations is the responsibility of the organization's leaders. These guidelines should include, but not be limited to the following (Walton, 1998):

— **Innovation.** Programs should be developed that meet the changing needs of organizational members and remain fresh by offering new and interesting activities to keep them exciting.
— **Continual Improvement.** Constantly looking for ways that programs can be improved keeps them fresh, energized, and meaningful. Program development is a dynamic process that should always be evolving toward relevant methods and processes.
— **Continuous Education.** Good organizations commit to continuous educational opportunities for staff members. College classes, seminars, and workshops should be

supported and encouraged for staff members to ensure competency and effectiveness in program and administrative areas.

— **Attention to Detail.** Programs in which details are important are generally superior to programs in which details are not an issue. Paying attention to details helps to ensure quality and success. There is an old saying that goes: "The devil is in the details," which reminds us those problems can occur when details are not attended to.

— **Pride.** Staff and volunteer members must have a strong feeling about the programs they are planning and must work diligently to provide customers with the best services possible. Pride is contagious, and it begins when everyone in the organization prides himself or herself on what the programs are accomplishing for their members. Pride includes planning and implementing new programs with as few mistakes as possible and eliminating mistakes or unnecessary aspects from existing programs.

— **Anticipatory Planning.** Program developers must be proactive in the sense that they look ahead to program needs for the future as well as those of the present. In order to do this, leaders must be on the cutting edge of program development and must maintain knowledge of issues and customer needs.

— **Teamwork and Responsibility.** Programs are by necessity developed and implemented in a cooperative process. Program leaders must have skills in developing effective teams of professional staff members, volunteers, invested staff members of other organizations, consultants, and even program participants in the overall development of programs. Shared input and responsibility requires leadership and management that is competent in developing collaborative, successful ventures.

— **Performance Measurements.** Program successes and outcomes can and should be validated through an evaluation process. Interviews, focus groups, surveys, pre/post tests, and observation are all legitimate ways to determine whether programs are meeting their objectives and whether they are successful from the participants' standpoint. Evaluations can be time-consuming but the results can assist the organization in developing better, more effective programs. They help staff members determine whether they are meeting the needs of their members, and they provide useful information when seeking support from outside funders.

Providing programs of the highest possible quality that meet or exceed the expectations of customers is the only way to ensure that an organization maintains integrity in its mission while providing opportunities of enhancement for its members.

A commitment to programs of the highest quality is the responsibility of everyone in an organization, and once this commitment is established, the focus of attention turns to the developmental process itself. There are three major **stages** of program development (Weis & Muller, 2015): (1) **Initial (Planning) Stage**, (2) **Middle (Planning/Implementation) Stage**, and (3) **Final (Evaluation) Stage** (See PIE, Figure 5.1 on the following page).

Figure 5.1

Stages of Program Development: Planning, Implementation, and Evaluation (PIE)

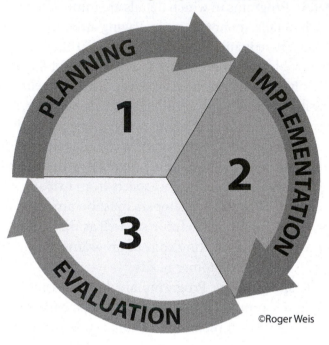

©Roger Weis

INITIAL (PLANNING) STAGE

Careful planning in this stage is important since it sets the groundwork for other activities throughout the program development process. Good planning should be a task-by-task process (Russell & Jamieson, 2008), although the sequence of tasks and modification or simplification of tasks depends on particular situations, and some tasks may not even be necessary.

Tasks are specific work segments or activities that are necessary to accomplish program objectives (Hardy, 1984). These tasks or activities may have a number of **Action Steps** as will be discussed further along. The development of tasks/action steps is the responsibility of the program or planning committee, and members of this committee are determined by the organization's leaders, usually a program director or another senior staff member. Tasks typically specify (1) which activities are to be completed to accomplish program objectives, and in what order; (2) who is responsible for completing various activities; and (3) when these activities are to be completed. Although tasks for specific programs may vary considerably, some standard tasks for consideration are listed below (Weis & Muller, 2015):

Task 1—Selection of a Planning Committee. Groups often have greater potential for creativity and thoroughness than individuals because of enhanced expertise, synergy, and opportunity to attend to details. Selecting an effective planning committee to develop specific programs is essential for successfully meeting organizational goals and planning programs that meet and exceed the expectations of its members. Although this is considered one *task*, it may involve many *steps*. And a well-planned committee should have as many *significant* **action steps** as is necessary. Planning members should include:

- ▶ staff and volunteer members who have knowledge and skills in program planning as well as in the particular content area of the program;
- ▶ individuals with particular knowledge and skills in areas of specific expertise relevant to program planning, such as marketing, finances, and volunteer coordination and risk management when these are needed;
- ▶ individuals, such as the members of the organization, who will benefit from the program, since these individuals can often add insight into the needs and desires of the membership in general.

Planning committee members are *responsible* for the following:

- ▶ developing a schedule of program planning meetings
- ▶ identifying and prioritizing other tasks or action steps according to what needs to be done first, second, and so on
- ▶ assigning a responsible person or persons to accomplish each task
- ▶ recording each aspect of the program plan on a **Program Planning Worksheet (PPW)** (see Figure 5.2 on the following page)
- ▶ implementing, monitoring, and reporting the progress of the program to the appropriate organizational leaders(s)

Task 2—Needs Assessment. The needs and desires of constituents should be identified and assessed so programs can be developed to focus on appropriate areas. **Needs** are usually considered as an individual *physiological, psychological, or social imbalance*. Edginton & Ford (1985) note that when an individual recognizes a deficiency in any of these areas, he or she has a need. Physiological needs might include deficiencies associated with the need for food, water, sleep, and sex. Psychological and social deficiencies might be harder to assess, but would include the need for companionship, social interaction, recognition, safety, love, achievements, and self-esteem.

A need, then, is the assessed difference between the ideal state of an individual and the actual condition of an individual as he or she is functioning in their environment. Communities, too, have needs as do states, nations, and all of society, and program planners should be aware of collective needs in developing programs. **Desires**, on the other hand, are considered wishes *that are perceived as something necessary* (Edginton, Edginton, Hanson, & Hudson, 1998). In this context, desires are differentiated from needs in that they are not necessary to sustain life, but they can also be considered in determining future programs (Weis & Muller, 2015).

Figure 5.2

Program Planning Worksheet

Date___/___/___

Name of Organization _____

Name of Program/Project _____

Program Coordinator_____

Program Committee Members:

Name	Address	Phone #	e-mail address
1.			
2.			
3.			
4.			
5.			
6.			

Program Objectives _____

_____

_____

Estimated Direct Income	Estimated Direct Expenses	Gain (Deficit)
Actual Direct Income	Actual Direct Costs	Gain (Deficit)

Action Steps from Work Tasks	Person(s) Responsible	Completion Dates

Evaluation Results_____

_____

Recommendations for Future Programs_____

_____

In the 1940s, Abraham Maslow advanced a general theory of human needs and motivation that still serves as a foundation and guide to understanding basic human needs. He identified physiological needs, safety needs, affiliation needs, esteem needs, and the need to become self-actualized. These needs are discussed in detail below:

1. **Physiological needs.** These include basic human needs for food, water, shelter, sleep, sensory gratification and could be satisfied by a supportive environment.

2. **Safety needs.** This category includes being relatively free from danger and might involve a safe home, neighborhood, or work environment.

3. **Affiliation needs.** These needs can be expressed in the desire to join with others in completing a project, making a family, or achieving a sense of belonging (fraternities or sororities). This need implores individuals to explore and develop relationships with friends, family, and co-workers.

4. **Esteem needs.** These needs are expressed in individual and collective desires for a sense of accomplishment or achievement. This satisfaction can be received externally, internally, or both. External esteem satisfaction comes from visible rewards such as a salary increase. Internal esteem satisfaction results when individuals realize a sense of accomplishment, success, and being counted on.

5. **Need for self-actualization.** Maslow described this need as a desire to become everything that one is capable of becoming. As self-actualization occurs, individuals reach out to assist others in becoming all that they are capable of becoming through empowering or mentoring activities (Maslow, 1943).

Maslow posits that individuals will work to satisfy needs in that order and it is only when basic needs such as safety and food are met that higher needs for esteem and self-actualization can be considered. Although research has failed to conclude a clear separation between the categories and the validity of Maslow's theory in general, it remains a foundational treatise on human needs and motivation.

Programs should only be developed that address important issues and needs of organizational members and should take into account the various life stages that individuals may be passing through. For instance, teenagers are passing through a very difficult stage of their lives as they struggle to develop and understand their identity, as noted in Erikson's Stage Theory in Chapter 4 of this text. At the same time, they are also often confronted with a number of issues such as smoking, alcohol and drug use, and premarital sex. A program that is designed to strengthen their system of values by offering them the opportunity to make a difference in someone else's life, for instance, could become a critical aspect to their personal development. These kinds of programs help teens develop a positive sense of **self worth** and the knowledge that they can and do make a difference (**self-efficacy**). Programs that also confront important issues head-on with facts, methods of handling situations, and the opportunity to teach these to others, such as younger children, can be an invaluable experience with lifelong implications. These experiences can allow them to develop communication and teamwork skills and even provide insight into future vocational possibilities.

An **assessment of needs** should be made prior to further program planning, and that can be done in a number of ways: (1) Researching and assessing existing data, such as published reports in newspapers, magazines, journals, and institutional bulletins can be essential in understanding the needs of individuals in general (Russell & Jamieson, 2008). (2) Assessing the needs and desires of organizational members firsthand can and should be done through interviews, focus groups, and and/or surveys that can be implemented periodically or at set times throughout the year. Interviews can be face-to-face, or a sampling of telephone interviews can be initiated. Individual interviews provide a focus of insight that cannot be duplicated by other methods. On the other hand, focus groups sometimes provide collective information that cannot be found through an individual process. And surveys can provide confidentiality that is virtually non-existent with the interview and focus group format and may provide for more open and honest responses (an example survey can be found in Figure 5.3 below). (3) A third method of understanding the needs and desires of constituents is through information already gathered for organizations that are a part of a state-wide, regional, or national association. These organizations often receive pre-planned programs addressing the needs of the general membership, which can be valuable and time saving.

Figure 5.3

Needs Assessment Survey

Kingston Community Center
Survey for New Programs

Please help the Kingston Community Center determine new program interests for the upcoming activity year. Complete the following anonymous survey and place it in the survey box located at the North entrance to the facility. Once you have done this, the front desk clerk will give you a coupon for 20% off any special class, workshop, or seminar. Thanks for helping your center be the best it can be!

PLEASE CHECK YOUR AREAS OF INTEREST:

❏ Aerobics	❏ Aquatics	❏ Arts & Crafts	❏ Athletics/fitness	❏ Basketball
❏ Bowling	❏ Computer class	❏ Culinary class	❏ Cycling	❏ Education
❏ Golf class	❏ Karate	❏ Racquetball	❏ Scuba	❏ Senior activities
❏ Trips	❏ Softball	❏ Volleyball	❏ Youth activities	

Comments and other suggestions:_____

_____

_____

©Roger Weis

Task 3—Review Developmental Theories, Competencies, Stages, and Issues. After assessing the needs of the constituents of an organization, it is also important to have an understanding of developmental stages they may be experiencing, along with an understanding of significant issues and trends that members may be challenged with (see Chapter 4). It is important to review developmental theories, competencies, stages (Erikson), and issues relevant to the needs of the membership and the mission of the organization. Although needs and desires are important, understanding developmental processes is equally important to crafting effective programs.

Maintaining an awareness of current and significant issues and trends provides program planners with the opportunity to address some of these issues through programs. Programs that address recognized needs, confront important issues, and focus on the overall development of individuals strikes a chord with members who realize the organization is focusing on their situation and providing programs directed toward their well-being (Weis & Muller, 2015).

Task 4—Incorporating Values and Character Education. Nonprofit organizations have a significant responsibility to assist members in becoming responsible individuals and citizens. This mandate dates back to the early part of the twentieth century when organizations such as the Boy Scouts of America, Girl Scouts of the USA, Boys and Girls Clubs of America, Camp Fire Boys and Girls, Girls, Inc., and the YMCAs and YWCAs focused a great deal of attention on character development, as they still do today (Edginton, Hudson, & Ford, 1999).

Values can be thought of as principles that guide our lives and the constructs that are important in our lives (Edginton et al., 1998). **Values education** occurs when nonprofit leaders assist members in defining and developing their values through select, organized methods. Values education should reflect: (1) the basic values of the community and society; and (2) parallel the values of the organization, but they (3) should not impose values upon members. Values such as honesty, justice, equality, and freedom, to list several, are values that can and should be encouraged by organizations, but must be accepted freely by participants, not forced upon them.

There are several effective ways to introduce values in a program. In the **direct-programmatic approach** values clarification and development is the main focus of the program. In other words, the program is designed and promoted as a values clarification/development program. This can be a very honest and effective approach, although some participants may be hesitant to be open regarding their value system.

Another effective way to introduce values education is through an **integrated-programmatic approach.** In this approach, values are introduced as part of the structure of the program and occur more *naturally* within the program's framework. This makes this approach very functional and prevents compartmentalization. For instance, the indoor soccer league might support the concept that all children make the team and there are no tryouts. It could also include the concept that all children will play an approximately equal amount of time and that all participants will shake hands with the opposing team members at the end of the game. Fairness, sportsmanship, and teamwork are just some of the values that can be presented within this framework. And finally, values are taught by **role modeling**. Organizational leaders inevitably provide examples of values for participants to consider through their decisions and actions, so it is important for these leaders to assess and monitor their actions in all facets of operational activities (Weis & Muller, 2015).

Another important concept to consider in program development is the concept of **character education**, or helping individuals internalize values such as honesty, integrity, equality, and fairness. It is one thing to clarify and develop a healthy system of values but it is another thing to live one's life in accordance with that system of values. Nonprofit leaders have the opportunity to develop programs that allow individuals to internalize values by clarifying, using, and reflecting upon them over and over again in various situations. Clubs and organizations, service learning opportunities (see Chapter 2), and other programs that promote continual use and reflection of values are essential to healthy individual development.

Quality programs combine (1) constituent needs with (2) an understanding of developmental stages along with (3) a focus on important issues or trends, and include (4) values and character education which can have a powerful impact on the lives of the members of any organization.

Task 5—Determine Program Objectives. Most nonprofit organizations have a **purpose** or a **mission statement** that spells out their reason for being in a general way (Weis & Muller, 2015). This statement usually refers to enhancing the quality of life of specific individuals in the community in some way, but it is so broad that organizations usually designate a number of definitive **goals** they plan to accomplish as a part of their purpose. For instance, an organization that plans to enhance the quality of life for socially/economically disadvantaged children might have goals of helping children develop competencies in health, education, recreation, and vocations. More specifically, the organization could set a number of **program objectives** or outcomes (Worth, 2017) for each of these areas (goals). For instance, in the area of health, a program objective could include having children become competent in personal hygiene, or in nutritional guidelines of some kind. An objective for education could be to improve the literacy rate or the percentage of high school graduates in a particular community. Program objectives are both measurable and capable of being accomplished in a set amount of time.

Setting program objectives provides motivation and direction for the program staff who can begin concentrating on developing action steps necessary for achieving set objectives. Having program objectives also provides a basis from which to measure whether or not goals have been achieved. The measurement process will be discussed in the evaluation phase of program development.

There are generally two types of program objectives: (1) **Qualitative.** This type of objective includes the various areas the program is designed to address or change, including needs, issues, situations, values, competencies, and/or life stages and ties in well with the "Outcome

Model" which lists program benefits or "outcomes" (Worth, 2017); and (2) **Quantitative.** This type of objective includes areas of the program that can be counted and observed, such as the number of program participants, the length and meeting times of the program, and financial considerations; this is very similar to "Outputs" in the Program Outcome Model (Worth, 2017). Both types of objectives need to be considered and documented on the Program Planning Worksheet prior to implementing a program.

Program objectives should be written in a certain way and include certain criteria (Edginton, Hanson, & Edginton, 1992; Weis & Muller, 2015):

- ► **Specific.** Program objectives should be clear and succinct.
- ► **Measurable.** There needs to be a way in which to measure whether or not program objectives are met.
- ► **Reality-based.** Objectives should be challenging yet reachable.
- ► **Useful.** Objectives provide program staff with direction and therefore must be helpful in guiding staff members toward achieving the purpose(s) of the program.
- ► **Linked to Needs.** Obviously, objectives must be linked to the needs, issues, competencies, values, and so on that the program is addressing and is designed to affect.
- ► **Inclusion of Program Concept and Format.** Including the program concept or idea and the program format in the objective helps to connect the purpose of the program to the overall program process. The program concept and format will be discussed in Task 6.

Setting purposeful objectives provides a foundation for the rest of the developmental process, and it is vital that objectives are well-written and defined. An example of a clear and effective objective follows:

The Teens for Seniors program provides teenagers in the Morganfield Boys and Girls Club opportunities to assist senior citizens attending the community center's day care program. Teens are trained to participate with seniors in social and recreational activities. Some of the intended objectives include:

- ► Involvement of a minimum of 10 teenagers in a program with a minimum of 25 senior citizens meeting at least once a week for social and recreational activities for a 3-month period
- ► Improved inter-generational understanding
- ► Increased flexibility on the part of senior citizens
- ► Decreased depression on the part of senior citizens
- ► Enhanced self-esteem of teenagers and senior citizens
- ► Increased sense of responsibility and caring on the part of the teenagers
- ► Improved teamwork, communication, recreation, socialization, and leadership skills on the part of the teenagers.

This kind of program provides opportunities for improving the overall health and well-being of both teenagers and senior citizens and allows the teenagers to develop a number of important skills and character traits that will be useful throughout their lives. This objective includes the program concept and format and addresses needs, issues, competencies, values, and life stages. The objectives for this program include both qualitative and quantitative areas that can be measured in various ways and the program is designed to be realistic, yet challenging in nature.

Measuring outcomes of programs is a highly important way for nonprofit organizations to report to their constituencies and sponsors successes in order to maintain viability, but there are other factors involved which will be discussed in the evaluation section.

Task 6—Selection of Program Concept/Format. Once the program objectives have been established, a program idea or concept must be determined along with a format that results in an effective process for reaching objectives. This is very similar to the United Way's **Activities** section of the Outcome Model which takes into consideration ways in which to fulfill its mission (Worth, 2017). There are a number of ways or program *approaches* that can be considered in determining the program concept (Edginton & Edginton, 1994; Weis & Muller, 2015):

▶ **Traditional Approach.** Relying on past successes within the organization to determine a program concept is referred to as the traditional approach. Reviewing past programs to determine how they can meet current objectives can be valuable for two reasons: (1) Less time and energy needs to be expended on the planning process since the program has been implemented previously; and (2) organizational members who have appreciated programs from the past often look forward to a repeat of those programs with anticipation. One disadvantage to planning programs from a traditional approach standpoint is that if current programs rely too heavily on past planning they may become uninspired by not taking into account changes in interests, issues, trends, and lifestyles. Taking traditional program ideas and adding new twists can help keep the program fresh and exciting.

▶ **Current Practice Approach.** Programs that are effective in one part of the country can often be effective in another part as well. Nonprofit leaders are usually open to sharing successful program ideas with each other in the field. This type of approach can save a good deal of planning time and lends legitimacy to the future success of the program. One disadvantage, however, is that sometimes a program that works in a large metropolitan area of the country may not work in a rural area, or vice versa. In a similar manner, a program that succeeds in the northeastern part of the country may not be as acceptable in the southwestern part, and so on. Both sides of the situation need to be taken into consideration before employing the current practice approach.

▶ **Expressed Desires Approach.** Offering members opportunities to express their desires for program selection through surveys, interviews, and focus groups provides them with a feeling of involvement and may provide the program staff valuable insights for program development. This information can also be valuable in reducing risk of developing programs for which there is little or no interest. Information provided by members is important and should be weighed with other factors in determining the program concept. For instance, some members may respond to what they "want" versus what they really needed.

▶ **Prescriptive Approach.** This approach is directed toward developing program concepts focused on members of the organization with special needs or special situations. This concentrated focus on specific individuals can have very important and far-reaching consequences and should always be considered in the overall scheme of program development. However, consideration should also be given to the fact that these programs are usually time-consuming and resource intensive and address the needs of only a select number of members and the approach may need to be used accordingly.

▶ **Innovative Approach.** Creating new programs from scratch can be challenging, exciting, and rewarding. Members of the planning committee should convene to discuss alternative program ideas in *brainstorming* sessions. These sessions include expressing any and all ideas without qualification, recording the alternatives, and returning later to discuss the feasibility of each idea. Each member of the planning committee should feel that his or her ideas are welcome while they are being expressed. The newness of the resulting program concept often creates a level of excitement and anticipation that other, more traditional program ideas may not incur. A possible disadvantage of this kind of program approach is that because of the newness of the program idea, more time and confusion in the planning and the implementation process may occur and some uncertainty may exist as to the potential outcome.

▶ **Combined Approach.** "Good organizational leaders incorporate some or all of the approaches above for creating options for program concepts" (Weis & Muller, 2015). Using successful program ideas from the past provides some continuity, certainty, and tradition. Incorporating program ideas that have been successful in other places may decrease the amount of time necessary for planning and provide a sense of certainty regarding the outcome. Inviting members of the organization to express their desires and needs gives them a sense of involvement while providing program staff members with valuable information. Developing specific programs for certain individuals in an organization indicates to those members that they are important and that their needs are being addressed. Finally, creating new program ideas can cause a sense of excitement throughout an organization. The combined approach to program development can be highly successful because it brings together information from numerous sources in making program decisions. Finding just the right approach to program development can be time-consuming, but being able to develop programs that create interest and excitement and that meet the intended objectives has a great deal of merit and is certainly worth the effort.

The selection of a program **format** is important because different program structures or formats provide different kinds of experiences for individuals. The way in which a program is structured is linked to the likelihood that customers will achieve desired benefits. For instance, a program for self-improvement may be structured as a workshop or seminar. A program designed to include physical competition may take the format of a sports league. Farell and Lundegren (1991) posit that the program format chosen should be directly linked to the experience desired for the customers and suggest five program formats: (1) self-improvement, (2) competition, (3) social, (4) participant spectator, and (5) self-directed. A great deal has been written about program formats in the leisure services field and Russell (2008) suggests more common approaches to program formats: (1) clubs, (2) competition, (3) trips and outings, (4) special events, (5) classes, (6) open facility, (7) voluntary service, and (8) workshops, seminars, and conferences. Each of these formats vary in terms of general characteristics and provide for a wide selection on program structure. Most experts agree that the program format is the structure or form the activity takes and that the format is one of the key ingredients in meeting customer expectations.

Task 7—Evaluate Resources. Another important consideration in the overall development of a program is the assessment of resources necessary for program delivery. Necessary resources may include any or all of the following (Weis & Long, 2011):

▶ **Space availability.** One of the first things to consider regarding resources is determining what type of space is necessary and then exploring the use of existing space within the organization or other areas and facilities.

▶ **Personnel.** Planners should develop a list of staff and/or volunteer members who are competent and available to develop a specific program. If an expert specific to a particular program is not already a part of the organizational team, one might be recruited as a volunteer or a part-time consultant or expert might be hired.

▶ **Finances.** Sometimes a program fee may need to be assessed to cover some expenses. It is also important to research the availability of sponsors to cover program costs.

▶ **Collaboration.** Some programs can be more successful if they are planned in collaboration with other organizations. Collaboration may take a little more time in the beginning, but often brings with it enhanced resources, increased services for more people, and more excitement and enthusiasm.

▶ **Supplies.** Planners must envision the supplies necessary for a successful program and develop a list. They must also determine which materials are already available and which materials can be borrowed, donated, or paid for through sponsorship. Businesses and service organizations often sponsor nonprofit organizations for several reasons: (1) it helps develop the community, (2) it enhances public relations, and (3) it builds morale among its members.

► **Constraints.** Attention also needs to be given to any possible constraints on a project such as legal conditions or general regulations. For instance, when working with special individuals there might be a limit of individuals per therapist or a limit of individuals in a specific recreational facility such as a pool.

► **Equipment.** The equipment necessary for the program must meet the needs of the program and the participants, and must be in good, safe condition.

All of these aspects are important to the success of programs and combined are similar to the concept of "inputs" in the Program Outcome Model (Worth, 2017).

MIDDLE (PLANNING/IMPLEMENTATION) STAGE

This is also a vital stage of program development, since the steps necessary for planning and implementing the program are designated and developed further. This is also the stage in which a supervisory plan is selected and the program is actually implemented (Weis & Long, 2011).

Task 8—Risk Management is Priority #1. Risk management is the prevention, control, and handling of risk associated with programs. Because individual and group safety and health are at stake, it is the most important step in the implementation of programs and should be the number one concern of all staff and volunteer members. Anything that could involve a loss of resources is considered a risk. A **risk management plan** involves looking at potential problems before they develop, eliminating them if possible, or managing them through training, warning, controlling, and/or insurance; all of this is to prevent injury, illness, damage, or another kind of loss.

Risk management is the most important step in program development, and the risk management plan for the program must be carefully thought out and implemented with clear instruction and communication. The main focus of the plan is to protect the program participants and the organization and involves three essential components:

1. **Identification of Risks.** Each program should be examined carefully for conditions or situations that could present risks. Program staff and volunteer members should become aware of obvious risks as well as not-so-obvious risks. Risks can include potential losses, accidents, injuries, illnesses, health threats, or damages. For example, a service learning project that includes cleaning up a section of the shoreline at a lake could involve the risk of being around water as well as potentially dangerous materials along the shore.

2. **Evaluation of Risks.** All risks are relative in terms of importance, and two questions can be asked in determining this:

   — What is the probability that the risk will develop into an accident, injury, loss, or damage of some kind?

   — If a loss of some kind occurred, how severe could it be?

3. **Handling Risk.** There are essentially three ways to handle risk:

   — *Prevention (Avoidance).* One of the first and most important areas of managing risks is to match participants with appropriate experiences. Following that, participant orientation, training, and appropriate communication and supervision are keys to preventing and avoiding risk (Russell & Jamieson, 2008).

   — *Risk Reduction.* Examples of risk reduction include clearly defined and communicated safety rules and well-thought-out procedures, including emergency procedures. In the case of the shoreline clean-up, having water safety equipment readily available, including life jackets, and advising participants to stay away from potentially dangerous cliffs or deep areas of the water would be examples of effective risk reduction approaches.

   — *Risk Retention or Transfer.* This refers to how a loss will be handled should it occur. In other words, which entity is responsible for the loss and responsible for payment of any damages (Van der Smissen, 1990)?

There are a number of forms to be considered in various stages of program activities and throughout the risk management process. The organization's legal counsel must review all written forms. Some examples of forms are included below:

— **Agreements** should be written between the organization and other community organizations that are involved with the program activity or where the activity may be conducted. This is done so that there is a clear understanding of expectations and roles between the sponsoring organization, the participant, and the community organization to which the service is provided, or for which an activity is conducted.

— **Participant Agreements.** These forms can be used to document that the participant understands that risks might be involved in the activity, agrees to abide by set safety rules, and agrees to perform as trained or instructed. These forms are also referred to as *Assumption of Risk Agreements.*

— **Waivers/Releases.** These two terms are often used interchangeably. Ordinarily, these forms state that the participant agrees not to hold the organization responsible if a loss of resource should occur. This kind of form is only valid if it is signed by an adult, and parents/guardians **can never legally sign the rights of children away (under the legal age of majority).**

— **Insurance.** Maintaining effective insurance coverage is the standard way of handling risk to prevent excessive or even devastating financial loss to an organization or entity. Insurance policies should be checked carefully to determine coverage prior to each program or activity.

Managing and keeping risk to a minimum and being certain that liabilities are adequately covered through insurance should be the highest priority of each and every staff and volunteer member of the organization. Once risk management policies have been established by the organization, each individual **should make every effort to follow the risk management policies relating to program development and other activities.**

Managing risk is a fluid and ever-changing process, and risk management procedures should be reviewed periodically to keep them up-to-date. Experts in the field of risk management, legal counsel, as well as key board and staff members should be involved in the development and periodic review of risk management procedures. Further information on liability, risk management, and insurance relevant to nonprofit organizations can be found in Chapter 7 of this text. Additionally, the following references are suggested: *Leadership in Recreation and Leisure Service Organizations* (1999) by Christopher R. Edginton, Susan D. Hudson, and Phyllis M. Ford; and *Legal Liability and Risk Management for Public and Private Entities* (1990) (Vol. 2) by B. Van der Smissen.

Task 9—Marketing and Promoting Programs. Bagozzi (1975) defines marketing as the facilitation of some form of exchange. Defined as such, marketing is an important process that can link nonprofit organizations with entities within their environment. These entities can include program participants, donors, governments, media, service collaborators, and others. Marketing is a vital process in a nonprofit organization because (1) the success of marketing campaigns often determines whether or not the organization will thrive; (2) it is not an optional process, whether it is done amateurishly or professionally, it inevitably will occur in some form; and (3) the exchange concept signifies that there is more to marketing than communication and that advantageous exchanges of something of value also occur (Andreasen & Kotler, 2008).

In the context of nonprofit organizations, the something of value is usually a type of community service offered to the public. In conjunction, individual members of the community have something of value to offer nonprofit organizations: their membership and participation in programs. These individuals may also serve as volunteers from time to time, so there is an exchange of value when the organization needs assistance and offers the opportunity for individuals to assist through their specific expertise and involvement. Anytime two parties like this have something that might be of value to each other it is referred to as a **market exchange.** The process that brings these two parties together is usually referred to as **marketing** or **promotion** (Hardy, 1984). The marketing and/or promotion committee of the board of directors should be involved in this process and should be very helpful in developing strategies.

Marketing and promotion are very important steps in the program development process, since programs are of little importance unless they are joined with individuals who need or desire to participate. In order to understand how individuals become attracted to particular programs, it is important to look at something commonly referred to as the four *Ps*, or the **marketing mix** (Wolf, 1999; Weis & Muller, 2015):

— **Product.** One of the most important elements in the marketing mix is the product and the quality of the product. In nonprofit organizations this typically means a program or service. In order for a program or service to be desirable, it must meet or exceed the expectations of the participants for them to be willing to pay for and participate in it. Staff members focusing on developing programs that individuals need, want, and desire and then ensuring that those programs are of the highest quality possible helps to effect strong and continued program participation. The reputation of the organization and of the staff is another important consideration in order for the product to be successful. Since people often select programs from organizations with a history of success and quality, this may be the most important consideration in product selection.

— **Promotion.** Some of the best programs are often *best-kept secrets* as well when they are not promoted aggressively and effectively. Promotional material for programs should obviously be directed toward potential program participants, but it should also be directed toward other members of the public who may become interested in the organization as volunteers, potential sponsors, on in some other capacity. It is important to remember that some of the best potential program participants include current members. One of the most successful forms of promotion is to current members, and this is referred to as **market penetration**, since the promotional activities are designed to further penetrate an already established group. *This group is also an excellent group to ask to convey program information to others.* Promoting programs to individuals who are not already members of the organization is called **market development** and can also be a very successful process. Making promotional material available to target groups that have a high probability of participation and providing similar promotional material to groups that are less likely to become involved is referred to as the **80/20 principal.** In other words, significant time, energy, and money may be spent on getting results that can be counted on in a big way while also spending time, energy, and money on lesser results, because those results are also important. For example, meager results may occur by spending a good deal of time and money to place flyers promoting programs for children on the windshields of cars in a local mall parking lot. The same and possibly less money could be spent on flyers that are delivered directly to children at the local schools, churches, or youth organizations. Both methods can be successful, but one will be more successful and cost less and should be given a higher priority. There are a number of ways to promote program opportunities:

▶ **Flyers.** Flyers need to be created that are attractive and appealing. They should contain appropriate information, graphics, and have some *open space* to make them easier to read and more appealing. Flyers should answer standard questions, such as (1) *What* is going to happen during this activity and *why?* (2) W*here* will the activity occur? (3) *Who* is organizing the activity? (4) *How* will it benefit the program participants? (5) *How much* will it cost? (6) *What* is the date and time(s) of the activity? (7) *Is there anything* the program participant should do in preparation for the activity? (8) Is *transportation* available for the activity? Any other questions that are applicable to upcoming events should also be answered. Graphics appropriate to the activity should be added, and sometimes a **registration form** may need to be added with spaces for appropriate information about when participants must register for an activity. Colored paper can be eye-catching and add to the appeal of a flyer. Most local printing companies can enlarge flyers to poster size when necessary. Flyers should be posted in highly accessible places well in advance of an activity, typically three weeks to a month. More advanced notice may be required for some programs. Members can be helpful in posting and passing out flyers in their neighborhoods, schools, or places of work. Contests and prizes for volunteers who bring participants in for program activities can also be effective. An example of a program flyer can be found in Figure 5.4 on following page.

▶ **Public Service Announcements (PSAs).** Promotional announcements should be provided to local newspapers and television and radio stations with information regarding upcoming services and program opportunities. Including local media in the overall marketing and promotion strategies is an excellent way to promote opportunities and most media organizations are more than willing to assist in promoting community activities. It can also be advisable to include a member of the local media as a **media sponsor** for a program. As a media sponsor a radio station, for example, might agree to do some extra on-air promotional spots and a live segment on the day of the activity. In return, the organization could mention the radio station as one of the sponsors on flyers, t-shirts (if there are any), and in public service announcements. The chances of an organization's programs being included in newspaper and radio spots depend on the excitement generated around a particular activity, the reputation the organization has for providing community services, and the relationships that have been developed with members of the media. The same type of appropriate information should be included in the public service announcement that would be included in a flyer (on the following page). An example of a public service announcement is included in Figure 5.5 (on page 203).

Figure 5.4

Promotional Flyer

MAKE A DIFFERENCE
in the life of a
Senior Citizen

You can make a difference in the lives of senior citizens in our community by joining the program at the Morganfield Boys and Girls Club. The Boys and Girls Club is located at 1618 Seawall Dr., behnd the Sourthwest Cinema.

The team program participants meet Thursday evenings from 7–8 p.m. to plan the project beginning April 19.

The project includes recreational activities, crafts, health and fitness, and joint service outings. The project will last 6 months culminating with a big splashdown pool and pizza party.

There is no program fee, but you must be between the ages of 13–17 and be a mamber of the Boys and Girls Club.

Call today for more information: Stefani Dowell,

762-3838

Morganfield Boys and Girls Club

©Roger Weis

Figure 5.5

Public Service Announcement

Morganfield
Boys and Girls Club
1618 Seawall Dr.
Farmington, DE 22904
Phone: 277-762-3808
E-MAIL: **MBCGA@ORG.COM**

N E W S   R E L E A S E

(For Immediate Release)

The Morganfield Boys and Girls Club is proud to announce the Teens for Seniors program beginning Thursday, April 19, 7–8 p.m., in the club facility located at 1618 Seawall Dr. just behind the Southwest Cinema. This program will involve teens between the ages of 13–17 spending quality time with senior citizens in local nursing homes and the community seniors center. The program will consist of recreational activities, arts and crafts, health and fitness activities, and a joint service project. The 6-month-long project will conclude with a huge splashdown pool & pizza party at the Morganfield Boys and Girls Club swimming pool. There is no cost for the program, but you must be a member of the Morganfield Boys and Girls Club. For more information on the program and membership into the Boys and Girls Club, contact Stefani Dowell at 762-3808.

©Roger Weis

- ▶ **Displays, Exhibits, and Demonstrations.** Displays are generally two-dimensional, while exhibits are typically three-dimensional, and both can serve as a great way to let the public know about upcoming events as well as about the organization in general. They can be used to attract program participants, volunteers, donors, or other interested parties to the organization. A simple display could be a flyer in the form of a *tent* left on the table of a business, school, doctor's office, or other appropriate location. A more sophisticated display might include a Velcro board with attractive materials attached. An exhibit could include some of the equipment used in various programs, such as lifesaving apparatuses, and can be displayed appropriately on tables or floors. Demonstrations are a more dynamic approach and can include past program participants demonstrating something they have learned or experienced or it could be the program leader(s) demonstrating an aspect of the upcoming activities. Demonstrations should be rehearsed in order for them to be successful.

- ▶ **Newsletters.** Businesses, service associations, and other organizations will sometimes let nonprofit organizations include program activity information in their monthly, quarterly, or biannual newsletters for free. This not only assists the nonprofit organization, but it also provides an additional service to their members. By using publishing software or obtaining sponsors, nonprofit organizations can also develop their own newsletters, which can become excellent outlets for program and service information.

- ▶ **Advertising.** It may sometimes be necessary for nonprofit organizations to pay for advertisements in local newspapers and on radio and television stations. Media organizations typically assist the nonprofit organization with content and layout and often provide advertising for a reduced rate. Many media organizations will also provide advertising if they sponsor a particular event or they may provide a **gift-in-kind**, which means that the advertising is the media's way of contributing to the nonprofit organization.

- ▶ **Personal Contact.** One of the most effective ways of letting the public know what is coming up programmatically is by word of mouth. People who have had good experiences within an organization often willingly and voluntarily tell others about program opportunities. A more formal way of communicating program information is through a **speaker's bureau** made up of staff members and/or volunteers who present program information at club and organizational meetings. This process is an excellent way to provide program information as well as to recruit volunteers and financial support.

- ▶ **Informational Packets.** Information in the form of packets, brochures, or newsletters can often be left with the local Chamber of Commerce, United Way, Better Business Bureau, and other key places throughout a community where families and businesses that are new to the community can find out about the organization.

► **Website.** Creating and maintaining a website with current program and organizational information gives both members and prospective members quick access to opportunities within an organization. Promoting the website through informational packets, flyers, signs, and any other means available will provide the organization with a great deal of exposure.

► **Social Networking.** By incorporating Facebook, Twitter, and Instagram for example, organizations can promote events by posting information and inviting individuals to join groups in an effort to keep informed on activities, special offers, volunteer opportunities, internships, and even career possibilities. Social networking can be a quick and easy way to promote just about anything an organization wishes to promote.

Designing and implementing promotional material and promotional campaigns is often done by staff members in association with volunteers who possess expertise in marketing and promotion. Most nonprofit organizations have a board committee or group of volunteers created with the primary purpose of promoting the organization, program activities, and any other services. When effectively designed and implemented, promotional activities can be both fun and rewarding.

— **Price.** Price is a significant aspect in the selection process of choosing a particular program, and if all things are equal, price can be the determining factor. Generally speaking, individuals select the product, service, or program that is the least expensive if quality and other factors are fairly equal. However, cost is sometimes associated with value, and a program must be perceived to have *real value* in order to be desirable. So it is important for an organization to keep cost at a minimum in order to be competitive and be cost-effective for its members, while establishing a sense that the program is of *real value*. The cost of the program must also fit into the budgetary requirements established for programs. Staff members of nonprofit organizations usually set pricing for programs, sometimes with input from board members, and with the approval of the board of directors. Organizations with national and/or regional affiliations often receive assistance in setting fair and effective prices. Most nonprofit organizations set up scholarships, a sliding scale system, and/or payment plans for individuals who qualify for financial assistance.

— **Place.** The location of the facility or space where programs or services are offered is a significant consideration. The location must first be accessible to the targeted group of potential participants. Sometimes this means making programs and services *outreach* activities that are delivered to the targeted group through mobile or satellite units. The facility or space must be a desirable location for programs and services and, above all else, it must be clean and safe and be perceived as clean and safe by the community. Program space must also adhere to local health, safety, environmental, and fire codes.

Promoting programs and services for a nonprofit organization is a vital and exciting aspect of program development and must be well thought out, comprehensive, and focused both on the present and the future. Organizations with an eye toward quality, which are effective at program and service promotion, are generally successful in attracting participants, volunteers, and financial support.

Task 10—Program or Project Budget. Successful nonprofit organizations require a **program** or **project budget** prepared in advance of each activity. This should be a separate budget from the **operating budget**, the budget the organization uses to operate on for a **fiscal** or financial year, but it folds into the operating budget. The program budget includes a total of the **estimated expenses** and a total of the **estimated income** or **revenue.** Estimated expenses include any projected costs for a specific program. These expenses might include such items as supplies and materials, equipment, postage, food, travel, and personnel hired just for a specific program. Estimated income would include any fees or contributions that are received for the use of a specific program. Estimated expenses and income can be summarized on a PPW such as the one in Figure 5.2.

Programs may be projected to have a **gain**, which means there is more income projected than expenses, or to have a **deficit**, which means the expenses are projected to exceed the income. Deficits are almost always listed in parentheses. Programs are usually planned to realize a gain or at least to break even, but some programs are considered so important they will continue to be implemented by an organization with the idea that the money will be made up in some other way. Once a program is completed there is a place on the PPW (see Figure 5.2) to include the **actual income** as well as the **actual expenses** and a space for the **actual gain** or **deficit.** This provides staff and board members with financial information regarding each program. For instance, the Teens for Seniors program mentioned previously might have an income based on projected sponsorships and expenses projected on the basis of planned activities. This would provide some budgetary guidelines for the program staff to work with. The actual income and expenses would be listed once the program was completed and would provide much-needed financial information for the program (See Figure 5.6).

Figure 5.6

Program or Project Budget

Program Budget for Teens for Seniors

	Income	Expenses	Gain/Deficit
Estimated	$500	$300	+ $200
Actual	$580	$380	+ $200

©Roger Weis

Income and expenses can be broken down further on a separate ledger for a detailed analysis of costs versus revenue. Recording expenses and revenues for each program on the PPW as well as in a ledger also provides financial information if and when similar programs are considered in the future.

Some organizations also keep an accounting of how much time professional and volunteer staff members spend with specific programs, along with how much overhead expense, such as utilities and rent, is incorporated in each program. This is sometimes referred to as **indirect** or **functional** cost. It may also be considered in the "Input" part of the Program Outcome Model (Worth, 2017) which helps weigh the benefits of the program or "outcomes" with the "inputs."

Task 11—Walk-Through/Rehearsal. Before the actual implementation of any program or activity, it can be a good idea to do a visual and/or physical walk-through or rehearsal. This provides the program committee a chance to visualize and prepare for most aspects of the program, such as where equipment is to be set and where staff and volunteer members are to be stationed. It provides the committee with the opportunity to estimate spatial needs and examine equipment, materials, and supplies. A walk-through allows committee members an opportunity to review checklists and to become familiar with the layout of the program areas. Most importantly, it provides them with time to review the risk management plan and to be certain all aspects of the plan are in place.

Task 12—Implementation and Supervision. The implementation step is the time in which the program or activity actually begins. The plans and steps that have been developed up to this date provide a structure and some guidelines on how to proceed with the program or activity. This is the time to follow carefully developed plans, monitor the progress of each aspect of the program, and make changes if necessary. Almost no program goes exactly according to plan, and ingenuity and flexibility are necessary character traits if and when things go awry.

Determining which leadership or supervisory style to adopt with specific programs is a lifelong endeavor (see Chapter 2). Studies indicate there is really no ideal leadership style for a given program (Edginton & Ford, 1985), which means the leadership or supervisory style depends on the circumstances, the maturity of the staff and volunteers, and other dynamics that are involved with each activity. It means that individuals in leadership positions must develop leadership and management skills and knowledge and be flexible enough to incorporate appropriate concepts and actions when necessary. For instance, incorporating the Tri-Dimensional Leader Effectiveness Model (Situational Leadership), described in Chapter 2, Figure 2.4, as a supervisory strategy allows a supervisor to be flexible and lead/manage differently under different circumstances. The same thing can be said of Collaborative Leadership, discussed in Chapter 2 along with Comprehensive Leadership, which is also outlined in Figure 2.6.

Good nonprofit organizations encourage leadership and management training for administrative program staff. These organizations typically provide training in the form of workshops, seminars, and conferences, sometimes offered as in-service opportunities. Some nonprofit organizations also support advanced, formal educational opportunities by offering financial assistance for tuition and/or rewards for advanced educational work (Weis & Gantt, 2009; Weis & Muller, 2015).

Task 13—Special Considerations. Staff and volunteer members should have training and should always be well prepared for special situations and individuals with special needs. Programs must be designed to meet the special needs of individuals, and often the diversity of individuals with special needs adds depth to program intent. Special needs may take the form of **medical problems,** such as diabetes, AIDS, or epilepsy. They could take the form of various **physical disabilities,** such as cerebral palsy and multiple sclerosis, or **psychological disorders** that include autism and psychosis, as examples. Severe **behavioral maladjustment** would include a condition such as attention deficit disorder (with hyperactivity). There are a number of **communication problems** that need to be considered, such as speech difficulties, hearing impairments, and language barriers (Weis & Long, 2011). Some of these conditions may require staff and volunteers with specific training and qualifications. Others may require a certain staff-to-member ratio, and even special materials and equipment. Policies and procedures for handling individuals with special needs must be in place prior to program development. These policies and procedures must be inclusive, fair, effective, and within legal guidelines. They must be reviewed and approved by the board of directors of the organization.

Another special consideration when developing programs is the issue of **abuse** and **neglect.** In the course of offering programs and services, nonprofit leaders sometimes encounter children, senior citizens, spouses, and others who may have been or are being abused or neglected. Some **characteristics** of individuals who have been abused may include (Weis & Long, 2011):

— Feelings of inadequacy
— Listlessness and depression
— Lack of joy and excitement
— Unexplained bruises and abrasions
— Difficulties with relationships
— Aggressiveness
— Reluctance to receive praise and/or physical affection
— Thin or emaciated appearance

It is important to note that there might be other characteristics to suggest abuse or neglect and that the presence of any of the characteristics above doesn't necessarily mean that abuse or neglect is occurring. However, if a program leader suspects abuse or neglect he or she should follow the guidelines listed below:

— Report the suspected abuse or neglect to a supervisor.
— The supervisor should contact the organization's director.

— The director may decide to gather further information if further information seems necessary. Oftentimes, however, immediate action is called for.
— If abuse or neglect is still suspected, it must be reported to the appropriate, local authorities as quickly as possible. In most instances, reporting possible abuse and neglect situations is a legal responsibility as well as being the right thing to do.
— An incident report should be completed documenting what occurred and what procedures were taken.
— Some organizations may require incidents of abuse and neglect be reported to a specific board member or committee.

If there is ever any question of abuse or neglect, it is imperative to follow the guidelines above and report suspected incident(s) without delay.

FINAL (EVALUATION) STAGE

The final stage of program development includes an effective and thorough evaluation process, which is important for a number of reasons: (1) it helps determine whether the program was successful and the program objectives were met; (2) the information is important in helping staff and volunteer members make constructive changes for the future; (3) it provides board members with the type of information important in determining if the organization is on the right track; (4) it gives program participants an opportunity to express their concerns, suggestions, and praise regarding activities that affect their lives; (5) the results may be reported to the media so that community members are kept abreast of the benefits of the organization; and (6) evaluation results are essential for accrediting bodies and financial sponsors, such as corporations or the United Way. This stage also includes the process of analyzing and reporting program results and making recommendations and changes for the future.

Task 14—Evaluation Process. There are essentially four activities that need to occur in an evaluation process (Edginton & Edginton, 1994):

— Determining which individual(s) should be involved in the process
— Determining what exactly needs to be evaluated
— Selecting the type(s) of evaluation
— Implementing the method(s) of evaluation

Which individuals should be involved in the evaluation process? There are a number of individuals who can and should be involved in the evaluation process. To begin with, the participants of the program are the primary individuals who need to be involved in the evaluation process because they are the individuals most affected by the program. If the participants are too young, or for some reason they are unable to respond to the evaluation, parents, guardians, or caretakers may be asked to assist. In addition to the participants, program staff, volunteers, collaborating agency members, sponsors, and anyone associated with the program can participate in the evaluation process.

What needs to be evaluated? Two major areas need to be measured regarding the success of the program to determine if the program met the program objectives and to what degree: **quantitative** measurements and **qualitative** measurements. In other words, did the program meet the numerical objectives, and did it make a difference and have a positive impact?

Numerical (quantitative) measurements could include the number of participants, the number of activities, and any financial objectives. Qualitative measurements help determine whether the program made a difference in specific areas such as knowledge, skills, health, and attitude.

In addition to providing information that helps to determine if objectives were met, evaluation processes can provide information regarding the overall quality of the staff, facilities, supplies, and materials. Other areas that can be examined include program accessibility and affordability, and any other aspect of a program that needs to be assessed.

Selecting the Type(s) of Evaluation. In general, there are two major types of evaluation. The first type can be incorporated at various stages of the program; the second type is used at the end of a program:

— **Formative Evaluation.** A formative evaluation can be implemented at various stages while a program is being implemented to help determine whether changes need to be made while activities are in process. The advantage of this type of evaluation is obvious: constructive changes can be made before the program ends. The disadvantage is that it is one more task that can be time-consuming and therefore difficult to include.

— **Summative Evaluation.** This type of evaluation is done at the end of the program and provides feedback to determine whether the program met its objectives, and it provides information for making changes to a program in the future. Incorporating a summative or final evaluation at the end of a program is simpler and less time-consuming, but the disadvantage is that it will not help address changes that may need to be made during the implementation of an activity.

Implementing Methods of Evaluation. Programs can and should be evaluated incorporating a number of different methods. Select methodology is discussed below:

— **Observations.** Observation can be a legitimate form of evaluation that provides the evaluator with personal and immediate information. Although not as objective and often not as formal as other methodologies, observation provides a sensory assessment that cannot be duplicated.

— **Interview.** Conducting interviews provides the evaluator with a broad range of information. Questions should be designed from general to specific, and flexibility should

Figure 5.7

Example Interview Questions

1. What did you think of the Teens for Seniors program?

2. Was the program beneficial? For whom?

3. What did you like best about the program? Least?

4. Was it offered at a convenient time?

5. Was the program accessible for you?

6. Were the trainers/counselors helpful?

7. What would you change about the program?

8. Would you recommend this program to others?

9. Is there anything else you would like to say about the program?

©Roger Weis

be built in to ask other questions based on the responses. Interviews can be done in person, via telephone and e-mail or any other viable way, and the issue of confidentiality should be addressed up-front. As an evaluation tool, interviews can be highly focused and valuable, but can be time-consuming. Example interview questions are listed in Figure 5.7.

The evaluator should remember to remain flexible and to insert other questions based on the responses of the interviewees.

— **Focus Group.** Recruiting several people together at the same time for interviews provides the evaluator with a broad range of information and a synergy that is difficult to duplicate with interviews. Again, questions should be designed from general to specific, and flexibility should be built in to ask other questions based on the responses of the participants. Questions can be patterned after the interview questions in Figure 5.7.

— **Evaluation Survey.** Providing program participants with a way to report their experiences and assuring anonymity with a survey increases the likelihood the responses will be objective and more honest (Russell & Jamieson, 2008). As with interviews and focus groups, questions should go from broad to specific and seek to assess any important aspect of a program. Questions can be turned into statements for use with the Likert Scale, and each statement should address only one aspect of the program. An example evaluation survey to be administered to the teenage participants is included in Figure 5.8 on the following page.

Figure 5.8

Example Evaluation Survey

Teens for Seniors Program

In order to help us evaluate the Teens for Seniors program and plan for future programs, we would like you to complete the following survey. The survey is anonymous and no one will know the result of your responses. When you have completed the survey, please drop it in the box marked "Surveys" on the table near the exit. Thank you for participating in the Teens for Seniors program and for completing the survey.

Indicate the number that reflects your response to each statement based on the following scale:

	1 Strongly Disagree	2 Undecided	3 Agree Strongly	4 Disagree	5 Agree
1. The Teens for Seniors program was effective.	☐	☐	☐	☐	☐
2. I am now more comfortable with senior citizens.	☐	☐	☐	☐	☐
3. The recreational aspects of the program were successful.	☐	☐	☐	☐	☐
4. The crafts aspect of the program was important.	☐	☐	☐	☐	☐
5. The health and fitness aspects of the program were effective.	☐	☐	☐	☐	☐
6. The joint service outings were successful.	☐	☐	☐	☐	☐
7. The trainers did a good job in preparing us.	☐	☐	☐	☐	☐
8. The meeting location was convenient.	☐	☐	☐	☐	☐
9. I would recommend the program to a friend.	☐	☐	☐	☐	☐

Comments/suggestions: _____

_____

_____

_____

_____

_____

— **Pre/Post Test or Survey.** Providing a pre-test to participants prior to a program and then providing the same test following a program is an excellent way of determining whether real changes and impact have been made (Russell & Jamieson, 2008). Knowledge, attitude, character, and skills are just a few areas that can be tested with a pre/post test to determine change. The pre-test and post-test must have correlative identification such as numbers and be completed by the same individual and scored accordingly. An example pre/post is included in Figure 5.9 on the following page.

The pre/post test measures the participants' perception of knowledge, attitude, skills, and self-esteem regarding their experience and would be given to teenagers prior to the beginning of the program and again once the program was completed. The resulting scores will help the evaluators determine the degree of effectiveness of the program in a number of different areas.

Search Institute

Although founded in 1958 to assist in implementing and measuring programs that affect the lives of youth, it wasn't until 1990 that the Search Institute initiated the 40 Developmental Aspects or "gateway assets" that have to do with individuals developing academically, socially, and emotionally to prepare for the many changing implications of the twenty-first century (http://www.search-institute.org/). Although originally designed for youth, the 40 Gateway Assets has been altered to be used with a broad range of age groups. Experts often state it is the most used and cited organization when it comes to determining developmental needs and ways to measure programs to determine if they are meeting those needs.

Since support of nonprofit organizations is based more and more on outcome-based information, this is an invaluable website to incorporate in overall program assessment. It has been used for years by the Big Brothers Big Sisters organization to help determine the effectiveness of its mentoring programs. Research is currently underway in five African countries to determine the value of experiential education on the overall development of youth.

World Vision incorporates aspects of the website in determining their effectiveness and the Salvation Army is starting to integrate youth development principles and practices in its network and even Capital One is incorporating the gateway aspects in developing programs to educate youth, teens, and parents on life skills regarding finances. Search Institute maintains a great reference site for books and citations; they offer numerous seminars and workshops along with maintaining a "shop" in which they sell books, CDs, DVDs, posters, and other educational materials. Working with Search Institute could be a "sea change" in the way you initiate, implement, evaluate, and promote programs to many different types of groups.

Although this sort of measurement provides indicators that help determine if a program is helping to meet the mission of the organization there are other ways to determine if it is meeting indicators across other dimensions. Robert Kaplan and David Norton (1992) developed a concept referred to as the Balanced Scorecard which has four perspectives:

Figure 5.9

Example Pre/Post Test

Teens for Seniors Program
Pre/Post Test or Survey

In order to help us determine various changes that might have occurred during the Teens for Seniors program, we would like you to complete the following Pre/Post Test. Be certain that your Pre-Test number correlates with your Post-Test number and thank you for participating in the survey and the program.

Indicate the number that reflects your response to each statement based on the following scale:	1 Strongly Disagree	2 Undecided	3 Agree Strongly	4 Disagree	5 Agree
1. I am comfortable being around senior citizens.	☐	☐	☐	☐	☐
2 Senior citizens can make a positive contribution to their community.	☐	☐	☐	☐	☐
3. I am making a positive difference in my community.	☐	☐	☐	☐	☐
4. I am able to lead recreational activities with senior citizens.	☐	☐	☐	☐	☐
5. I am able to lead crafts activities with senior citizens.	☐	☐	☐	☐	☐
6. I can work effectively with senior citizens in making a difference in our community through service projects.	☐	☐	☐	☐	☐
7. I feel good about myself.	☐	☐	☐	☐	☐

Comments/suggestions: _____

_____

_____

_____

_____

_____

_____

©Roger Weis

1. **The financial perspective,** including financial performance indicators.

2. **The customer or client perspective,** including measures of customer satisfaction.

3. **The internal business perspective,** including measures of operational efficiency and quality.

4. **The innovation and learning perspective,** including measures of the organization's ability to adapt to changes in the environment (Murray, 2010, p. 446).

A variation of this and simplification of the Balanced Scorecard type of measurement was offered by Rob Paton (2003) specifically for nonprofit organizations that is referred to as the Dashboard. The Dashboard proposes two questions: (1) Does the program/project reach its intended purpose and, (2) is the organization operating efficiently?

Effective evaluation processes can be very helpful in determining whether or not programs are meeting their objectives and whether they are quality programs. The process also encourages communication between program staff members, volunteer members, and participants and provides helpful program information for the future. This information can also be used to develop funding, as a part of the promotion process, and for marketing processes as well.

Task 15—Record and Report Results. Evaluation results need to be assimilated and recorded on the Program Planning Worksheet and maintained in a permanent file for future reference. This can provide invaluable information for future programs. The results of each program should be discussed by the program and volunteer staff members and with the participants when applicable. Program evaluation results are sometimes reviewed by the program committee of the board of directors and even by the entire board of directors. They may also be used as a part of personnel evaluations. The results of successful programs should also be reported to the media and included in the organization's promotional material.

Task 16—Formulate Recommendations for Future Program. Program staff and volunteer members, along with a select group of program participants should discuss recommendations for future programs based, in part, on the resulting program evaluations. Recommendations for future programs will provide insight for the focus of programs and can be recorded on the Program Planning Worksheet and filed for future reference.

Providing programs that *meet and exceed* the expectations of customers and provide them with positive outcomes is both exciting and rewarding, and it requires a good deal of expertise in planning, implementation, and evaluation. This customer-centered/benefits approach to program development provides a step-by-step planning process intended to offer guidance and support for program development. Work tasks can be divided up into program planning steps. As mentioned earlier in this chapter, programs can and often do change directions in all stages for one reason or another, and flexibility and innovation are required characteristics for leaders in the nonprofit area. A simplified, simulated program plan is included in Figure 5.10.

Figure 5.10

Simulated Program Plan

Date _09_ / _25_ / _17_

Name of Organization _____ Morganfield Boys and Girls Club _____

Name of Program/Project ____ Teens for Seniors ____

Program Coordinator_____ Julie Weston ____

Program Committee Members:

Name	Address	Phone #	e-mail address
1. Julie Weston	1407 Wall St.	762-4791	j.weston@b&gca.org
2. L. W. Perdue	131 Camile Dr.	762-0101	lw.perdue@bas.org
3. Vivian Perdue	7229 Opal St.	753-1098	v.perdue@bas.org
4. Virginia Kenova	1413 Carol Dr.	759-2038	vkenova@lol.org

Program Objectives The Teens for Seniors program provides teenagers in the Morganfield area opportunities to assist senior citizens attending the Westview Day Care program. Teens will be trained to participate with seniors in social, cultural, service, and recreational activities. Intended objectives include:

— A minimum of 10 teenagers involved in a program with a minimum of 25 senior citizens meeting once a week for activities

— Improved inter-generational understanding

— Increased flexibility on the part of senior citizens

— Decreased depression on the part of senior citizens

— Enhanced self-esteem of teenagers and senior citizens

— Increased sense of responsibility and caring on the part of teenagers

— Improved teamwork, communication, recreation, socialization, and leadership skills on the part of the teenagers

Estimated Direct Income $340	**Estimated Direct Expenses** $500 (sponsorship)	**Gain (Deficit)** $160
Actual Direct Income $270	**Actual Direct Costs** $480	**Gain (Deficit)** $210

Action Steps/Work Tasks	Person(s) Responsible	Completion Dates
1. Formulate Committee	Weston	October 1
2. Conduct Needs Assessment	V. Perdue	October 10
3. Review Developmental Theories, Issues, and Values	Weston	October 11
4. Determine Program Objectives	Committee	October13
5. Develop Program Concept and Format	Weston	October 14
6. Evaluate Resources	Committee	October15
7. Identify Potential Program Risks	Committee	October 20
8. Prioritize Program Risks	Committee	October 20
9. Develop Plan for Handling Risks	Committee	October 21
10. Evaluate Insurance Coverage	Weston	October 22
11. Prepare Participant Waiver Forms	Committee	October 23
12. Meeting to Develop Plan for Promoting Program	Committee	October 25
13. Develop Flyers & PSAs	L. W. Perdue	October 26

Figure 5.10

Simulated Program Plan (Page 2)

Action Steps/Work Tasks	Person(s) Responsible	Completion Dates
14. Develop Promotional Event	V. Perdue	October 27
15. Establish Program Budget	L. Perdue	November 1
16. Plan for Special Considerations	Weston	November 5
17. Post Flyers	L. W. Perdue	November 9
18. Release PSAs	L. W. Perdue	November 9
19. Conduct Promotional Event	V. Perdue	November 9
20. Walk-Through/Rehearsal	Whole Committee	November 10
21. Participants Sign Waiver Forms	V. Perdue	November 15
22. Implement and Monitor Program	Whole Committee	December 1
23. Conduct Formative Evaluations	V. Perdue	January 15
24. Conduct Final Evaluations	V. Perdue	March 1
25. Record Results on PPW	Kenova	March 5
26. Report Results to Board and Media	Weston	March 6
27. Formulate and Record Future Recommendations (PPW)	Whole Co	March 15

Evaluation Results The Teens for Seniors program was evaluated primarily through observation and a final evaluation.

A summary of the evaluation administered to the teenage participants follows:

Summary of Evaluation
Number of Respondents: 10

Statement	Average Score
1. The Teens for Seniors program was effective.	4.9
2. I am more now more comfortable with senior citizens.	4.5
3. The recreational activities were successful.	4.3
4. The crafts aspect of the program was important.	4.4
5. The health & fitness aspects of the program were effective.	4.6
6. The joint service outings were successful.	4.8
7. The trainers did a good job in preparing us.	4.1
8. The meeting location was convenient.	4.7
9. I would recommend the program to a friend.	5.0

Comments/Suggestions: I loved the program and would do it again!

Need more time for preparation.

Training could have been more comprehensive.

Recommendations for Future Programs

Based on observation, informal interviews, and the final evaluation, it seems that the program basically met the objectives and in some cases exceeded expectations. Although requiring a good deal of resources in terms of personnel time, it is recommended that the program be repeated annually or more often if appropriate. Suggestions for changes include a longer preparation time and a more thorough training period.

©Roger Weis

A PLAN TO IMPROVE CUSTOMER SERVICE

In addition to providing the best programs possible, organizations must also strive to deliver the best **customer service** as well (Russell & Jamieson, 2008). Customer service is anything that helps a customer or member realize the full value of a product or service (Davidow & Uttal, 1989). This could include providing effective information and assistance whenever and however it is needed. Davidow and Uttal (1989) developed a six-point plan to address customer service:

1. **Devise a service strategy.**

   This involves understanding what customers or members expect then developing services to match those expectations. This helps an organization prepare plans for many different scenarios.

2. **Encourage top management to set examples.**

   It is important that top level management walk the talk and have a genuine passion for great customer service and demonstrate that passion every day. It needs to be understood that customer service is everyone's job not just those working on the line.

3. **Concentrate on motivating and training employees.**

   The first step in this part of the process is to hire the best personnel possible then train them in the most effective ways of solid customer service for the organization. Always acknowledge personnel when they succeed with good customer service strategies and activities.

4. **Design services that make good customer service possible.**

   The kind of services that will most often be needed can be anticipated and a system designed to meet needs efficiently and effectively (Weis & Muller, 2015). Constantly reviewing customer service strategies helps an organization stay in touch with customer and membership needs.

5. **Invest in service infrastructure**.

   To be successful, organizations must invest in the kinds of resources that will help employees deliver the best customer service possible. Computer hardware and software need to be updated constantly with a good support system and training readily available. Leaders must consistently assess that the infrastructure matches the needs of customers.

6. **Monitor achievement of customer service goals.**

   Continuous monitoring of the success of customer service is essential in being certain that customer service goals are being met. The monitoring process can take the form of focus groups, individual interviews, and evaluation surveys for example and should be a priority of any organization that wants to succeed. This kind of information can be essential for improving processes and activities and maintaining a strong base of customer respect and support.

SUMMARY

Programs should be designed to meet the objectives and goals of the organization and to meet and exceed the expectations of the customers while providing them with positive outcomes. This customer-centered/benefits approach to program development requires that staff and volunteer members be committed to the organization, to quality programs, and to the customers or members. Programs must be designed to meet and exceed the general standards and expectations of the constituents.

Program development can be divided into three interrelated stages: (1) Initial (Planning) Stage, (2) Middle (Planning/Implementation) Stage, and (3) Final (Evaluation) Stage (PIE). Each of these stages can be divided into specific steps that can be modified or simplified depending on the circumstances. The sequence of steps can also be changed if necessary.

The Initial Stage of program development is important because it builds the foundation for later stages. This stage includes selecting a program committee to organize the project, surveying membership needs, reviewing developmental theories and relevant issues including values and character education, and then determining objectives for the program. Once program objectives have been decided, a program concept and format must be developed to ensure the objectives are achieved. This stage is concluded once resources necessary for the program, such as personnel, time, space, and money, are evaluated.

The Middle Stage of program development begins with the most important step in the whole planning process, developing a system to keep all risks involved in any program to an absolute minimum. The next step in this stage is to create a comprehensive marketing plan for generating promotional material. Another step in this stage is to design a Program Budget in order to record the estimated and actual expenses and the income for each individual program.

Conducting a walk-through or rehearsal for each program allows the program staff to visualize and prepare for most aspects of a program. Understanding leadership and supervisory styles is also important, so nonprofit leaders can incorporate appropriate concepts and actions when necessary in supervising others in program delivery. And finally, being trained and prepared for special situations and individuals with special needs is vital to the overall success of program development.

In the Final Evaluation Stage, the program must be evaluated to help determine whether it was successful and met its objectives. This information can also be helpful for staff and volunteer members in making changes for future programs as well as for sponsoring organizations to determine if their sponsorship is worthwhile. Some ways programs can be evaluated are through observation, interviews, focus groups, and surveys.

Program results should be recorded on the Program Planning Worksheet and reported as is appropriate. Reports might be made to a board of directors or to a committee within the board. Other reports may be presented to sponsoring entities, to the news media, and they may be included in the organization's communications materials. It is particularly important that recommendations for the future be recorded and kept readily available for future programming staff.

This chapter addressed, in part, the competencies of the Nonprofit Academic Centers Council (NACC) including those of Nonprofit Program Planning, Nonprofit Marketing, and Nonprofit Risk Management.

REFLECTION AND APPLICATION

1. How can the concept *customer-centered/benefits approach* help you in planning effective programs?

   _____

   _____

   _____

   _____

   _____

2. What are the advantages to this kind of approach?

   _____

   _____

   _____

   _____

   _____

3. Describe the key parts of a program objective.

   _____

   _____

   _____

   _____

4. What is the difference between a program concept and a program format?

   _____

   _____

   _____

   _____

5. How does a program budget fit into the fiscal operational budget?

_____

_____

_____

_____

_____

6. Design a needs-assessment plan to develop a program scenario.

7. After developing a program scenario, design a risk management plan.

8. Using the same scenario, develop a comprehensive marketing plan.

9. Finally, develop a plan to evaluate the program.

10. Develop a list of nonprofit leaders to see about shadowing the staff during a day a program is implemented. Describe what you experienced:

_____

_____

_____

_____

_____

_____

_____

_____

_____

_____

_____

_____

_____

_____

_____

_____

_____

REFERENCES

Andreasen, A. R. & Kotler, P. T. (2008). *Strategic Marketing for Non-Profit Organizations,* (7th ed.) Upper Saddle River, NJ: Pearson

Bagozzi, R. P. (1975). Marketing as exchange. *Journal of Marketing, 39:*32–39.

Cobb, A. T. (2012). *Leading project teams: The basics of project management and team leadership.* Thousand Oaks, CA: Sage.

Davidow, W. H., & Uttal, B. (1989). *Total customer service: The ultimate weapon.* New York: HarperCollins.

Edginton, C. R., Edginton, S. R., Hanson, C. J., & Hudson, S. D. (1998). *Leisure programming: A service-centered and benefits approach.* St. Louis, MO: Wm. C. Brown.

Edginton, S. R., & Edginton, C. R. (1994). *Youth programs: Promoting quality services.* Champaign, IL: Sagamore Publishing.

Edginton, C. R., & Ford, P. M. (1985). *Leadership in Recreation and Leisure Service Organizations.* New York: John Wiley and Sons.

Edginton, C. R., Hanson, C. J. & Edginton, S. R. (1992). *Leisure Programming: Concepts, Trends and Professional Practice* (2nd ed.). Dubuque, IA: Wm. C. Brown.

Edginton, C. R., Hudson, S. D., & Ford, P. F. (1999). *Leadership in recreation and leisure service organizations.* Champaign, IL: Sagamore Publishing.

Farrell, P., & Lundegren, H. M. (1991). *The Process of Recreation Programming: Theory and Technique.* (3rd ed.). Venture Pub.

Hardy, J. M. (1984). *Managing for impact in nonprofit organizations.* Erwin, TN: Essex Press.

Kaplan, R. S., & Norton, D. (1992). Using the balanced scorecard as a strategic management system. *Harvard Business Review, 70(1).*

Kerzner, H. (2009). Blog. Retrieved from http://www.drharoldkerzner.com/blog/

Maslow, A. H. (1943). A theory of human motivation. *Psychological Review* July, 370–96.

Murray, V. (2010). Evaluating the effectiveness of nonprofit organizations. In D. O. Renz & Associates (Eds.). *The Jossey-Bass handbook of nonprofit leadership and management* (3rd ed.). San Francisco, CA: Jossey-Bass.

Paton, R. (2003). *Managing and measuring social enterprise.* Thousand Oaks, CA: Sage.

Russell, R., & Jamieson, L. (2008). *Leisure program planning and delivery.* Champaign, IL: Human Kinetics.

Van der Smissen, B. (1990). *Legal liability and risk management for public and private entities* (Vol. 2). Cincinnati, OH: Anderson.

Walton, M. (1998). *The Demming management model.* New York: Perigee.

Weis, R. M., & Gantt, V. W. (2009). *Knowledge and skill development in nonprofit organizations.* Peosta, IA: eddie bowers publishing co., inc.

Weis, R. M., & Long, R. F. (2011). *Leading and managing nonprofit organizations.* Peosta, IA: eddie bowers publishing co., inc.

Weis, R., & Muller, S. (2015). *Leading and managing nonprofit organizations.* Peosta, IA: eddie bowers publishing co., inc.

Wolf, T. (1999). *Managing a nonprofit organization.* New York: Prentice Hall.

Worth, M. J. (2017). *Nonprofit management: Principles and practice* (4th ed.). Thousand Oaks, CA: Sage Publications, Inc.

FINANCIAL PROCESSES AND FINANCIAL DEVELOPMENT

The role of financial resource development and management in successful nonprofit organizations continues to gain importance and appreciation as a result of a number of significant changes in the nonprofit sector. What started as one of the natural strategies through which people expressed their early voluntary spirit and organized to build the country, has become a measurable part of the gross domestic product, employment, and human services delivery system. The sector has grown into what many call the "third sector," taking its place of importance alongside of the for-profit business and government sectors of society.

What was once considered to be an afterthought or necessary evil, finding the money to pay the costs of voluntary actions, is now considered one of the most important elements of effective nonprofit sector leadership. Nonprofit programs once operated from a perspective that good work would naturally translate into sustainable funding. A lot has changed and continues to change nonprofit funding. Difficult economic times bring a pressure that can promote a **zero-sum** perspective that makes nonprofit leaders feel like they are competing with each other for a limited and shrinking pool of funds. Shifting political focus often accompanies economic challenges and can promote devolution of government relationships with human services. Government devolution is a complex process involving changes in regulation, funding, and service delivery. It is a shift in the responsibility for providing and funding services from government to the community (Weis & Muller, 2015). In some cases, if a profit can be generated, the business sector responds to the opportunity. However, for the vast majority of human service programs and services the nonprofit sector is the only system available to respond. The financial resources of the nonprofit sector are significantly less than those in government. So, the nonprofit sector needs the highest possible quality financial development and management to respond to the shift in funding support.

Nonprofit sector leaders recognize the critical intersection of the organization's successful response to community needs and the **public will** necessary to support and sustain the work. The case for sustainability is based on the value the community places on the services provided, regardless of the funding sources. The assumption is that if the services are valued, the financial resources will follow. While it may not always be the case, it is one basis upon which leadership is increasingly committed to demonstrating program value and effective **financial stewardship**. This framing of the role of financial resources in the nonprofit sector requires everyone working in the sector to have an appropriate level of related appreciation, understanding, and skills. For example, people working in the delivery of programs and services for large nonprofit organizations, at a minimum, need to be able to participate in program budget development and appreciate the role their programs play in building and maintaining public support for the organizations. A large proportion of the nonprofit sector is composed of small- to mid-sized organizations in which most staff members are required to play a range of financial roles that may include fundraising, budgeting development, and financial reporting, among other responsibilities. A lot of the detailed financial resource development and management work may be done by specialists, including bookkeepers, accountants, tax preparers, financial managers, etc. However, a successful career in the nonprofit sector, regardless of role, is supported by quality financial resource development and management skills and the ability to work effectively with specialists (Weis & Muller, 2015). Nonprofit leaders want staff who understand the importance of financial resource development and management and who have related skills to bring to the organization.

This chapter is dedicated to promoting a fuller appreciation and understanding of the role of financial resource development and management in the ongoing leadership and operation of nonprofit organizations. There are three major areas to consider in this chapter regarding fiscal matters: (1) financial management or budgeting, (2) financial processes or accounting, and (3) financial development or fundraising. The chapter will explore these three areas, how they relate, and how they are integrated with other aspects of organizational leadership and development.

FINANCIAL MANAGEMENT OF BUDGETING

Good nonprofit financial management involves an annual planning process that is typically a part of a five-year rolling plan for financing the organization. At the end of each year, the plan rolls forward one year so that at any given time the organization has a financial plan for the next five years. The financial plan describes how the organization will cover the cost of its operations. The term "budgeting" is often used to describe this planning process. The resulting **operating budget** is an organization's plan for the financial or **fiscal** year that specifies how much **income** or **revenue** it expects to generate and how much it anticipates it will cost in **expenses** to operate for the same period. A simplified "income and expense" operating budget is present in Figure 6.1.

Figure 6.1

Typical Nonprofit Operating Budget for a Fiscal Year

Income		Expenses	
Membership Fees	$95,000	Salaries	$ 93,000
Program Fees	27,000	Benefits	17,000
Special Events	20,000	Activity Supplies	14,000
United Way	15,000	Utilities	24,000
Foundation Grants	12,000	Facility Cost	10,000
Annual Campaign	25,000	Telephone Cost	9,000
Total	194,000	Postage	3,000
			23,000
			194,000

©Roger Weis

A fiscal year often aligns with the calendar year, from January 1 to December 31. Other fiscal years are chosen because the work of the organization aligns with other budget processes, like the traditional school year of September 1 to August 31, the typical government budgeting year of July 1 to June 30, or a different fiscal period dictated by another funding source like United Way or a grant making foundation. A nonprofit organization can select any dates for its fiscal year as long as it specifies these dates in its articles of incorporation and has a financial management system that allows it to track and report budget activity at any given time during the period (Weis & Muller, 2015).

As shown in Figure 6.1, the operating budget is generally divided into two major sections, **income** or **revenue** and **expenses.** These sections are often further divided into additional levels of detail by identifying **income categories** and **expense categories**. Each specific expense and income category is listed on a "separate line" with a certain dollar amount shown to the side, and for this reason these categories are referred to as **line items.** It is up to the organization to decide which line items (or categories) to include. For instance, in the expense section, all salaries may go in one line item and employee benefits may make up another. In the income section, all membership fees may be listed as one line item while program fees may make up another (Weis & Muller, 2015).

Developing a Budget

Budget development is the core of the financial planning process, and it is important to have specific guidelines to follow when developing the budget that will help support the organization for the coming fiscal year. Each nonprofit organization needs to develop its own budgeting guidelines, in alignment with the size and scope of the organization's finances, to most effectively engage the human resources available, and to complement the management and leadership approaches in practice. The following steps are recommended in preparing a budget and are derived in part from Wolf (1999); Weis & Muller (2015); and Zieltow, Hankin, and Seidner (2007):

Step 1: Develop a List of Expenses. Budgets need to be prepared months in advance of a fiscal year by the administrative staff, with input from the program staff and guidance from financial committee members of the board of directors. These individuals must consider and make a projection of all of the expenses necessary to operate the organization for a fiscal year.

Administrative staff members should (1) look at expenses from previous budgets to develop a sense of what costs have been in the past, (2) estimate any changes in those costs, and (3) envision future needs and what those needs will cost the organization to operate effectively. To be as accurate as possible, leaders should seek input from all staff members of the organization, as well as from board members, before making projections about expenses. Expenses should be estimated on the high side, with room for unexpected expenses should always be considered.

Step 2: Determine Sources of Revenue. Once a list of projected expenses is developed, a process follows to determine sources of income. Administrative leaders, with input from the program staff and guidance and approval from the financial committee of the board of directors, develop a list of sources of revenue to pay for the projected expenses. This can be accomplished by (1) looking at revenue sources from previous budgets to get an idea of potential areas of income generation and by (2) looking at new areas of financial development. Many organizations have a financial development committee comprised of staff and board members whose job it is to generate potential revenue sources. Income projections should be kept on the low side, and allowances must be made for possible discrepancies in income projections and lower-than-projected actual income outcomes.

Step 3: Comparing Expenses With Revenue. Once the projected revenue and expense lists have been developed, it is time for the administrative staff and financial committee members of the board to determine whether the projected revenue will cover projected expenses. If the projected revenue covers or exceeds the projected list of expenses, then the budget could move forward toward the approval phase of the budgeting process. If, on the other hand, the projected revenue does not cover the projected list of expenses, then a number of considerations can be undertaken.

First of all, each administrative and program need should be evaluated carefully. After close scrutiny, some of the expenses may be eliminated, or at least the cost reduced. One way to do this would be through a process referred to as **zero-based budgeting** in which no historical base is recognized for expenses and each expense line begins with a clean slate. This process provides an opportunity to examine exactly what is needed to cover the cost of each organizational need. For instance, in looking at telephone costs, it could be advantageous to consider other, less expensive telephone service providers, as long as the service is still effective. A change in providers can save an organization hundreds or even thousands of dollars each year.

The same process could be used in hiring a consulting firm for accounting and bookkeeping processes or any number of other organizational operations, rather than maintaining full-time staff for these functions. Even though it is generally more time-consuming, zero-based budgeting can be very effective in eliminating unnecessary expenses and should be considered when balancing expenses with income. Although often efficient, it may also lead to some uncertainty if/when personnel expenses come into play. Another way to meet organizational costs would be to look at the revenue side of the budget to determine other ways to enhance or develop new income streams to cover expenses.

Step 4: Setting Administrative and Program Priorities. Once expense and revenue potential have been reviewed and assessed, organizational leaders should schedule a priority-setting session. This session should help in determining the need for specific programs and administrative operations. Several key questions need to be asked in this session:

1. Which programs are central to the purpose of the organization?

2. Which programs are cost-effective and how important is this consideration?

3. Which administrative operations are essential to the overall success of the organization, and which ones can be altered or eliminated, if any?

When these questions have been addressed thoroughly, organizational leaders will be better prepared to select the best path for the organization to pursue for the coming fiscal year.

Step 5: Adjust and Balance. Once projected expenses and revenue potential have been carefully examined and a list of priorities selected, the next step involves listing expenses and income figures on a budget sheet and balancing those figures. Generally speaking, the projected expense side of a budget should balance with the total figure for revenue. Each program may not be cost-effective, or even cover all of the expenses for the program, but the overall budget must balance.

The budget process so far has skewed the figures so that expenses are projected on the high side and revenue estimates are projected on the low side. If the budget actually ended up as projected, the "extra" money for a fiscal year could not be used as a form of profit to be used where needed in the organization. This money must be used within the organization in some manner, so that the expense side of the budget balances with the revenue side. This is often done by incorporating this money in a contingency or reserve fund that will be discussed later in this chapter.

Step 6: Budget Approval. Following the development of a budget, only the board of directors can approve the budget. This is often done by first having the finance committee of the board review a proposed budget and then forward their recommendation to the full board for final approval. Board members must be fully knowledgeable regarding any expenses that are to be incurred and confident about the revenue that is to be generated. Members should have an opportunity to ask questions about the legitimacy of any and all expenses and the accuracy and certainty of income projections. Board members are ultimately accountable for fiscal matters of an organization, and therefore they should challenge each line of the budget to be as certain as possible the organization is on a responsible fiscal path.

When they sign off on a budget, members of the board are exercising their fiduciary responsibility to set parameters for the budget and therefore for the operation of the organization and its programs and services. When the board votes to approve a budget, they are implicitly agreeing to a level of financial development necessary to sustain expenses for programs and administrative operations.

Step 7: Monitor and Amend. Once the budget has been approved and put into place, it must be continually monitored. A budget is only a carefully thought out fiscal projection for the coming year, and a number of things can and often do happen to warrant monitoring and sometimes alteration. It is important that key members of the staff and board monitor the budget at least on a monthly basis. It is also important that provisions are made to amend the budget when necessary and possible (Weis & Muller, 2015).

Most organizations have included in their constitution, charter, and/or bylaws policies as to when budget amendments can be made. Amending the budget once or twice a year provides an organization with some flexibility without necessarily going to extremes. Revisions should be carefully thought out and should reflect the changes that necessitated the revisions in the first place. "Revised budgets" must also be presented to, studied, and approved by the board of directors, as designated by the policies regarding budget revisions.

Project or Program Budget

Nonprofit organizations typically pursue their missions by delivering programs and services to the community. Developing a budget for each program or service is an important part of the overall financial management process and is referred to as **project or program budgeting**. A separate budget for each program allows the organization to estimate income and expense lines for each and then to analyze these income and expense lines once the program is completed. Allocating the right amount of financial and human resources to each program the organization provides links the budgeting process directly to the strategic planning. An organization with a high quality strategic plan has already done some of the work to create a program budget (Zietlow et al., 2007). This budgeting process is also known as **functional accounting**, or **cost center accounting** when referring to record-keeping procedures, and it allows an organization to assess income and costs on a project-by-project basis (Weis & Muller, 2015).

A program budget includes the **direct income** and **direct expenses** associated with conducting a specific program. For instance, CPR classes presented by the local American Red Cross require specialized instructor skills, equipment, and space rentals and are often paid for through a fee paid for by the participants. It is fairly simple to estimate the direct expense and income for these types of programs and to determine actual expenses, income, and gain or deficit once the classes are completed. It is a good practice to analyze program budgets once completed in order to continue to learn about the costs of related expenses and the level of interest and capacity or willingness to pay fees among the target populations. This practice helps program staff conduct effective budgeting over time.

The projected income and expenses, as well as the actual income and expenses of each program, can be placed on a Project or Program Budget (see Figure 6.2) and added or attached to a Program Planning Worksheet (Figure 5.2) with the total figures recorded on the worksheet. Quality budgeting involves formal commitments and guidelines to planning, implementing, reporting, and analyzing program budgets. In most nonprofit organizations, project or program budgets are combined in the development of the operating budget, which also includes the other expenses and income beyond the projects or programs (Weis & Muller, 2015).

Some nonprofit organizations require program budgets to include the management and support costs (administrative/overhead) that are associated with the conduct of each program, and the organization often devises a formula to determine these **indirect costs** for each program budget. Costs can be calculated for the percentage of staff time, space and utility allocation, marketing material development, phone service, and others designated as indirect costs to each program. This information provides leaders with an idea of the overall costs, direct and indirect, associated with each program and may help in determining the program's overall financial desirability.

Figure 6.2

Project or Program Budget

Direct Income		Direct Expenses	
Registration Fees	$13,000	Part-time Salaries	$4,000
Concession Fees	9,000	Materials and Supplies	3,000
T-shirt Sales	8,000	T-shirt Costs	5,000
Total	$30,000	Promotion	3,000
		Total	$15,000
			$30,000
			−15,000
		Gain/(Deficit)	$15,000

©Roger Weis

Project or program budgeting has a number of benefits:

1. It provides a detailed analysis of each program for the purpose of cost effectiveness and priority setting.

2. It helps determine the revenue-generating possibilities of each program.

3. It can be used as a tool to seek financial support from community service groups, foundations, and/or corporations if programs are determined to be important, but not necessarily cost-effective.

4. It provides leaders of organizations with a program-by-program analysis of specific budgets and tells them how the estimates and results fit into the overall budgeting process.

Along with measuring the quality results of programs, the budget may provide information that is helpful for using the **balanced scorecard** (Kaplan & Norton, 1992) as well as information if Rob Paton's (2003) **dashboard** is involved in determining the value of select programs.

Figure 6.3

Contingency/Reserve Fund

Income		Expenses	
Membership Fees	$430,000	Salaries	$520,000
Program Fees	270,000	Benefits	213,000
United Way	128,000	Materials/Supplies	119,000
Special Events	96,000	Contingency/Reserve	72,000
Total	$924,000	Total	$924,000

©Roger Weis

Contingency/Reserve Funds

The financial health of a nonprofit organization can be significantly impacted if there is a plan to generate excess income that can be used for unexpected needs or expenses—the contingency part—as well as for new equipment, renovations, or growth of any kind—the reserve part (Wolf, 1999) (Weis & Long, 2011). When heating units break down, roofs leak, and community outreach vans wear out, a contingency fund is vital to ensuring the continuation of needed programs, regardless of unexpected circumstances. Most organizations allocate a certain percentage, such as between 5–10% of their annual income to this fund, although it may be higher depending on the probability of need. This extra income is listed on the expense side of the budget and may be divided up as a contingency and a reserve fund or combined as in Figure 6.3.

Several factors need to be examined prior to creating a contingency/reserve fund (Weis & Long, 2011):

▸ **Probability of need.** The larger, more complex, and more facility/equipment-based an organization, the more possible flexibility in programs and the more repairs or replacements for facilities and equipment could be required.

▸ **Probability of growth.** The more probable some kind of growth is in the foreseeable future, the greater need for significant contingency/reserve funding sources.

▸ **Consistency of income or revenue.** The less consistent income predictability and reliability, the greater the need for contingency/reserve funds to maintain operations.

▸ **Cash-flow concerns.** Organizations also may experience cash-flow problems when bills need to be paid before there is adequate income. With a reasonable reserve fund, an organization can borrow from itself.

▶ **Relative stability of the organization.** If the organization is constantly changing leadership and/or is a relatively new organization, the fund should be larger to support unanticipated changes that may occur.

When an organization has adequate financial resources in the contingency fund, it should allocate the rest to a reserve fund that is kept in a carefully selected interest-bearing account, approved by the board of directors. A number of organizations maintain as much as 25–50% of a year's budget in the contingency fund, and others maintain a good deal more. Evidence of financial health is found in the thoroughness of planned contingency/reserve funds and the commitment the organization has to their long-term development.

Sometimes an organization's contingency/reserve funds become significantly large and may become a disincentive to funders and supporters, because it could look like the organization has more money than it needs. One way to manage this dynamic is to place a portion of these funds in an **endowment** which has special rules and restrictions. Generally speaking, only the interest generated from this kind of an account can be used for the designated purposes for which the endowment was established. This means that the principle will remain in perpetuity (forever) (Worth, 2017). With good management, it can also grow over time. Nonprofit organizations often establish endowments to support a portion of their ongoing operating budget to insure financial health when other sources of funding decline and/or to allow them to put a larger portion of their other funds into the delivery of programs and services. It is also common practice for endowments to be established to support particular programs that are important to the organization's mission but difficult to fund. The funds contained in endowments can be switched to other uses by an action of the board of directors, if and when it becomes necessary. However, effective financial management involves the establishment and long-term maintenance of endowments as a way of helping insure financial sustainability of the organization and its programs (Zietlow, Hankin, & Seidner, 2007).

Cash Flow

In the budgeting process, income and expense projections are made for an entire fiscal year, as a part of the broader or rolling multi-year financial planning process. An annual budget can only indicate how things are supposed to come out at the end of a year, but it does not indicate how much money is needed or available at any given point in the year. Since organizations may incur more expenses in one part of the year than in another, and since the level of funds coming into the organization may vary significantly from one month to another, it is important to know how much money is available for expenses throughout the year. **Cash-flow** projections, or projecting and maintaining an organization's expenses and income on a month-to-month basis, help to keep the organization solvent and able to cover its expenses (Weis & Long, 2011).

To conduct a cash-flow analysis, both expenses and income are laid out on a computer-generated spreadsheet (if possible), with separate columns for each month. The first column lists the total yearly budget, and each horizontal row lists each budget line item. Listed next to each item is the amount of expense or income expected for that item in each particular month. For example, if salaries for the organization total $360,000, and if that is consistent from month to month, then the line item for salaries would read $360,000 as the annual total, followed by the monthly totals of $36,000 for each month. The first three months would appear accordingly:

	Total	January	February	March
Salaries	$360,000	$30,000	$30,000	$30,000

On the other hand, if all the money for a special event came in March, the line item "Special Event" would look like this:

	Total	January	February	March
Special Event	$37,000	0	0	$37,000

A careful projection of cash flow requires that each expense item and each income item be calculated to determine the availability of money in relation to expenses for each month. There can be uncertainty regarding the exact amount of an expense item, and it is best to be conservative and estimate on the high side. It is also advisable to be conservative with the income items, to underestimate the amount, and to estimate the time of the deposit later than expected.

Once all of the projected monthly income and expense items have been listed, a monthly net income (or deficit) is calculated by subtracting total expenses from total income for that particular month. For example, if the organization anticipates $45,000 of income for the month of January and anticipates spending $44,500, then there is a net income for January of $500. If in February the anticipated income is $43,000 and expenses are anticipated to be $43,500, then the anticipated net deficit is $500 for the month of February (see Figure 6.4 on following page) (Weis & Long, 2011).

Monthly financial projections are important because each one affects a cumulative flow of cash. The cash-flow summary is indicated at the bottom of Figure 6.4 and begins with an opening cash balance or the amount of money on hand at the beginning of the month. The net monthly income (or loss) is added (or subtracted) from this amount for the ending or cumulative cash balance for the month. This bottom line indicates the amount of money the organization should have to begin the next month.

Figure 6.4

Cash-Flow Analysis

Expected Income	January	February
Membership Fees	$25,000	$25,000
Program Fees	16,000	14,000
United Way	4,000	4,000
Total	$45,000	$43,000
Expected Expenses		
Salaries	$31,000	$31,000
Benefits	6,000	5,000
Utilities	4,500	4,500
Facility Rent	3,000	3,000
Total	$44,500	$43,500
Monthly net income (or loss)	$500	($500)
Cash-flow summary		
Opening Cash Balance	$200	$700
Monthly Net Income (or Loss)	500	(500)
Ending (Cumulative) Cash Balance	$700	$200

©Roger Weis

Developing cash-flow projections approximately six months in advance of the coming fiscal year helps to prepare for and prevent any potential shortfalls. If the organization still falls short at some point, money can be borrowed or moved from a contingency/reserve fund. If this is not possible, money can be borrowed through a commercial lending institution. The board should take the lead in this process and seek a low or no-interest loan.

This chapter began with the idea that financial resource development and management practices and skills are becoming increasingly important to the success of nonprofit organizations and for careers in the sector. Everyone who works in the nonprofit sector has some level of fiscal responsibility, and it is important that all staff members have at least some knowledge of and input into financial matters. It is equally important that senior staff and board members are highly knowledgeable in the fiscal matters of the organization, particularly since senior administrators are responsible for preparing budgets and other financial processes and since board members are ultimately responsible for overall finances and the approval of finances. Delivering quality, effective programs from a financially sound foundation is a major factor in assuring organizational success, demonstrating quality stewardship of the public trust, and sustaining the programs and services needed in the community.

FINANCIAL PROCESSES

Since so many people rely on nonprofit organizations for the delivery of important programs and services, it is essential that these organizations maintain accurate financial records and that these records be open for review and examined annually by an independent auditor. **Accounting** is the term used for financial record keeping, and there are two main types of accounting methods. One is called **cash-basis accounting** and the other one is called **accrual-based accounting** (Weis & Long, 2011).

Cash-basis accounting may be the most familiar type of accounting being practiced in nonprofit organizations, since most people use this type of approach with their personal finances. With cash-basis accounting, financial transactions are recorded only when cash changes hands. Records are made only when money is deposited in an account or when money is withdrawn from an account or a check is written from an account. This system is beneficial in its simplicity, straightforwardness, and quickness. It does not, however, take into account any unpaid bills that are outstanding or any money that might be owed to the organization.

With an accrual-based accounting system, on the other hand, money that actually changes hand, whether through a deposit or a withdrawal, is recorded and money that is owed to an organization and owed by an organization is recorded as well. The advantage of this system is that it represents an organization's actual financial status at any given time much more accurately (see Figure 6.5). The disadvantage is that it is a more complex and time-consuming process.

Figure 6.5

Cash Versus Accrual

	Cash	Accrual
Beginning Cash in Bank	$10,000	$10,000
Purchased Materials (Payable)	0	−500
Membership Commitment (rReceivable)	0	5,000
Ending Cash in Bank	$10,000	
Net Worth		$14,500

©Roger Weis

Still another option for an organization is to incorporate a **modified cash-basis accounting** system. With this system most accounts are kept on a cash basis with the exception of a few accounts that need to be monitored closely because of the amount of funds that may move in and out of the account throughout the fiscal year. For example, an organization might incorporate a cash-basis system for all of its income lines with the exception of membership fees, if membership fees can be paid over a period of time. This system would provide information on memberships that have been paid in full, yet keep track of those that are being paid over a period of time. This same system can be used for paying bills. Bills that are paid in full using a cash-basis accounting system would be recorded, while select bills that may take some time to pay could be recorded through an accrual-based system. For instance, major equipment purchases that are being paid for over an extended time period could be recorded with the accrual-based system. This modified cash-basis accounting system is often used for paying federal and state taxes as well, which involves withholding money from employees' salaries on a regular basis and using that money for paying the appropriate taxes (Weis & Long, 2011).

Fund Accounting

Income and expenses that are designated for the sole purpose of operating the organization are sometimes referred to as **operating funds** or **unrestricted funds**, which means they can be used for almost any aspect of the organization's operations. Some smaller organizations that operate exclusively on unrestricted funds are often able to develop a budget for income and expenses on a simple format referred to as a **single fund budget.** Larger, more complex organizations have unrestricted operating funds and often have fund accounts that are used for a number of other areas as well. One such example might be a special project in which funds would be **restricted** just for that project. Another reason to have an additional fund account is to separate the accounting for grant funds from the accounting for operating and other funds.

Operating funds and additional funds can be recorded on the same budget sheet, which is referred to as a **multiple fund budget**. Each fund is separate from the other, each with its own categories of revenue and expenses (see Figure 6.6).

The operating budget is listed first on the left-hand side of the budget. A special project (restricted) is summarized in the second column, and the third column represents a project sponsored by a grant. The sum of the three columns is represented in the fourth column. A multiple fund budget is more beneficial than a single fund budget when more than one fund is necessary because it provides quick access to the records of separate funds at one time and allows a review and comparison of all funds at the same time.

Figure 6.6

Multiple Fund Budget

	Operating Fund	Project Fund	Grant Fund	Total
Income				
Membership Fees	$800,000			$800,000
Program Fees	320,000			320,000
United Way	32,000			32,000
Annual campaign	64,000			64,000
Contributions		$87,000		87,000
Grant			$212,000	212,000
Total	$1,216,000	$87,000	$212,000	$1,515,000
Expenses				
Salaries	$720,000	$47,000	$132,000	$899,000
Benefits	253,000	24,000	43,000	320,000
Supplies	57,000	15,000	32,000	40,000
Utilities	66,000			66,000
Facility Rent	47,000			47,000
Contingency/Reserve	72,000			72,000
Total	$1,216,000	$86,000	$207,000	$1,509,000

©Roger Weis

Financial Statements

Two types of financial statements provide information relevant to the financial well-being or financial condition of organizations, the **balance sheet** and the **income statement** (Zietlow, Hankin, & Seidner, 2007). The balance sheet (see Figure 6.7) is like a snapshot of the organization's financial condition, providing information as of a particular date, and that date is usually the last day of the month of the last month of the fiscal year. Half of the balance sheet lists all of the organization's assets or those things it owns. The other half lists the organization's liabilities (all that it owes) as well as its net assets or fund balance. Each half adds up to the same total number, hence the term *balance sheet*.

Figure 6.7

Balance Sheet

Assets	
Current Assets	
Cash	$13,300
Accounts Receivable	15,200
Prepaid Expenses	16,300
Total Current Assets	$44,800
Noncurrent Assets	
Fixed Assets (land, buildings)	$110,000
Grants Receivable	16,300
Total Noncurrent Assets	$126,300
TOTAL ASSETS	$171,100
Liabilities and Net Assets	
Liabilities	
Current Liabilities	
Accounts Payable	$17,200
Deferred Income	10,500
Total Current Liabilities	$27,700
Noncurrent Liabilities	
Mortgage	$91,000
Total Noncurrent Liabilities	$91,000
Net Assets	
Unrestricted	$23,000
Restricted	$7,700
Net Income/(Loss) YTD	$22,000
Total Net Assets	$52,300
TOTAL LIABILITIES AND NET ASSETS	$171,000

©Roger Weis

The **balance** exists between the assets on the one hand and the liabilities and net assets on the other. Mathematically speaking, it would look like this:

Assets equals Liabilities plus Net Assets, or A = L + NA

This formula makes calculating the **fund balance** easy, since it is determined by subtracting the amount the organization owes from how much it owns:

Net Assets equals Assets minus Liabilities: NA = A − L

Balance sheets may first appear to be complicated, but understanding each section helps to reveal the overall financial picture of an organization (Konrad & Novak, 2000). Reviewing the **asset** section of the statement in Figure 6.7 indicates what the organization owns in terms of cash in the bank, land, buildings, and equipment, as examples. Since most balance sheets are prepared on an accrual basis, they also include all the money owed to the organization as an asset. These are often referred to as **accounts receivable** and might include money owed to the organization by way of membership payments that are on a schedule or grant money that has been committed but not received. The asset section may also indicate a line for **prepaid expenses** that might include expenses for an activity or event that is occurring in the next fiscal year or some other expense that had to be prepaid.

The asset section of the balance sheet is divided into **current assets** and **noncurrent assets**. Current assets include cash or any item that is expected to become cash within the next year; noncurrent assets are those items that are not as liquid (currently available to be used) and may not be paid for two years or more in the future, like those from grants or pledged contributions from individuals.

The other half of the balance sheet includes the organization's **liabilities**, or what it owes to others. This section is divided up as well, into **current liabilities** and **noncurrent liabilities**. Current liabilities include money that the organization owes in terms of unpaid bills (**accounts payable**) and any revenue or income that has been collected for activities that will not occur until the next fiscal year (**deferred revenue** or **income**). Longer-term obligations, such as **mortgages**, are classified as **noncurrent liabilities**, since they are not due in the next fiscal year.

Once all of the liability categories are totaled and subtracted from the total assets, the difference results in the **net assets**. Net assets are classified into one of three categories as established by the Financial Accounting Standards Board, which establishes financial accounting and reporting standards that are followed across the sector (Weis & Long, 2011):

▶ **Unrestricted net assets** include income from contributions and grants and any other earned income or income from investments that is not restricted for use and can be used for any purposes as determined appropriate by the organization.

▶ **Temporarily restricted net assets** are those assets that are temporarily restricted by donors until that restriction has been met in the future.

▶ **Permanently restricted net assets** include donor-imposed requirements that will never be removed.

Looking at the total net assets in Figure 6.7, it would appear the organization is in good financial shape with a net worth of $52,300. Closer examination of the balance sheet shows that only $13,300 is actual cash in the bank and $15,200 is listed as accounts receivable. A large portion of the asset section includes fixed assets such as land and buildings ($110,000), which is not liquid (not available) and would have to be sold in order for funds to be available to cover any debts the organization might have.

Since the balance sheet must include all the assets and all liabilities of an organization, it is an excellent tool for board and staff members to use when making major financial decisions. It is also an important barometer for prospective board members, funders, and regulators to determine the financial health of an organization prior to any commitments or designations. It is a much better indicator of financial health than a financial statement, which will be examined next, but because individuals are often mystified by all of the numbers and jargon, most people are content to review only the financial statement. But an organization can have a significant net worth and look healthy on a financial statement, yet have a large amount of money invested in a non-liquid asset, such as a building, and therefore appear less healthy on a more detailed balance sheet. This is why the balance sheet should be examined prior to any important financial decisions.

While the balance sheet provides us with information about an organization's financial health at a particular moment in time, the **income statement** summarizes financial activity over a period of time, usually a month or a year. It contains historical financial information and information about the sources of an organization's revenue and expenditures. Since revenue and expenditures are divided into sub-categories, it provides detailed information on each source of revenue and where expenses are going. The income statement indicates whether an organization has a surplus or a deficit over a period of time, and it is calculated by subtracting expenditures from total revenue and is carried forward to the balance sheet. An income statement can include the fund balance at the bottom portion of the report, particularly in the case of year-end audited statements.

A monthly financial or income statement designed like the one in Figure 6.8 provides a view of the progress being made on revenues and expenses, as well as activity for the month that was recently completed and all of the activity thus far this year, and it compares both to a monthly and annual budget. The sample in Figure 6.8 presents an organization that is halfway through the fiscal year, since the statement covers the period from July 1 through December 30. Focusing on the revenue half of the budget, it might be expected that approximately 50% of the budget would have been met halfway through the fiscal year. The income or revenue that is indicated for the first six months totals $144,000 of an annual budget of

Figure 6.8

Income Statement from July 1 to December 31

	Current Month		Year to Date	
Revenue	**Actual**	**Budget**	**Actual**	**Annual Budget**
Membership	$12,000	$12,500	$74,000	$125,000
Program	5,000	4,000	27,000	53,000
United Way	2,000	2,000	12,000	24,000
Annual Campaign	5,400	4,000	31,000	62,000
Total Income	$24,000	$22,500	$144,000	$264,000
Expenses				
Salaries & Benefits	$14,000	$13,700	$84,000	$171,000
Supplies/Telephone	700	800	4,200	9,000
Postage	1,600	1,200	8,800	15,000
Travel Expenses	1,100	1,000	7,000	16,000
Mortgage Interest	3,000	3,000	18,000	36,000
Contingency/Reserve	0	0	0	17,000
Total Expenses	$20,400	$19,700	$121,000	$264,000
Net Income (Loss) YTD	$4,000	$2,800	$23,000	0

©Roger Weis

$264,000, which equals 54%. This is a good sign that the organization is progressing well toward its overall goal of $264,000 in revenue for the fiscal year.

Looking at the expense half of the budget, the organization has spent $121,000 of an annual budget of $264,000; this equals 46% of the budgeted amount for the first half of the fiscal year. Based on the information provided by this financial statement alone, revenue seems to be accruing in a reasonable fashion, and expenses seem to be under control for the first half of the fiscal year. But a more accurate fiscal picture can be determined by looking "behind the numbers" at each category to understand the organization's fiscal status in-depth. For instance, $74,000 has been generated in membership fees, which is 59% of what is budgeted in the membership line for the year ($125,000). This appears to be a positive figure, but what if the organization has completed a major membership campaign and expects far fewer members in the next half of the year? It still needs $51,000 in this category to meet the budget, and it needs to be certain that plans are in place to generate this income. Similarly, the organization has only spent 46% of its allocation for expenses in the first half of the year, which is also a good indication of positive fiscal health. Key board and staff members need to monitor the expense side of the budget continually to be certain that expenses are kept at the same conservative level for the remainder of the year to insure fiscal health (Weis & Long, 2011).

Continually examining balance sheets and income statements provides board and staff members with the information they need to make effective financial decisions that often have a direct bearing on the overall success of the organization. Providing a narrative with statements offers additional, in-depth information on financial categories and helps prevent any unwanted surprises down the road.

Controls

In handling money within an organization, a number of irregularities can occur, either intentionally or unintentionally. One of the most important responsibilities of the board of directors is to establish **fiscal controls** that protect individuals and the organization from irregularities and mistakes. For example, it is generally accepted that fewer fiscal irregularities will occur if there are at least two people involved with financial transactions, each double-checking the decisions and actions of the other. Similarly, the board should design all financial processes and policies with a significant number of **checks and balances** to insure fiscal integrity (Weis & Muller, 2015).

One of the most important steps in establishing reliable financial procedures is for the board to require that two people be involved in processing all payments. For example, a key administrator who is familiar with the budget and with specific financial expenditures should approve payment. A board member involved with the financial committee should receive the approval for payment and be responsible for writing checks and monitoring this procedure for other board members.

Each payment transaction requires documentation, and one simple way of providing this is to create a stamp that is placed on each invoice that arrives with the following designations and then filled in with the required information as the transaction moves through the established process (Wolf, 1999):

Date Received:

Date Paid:

Account:

Check Number:

Approved:

On the day the invoice is received, it is stamped and the date is recorded on the first line. The assigned staff member determines which budget line item account is to be used to make the payment, records the appropriate account title or number on the third line, and signs or initials to indicate approval for the payment to be made. The assigned board member receives the invoice with all the information in place and writes the check, recording the check number and the date it was written in the appropriate stamped space on the invoice. All payment records should be systematically filed for future referral and review by an auditor.

Another important control on writing checks is to set a policy that checks cannot be made out to the same individual who is signing checks, or that at the least there must be a counter signature on those particular checks. This process—of having two people sign certain checks—could also apply to expenditures exceeding a certain amount, such as $1,000, or whatever amount the board deems appropriate. A formal policy to this effect, with the names of those approved to sign checks when needed, must be on file and available for consultation.

With a similar commitment to formal procedures, a system of careful controls must also be incorporated for the handling of incoming money so that both a staff and board member are included. Incoming funds must be received, recorded, and deposited promptly. Deposit slips should be checked with records periodically, and any significant irregularities must be reported to the board.

The organization must be protected from loss of income through either intentional or unintentional irregularities. One way to do this is through the process of **bonding**, which is a form of insurance for fiscal matters. Because premiums for the bonding process vary with the amount of money under protection, careful consideration should be given to determine this amount to be covered and the cost of bonding. One way to designate this amount would be to determine the largest amount of money that could be in the bank at one point and increase that figure by 20% (Wolf, 1999). This amount should comfortably protect the organization, its staff, and its volunteers without excessive bonding premium costs.

Physical controls and security measures are equally important in protecting organizations from financial loss, or worse. Financial transactions that are conducted with electrical or mechanical equipment, such as cash registers, have a small likelihood of error. Equipment must be checked regularly for proper functioning and accuracy. Financial transactions that are conducted online must follow security protocols and include appropriate protections. Financial records should be kept in fireproof cabinets. Offices should have adequate fire and burglary protection and should install properly functioning security systems. If large amounts of money are expected to come into the organization at one time, as with a special event, hiring security police should be considered.

Reporting Requirements

Nonprofit organizations must file a number of reports each year to maintain their nonprofit status and demonstrate fiscal responsibility. Financial reporting procedures for organizations vary from state-to-state, and it is important that each organization check individual state regulations regarding reporting requirements.

Most nonprofit organizations are required to complete an **annual tax return** with the IRS that is called a **Form 990.** This form includes information on all income and expenses of the organization in support of its tax-exempt status. Failure to comply with this requirement could lead to significant civil and criminal penalties. If an organization receives income exceeding $1,000 that is not related to the tax-exempt purpose of the organization (excluding income from investments) it must be recorded and filed on a **Form 990-T** with its Form 990. Determining which income this might include can be difficult and is best determined by the individual who does the annual audit and who knows the related tax regulations.

Some general understanding of tax regulations will help illustrate the importance of having knowledgeable people involved in this aspect of the organization's financial management. For example, all organizations that have employees must withhold income taxes, social security, and Medicare from their pay and report this amount to the IRS. If a nonprofit organization is not a 501(c)3, it must also pay federal unemployment taxes (**FUTA**) on salaries that are reported on **Form 940.** Employers must prepare a **W-2 Form**, which is the annual wage and tax statement, for each employee. This must be mailed to each employee by January 31, and a copy must be filed with the IRS no later than February 28 of each year. Non-employee compensation paid in amounts exceeding $600 must be reported on **Form 1099-MISC**, filed with **Form 1096** and filed with the IRS annually. If an organization receives a gift of property, other than money or securities, it must file a **Donee Information Report Form 8282** with the IRS if the amount of the gift exceeds $500. These examples illustrate the importance of having an in-depth understanding of the tax regulations in order to insure that the nonprofit organization is in full compliance.

Recording and Reporting Systems

It is essential that nonprofit organizations have quality policies and procedures for recording and reporting all aspects of their financial processes. This often starts with how the recording and reporting process is designed. Prepackaged accounting computer software is readily available to handle accounting needs and even the smallest of organizations can benefit from the use of these often-inexpensive programs. Customized accounting software packages that include links to membership and fundraising packages can also be purchased through accounting or software firms that specialize in the work of nonprofit organizations. Computerized spreadsheets are an important tool in recording and analyzing income and expenses, determining cash flow, and maintaining membership and fundraising records. They are also readily available as prepackaged software, or they can be obtained in a more customized fashion. Affiliates of national nonprofit organizations may also be able to acquire software packages designed specifically for their organization from their national headquarters. Another good source of such resources can be found in the state association of nonprofit organizations and their National Council of Nonprofit Associations.

Some organizations find it less expensive and/or more expedient to contract accounting procedures, payroll systems, and other record-keeping and meeting form requirements to firms that specialize in these processes. These firms are generally more accurate and can relieve the organization of unwanted and often time-consuming tasks.

Organizations with the best of intentions and purposes can help develop their effectiveness, in part, by maintaining appropriate financial records and reporting those accounts in a timely and appropriate manner. An effective accounting and reporting process adds to the overall success of the organization and helps to assure staff and volunteers, participants, contributors, and other community members of the organization's financial integrity.

FINANCIAL DEVELOPMENT

The development of the financial resources needed to successfully operate a nonprofit organization includes an increasingly sophisticated field of practice. Financial development and fundraising are not synonymous. Fundraising is just one aspect of financial development. The nonprofit sector has its roots in a number of traditional methods of acquiring financial support. The notion of individual financial contributions was a key to the early years of the founding of this country by the way in which successful voluntary action generated charitable contributions of support. The tradition continues as individual donors contribute enormous sums of money to nonprofit organizations. The idea that people would pay a fee for a valued program or service from a nonprofit organization has been a common practice throughout most of the modern history of the sector. And, government departments and other organizations have provided funding to nonprofit organizations in support of the delivery of important programs and services to the community for decades. Nonprofit sector financial development includes these and many other methods of acquiring the resources needed. Increased value is being place on nonprofit organizations that have a strategic and diversified set of sources of funding support. A nonprofit organization with diversified sources of support is considered to be healthier and better able to withstand shifts in funding from any one stream of revenue. Therefore, this section will focus on the range of funding strategies nonprofit organizations incorporate into their financial development.

Modern nonprofit organizations must construct a thorough and comprehensive financial development plan in order to successfully meet their financial needs. Some pre-requisites for the financial development plan include the following **criteria** (Weis & Muller, 2015):

▶ *A clear and focused mission or purpose.* It is much easier to generate income and gain support for a nonprofit organization when the purpose of the organization is clear and highly desirable. The mission must be clear, understood, and important to community members.

▶ *An overall reputation for integrity.* Before any fundraising efforts are initiated, the organization must have developed a reputation for dependability and quality. For new organizations, the reputation can be associated with that of the volunteer board members and staff members.

▶ *A history of program success.* Individuals like to support organizations that are successful and that enhance their communities. Some history of program success implies the probability of future success.

▶ *Professional staff members and committed volunteers.* Individuals like to support organizations that have competent and committed leaders. Proven leadership provides confidence in community support.

▶ *Clear and proven needs for financial support.* Community members are more likely to provide financial support to an organization that is generating money for specific needs that have been clearly established.

▶ *Administrators with experience and skills in financial development.* In addition to having clear needs for financial support, an organization must have individuals with specialized skills in developing support. Technical and people skills are essential in building a financial base.

There is some truth to the axiom "actions speak louder than words." Organizations with a proven record of success and with the potential to develop and maintain a financial base will have a much easier task developing financial support. In order to have organizational information readily available for financial development efforts, many organizations prepare a **case** or **case statement** in advance of such activities. Aspects of a case statement are discussed next.

Case Statement

The case statement is prepared information that can be used for public relations and/or financial development activities. Any and all information can be extracted from the case statement to be used for appropriate purposes. The case statement forms the basis for all of your donor communications and asks, and provides a valuable resource to everyone who is soliciting donations on your behalf (Bray, 2008; Garecht, 2016). Basically, the case statement includes (1) the history of the organization and its mission, (2) what it plans to do or become/ strategic plans, and (3) reasons it will be successful with forthcoming contributions (Brinckerhoff, 1994).

The case statement should describe the importance of the organization and list some of its projects or activities that work toward its purpose or reason for being. It needs to include a specific list of projects that, with appropriate funding, could make further differences in the lives of individuals in the community. And it should include a list of program or project successes as proof of consideration for support (Seiler, 2003).

Fundraising consultant and practitioner Dan Conway states that the case statement should answer these questions: Who are you? Why do you exist? What is distinctive about you? What is it that you want to accomplish? How do you intend to accomplish it? How will you hold yourself accountable?

Whether the case statement is a written document or a database of information on the organization and the community, it should be a fluid instrument capable of being changed quickly as new data is revealed. It can save individuals within the organization a great deal of time searching files for effective information, and it provides potential participants, partners, and contributors with invaluable assistance in making decisions for engagement or support (Weis & Muller, 2015).

The Board's Role in Financial Development

The involvement of board members is critically important to the overall success of developing finances in a nonprofit organization. There are typically **five (5) ways board members get involved in financial development**. First of all, (1) as the primary stewards of the organization, board members have an overall fiduciary responsibility. This is not a day-to-day assignment, but is generally realized by working through the Chief Executive Officer (CEO), Executive Director (ED), or assigned administrator sometimes referred to as the Chief Financial Officer (CFO). Additionally, (2) board members can play a strategic role in helping to determine both the kinds of financial development activities that will occur and the goals of those activities. They can bring expertise, experience, connections, commitments, and their time and energy to the diverse set of financial development activities that the organization engages to fund its ongoing operation and sustainability. Organizations that do not include board members in financial development meetings are missing out on valuable resources and may be acting contrary to organizational by-laws (Worth, 2009).

Board members can (3) also provide key leadership in fundraising activities by their participation, guidance, and inspiration. Some board members are selected because of their experience and expertise in generating funds and should be called upon accordingly. Other board members may not have significant financial expertise but (4) their connections with community leaders provides access to other potential donors, linkages to prospective partners and collaborators, and support for other types of investments (such as contracts for services). Board members can help identify donors and can serve as door openers for prospective gifts. With few exceptions, (5) board members should be asked to contribute financially to the organization and should be a part of the process in organizing and soliciting other contributions.

Although staff members have developed more and more expertise in financial development, not involving board members can leave a tremendous void in the overall development process. An explanation of the board member's role in financial development should be one of the first things the nominating committee provides when recruiting potential board members.

Once a member has been selected, this same role must be reiterated in the board's orientation and training sessions. Committed and informed board, staff, and volunteer members along with organizational integrity combine to make the best formula for financial stability (Weis & Muller, 2015).

The Development Committee's Role

One of the most important factors in successful financial development is the creation of a cohesive development committee that has effective leadership, vision, and commitment (Conway, 2003). The *core* **development team** is made up of board members that include representatives from the development and finance committees, the development committee chairperson, and the board chairperson. Other volunteers from the community may also be included on the development team. Key individuals from the staff side of the organization should be involved, including the ED, the development director, other professional and support staff members, and paid consultants, when appropriate. It is always good to have professional staff members involved who are leading key programs that are central to the organization's mission. Since all board and staff members are expected to contribute to financial development in one way or another, everyone needs to be involved in the development process at appropriate times.

In many nonprofit organizations, the **development committee** works with the development director (or a staff member assigned the responsibility) to (1) determine financial needs, (2) develop a plan that strategically integrates all the methods of financial development, (3) implement that plan, and (4) monitor and amend the plan when necessary as the plan unfolds. This would often include financial plans for the short-term such as a fiscal year as well as strategic, long-range development plans. The case statement, mentioned previously, is an invaluable tool in assisting with all of the steps above.

Some organizations seem blessed with great leadership when it comes to matters of finance, while others struggle in their **recruitment** of quality staff and board members. Good leaders are generally attracted to an organization because of the mission or purpose and the organization's reputation for success and integrity. Recruitment of development committee members should be done just as it is with other board members, incorporating job descriptions and a matrix of specific skills and tasks. Once development committee members have been recruited, they can be *empowered* by a number of strategies (Grace, 2003):

- ▶ broad participation in the overall process, from planning, to setting goals, to implementation, to evaluation
- ▶ training
- ▶ coaching and practice
- ▶ clear and effective communication process
- ▶ providing experienced mentors with each team

► continually reminding team members of the importance of the development activity to the overall mission of the organization

Because of the nature of their work, it is essential to organize the development committee into an effective team. Successful teams often demonstrate a number of the same qualities (Rosso, 1996):

► highly productive teams have developed a similar vision and are able to share that vision with others
► hierarchy is almost nonexistent, and communication is open and respectful
► the organization is highly supportive of the committee's work
► team members rely on empowerment of each other and develop an effective level of synergy
► the team is open to new ideas and works hard to reduce misunderstandings

Recruiting and maintaining a highly effective development committee needs to be one of the top priorities of the ED, development director, and the board chair. They must understand what kinds of individuals are important in building an effective development team, and they must be able to maintain that committee at the highest level of success. The development committee can and should be involved in one way or another in all of the activities discussed below.

Developing a financial base for any organization should be a comprehensive process involving the following possibilities, where appropriate: membership fees, program fees, special events, product sales, residential campaigns, United Way support, annual campaigns, capital campaigns, deferred gifts, and grant support. A key to long-term financial health is the selection of a strategic set of these financial development methods, which are closely monitored and adjusted periodically to respond to changing circumstances and the revenue generated by each method (Weis & Muller, 2015).

Membership and Program Fees

It is common for facility-based and a number of non-facility based organizations to use a membership fee and some additional program participation fees in order to help insure that their operating costs are paid on an ongoing basis. A membership fee (1) provides funds for operating the organization and (2) gives members the sense that they belong to the organization and are committed enough to pay a fee. It also (3) provides members with a sense that they are supporters of the organization's core values and mission. Program fees can be used to cover some of the direct expenses associated with certain programs, such as specialized instructor skills that are not typically found on the staff. There are a number of questions that need to be asked regarding membership and program fees (Weis & Muller, 2015):

WHO SHOULD MAKE UP THE MEMBERSHIP OF AN ORGANIZATION?

Membership in organizations is generally based on (1) the purpose of the organization and (2) the guidelines established by the board in the bylaws and/or membership policy of the organization. For example, a nonprofit organization whose purpose it is to enhance the lives of children in the community should specify age, geographical parameters, and any other considerations.

HOW MANY MEMBERS SHOULD AN ORGANIZATION HAVE?

Organizations generally set a limit on the number of members and program participants that can be served effectively:

1. **Space analysis.** The number of participants allowed for a given space is first of all determined by community policies, usually by the local fire department. Beyond this legal control, organizations may wish to limit the number of participants so there is adequate space for effective and safe program implementation.

2. **Resources.** An analysis should be done to determine an effective staff, faculty, and/or volunteer ratio with program participants. In most cases, a predetermined ratio of staff to program participants is set by organizational policy and in some cases, such as therapeutic settings, the ratio may be set by law or professional standards. It is also important to assess the quantity of supplies, materials, and equipment available for adequate programming.

3. **Budgetary considerations.** It is important to consider the number of members and program participants necessary to meet the specific line items of the budget dealing with membership and program participation. This is essential if the program budget is based solely on a program fee or as a part of the membership fee. If the program cost is being supported by other sources of funding, the number of members and participants can still be useful to have a sense of what to charge or what needs to be raised in additional funds.

4. **Tradition.** Some organizations have a tradition that limits the number of members and program participants and others have a history of including a larger number of members. Traditions can be changed, but they should at least be considered in the overall discussion to determine individual numbers for an organization and for specific programs.

HOW ARE MEMBERSHIP AND PROGRAM FEES DETERMINED (PRICING)?

Determining the cost for memberships or a fee for a specific program in any organization is tricky, but a number of aspects should be considered:

1. **Mission and policy.** If the mission of the organization is to serve economically disadvantaged individuals, then this must be considered in establishing any fee, membership or otherwise. Many nonprofit organizations set some of their fees on a **sliding scale** basis, meaning that the fees for individuals who need assistance can be based on their income-to-expense margin or cash availability. Additionally, some organizations set up a **scholarship program** for people in need. Even if the organization's mission has nothing specifically to do with serving the economically disadvantaged, nonprofit organizations are created to provide a service and should be priced accordingly.

2. **Budgetary requirements.** Just as budgetary requirements must be considered when determining the number of members or program participants an organization should engage, it must also be considered when setting a price for membership or specific programs. Membership and program fees often make up a substantial portion of an operating budget and are therefore necessary for the overall financial health of the organization. The amount of the budget being generated by other financial development methods informs the pricing process.

3. **Tradition.** The organization's history should also be considered in the mix of determining membership and program prices. If an organization has a tradition of setting memberships or program fees at a certain level, the community comes to expect that range of pricing. Pricing can and often does change, but gradual, conservative changes are much easier to accept and deal with than radical, major changes in pricing. This can impact the overall blend of financial development methods and goals set for each.

WHAT DOES A MEMBERSHIP CAMPAIGN CONSIST OF?

Many organizations develop a special campaign, referred to as a membership campaign, to recruit new members. Whether motivated by a need to increase membership or to respond to an opportunity to provide new or additional programs to different parts of the community, a membership campaign should be designed to stimulate a great deal of enthusiasm and interest in the organization and can last from a few weeks to several months, and even longer. A well-designed membership campaign can be a way of increasing the flow of funding through this financial development method. The goals set for this method must be closely coordinated with the other methods that make up the overall financial development plan. Quality membership campaigns consider the following:

1. **Special Offers.** Membership campaigns often include special offers during the campaign. These may include a reduced cost for membership, extended membership for a standard cost, additional memberships at a reduced rate (see Figure 6.9), current members receive a discount for their annual fee when they bring in new members, and free or reduced program fees for sign-ups during the campaign. Any innovative special offers that will attract new members to the organization should be considered.

2. **Kick-off.** Effective membership campaigns often have a *kick-off* event, an activity that begins the campaign with a whirl of excitement and activity. The kick-off can be an event that includes information on the organization and special offers involved with the campaign. Door prizes, entertainment, surprises, and free food are all likely to enhance the excitement surrounding the campaign. Local celebrities and the media should be invited along with the members of the organization. The kick-off event can also be an opportunity to bring broad public attention to the mission of the organization and a source of attention and support for other methods being used in the financial development plan. For example, materials and media activity being prepared for the membership campaign can be designed to also support ongoing individual donor development and cultivation. Potential donors can also be invited to the kick-off as an opportunity to get quickly acquainted with the mission.

3. **Flyers, Public Service Announcements (PSAs), Twitter, Facebook, Instagram, and Signs.** Attractive, informative flyers should be created and posted strategically throughout the community several weeks prior to the kick-off and the beginning of the campaign. Public service announcements should also be sent to the media prior to the beginning of the campaign. Businesses will often donate space for display and marquee signs to promote the campaign. Twitter accounts, Facebook, and Instagram are great avenues to promote any campaign. Any materials developed for a membership campaign can also have uses in other financial development methods if designed with multiple uses in mind.

4. **Contests.** Introducing contests for the campaign adds excitement and interest, helps create a sense of ownership for staff members, volunteers, and members, and has a strong potential for increasing membership enrollment. Prizes can include days off for staff members and t-shirts for volunteers and members. Grand prizes or drawings for contest participants can include free trips donated by local travel agencies.

Figure 6.9

Reduced Membership Promotional Flyer

Buy One Membership
In the Morganfield YMCA
and Get the Second Membership
at ½ Price!!

That's right. When you sign up for membership in the Morganfield YMCA, you can bring along a friend for just half price if you both register during the month of June! This 12-month offer is good for current and new members.

Membership includes full use of the facility:

- Olympic size pool
- Fitness center
- Youth center
- Career development center
- Giant whirlpool
- Racquetball courts
- Adult and youth sport leagues

For more information on this great offer,
contact Darcy Young at 750-9622.

Hurry, offer ends soon!

©Roger Weis

Special Events

A special event fundraiser is an activity designed with the primary purpose of generating income for an organization and with secondary objectives that could include increasing public awareness, entertainment, health and fitness, enhanced knowledge and awareness, and fun. Special events have the potential to generate enormous interest in the organization while also developing funds. Special event fundraisers come in many, many forms and are limited only by imagination. There are a lot of resources available to help development committees make decisions about the methods they will undertake and about the process of planning for these activities (Mintzer, 2003). When planning special events, the following criteria should be considered (Weis & Long, 2011):

1. **Safety.** The most important aspect of a special event or any activity in an organization is keeping risks and health hazards to an absolute minimum. For all special events, a conscious effort must be made to follow the guidelines for managing risks listed in Chapter 7.

2. **Community Need.** The most successful special events are those that most effectively fulfill needs of the community or a targeted group. Events that focus on sports, health and fitness, or the arts, as well as any activity that fulfills specific need in a meaningful way—such as an educational event—are sure to succeed.

3. **Creative and distinctive.** Special events should be distinctive in order to appeal to a wide range of interests. For instance, *-thons* have a long and proven history of being successful and a twist on a *-thon* might be to have a *volunteer-a-thon* instead of a *walk-a-thon*. It is a little different than a typical *-thon* and it provides services to the community. The notion is that participants get pledges of a set amount of money for each increment of the event that they accomplish to be paid upon completion of the event, such as a set amount for each mile walked, each hurdle jumped, hours volunteered, and so on. Special events vary as widely as people's imaginations, from carnivals to bingo and from "pies in the face" to silent auctions. Choosing the right kind of event to best match the interests and energies of those who are sought as participants/donors is the real trick to successful special events.

4. **Natural Connection.** Special events that have some kind of a natural connection to the organization can sometimes be easier to implement than others. An example might be a YMCA that develops a bicycle or running race. Health and fitness are two areas that YMCAs typically incorporate in their programs, so they would have access to expertise in those areas as well as access to members with those interests.

5. **Organization and Promotion.** To be successful, special events have to be planned and promoted well, just like any other program. The program development section in Chapter 5 contains detailed steps to follow in developing a program. The goal here is to make sure that the people who are targeted as participants/donors for the special event are aware that it is happening and motivated to engage and donate.

6. **Fundraising Potential.** Regardless of how creative or well-planned an event is it has to have the potential to raise money. Finding a high quality fit between the interests of those who are targeted as participants/donors and the special event being planned is the primary key to success. Corporate and association sponsorships can be solicited to cover many or all of the costs. It is also important to keep expenses as low as possible, while maintaining a quality event.

Product Sales

The Girl Scouts of America have taken product sales to great heights with their acclaimed Girl Scout cookie campaign that results in tens of millions of dollars for local councils around the country each year. It has a double benefit in that it is also an educational program for participants who are learning about small business management while selling cookies and generating funds for the organization. Other organizations are successful selling candy, calendars, popcorn, teddy bears, and fruit, to mention only a few of the items sold each year for nonprofit causes. Selling products can be very successful if a few key factors are incorporated (Weis & Muller, 2015):

- ► Make safety the number one priority.
- ► Be certain to have a large and responsible sales force.
- ► Develop an effective communication system.
- ► Select products that are popular and easy to sell.
- ► Provide appropriate and adequate incentives.
- ► Establish a clear beginning and end date.
- ► Try to buy products on consignment.
- ► Develop an effective control system for money.

Product sales also help promote the organization and provide members of the organization an opportunity to develop ownership by assisting the fundraising process.

Online Fundraising

Online fundraising matters because it is becoming a growing portion of organizational budgeting. An increasing number of individuals and corporations are contributing through online fundraising. This kind of fundraising usually begins with a website or a Web page. The message is clear and strong and the contribution can be done quickly (Andersen & Higman, 2011). It needs to be continually monitored with up-to-date communication and information, including opportunities for donors to offer feedback. But once a competent system is established, monitored, and updated it can become one of the simplest and most encouraging sources of support for any nonprofit entity.

Residential Campaigns

A number of nonprofit organizations, particularly national health organizations with high visibility, have great success with **residential campaigns**, in which individuals in specific communities are asked to approach their neighbors requesting support for an organization. This type of campaign is highly organized, yet personalized at the same time, as neighbors are approaching neighbors for support and participation.

Residential campaigns usually begin with paid or volunteer staff members within the organization calling individuals in various neighborhoods using a specialized phone book that is divided by neighborhoods within communities. Any advance work that can be done to identify potential supporters by neighborhood will increase the success with the first level of recruiting participants for the campaign. Since the first level of participation requires a sizeable commitment, any advanced connection to the organization or the person doing the calling can increase the potential for agreement to join. The individuals who are called are asked to represent the organization within their neighborhood and are then sent a packet of material that may include the following:

- A letter of explanation describing in detail the campaign and the volunteer's role
- Information on the successes of the organization in addressing specific problems
- A list of names and addresses of other individuals in the neighborhood
- A solicitation letter to be given to each individual on the neighborhood list along with a return envelope
- A large, return envelope where all checks can be sent to the organization upon completion of the campaign

Once an individual has been recruited to coordinate the neighborhood campaign, he or she may be reminded occasionally by the organization about the campaign goal and any deadlines. There is usually a packet or kit goal for each neighborhood that is set at a reasonable level. Residential campaigns designed as such can be very successful, particularly when (1) the organization is recognizable and the purpose desirable; (2) the campaign is well organized; and (3) the solicitation approach is personalized, such as neighbor-to-neighbor. Once people have had a good experience participating in a residential campaign and are celebrated and recognized for their success, they make good candidates to serve in this capacity again or to be interested in moving into other financial development roles with the organizations. Successful residential campaigns result in tens of millions of dollars for nonprofit causes across the country each year.

United Way

Local United Way organizations are designed in part to be an umbrella organization that collects contributions for distribution to other organizations. The money United Way raises was previously **allocated** to organizations based on (1) need, (2) numbers of individuals served, and (3) types of programs. The United Way currently depends more on the **outcome model** in determining allocations. United Way affiliated organizations are required to submit information on (1) **Inputs,** or a list of resources dedicated to the program along with restraints such as policy or legal regulations, (2) **activities,** or the kinds of programs offered to fulfill the organization's mission, (3) **outputs,** which includes mostly quantitative data about number of participants and number of hours involved to mention several, and (4) **outcomes,** or the qualitative benefits such as enhanced knowledge, improved values systems, healthier lifestyles, and better behavior. An organization such as a community-based health and wellness center that has a strong capacity for fundraising through membership or program fees may not receive as much United Way support as a Big Brothers Big Sisters organization that provides important services with no membership or program costs to its members. United Way is increasingly focusing is allocation decisions on community issues that are determined by input from the community. This process is typically narrowing the focus of its funding and reducing the number of organizations and/or the amount of funds received by each organization.

An organization that is interested in becoming a United Way affiliated agency should review the organizational funding requirements prior to making application to see if it meets the standards and to understand any restrictions. Organizations that apply and become affiliates of the United Way must reapply for support each year. An **allocation committee** made up of local community volunteers determines the amount of money allocated to each organization. Most United Way funds are generated through a **payroll deduction** process in which individuals designate that a certain amount of money be withheld from their paycheck and contributed to the United Way or a specific organization affiliated with the United Way. In many communities, United Way also allows individuals to select among its affiliates the organization that will receive its donation. This has the impact of reducing the amount of money available for United Way to distribute. This financial development method has proven to be one of the most successful in history.

Annual and Capital Campaigns

An **annual campaign** is designed to generate funds for operating expenses and these funds can be passed on to members in the form of reduced membership and program fees, or in some cases fees may be eliminated (Weis & Muller, 2015).

Annual campaigns are highly organized with a chairperson, division leaders, team captains, meeting dates, fundraising material, and financial goals (see Figure 6.10). One hundred percent of the board of directors should be involved in the annual campaign, from participating as chairperson or division leaders, to recruiting division leaders on or off the board, recruiting team members, and making donations. **Campaign leaders** must be respected members of the community with a commitment to the organization and can be made up of board members and other members of the community in general.

The overall **campaign chair** should be someone who has a great deal of respect from the community, is committed to the purpose of the organization, and is able to organize and motivate others. The chair is sometimes a board member of the organization, but not always.

Figure 6.10

Annual Campaign Organizational Chart

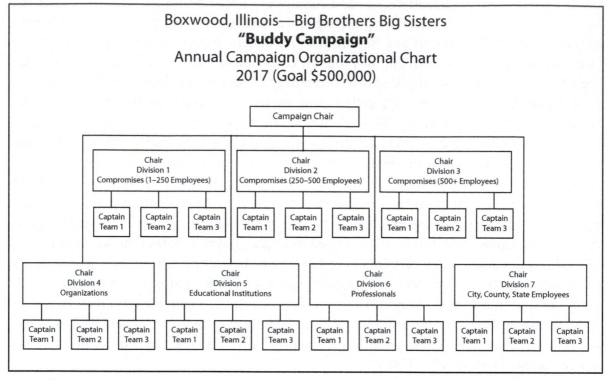

©Roger Weis

The community should be divided up into segments that make sense in the given community. Segments could include such divisions as small, middle-sized, and large business divisions, an educational division, a professional division, an organizational division, a division that includes city, state, and federal employees, and so on. Each division should have a leader who can organize his or her segment into teams with team captains. Each team is responsible for generating a certain amount of money from an assigned section of the division, and that amount, combined with other teams, is the goal for the division.

A **prospect list** must be established for each division. Special consideration should go to individuals, corporations, and associations with natural ties to the organization such as board members, staff, and volunteer members, members, parents of members, firms represented by members, previous members, previous contributors, community-minded corporations, and service associations. Prospects may also be selected from the Chamber of Commerce list and even from the yellow and white pages, although this should be a lesser priority as a method of developing prospect lists. Lists should be reviewed after each annual campaign and cultivated by the members of each team to reflect the results of the experience. This provides a list of donors or prospective donors based on the experience of the team, increasing the odds of meeting future fundraising goals with the annual campaign.

The **solicitation process** for an annual campaign should be highly organized, but personable. Telephone calls, face-to-face meetings, and direct-mail contacts between team members and prospects are very important and produce the best results. Often, a campaign will have an appealing **theme** and purpose, such as the "Buddy Campaign" in Figure 6.10, and this theme and purpose will be reflected and explained in the campaign material. This provides some focus for potential prospects and helps assure them that their money is going to make a difference in a specific area within the organization. Meetings should include an informational and inspirational **kick-off** event followed by a number of **update** or **report meetings.** All of these meetings should be both informative and inspirational. Although annual campaigns should be planned a year in advance, the actual campaign is relatively brief, lasting from two to four weeks.

Organizational staff members usually play support roles in an annual campaign, developing materials (see Figure 6.11 on following page), organizing meetings, keeping records, supporting the volunteers in their fundraising efforts, and organizing the kick-off event and closing celebration.

A **capital campaign** is designed to generate funds for capital expenditures such as new buildings, renovations, major equipment purchases, and endowed educational positions (Weis & Muller, 2015). A capital campaign is highly organized, like an annual campaign, and involves the selection of a chair, division chairs, teams, and team captains. It also has a financial goal, campaign materials, and scheduled meeting dates. Unlike an annual campaign, a capital campaign is typically designed to raise larger amounts of money and the campaign period is usually longer. This period can last from several months up to one or two years, and even longer in some circumstances. This is in part the result of the challenge typically encountered in raising funds for capital development.

Fundraising **consultants** are often hired to coordinate capital campaigns because of their expertise and so that staff members can concentrate on other duties, although the staff should be involved in a support role. The consultant may first conduct a **feasibility study** to determine (1) whether the community believes in the goal the campaign is addressing and (2) whether the community would be willing and able to support the campaign. If the feasibility study results are positive, the consultant often serves as the overall advisor and/or professional coordinator of the campaign. Capital campaigns can result in some great opportunities to serve communities, but they can also extract a great many resources from the community and should only be considered if real needs exist and if the community is willing to support the campaign. One potential negative side effect of a successful capital campaign is that donors may choose not to contribute to the organization when other requests for support come their way, and should be considered when identifying prospect lists for a capital campaign.

Figure 6.11

Flyer for Annual Campaign

Boxwood, Illinois—Big Brothers Big Sisters (BBBS)

"Buddy Campaign 2017"

CAMPAIGN GOAL $500,000

The Boxwood, Illinois, Big Brothers Big Sisters program matches children from single-parent families with caring, adult mentors for the purpose of friendship and guidance. The organization averages approximately 350 matches each year. The Big Brothers Big Sisters program of Boxwood is affiliated with the National BBBS organization. The Boxwood program has proven to be a deterrent to unacceptable behavior, drugs and alcohol abuse, and school absenteeism. It has fostered positive character development and provided opportunities for young children between the ages of 6–17 that might not have them otherwise. Won't you help? BBBS charges no fees to the families who participate, and the organization operates primarily through corporate and private contributions. You and/or your organization can choose to be a "Buddy" at several different levels:

Universal Buddy $5,000
Galactic Buddy $2,500
Solar Buddy $1,000
Super Nova Buddy $500
Super Buddy $200
Buddy......................$100

Just fill in information below, attach it to your check, and return it to the BBBS Buddy Campaign team member who contacted you. Any amount is greatly appreciated. Thank you so much for being a buddy to children who really need one!

_____   _____
Your Name   Corporation (if applicable)

_____   _____
Address   Phone Number

_____
Amount Contributed

©Roger Weis

Corporate and Service Club Support

Whether the support is for a special event, an annual campaign, capital campaign, or some other financial development method, corporate and club support can be essential. If cultivated effectively, corporations and service clubs, such as the Rotary or Lions Clubs, can become key allies for nonprofit organizations:

1. First of all, service clubs have a primary interest in the well-being of a community. Local corporations are also typically invested in the quality of life in the community. Increasingly, corporations are considering a dual bottom line of profit and social good. Their employees and colleagues, along with their families live and work in the communities in which they are located, and it is in their best interest to provide support to nonprofit organizations.

2. Another reason corporations and clubs often support nonprofit causes is that this support usually boosts the morale of the employees and members. Supporting nonprofit causes can enhance loyalty and positive feelings among employees and club members.

3. Finally, supporting nonprofit organizations establishes a strong public image and influences public opinion favorably.

When seeking funding support from a corporation or club, it is important to research the organization regarding their work and community involvement. Prior to seeking an interview to present a case for support, a proposal should be carefully prepared listing reasons the corporation or club should support the organization. The corporation or club will also want to know what the benefits to its organization will be if it supports the organization.

It's a good idea to offer the corporation or club sponsorship at several different levels and to seek an introduction through a board member or other community leader. Regardless of the results, the organization should be gracious in its relationship with the corporation or club, because a decision not to provide support today could be different the next time a request is presented. Individuals should always be thanked for their support in the most appropriate manner.

Planned Gifts

Planned gifts come in three forms, (1) **current outright gifts,** (2) **expectancies, and** (3) **deferred gifts** (Regenovich, 2003). **Current outright gifts** of assets such as stock, real estate, and personal property are considered planned gifts because of their value and that they are combined with other assets. The organization can keep the asset or sell it, as they choose. Another current outright gift is a **charitable lead trust** that pays income to the organization for a set period, and when completed the principle returns to the donor. An **expectancy** is a promise from a donor to make a gift at a future date, which can be revoked at any time. Bequests, retirement plans, IRAs, and life insurance are all expectancies that allow a donor to promise a contribution. The funds pass to the organization named as a beneficiary at the donor's death. Expectancies may be revoked by the donor at any time.

Deferred gifts involve the irrevocable transfer of money or property that will not be available to the organization until a set time in the future. Once established, the deferred gift is complete, providing an income tax deduction for the donor. The organization receives its benefit at a future event (the donor's death) or the expiration of a specified term. There are two common forms of deferred gifts, (1) a **charitable gift annuity** and (2) a **charitable remainder trust**. The charitable gift annuity is a contract where the donor transfers cash or property to the organization. The organization agrees to pay a set amount each year until the donor's death. The charitable remainder trust is created with a legal trust document that transfers cash or property to the organization. In return the donor receives income from the trust for life or a specific term not to exceed 20 years (Regenovich, 2003).

Since donors benefit from tax incentives and from the feeling that they have helped the community, and since organizations benefit from the financial aspects, deferred giving is a mutually beneficial process, but it has to be organized and promoted. The first step in organizing a deferred gifts program is to (1) form a committee consisting of an attorney, a banker and/or an accountant, and a marketing specialist. These committee members can be board members or other members of the community, with staff members in supporting roles. The committee members must then (2) decide the type of deferred gift plans the organization would like to initiate and (3) design marketing material that describes the plan and the ways donors can be involved. (4) A prospect list needs to be developed along the same lines of developing a prospect list for an annual or capital campaign. Once the list is ready, (5) contact should be made in person, over the telephone, and/or through a mail campaign. (6) Seminars describing the plans should also be considered, with the public invited.

Although a deferred gift program usually does not benefit an organization immediately, the long–term benefits can be astounding, and the benefits to donors are significant. Because of the minimal cost invested, the volunteer nature of the process, and the financial potential, seeking deferred giving should be an organizational priority.

Grant Support

Grant funds are typically viewed by the funding source as support for innovation in their specific fields of interest. The underlying assumption is that individual donors and program participants are unlikely to be able or willing to pay for the start-up costs of developing new programs and services, but once proven effective, they will be more likely to support the ongoing operation. Given that framing, most grant making organizations view their funds as a rare source of support for testing new programs, reaching out to new populations, or experimenting with creative approaches to program delivery.

A wide range of organizations use competitive grant making processes to distribute their resources in pursuit of their missions and interests. Different levels of **government** frequently use a grant making to distribute funds to promote innovation in addressing a critical social issue or challenge. **Corporations** often engage in grant making to distribute resources from their profits to help improve the community in which they do business and to participate in cause-related marketing to help enhance their public image. Individuals, families, corporations, and communities create philanthropic organizations (foundations) to focus funding attention on selected issues, needs, or communities. Many of these efforts are organized as **operating foundations**, which generally means that they do not have endowments and must acquire the funds that are distributed through grant making and/or by operating programs and services in support of their interests. **Endowed foundations** place funds in endowments, using the interest generated by the investment of the principle for grant making. IRS regulations promote philanthropy by allowing a tax deduction for donations made to foundations with their public benefit missions. The IRS promotes endowed philanthropy by requiring that a minimum of 5% of the net asset value to be given for public purposes each year. Over time this means that the endowment is able to generate more than that amount, with the difference being added to the principle and supporting its growth (Orosz, 2000).

As foundations accomplish their missions through the successful efforts of the organizations that they fund, they are typically very eager to connect with those working in their fields of interest. Lists of foundations and descriptions of what they support can be found online and in hard copies located in libraries around the country. The Internet facilitates connections and most grant making organizations have quality sites that offer detailed information about their interests and processes. The same commitment to transparency encourages organizations to be members of the Foundation Center and participate in their online directory, www.fdnenter.org. The directory is an electronic clearinghouse search engine that facilitates locating grant opportunities (Sargeant, Shang, & Associates, 2010). Another cite to consider is The Foundation Center (www.foundationcenter.org/) for lists of thousands of different opportunities.

The government is not designed to address actively all of the needs of each individual citizen. Billions of dollars, therefore, are set aside each year for government agencies to provide funding in the form of grants to individuals and organizations that propose to address some of the needs in communities. With the same commitment to facilitating quality communications and promoting ease of connection to grant making opportunities, most government funding sources turn to the Internet. For example, the U.S. Department of Health and Human Services manages www.grants.gov which offers a quality search engine for a very large portion of Federal funded grant making open to nonprofit organizations. In addition, the Catalogue of Federal Domestic Assistance (www.cfda.org) maintains information on almost all federally funded grant programs. With the success of such Internet sites as a model, more and more government departments at all levels of government are using their official websites to help promote grant making opportunities. Connecting to government funding opportunities can be supported by developing relationships with local, regional, and national political representatives whose job it may be to provide funding for worthwhile projects. Developing and maintaining communications can help insure connections whenever resources become available.

The sheer volume of grant making opportunities can make the search process challenging, particularly for small nonprofit organizations with limited staff resources. One frequently used approach to identifying potential grant making opportunities is to **participate in professional networks**, asking other nonprofit organizations in the local area that work on similar issues to learn what foundations they have applied to with success. Cultivating these types of relationships with other organizations can pay dividends over time. Look for opportunities to network through professional associations and community gatherings like the United Way Agency Directors Association and its regular meetings. Grant making organizations often use these associations and gatherings to promote their goals and opportunities to apply for funding support.

There are resources available to support the grant seeking process. Many nonprofit organizations have grant development departments that maintain this information and also provide instructional methods on completing applications and writing proposals for funding. Network organizations, associations, and educational institutions frequently offer support to the grant making process for their members, including grant writing training. Consulting firms and individuals are available to support grant seeking efforts for a fee. In addition, most grant making organizations are eager to support the application process in order to facilitate effective connections to those doing the most creative work in their areas of interest. Once a potential grant source has been identified, it is important to invest time in building a quality relationship with the organization's representative to help insure that the resulting application for funds meets all expectations and is successful.

Traditionally, an application for grant funds is presented in the form of a **proposal** that makes a compelling case for the alignment between what the project needs funded and the interests of the funding source. In addition to a written proposal, many grant makers (foundations and government) have a number of forms that must be filled out exactly as they are requested. With the increasing use of the Internet online applications, the forms include the typical prompts, space limits, and information requirements, not allowing submission until they are completed correctly. This type of online application may replace or be synonymous with the proposal for some funding sources. In completing an application or developing a proposal for a grant, it is always essential to *follow the directions* just as they are listed.

Although the requirements for grant proposals may vary greatly across funding sources, there are some typical sections proposals often include. The following are recommended to help guide the development of grant proposals and are derived in part from Weis and Muller (2015), Weis and Long (2011), Orosz (2000), and Sargeant et al., (2010):

1. **Introduction, Abstract, or Summary.** This section is usually brief and to the point. It should include the name of the applicant, the name of the funder from which the money is requested, the amount of money requested, and for what time period. Beginning the content area with detailed information regarding the problem or situation can be a strong start. It is a good idea to describe the program or method that is being proposed to address the problem, along with the program objectives. The program should be innovative and should clearly address the problem or problems. Information should be provided regarding the credibility of the organization and the credibility of the staff that would be developing the program. This section should be written in clear and concise language.

2. **Problem Statement or Statement of Need.** The problem statement or statement of need often follows the introduction. This section asks for expanded information regarding the problem or opportunity on a local basis and a description of the constituencies being served. The applicant may include quotes and paraphrases from local experts and officials if they emphasize the importance of the problem or opportunity. Information can point to community members affected by the situation, and quotes from some of these people can be provided. Incorporating vital statistics is also important. If the situation exists in other areas, regions, or localities, this information may also be included. If possible, a connection should be made here with the organization's background and the problem or opportunity.

3. **Program Objectives.** Program objectives describe *what* is to be accomplished through the program and is therefore an *outcome-based* concept. Objectives should be clear, specific, and measurable and should include established timelines for completion. They should be challenging, yet realistic. The evaluation of the project will assess the achievement of these objectives. Results anticipated beyond the funding period and information regarding the evaluation process may also be mentioned.

4. **Program Description or Methodology.** This section should describe the program activities in detail and answer the question of *how* the objectives will be reached (*outputs*). The program section describes the project staff and often includes resumes from key individuals, particularly the coordinator, attached as appendices. Timelines for activities need to be included and schedules for activities can be a part of the methodology section or attached as appendices.

5. **Evaluation.** The purpose of an evaluation is to determine whether adjustments need to be made to a project (**formative evaluation**) and whether the project was effective in achieving the objectives (**summative** or **final evaluation**). Also, it is often important to provide accountability to funders.

    A good practice is to provide a set of **key evaluation questions** that align with the program objectives. Providing the answers to these questions will allow the organization to demonstrate progress and success experienced during the grant.

    Evaluations may be done through a number of methods, including surveys, interviews, focus groups, and journals. Pre/post tests can also be administered to participants to determine changes from the beginning of a project to the end. Specific data, which might come from an educational institute or a health organization, for example, can also be recorded at the beginning of a project and then be recorded again at the end to calculate any significant changes. For more detailed information on conducting evaluations, see Chapter 5, "Program Development."

    This section should express a willingness to work with an external evaluator and describe how the results of the evaluation are to be recorded and reported.

6. **Organizational Expertise.** This section is used to demonstrate why the organization is the right one to take on the proposed project. There are several things that can be included to support this case, such as the mission, the qualifications of the staff, established expertise, and particular skills, technologies, or capacities.

7. **Future Plans.** If there is a need for a project to continue, many foundations and governmental sources like to know what will happen when the grant ends. Sometimes this can be accomplished by pulling the project into the organization's operating budget. Rearranging staff responsibilities and re-prioritizing existing supplies, materials, and other costs might do this. Another possibility is to institute some program fees, develop special events to support the project, and/or develop corporate sponsorships. Yet another proven method for future funding is to seek additional grant support. There is almost always a way to continue funding a project that should continue.

8. **Budget.** The budget for a project is guided by what is needed for a successful project and by what is available from the funder and other sources. The budget should indicate that all expenses for the project will be met in some way. The income side of the budget should include income that has been confirmed, as well as income that is anticipated. Expenses should be realistic and as minimal as possible without sacrificing quality

or important aspects of the project. The budget for a grant includes specific expenses and does not usually include a miscellaneous line. The budget should also include a narrative description where additional information will help explain any unusual or critical items.

9. **Additional Support.** Funders typically prefer that they are not being asked to fund the total cost of a project and want to see a description of any other sources of support, including funds from the organization itself. Support from other sources can demonstrate a sense of credibility and value others have placed in a project, and, where appropriate, show how the project may be funded after the grant funds being requested.

10. **Appendices.** This section should be used sparingly but provide copies of pertinent documents that support the case made in the proposal, such as related policies, reports, financial statements, key staff resumes, etc.

In addition to the counsel offered in the above outline, a grant proposal needs to demonstrate to the funding source (Long & Orosz, 1995):

- ► the creativity and innovation of the project
- ► how the project fits the funders' interests
- ► the commitment to doing the project whether grant is funded or not
- ► that the organization has the expertise needed to succeed
- ► that the goal is on improving the lives of people and not just making the organization better
- ► that the organization is working with people and not doing things to them
- ► that the organization is taking a comprehensive approach to the problem or opportunity and show how the project fits
- ► that the organization is working collaboratively with other organizations that are working with the same problem or opportunity

In addition, it is good advice to keep the proposal concise and to the point, do not oversell the project, and personalize the proposal to the funding source's interests. It is never a good idea to write one grant proposal and send it to a bunch of grant making organizations. It is definitely worth the effort to write the proposal so that the reviewers can see that the applicant believes that there is a strong fit between their need for funding and the grant making organization's interests.

A FINAL THOUGHT

In all aspects of financial resource development and management, it is critical that staff, board, and volunteer members follow the guidelines and policies of the organization regarding financial matters, and that the integrity of the individuals involved and that of the organization are always maintained. The **ethical culture** that is described in Chapter 2 is exactly the culture that must exist in all areas of finance. Maintaining openness will result in the community developing a confidence and trust in the organization and the individuals who are a part of it. Being able to explain and be accountable for financial activities also leads to community trust and is an integral ally in all financial matters.

A high quality ethical culture on all financial matters is integrated with the other aspects of organizational leadership and development. The integrity, honesty, and character that it reflects is a direct product of ethical organizational leadership. As presented in the Chapter 2 description of the importance for nonprofit leadership to incorporate generative or creative elements into their work, this chapter also seeks to promote a balance among fiduciary, strategic, and generative roles for leadership (Chait, Ryan, & Taylor, 2005). For nonprofit leaders to focus too much attention on any one of the three areas of organization development will lessen the impact of their work. High quality practice in financial resource development and management is most effective when it is accomplished in close alignment with quality strategic planning and generative organizational development.

SUMMARY

This chapter is divided into three major areas regarding fiscal matters: (1) financial management or budgeting, (2) financial processes or accounting, and (3) financial development or fundraising.

Managing finances includes the process of developing a budget, which is a financial plan for an organization. Creating a budget should follow certain steps, such as developing a list of expenses necessary for the organization to operate for a fiscal year. A next logical step in developing a budget should be to determine available resources for the coming year. Once this is done, a comparison of expenses to revenue should be made to determine whether the revenue projections are adequate for the anticipated expenses. Following this, organizational leaders must meet and set program and administrative priorities for the fiscal year.

Once these priorities are set, expense and income figures should be placed on a budget sheet and balanced. Following this, the board of directors approves the budget and, along with staff members, monitors, and in some cases adjusts, the budget at specific times in the fiscal year.

Other important budgetary considerations include a project or program budget that allows program leaders to project and calculate expenses and income lines for specific programs. A contingency/reserve fund is necessary so that nonprofit organizations can address unexpected expenses, potential growth, or other concerns and opportunities. Keeping a positive cash flow for expenses is important, and preparing a month-by-month cash-flow analysis is critical in managing a budget.

The term used for financial record keeping is *accounting*. Organizations either use a cash-basis accounting system, in which financial records are made only when cash changes hands, or they use an accrual-based system, in which records are made when money changes hands, and in addition, money owed by an organization and owed to an organization is accounted for as well. Many organizations also employ a modified cash-basis accounting system, in which some records are kept on a cash basis and others on an accrual-based system.

Unrestricted funds are funds that are designated for the sole purpose of operating an organization and are often kept on a single fund budget. Special projects and funds restricted for specific purposes must be noted separately and are often recorded on a multiple fund budget in a separate area from the operating funds.

A balance sheet provides a thorough look at the assets and liabilities of an organization at one particular point in time, usually the end of a fiscal year. An income statement summarizes financial activity over a period of time, usually a month or a year. Both provide valuable analytical information on the current and overall financial status of an organization.

Expenses and income must be controlled carefully. This usually entails having a specific checks and balances system involving at least two individuals within the organization. Bonding, which is a form of insurance, is a necessary process to protect the organization from loss of income through either intentional or unintentional irregularities. Other controls include making sure there is physical protection for records and finances.

Most nonprofit organizations are required to complete a number of forms that verify their tax-exempt status. These organizations must also withhold income taxes and social security from pay and report this amount to the IRS. Prepackaged accounting software is readily available to assist organizations with accounting needs. Some organizations contract accounting procedures to firms that specialize in these procedures.

Modern nonprofit organizations must construct a thorough and comprehensive financial development plan involving a number of revenue producing areas. Many nonprofit organizations require a membership fee to provide funds for operating the organization and providing members with a sense of ownership. Program fees may also be charged for special programs and are designed to cover some of the direct expenses involved.

Special events can also be effective in developing revenue and should be planned as carefully as all other programs. Product sales, if planned correctly, can provide substantial revenue, and United Way affiliation can be a significant source of funds. Annual campaigns provide money for the operating budget and help keep membership and program costs low. Capital campaigns provide much-needed funds for new buildings, renovations, major equipment purchases, and other major expenses.

Deferred gifts are mutually beneficial to nonprofit organizations as well as providing tax breaks for the donors, and grant support can infuse funds for special projects and community needs. Corporate and service club support is also mutually beneficial by providing support for organizations and providing a morale boost and good public relations to the corporation or club.

This chapter addressed, in part, the Nonprofit Academic Centers Council (NACC) Competency Requirements of Fundraising Principles and Practices and Nonprofit Accounting and Financial Management.

REFLECTION AND APPLICATION

1. Describe how financial budgeting, accounting, and development are interrelated:

   _____

   _____

   _____

   _____

   _____

2. What are the steps in developing a budget? List the steps and be prepared to discuss:

   _____

   _____

   _____

   _____

   _____

3. How does a program budget fit into the overall budgetary scheme?

   _____

   _____

   _____

   _____

   _____

4. Define the roles of contingency and reserve fund and be prepared to discuss:

   _____

   _____

   _____

   _____

   _____

5. What are the differences between an annual and capital campaign? Discuss.

_____

_____

_____

_____

_____

6. Describe how membership and program fees are determined:

_____

_____

_____

_____

_____

7. Make a list of what needs to be included in the case statement used to guide the creation of a comprehensive financial development plan:

_____

_____

_____

_____

_____

8. Develop a list of the sections of a grant proposal:

_____

_____

_____

_____

_____

_____

_____

REFERENCES

Andersen, K., & Higman R. (2011) *Online fundraising.* Nonprofit Management 101, San Francisco, CA: Jossey-Bass.

Bray, I. (2008). *Effective fundraising for nonprofits: Real-world strategies that work* (2nd ed.). Berkeley, CA: Nolo.

Brinckerhoff, P. (1994). *Mission-based management: leading your not-for-profit into the 21st century.* Dillon, CO: Alpine Guild Books.

Chait, R. P., Ryan, W. P., & Taylor, B. E. (2005). *Governance as leadership.* Hoboken, NJ: John Wiley & Sons, Inc.

Conway, D. (2003). *Practicing stewardship.* Eugene R. Tempel (Ed.). San Francisco, CA: John Wiley & Sons, Inc.

Garecht, J. (2016). How to write a case for support for your non-profit (Part I). The Fundraising Authority. http://www.thefundraisingauthority.com/strategy-and-planning/nonprofit-case-for-suppor/

Grace, K. S. (2003). *Leadership and team building.* Eugene R. Tempel (Ed.). San Francisco, CA: John Wiley & Sons, Inc.

Kaplan R., & Norton, D. (1992). Using the balanced scorecard as a strategic management system. *Harvard Business Review, 70*(1), 71–79.

Konrad, P., & Novak, A. (2000). *Financial management for nonprofits: Keys to success.* Denver, CO: Regis University, School of Professional Studies.

Long, R. F., & Orosz, J. J. (1995). *Approaching the foundation: A useful U.S. model. Philanthropy,* Australian Association of Philanthropy, Inc., Sydney, Australia.

Mintzer, R. (2003). *The everything fundraising book.* Avon: MA: F+W Publications Company.

Orosz, J. J. (2000). *The insider's guide to grantmaking: How foundations find, fund, and manage effective programs.* San Francisco, CA: Jossey-Bass, Inc.

Paton, R., (2003). *Managing and measuring social enterprise.* Thousand Oaks: CA: Sage.

Regenovich, D. (2003). *Establishing a planned giving program.* Eugene R. Tempel (Ed.). San Francisco, CA: John Wiley & Sons, Inc.

Rosso, H. A. (1996). *Rosso on fund raising: Lessons from a master's lifetime.* San Francisco: Jossey-Bass.

Sargeant, A., Shang, J. and Associates. (2010). *Fundraising principles and practices.* San Francisco, CA: John Wiley & Sons, Inc.

Seiler, T. L. (2003). *Developing and articulating a case for support.* Edited by Eugene R. Tempel. San Francisco, CA: John Wiley & Sons, Inc.

Weis, R., & Long, R. (2011). *Leading and managing nonprofit organizations.* Peosta, IA: eddie bowers publishing co., inc.

Weis, R., & Muller, S. (2015). *Leading and managing nonprofit organizations.* Peosta, IA: eddie bowers publishing co., inc.

Wolf, T. (1999). *Managing a nonprofit organization.* New York: Prentice Hall.

Worth, M. J. (2009). *Nonprofit management: Principles and practices.* Thousand Oaks, CA: Sage Publications, Inc.

Worth, M. J. (2017). *Nonprofit management: Principles and practices.* Thousand Oaks CA: Sage Publications, Inc.

Zietlow, J., Hankin, J. A., & Seidner, A. G. (2007). *Financial management for nonprofit organizations: Policies and practices.* Hoboken, NJ: John Wiley & Sons, Inc.

7

RISK MANAGEMENT

Providing a safe and secure experience for all constituents, volunteers, and staff members must be among the highest priorities for nonprofit leadership and their organizations. **Risk** is inherent in every aspect of life, and nonprofit organizations are certainly not exempt from this reality, but they need to develop guidelines for understanding and dealing with risk in the most effective ways. Although insurance acquisition is primarily a task for administrators, developing and maintaining an effective risk management plan is the concern of board members, administrators, and program leaders.

Across the nonprofit sector, organizational leaders accept the principle that no program is totally safe and that risk is an inherent part of doing business. In many parts of the world, program participants often assume a large part of the responsibility for risk. But in the United States, participants are far less likely to accept as much personal responsibility for risk, and acceptance of responsibility varies from activity-to-activity and from one age group to another. This perspective on risk has produced a climate of **litigation** where people are quicker to turn to the law and engage the court system to determine responsibility and accountability. The resulting increased legal action has pushed liability insurance costs higher. As a result, organizations are having to bear varying and increasing degrees of responsibility and are forced to be as prepared as possible with adequate insurance coverage and a comprehensive plan for managing risks. The more thoroughly the plan is implemented, the more effectively risk is managed. If the legal system is engaged, a high quality risk management plan that is being consistently implemented will help support the organization during the process.

This chapter explores the types of risk that are typically found in nonprofit organizations, the management of risk, the case for risk management planning, and the development of a comprehensive risk management plan. Specific risk management guidelines for program activities that involve complex logistics and unusual potential for risk will also be examined. The chapter concludes with a review of relevant risk management processes and forms and the role insurance plays in providing financial relief for losses.

WHAT IS RISK AND RISK MANAGEMENT?

A **risk** might be considered as any threat to a nonprofit organization's ability to accomplish its mission (Jackson, White, & Herman, 1997). David Belmont, Chief Risk Officer *Commonfund*, states

> "For a nonprofit, mission-driven organization, risk may best be defined in a more strategic sense as the possibility of a failure to meet the organization's implicit or explicit commitments to its beneficiaries arising from its inability to deliver sufficient cash flow to meet dynamic near-term liabilities while earning a long-term return in excess of inflation" (Belmont, 2015).

Asset–liability management is a form of risk management that nonprofit organizations should consider as a way to increase the odds of having the financial assets required to achieve their mission. This type of risk management begins by focusing on the organization's endowment. While the endowment exists to fund future liabilities, it is essential to maximize earnings to maintain asset values. Investment policy will depend upon the institution's reliance upon the endowment for financial and strategic direction. The larger the reliance upon the endowment, the more restricted the investment policy (Belmont, 2015).

Belmont (2015) recommends looking at the organization's financial and strategic dependencies. Financial dependencies are exposed by examining capital spending, donations, grant funding, endowment returns, programming income, and committed expenditures. Strategic constraints are revealed by examining the assumptions in expected endowment returns and the anticipated endowment income as described in the institution's strategic plan. This information can be used to run short- and long-term analysis scenarios where the risk management team envisions and analyzes potential outcomes by considering different scenarios. This process can be very effective provided the risk management team is thorough and takes most likely scenarios into account when conducting their analyses.

Threats to a nonprofit organization take a number of different forms beyond that of the institution's endowment, including potential risk to people, property, income, and reputation in the community. According to Worth (2017), risks for nonprofit organizations usually fall into one of these four categories:

- ▶ People: Board members, clients, volunteers, staff, the public
- ▶ Property: Buildings, facilities, equipment, materials, copyright, trademarks
- ▶ Income: Sales, contributions, grants, donations
- ▶ Goodwill: Reputation, stature in community, ability to raise funds and appeal to volunteers

While risk can never be managed away, nonprofit organizations can develop a framework and a *culture* for both understanding and addressing risk in the most effective manner.

Risk management is an attitude and commitment of everyone associated with the organization for dealing with potential threats to individuals, income, property, or reputation. The willingness to take risk depends on many factors, including the people who are involved and in charge, the organization's history with risk, and the financial conditions (Brinckerhoff, 2009). Risk is also relative. Small nonprofits are immune suppressed versions of larger, more resource-rich organizations, where a poorly managed risk that gives a large well-resourced organization a minor setback might lead to the demise of a small nonprofit. Accordingly, small nonprofits are exceptionally attuned to risk mitigation geared toward survival. It is not whether a risk is simple or complex that is the crucial factor in determining if it needs to be managed, rather risks that have critical institutional consequences require serious oversight.

A culture of risk management in an organization is illustrated by the thoroughness and application of a comprehensive plan for managing risk. Good risk management plans are carefully undertaken and result in well thought out implementation procedures that are successfully integrated into the ongoing operation of the organization. They should be aimed at protecting people, property, income, and the reputation of the organization (Weis & Muller, 2015).

A dramatic and industry-changing example of poor risk management resulting in loss of reputation occurred at the beginning of the twenty-first century. During this time, a series of large corporations (e.g., Enron, Lehman) were involved in accounting scandals that unfairly resulted in investors losing millions of dollars. As a result of these scandals the U.S. Congress passed the Public Company Accounting Reform and Investor Protection Act in 2002. This act is more commonly called the Sarbanes-Oxley Act (SOX), after Senator Paul Sarbanes and Representative Michael Oxley, who were the legislation's main sponsors (Jackson, 2006, p. 3). Even though this act was focused on public companies, the effect has been enhanced accountability among both the nonprofit and private sectors (Jackson, 2006, p 5).

Accountability and transparency remain headline issues in 2016 with media coverage regarding misuse of donated funds by organizations such as the United Way, Wounded Warriors Project, and the American Red Cross, where a much smaller portion of donations were actually making it to the intended populations than would represent best practice. These organizations were viewed as having failed in their duties of accountability as well as adherence to their missions. For some of these organizations, such as Wounded Warriors, the consequences of these findings being made public have threatened their continued support by individual donors who may choose to put their dollars to work where they will be applied more directly to the target population.

These incidents and other similar cases where nonprofits and charitable foundations have been accused of being either totally fraudulent or lining the pockets of the founders rather than helping the target population, have caused the public to lose trust in the entire sector and led to calls for more government regulation. To avoid passage of additional heavy-handed government accountability and regulatory legislation, leaders within the nonprofit sector should work toward adopting the practices laid out in the SOX legislation as best practice. This would improve standard business practice, enhance transparency, and increase the public's trust in the nonprofit sector. For any given nonprofit organization, adopting these practices would represent a major step toward reducing or managing risk.

With transparency and accountability to the public and stakeholders in the forefront of the news and active legislation efforts, it is essential that every nonprofit develop a formal risk management plan. The nonprofit sector relies heavily upon government contracts and restricted grants, which places the industry at greater financial risk than the for-profit industry. This type of funding virtually guarantees a deficit because these types of contracts create working capital needs and provide for funding that typically arrives after expenses are due (Roberts et al., 2016). These funds are also frequently delayed in payment by fluctuations in economic circumstances within the funding organizations.

In the same way that Enron and other high-profile corporate scandals were commonly viewed as a product of poor ethics and oversight, the credit market meltdown of 2008 and resulting financial crisis were blamed on ineffective risk management by corporations and their boards of directors (Katz & McIntosh, 2015). This resulted in the added expectation for an organization's board of directors. They are now expected to take a leading role in overseeing risk management, including forming structures and enforcing policies.

While we know that there is no way to eliminate risk, it is important for executive directors to become well-informed regarding the company's risk profile, to discuss and evaluate risk scenarios with the board and to ensure the adequacy of their collective efforts to address potential risks. The goal should be to make sure that potential risks are understood and appropriately managed. The Executive Director (ED) and staff are responsible for managing the risks, while the board of directors' role should be one of oversight (Katz & McIntosh, 2015).

Within this social context where nonprofits are being held to higher and higher standards for transparency and accountability, the Nonprofit Risk Management Center (www.nonprofit risk.org) proposes **10 reasons** why nonprofit organizations need **risk management plans**:

1. Risk management plans help the organization protect clients, staff, and volunteers and other individuals in the community from harm.

2. Nonprofit organizations are like any other institution: they are vulnerable to claims and lawsuits alleging damages and injuries due to operational activities and are not exempt from punishment because of their altruistic mission.

3. Accidents and other adverse situations can often be prevented with a carefully thought out plan.

4. Nonprofit organizations often undertake projects collaboratively with other entities, and it is essential that organizations have a comprehensive plan that protects collaborative partners as well.

5. Part of a risk management plan prepares organizations to forecast, prevent, and cope with difficulties stemming from a crisis in public confidence or negative publicity.

6. Prospective board, staff, and volunteer members will be far more attracted to an organization with an integrated risk management plan in place. All three groups are interested in strategies used to protect members and preserve the organization's assets.

7. A good risk management plan can preserve various categories of assets and enable the organization to concentrate its focus on fulfilling its mission.

8. Although some finances are necessary in funding the risk management plan, it will enable the organization to conserve financial resources in the long run by preventing the loss of finances in unexpected situations.

9. A risk management plan allows the organization to concentrate the majority of its financial resources on realizing its mission, rather than on accidents and other unanticipated incidents.

10. Having an effective plan for managing risks focuses attention on safe and productive operations and allows the organization to offer more programs and activities within the framework of a positive environment.

Nonprofit organizations should schedule comprehensive assessments of potential risks to the organization. These assessments should occur at least annually by the board of directors or this task might be delegated to a formal risk management committee made up of members of the organization with a variety of areas of requisite expertise. The assessment process should be carefully planned, conducted, and documented. The risk management committee should begin by reviewing the organization's strategic plan and look to see that the:

► organization's activities meet target population's needs
► community input is solicited to determine whether the activities are benefiting the people they are designed to help
► mission statement is clear and reflects the values and people served
► strategic plan is written in a way that will help achieve the mission
► strategic plan was written with input from all stakeholders
► strategic plan accounts for changes in the community as well as the organization
► strategic plan identifies challenges facing the organization
► strategic plan sets goals and measureable objectives that address these challenges
► strategic plan integrates the activities around the mission

- ▶ strategic plan prioritizes the goals and establishes timelines for their accomplishment
- ▶ strategic plan establishes an evaluation process that includes performance indicators to measure progress
- ▶ budget allocations are aligned with the strategic plan
- ▶ strategic plan is communicated to all stakeholders

Review of the strategic plan should be followed by an examination of current policies. This includes all manuals and handbooks that are used to instruct employee work practices. Nonprofit organizations should have up-to-date policies that guide relationships between staff and management. In recent years, there has been a significant increase in lawsuits regarding wrongful termination, harassment and discrimination, disagreements about promotions or salary, and other related issues.

Once a clear understanding of the mission, strategic plan, and current policies have been established, the board of directors or risk management committee can begin identifying and mitigating risks for the nonprofit organization. If a separate risk committee rather than the full board of directors is determined to be the appropriate way to manage risk, it might take on some of the following roles:

- ▶ Create a robust process for identifying, managing, and monitoring critical risks; oversee implementation of that process; and ensure it is continuously improved as conditions change.
- ▶ Provide timely advice and guidance to the board of directors and ED on critical risk issues.
- ▶ Engage in an ongoing risk management dialogue with the board and ED as conditions and circumstances change and new opportunities arise.
- ▶ Oversee organization-wide risk assessments, including identification and reporting of critical organizational risks.
- ▶ Oversee the management of those risks having the significance to warrant the attention of a separate board-appointed committee composed of individuals with the requisite expertise.
- ▶ Help the board coordinate activities of the various standing committees with risk-associated discussions and initiatives.
- ▶ Watch for dysfunctional behavior in the organization that could weaken the effectiveness of the risk management process or lead to inappropriate risk-taking.

The risk committee charge/bylaws should clarify that the committee's activities support the board's overall risk oversight goals and responsibilities. With respect to specific risks the risk committee is assigned to oversee, care should be taken to watch for overlaps with other committees such as the audit committee (Beaumier & DeLoach, 2011).

Many of these lawsuits have included the organization, management, as well as board members. Because of the legal implications, personnel policies should be reviewed at least once a year by an outside expert in employee-related laws and regulations. Ensure that all management employees are well-versed on these policies. It has been common practice for courts to interpret actions by organizational personnel as representative of the organization's preferred course of action, superseding related documented policies. This means that management must follow written policies or risk having courts rule as if their actual practices are the official policies (McNamara, 2013).

The implementation of high-quality risk management plans over time is the only way to create a culture in which the organization can be free to pursue its mission without being limited by fear of risk. To complement the above list of reasons a nonprofit organization needs a risk management plan, the Nonprofit Risk Management Center provides a Hallmark Tool that allows organizations to examine the quality of its plan and its implementation. The Tool is designed to inspire thoughtful risk-taking, illuminate **risk management hallmarks** in risk-aware organizations, and provide specific and practical guidance for strengthening risk management practices. The following are the hallmarks of a nonprofit organization that is risk-aware:

1. Takes more risks than it avoids

2. Heralds a risk management champion

3. Guided by reality, in addition to scary headlines

4. Is bold, but smart

5. Cultivates a "can do" attitude among paid staff and volunteers

6. Sees the whole iceberg not just the tip

7. Understands that hindsight is not 20/20, but it is better than being blindfolded

8. Tells it like it is

9. Is transparent with insurance partners

10. Values the journey, not just the destination

11. Engages the board in the battle

12. Looks at risk from everyone's perspective

As with hallmarks in any arena that serve as goals and guides, these are offered to help nonprofit leadership measure the context in which they work with the issue of risk. A well-managed nonprofit organization is not limited by the fear of risk and is free to actively pursue its mission.

Another reason to develop an effective risk management plan is that the types of legal actions that can be taken against nonprofit organizations are almost limitless. Risk management planning can help prevent many situations that might lead to a lawsuit. Some of the more **common types of lawsuits** against nonprofit organizations are listed below (Weis & Muller, 2015):

1. Accidents are the basis of the largest number of lawsuits filed against organizations. When someone causes an automobile accident, for instance, or creates some other dangerous condition that results in an injury, it is referred to as a **tort.** Under tort law, liability is typically based on negligence that implies the person causing harm did not exercise a degree of care that a reasonable person in a similar situation would exhibit.

2. A negligent act might be an indirect cause of an accident. For instance, an accident might occur while taking teens through leadership training at a high ropes course. The organization might be held liable for a broken limb, based on the fact the ropes course instructors had not been properly trained. The organization might also be held liable if the instructors had not been properly screened and did not have adequate certification. Improper screening of staff and volunteer members is the basis of many claims against nonprofit organizations each year.

3. Board members might be sued if practices based on organizational policy that they have set resulted in negligence and/or injury or some other form of harm. For example, if a program participant is hurt on the diving board at the local YMCA and their policy allows the diving board to be present, then board members as the legal body that approved that policy are open to potential legal action.

4. Unfair employment practices are a large source of legal action. Some areas that are frequently a part of such legal action include discrimination, wrongful dismissal, sexual harassment, and other employment-related acts.

5. In addition to organizations and directors being sued by people who allege injury, the appropriate government office for fines and penalties can also sue them.

Another arm of the government, the Internal Revenue Service, can also file claim against board members for the organization's failure to file tax forms or for breaching other IRS rules. Although board members should certainly take great care in their duties as board members, the number of lawsuits filed is relatively small and most claims derive from the area of employment.

Different experts in the field of risk management propose a variety of **strategies for managing risk**. However, there seem to be **five steps in the process of managing risk** (Herman & Head, 2002; Herman, 2005):

1. **Consider the Context.** The environment in which a nonprofit organization operates is changing constantly and needs to be considered and reviewed on a regular basis and be a starting point when any risk management issue surfaces. Changes in staff and volunteers, funding patterns, appetite for risk, experience with legal actions, and economic and political shifts can all impact an organization's view of risk or how it manages risk.

2. **Identify Risks.** Each operation, program, or activity presents conditions or situations that might present risks. Both obvious and not so obvious risks must be explored. For example, a service program that involves cleaning up debris along the bank of a lake presents some potential risk of drowning along with the possibility of being harmed from dangerous debris/materials or wildlife. Identifying risk should be done on a regular basis to respond to changes in the context. A good practice is for a group with diverse perspectives to periodically review the organization's work and brainstorm to consider risks, both current and potential.

3. **Evaluate Risks.** There is no single or preferred way in which to analyze, review, or rank the list of risks identified in step two. Determining the relative importance of risks can be accomplished by asking the following questions:
   ▶ What is the probability that a risk will result in an accident, injury, illness, or damage?
   ▶ How severe would the loss be if it occurred?

4. **Decide What to Do and Take Action.** This step requires the most commitment of time and diligence in making decisions about the actions that will be taken to address those identified risks. It is important to start by considering the three basic ways to handle risk:
   ▶ **Prevention (Avoidance).** Matching participants to appropriate experiences is one key to preventing and avoiding risk, as is effective orientation, training, and appropriate supervision.
   ▶ **Risk Reduction.** Providing safety rules and well thought out emergency procedures are examples of risk reduction. In the case of the lake clean-up above, following safety procedures regarding how close individuals should get to the water's edge and providing effective materials such as gloves, orange vests, and/or life jackets are ways to reduce risk. Clear communication is also important in risk reduction.
   ▶ **Risk Retention or Transfer.** Risk retention or transfer refers to how a loss will be handled should it occur. That is, who is responsible for the loss and how will the financial loss be covered?

5. **Monitor and Adjust.** It is important to regularly review risk management policies and practices, particularly after a risk issue has been handled. This allows the organization to learn from experience, improving the policies and practices or eliminating those that no longer apply. This step keeps the risk management plan current and easier to apply.

Experts with the Nonprofit Risk Management Center propose four somewhat different strategies for managing risks that align with and support the pursuit of the goals set with the use of the Hallmark Tool presented earlier in this chapter:

1. **Avoidance.** Most nonprofit organizations will simply not offer a service or conduct an activity if it is considered too risky and will curtail programs or services if risks cannot be managed well. For instance, providing a zip line at a Boys and Girls Club swimming facility could be great fun, but the inherent risk might far outweigh potential benefits.

   A number of nonprofit organizations that transport members or clients are scrutinizing this activity more closely and deciding it might not be cost- or risk-effective. If the risks outweighs the benefits, but completely stopping an activity impairs the mission of the organization, another technique—modification—can be considered.

2. **Modification.** This implies changing the activity so that it can still be implemented, but within modified boundaries, so the potential for harm is within acceptable limits. Modification might be as simple as screening volunteers more carefully, taking hazardous materials away from a fence next to a YMCA, or removing the diving board from the Salvation Army pool area.

   With the example of transporting clients or members above, some modifications that could keep a program within acceptable limits might include:

   ▶ Making sure driver licenses are up-to-date and that no driver transporting members has an unsafe or unacceptable driving record.
   ▶ Providing drivers with training relevant to safe driving, accident procedures, emergencies, and other proper vehicle operation procedures.
   ▶ Conducting regular vehicle inspections and maintenance, and removing or fixing any unsafe vehicles.
   ▶ Maintaining records on all risk management procedures.

   Modifying activities increases safety throughout operations and activities while still allowing activities to continue within the revised framework. Making these modifications sends a clear message to members and personnel that safety is the number one concern of the organization and helps advance a quality risk management culture.

3. **Retention.** If an organization decides that it will retain the risks inherent with a certain practice, then it must be prepared to handle those threats if they occur. For instance, if an organization decides not to purchase insurance for the loss of money, then it should consider a contingency fund that could handle financial losses that might occur from theft or some other event. To manage risk, the organization should anticipate what losses potentially might occur in various areas and decide the extent that those risks could be managed. This type of projection and planning should be ongoing, since potential losses might increase or decrease, from case to case, and the organization must be prepared to handle them.

4. **Sharing.** Working with another institution to share the risks or the financial consequences is another method of managing risk. Agreements for sharing with other institutions might include other nonprofit organizations, insurance companies (through premiums), or through some other contractual agreement. This option is also referred to as *transfer*, since it is possible to transfer risk to another party. It is, however, almost impossible to fully transfer the risk for an activity to another party and maintain responsibility for the activity.

    For instance, a nonprofit organization has purchased what it deems to be adequate fire insurance, after which a fire occurs. The insurance might cover the cost of property and injury, but not cover the loss of membership or program fees if programs are not operating or the serious damage to the organization's reputation for poor safety practices and not managing risk effectively. In this case, financial loss has not been completely transferred and the organization might still experience damage to its reputation.

THE PROCESS FOR DEVELOPING A RISK MANAGEMENT PLAN

Administrative leaders and board members should undertake the development and implementation of risk management plans with input from staff members, volunteers, organizational members, and other constituents. Another consideration is to involve a specialist in risk management to provide guidance in the development of a plan. The organization might wish to confer with other specialists as well, such as a human resource professional to examine the employee handbook, an accountant to help in developing financial and accounting controls, and an insurance professional to review related policies and insurance coverage. Many nonprofit organizations seek to include people with this expertise among their board and committee membership. Ideally, representatives with this range of needed expertise will be included in a **risk management committee** to guide the planning process and oversee the long-term development of the plan (Herman, 2005). Although there are any number of approaches to developing a quality risk management plan, this section will concentrate on the four-step process recommended by the Nonprofit Risk Management Center (Jackson, White, & Herman, 1999):

STEP 1. DEVELOP RISK MANAGEMENT GOALS AND A POLICY STATEMENT

The first step in developing a risk management plan is to determine the goals of the plan. The goals are set in collaboration with the ED and the board of directors along with input from a Risk Management Committee, although *only board members can actually approve the final plan*. In addition to setting goals, this group must also design a brief (one- or two-sentence) risk management policy statement expressing the organization's commitment to managing risk and outlining what individuals throughout the organization can do to support the risk management plan. The risk management policy statement can also be used to demonstrate to others the seriousness with which the organization is taking this important issue.

One of the first steps in establishing goals is to review reasons that it is important to have a risk management plan. An extensive list is presented earlier in this chapter, which includes the desire to reduce accidents, which also lowers insurance rates. Other reasons might include the discussion of prevention activities that can occur before any threat or loss and activities that can occur in response to a threat or loss. A thorough review of how the organization's programs and services will help determine what can be done to address these risks and others.

Based on the list of reasons for taking action that surface from this initial review effort, the Risk Management Committee can develop three or four specific goals for the risk management program, such as:

1. To protect the organization's financial assets.

2. To provide a safe and healthy environment for staff members, volunteers, and constituents.

3. To develop plans for any crisis that should occur.

4. To confirm that insurance is adequate and cost effective.

After determining the goals of the risk management plan, the next step is to write a **risk management policy.** The risk management policy is derived from the program goals. The policy should reflect the goals of the program and point to actions that others can take in the risk management efforts. A mock Scottsdale Salvation Army policy statement is included below:

> The Scottsdale Salvation Army's number one priority is to protect its people, property, income, and reputation through the practice of effective risk management. The organization's board, staff members, and volunteers are dedicated to maintaining the safety and dignity of all constituents.

A risk management policy can and should appear on all important documents associated with the organization, and it should be emphasized more than anything else the organization promotes.

STEP 2. DETERMINE RESPONSIBILITY OF THE RISK MANAGEMENT PROGRAM

With consultation from the board of directors, the ED should assign responsibility for developing and implementing the organization's risk management program to the Risk Management Committee. In addition to key staff, board members, and constituents, experts from appropriate fields may be included in the committee to make sure that the needed expertise is available. Areas of expertise needed might include:

- insurance
- legal area
- public relations
- safety
- program development
- content areas aligned with the programs and services of the organization

The composition of the Risk Management Committee will vary with the type of risks associated with the organization and might change over time as programs and services change and risk changes. There is also benefit to having people involved with the committee who have personal knowledge of the types of risks associated with the programs and services of the organization, which may be found among its constituent groups and program participants (Herman, 2005).

The Risk Management Committee should consider dividing into subcommittees to address various operational categories. These categories could include: program, finance, building and grounds, governance (board operations), and public relations, to mention several. The subcommittees would be charged with designing materials for in-service training as well as ensuring that the training is conducted, which should be ongoing. The greater the involvement of everyone in risk management training, the greater the possibility that risk management will be understood as the highest priority and practices across the organization.

STEP 3. DEVELOP A WORKING PLAN FOR THE PROGRAM

The first step of the Risk Management Committee is to develop an action plan and assign responsibility and completion dates for each part of the plan. Committee and subcommittee tasks are listed next:

- Discuss the four steps of risk management.
- Identify key subcommittees and determine responsibilities.

► Begin risk identification and analysis by subcommittee.
► Review, analyze, and consolidate subcommittee findings.
► Set priorities for risk management (top, moderate, low).
► Determine appropriate risk management technique.

A. Discuss the Four Techniques of Risk Management

Identifying techniques of risk management provides a framework for the work of the Risk Management Committee. A brief summary of the four stages in the typical risk management process follows:

1. Recognize and Identify Risk

The first stage in managing risk is to gather the Risk Management Committee together for a brainstorming session to identify what might possibly go wrong in the organization. Such a session begins with a discussion of potential threats to people, property, income, and reputation. Many risks are generic in that they are virtually present within any organization, such as wet floors following cleaning, the potential for theft, or allegations of improper hiring or firing. Other threats can be unique to specific organizations, such as sexual abuse within a youth organization, or a malpractice suit against an organization for providing free legal services. The facilitator for such a brainstorming session should be someone with expertise in both facilitation and risk management, whenever possible.

2. Assess and Prioritize Risk

Once potential risks have been identified, the committee can begin evaluating the risks mentioned and determine the probability of certain risks materializing, how often they might occur, and what would happen if they did occur. Following this evaluation, the committee (or subcommittee) can begin assigning a high, moderate, or low grading for risks based on their probability and severity.

Once labels of High, Moderate, or Low are assigned to each risk, the committee can look at those risks with a High rating to determine if the organization should avoid the activity, provide appropriate insurance for the activity, and/or manage the risk with specific actions. An activity that is placed in a Low priority might be postponed until those activities in the top and moderate categories have been addressed.

3. Select and Initiate Effective Risk Management Techniques

The four risk management techniques explained earlier are briefly reviewed below:

► *Avoidance.* Eliminate all activities that are deemed too risky.
► *Modification.* Restructure the activity so identified threats are within acceptable limits.

▶ *Retention.* Accept all risks and prepare for potential consequences.
▶ *Sharing* (transfer). Share potential consequences with another entity, such as an insurance company.

This implementation phase is a critical part of risk management. Expectations for the results of using each technique should be clear, measurable, and easily observed. This entire process needs to be explained carefully to board, staff, constituents, and anyone else who could be affected by the process.

4. Continually Monitor and Change the Risk Management Program When Necessary

This stage of the risk management process is also important because it involves members of the Risk Management Committee evaluating the plan that is being implemented and determining if it is having the desired effect. The committee needs to assess whether or not the plan is working. If not, it needs to modify the plan to make it more effective. Monitoring the plan requires a structured communication process in which members can interact with each other at scheduled times as well as at impromptu times to assess and make adjustments.

B.   Identify Key Subcommittees and Determine Responsibilities

Because of the complex nature of developing a risk management plan, sharing the responsibilities with subcommittees simplifies the process and can make it more effective by having the right expertise involved in each element of the planning. Subdividing tasks by the organization's different operations is one way to address this complexity. Following are some of the typical subcommittees:

▶ **Programs.** All identified programs can be assigned to a subcommittee specifically established for this operation. Another way to do this would be to have a subcommittee assigned to categories of programs, such as special events, facility-based programs, or field trips. Each of these areas can involve unique and significant risk that might need to be addressed.
▶ **Fundraising activities.** Fundraising activities present a unique set of risks. Controls and security processes for handling money need to be carefully spelled out for all to know and follow. Careful consideration should also be given in developing a system of controls that virtually prohibits any possible impropriety.
▶ **Administrative operations.** Administrative activities actually have a great potential for threat or loss when areas such as physical facilities, employment practices, office policies and procedures, computer equipment and data, and the accounting and financial operations of the nonprofit organization are considered.

▶ **Governance (board operations).** The legal and fiduciary responsibilities of a board of directors is significant, and examining the operation of the board, including legal documents, bylaws and articles of incorporation, is an important part of risk management planning. The procedures for board minutes, orientation programs, and operating policies and procedures should also be a focus of risk management.

A Risk Management Project Task Worksheet can be used to assign responsibilities and to track progress. A sample task sheet similar to the one suggested by the Nonprofit Risk Management Center is presented in Figure 7.1.

Figure 7.1

Risk Management Project Task Worksheet

| *Organization:* | Lexington, Kentucky Family YMCA | |
| *Date:* | November 15, 2016 | |

Task	**Leader**	**Start/Finish Dates**
Risk Identification	11/15–12/15	
Special Events	Jeffery Howe	
Field Trips	Ann Sakona	
Sports Leagues	Jeremy Fishe	
Fundraising	Roland Gunn	
Administration	Sandy Lynd	
Governance	David Monahan	
Review Subcommittee Findings	David Monahan	12/15–12/31
Establish Priorities	David Monahan	01/10–01/30
Evaluate and Select Techniques		
Special Events	Jeffery Howe	
Field Trips	Ann Sakona	
Sports Leagues	Jeremy Fishe	
Fundraising	Roland Gunn	
Administration	Sandy Lynd	
Governance	David Monahan	
Document the Program	Sandy Lynd	03/15–03/30

©Roger Weis

C.   Begin Risk Identification and Analysis by Subcommittee

Each subcommittee needs to begin analyzing risk potential for the assigned area of the organization. Committee members should be thorough in their efforts to identify risks. There are a number of tools available to help committee members identify potential risks. Several tools are discussed below:

▶ **Surveys, Checklists, and Questionnaires.** Forms that help organizations identify potential risks are sometimes referred to as **exposure analysis forms** (as in exposure to risk). These forms are developed by insurance companies and businesses specializing in risk management and can be helpful to nonprofit organizations in identifying risks. Risks can sometimes also be determined by focusing on the questions asked with insurance applications.

▶ **Internal Documents.** Documents and records, including bylaws, employee manuals, the annual audit, policies and procedures manuals, board and committee minutes, annual reports, fundraising materials, marketing flyers, accident reports, and other informational documents can be valuable clues as to where risks might be found in the work of the organization.

▶ **Financial Statements and Records.** Financial records, such as annual reports, monthly statements, and audit reports, might be helpful in determining whether there are any threats in financial controls and other risks.

▶ **Workflow.** Analyzing all of the processes involved with delivering core services will help determine if there are any problem areas. Areas to check include registration procedures, service delivery, complaints, grievance resolutions, and the monitoring and supervision of staff and members. Marketing, employment, and fundraising procedures are other areas to be considered.

▶ **Personal Inspections.** Going over paperwork can assist in determining risks, but walking around and personally examining facility areas, financial safeguard systems, and other types of potential areas of risk can provide additional knowledge regarding potential losses. Personal examinations should be done at different times during the daily schedule so that numerous types of activities can be observed and assessed.

▶ **Interviews.** In addition to surveys and questionnaires, conducting personal interviews can provide in-depth information regarding potential risks. Interviews should be conducted with those individuals who know more about existing risks than anyone else: staff members, volunteers, constituents, and any other parties that interact with the organization.

▶ **Loss Histories.** Identifying losses that have occurred in the past will help to ensure that history does not repeat itself and that the organization can provide safeguards against any trends with particular situations. It is also a good idea to examine what has happened in similar organizations, a process referred to as **benchmarking** (establishing a standard of practice by which the organization will measure its results).

D.   Review, Analyze, and Consolidate Subcommittee Findings

Once the subcommittees have collected their information and recorded it on the Risk Management Project Worksheet (Figure 7.1), the full committee should review the information. A number of mutual risks might be common to most areas, such as potential for child abuse, automobile accidents, or injuries, and these can be consolidated on one worksheet. A separate worksheet can be kept for risks unique to specific areas, such as employment procedures. Risks identified by one subcommittee that apply to another area that have not been identified by that subcommittee can be added at this point.

E.   Set Priorities for Risk Management (high, moderate, low)

After risks have been identified, subcommittees begin an assessment of the potential for each risk. Projections must be made for the chances that a loss will occur (*frequency*) and its probable effect (*severity*). **Frequency** indicates the probability a risk will actually occur and how often it might occur. **Severity** measures the probable effect and cost and negative impacts to the organization if the loss occurs. Each risk can be graded as high, moderate, or low for both frequency and severity (see Figure 7.2).

Assigning grades to potential risks can be challenging, to say the least, but looking at past history and assessing current operations can help subcommittee members assess and project the frequency and severity. Looking at each past operation to see if there have been injuries—thefts and fires, for instance—and considering the effects of these losses can help determine the grading of potential losses. Although it remains only a projection of losses, it has become a calculated and informed projection.

Once all risks have been graded, they can be divided into high, moderate, and low priorities. For example, incidents within the category of sports leagues, where there is a high potential for severity along with a high possibility for frequency, would certainly go to a high risk priority level. Something with a more moderate level of frequency and severity, such as a special event, would be listed as a moderate priority, and so on.

Categories that receive the highest priority have the potential of being highly detrimental to a nonprofit organization. These categories should be looked at closely to see if the

Figure 7.2

Risk Identification Grades

Risk	Severity			Frequency		
	H	M	L	H	M	L
Special Events		X			X	
Field Trips	X					X
Sports Leagues	X			X		

©Roger Weis

organization should avoid the risk altogether or transfer a part of the responsibility of the risk to another party, such as an insurance company. Categories of risk that receive a lower priority for severity and frequency might not require such strong actions, but still must be assessed and evaluated. All three categories require close attention.

F.   Determine and Establish Appropriate Risk Management Techniques

Once risks have been identified and prioritized, attention should turn to managing risk through various techniques. Sometimes an area requires a combination of techniques. For instance, field trips would certainly require the purchase of insurance covering travel and potential incidents that might occur during the trip. A screening and driver training program could also be put into place. This would help to promote safety and lower the cost of insurance premiums. The organization might, instead, choose to contract a part of the responsibility of the field trips to another party, such as a charter bus organization. This would still require some insurance, but some of the liability associated with the trip would have been transferred to the bus company.

Once strategies have been identified and put into place for the high level risks, attention can be focused on other priorities, and techniques can be put into place for these as well. For instance, special events were assessed at a moderate level for frequency and severity (see Figure 7.2). Checking existing insurance might reveal that it is adequate and that no additional insurance is required to satisfy the severity grade. Providing adequate staff and volunteer risk management training, along with appropriate waivers (discussed later in this chapter) for participants might be all that is required for this category.

STEP 4.   DOCUMENT, IMPLEMENT, AND MONITOR THE PLAN

After techniques for every risk are established for managing various risks, documentation processes need to be refined or put into place, along with plans to monitor the ongoing implementation of the plan. Piecing together worksheets and documents produced during the overall process will result in a Risk Management Manual to facilitate implementation. This manual can be invaluable for helping everyone in the organization manage risk effectively.

A number of items should be included in the manual:

- ▶ Risk management policy statement and goals
- ▶ Responsibilities of the Risk Management Committee
- ▶ Job descriptions for committee members and subcommittee members
- ▶ A list of all members including addresses, phone numbers, and e-mail addresses
- ▶ A synopsis of the work that went into developing the manual
- ▶ A list of techniques and monitoring methods for each identified risk
- ▶ Crisis and emergency management plans
- ▶ Copies of Risk Management Committee reports
- ▶ A summary of the organization's insurance coverage

Putting together a Risk Management Plan and Manual will take some time, but it is an important investment in the long-term well-being of the organization and all of its constituents.

Once strategies have been developed and a formal plan exists, the committee must decide how to implement the plan. Responsibilities, deadlines, and objectives for the plan need to be developed in order for it to be effective. An introduction of the plan including an explanation of the overall organizational approach and commitment to risk management must be presented to everyone involved, with required training for staff and volunteer members.

The Risk Management Committee must monitor the plan continually through established methods of collecting information. They should evaluate the effectiveness of the plan on a reoccurring basis. Because the organization and the populations they serve change, every aspect of the plan should be reviewed and revised on a regular basis. This review and revision process should be done as needed, but with a formal review process occurring annually. Good risk management plans become part of an organization's culture, enabling it to focus on its mission and improve the chances for success.

RISK MANAGEMENT GUIDELINES FOR SPECIFIC PROGRAM ACTIVITIES

Some programs are associated with higher risk activities and, therefore, might require more specific guidelines. Program activities such as water sports, team sports, some special events, and other programs with complicated logistics seem to take on lives of their own. These activities can be managed more effectively with guidelines tailored to the distinctive nature of each activity. In a sense, risk management guidelines for specific program activities become a *plan within a plan*. In other words, guidelines for specific activities fit into the overall risk management plan. Although each of these programs or activities need to be considered separately, the guidelines included in Figure 7.3 can be beneficial in managing risk for a number of different kinds of program activities (Edginton, Hudson, & Ford, 1999).

Each activity should be examined carefully to make sure that all identified risks are graded low enough to be acceptable or the committee needs to ensure modifications (e.g., helmets, gloves, lifeguards, trail guides, and safety equipment) are made. It is also important that personnel have the appropriate credentials and training; that participants are of the right age and skill level; that the facilities and equipment are safe and effective; and that no avoidable risk exists following detailed planning. Consider the following when applying the guidelines in Figure 7.3 in developing plans for each program and activity (Weis & Muller, 2015):

I. **General Description**

    A. **Name of Program or Activity**

        Appropriately naming a program or activity helps staff members, volunteers, and participants to begin forming a mental picture of what might occur, including any

Figure 7.3

Risk Management. Guidelines for Specific Activities

I.	GENERAL DESCRIPTION	
	A.	Name of Program
	B.	Type of Activity
	C.	Level of Activity
II.	DATES AND TIMES	
	A.	Dates
	B.	Times
III.	GOALS AND OBJECTIVES	
	A.	Organizational
	B.	Activity
IV.	LOCATION	
	A.	Site/Area
	B.	Weather
	C.	Routes
	D.	Facilities
V.	TRANSPORTATION	
	A.	Mode
	B.	Routes/Destinations
VI.	PARTICIPANTS	
	A.	Number
	B.	Skill Level
	C.	Characteristics
VII.	LEADERS	
	A.	Number/Roles
	B.	Qualifications
VIII.	EQUIPMENT	
	A.	Type and Amount
	B.	Control
IX.	CONDUCTING THE ACTIVITY	
	A.	Pre-Activity Preparation
	B.	Group Control
	C.	Teaching/Instruction Strategy
	D.	Time Management
X.	EMERGENCY PREPAREDNESS	
	A.	Policies
	B.	Health Forms
	C.	Telephone Numbers

©Roger Weis
Adapted from Edginton, Hudson, and Ford, 1999.

potential risks. Organizers can begin to brainstorm for potential risks. For instance, a swimming activity might conjure up images of drowning, hypothermia, or choking. A baseball league will include equipment—such as bats, bases, and fences—that can cause bruises or broken bones. Even something as seemingly harmless as an arts and crafts program might include potentially hazardous materials, such as cutting instruments, electrical tools, or heat from the use of a kiln.

B. Type of Activity

Determining what will take place during each program or activity will help in designing the appropriate risk management techniques.

C. Level of Activity

Using industry-appropriate terms when describing the skill levels associated with each activity is also important. Terms such as *beginners*, *advanced-beginners*, *intermediate*, and *expert* might suffice. Sometimes activities have their own set of terms in describing skill levels, but the most important rule is to use terms that everyone understands, staff and participants alike. If there is uncertainty, include a clarifying description of participant skill level requirements.

II. Dates and Times

The designation of dates and times is important so that contingency plans can be made for events that will be held outdoors, in case of inclement weather. Another consideration is timing: an event held outdoors in the summer will have a longer opportunity for daylight than if the same event were held in the winter. It is also important to plan things so that activities do not last so long as to unduly fatigue leaders and participants and so that each group receives adequate breaks and refreshments. The possibilities for fatigue and overstimulation should be considered when planning a long event, so adequate downtime and refreshment breaks should be built into the schedule.

III. Goals and Objectives

Listing and understanding goals and objectives is imperative to the overall success of the activity. Understanding purpose gives direction to the activity and some guidelines for what risks might be acceptable or not. Objectives need to be clearly written with specific, projected outcomes. These objectives should be as inclusive as possible, stating skill, knowledge, emotional, spiritual, and/or physical attainment sought as appropriate. Both leaders and participants should have a clear understanding of the objectives.

IV. Location

The selection of a location for a program influences the potential type and severity of risks that might be involved.

A. Activity Site or Area

The activity site or area should be described by name and/or details might be listed that allow participants to find the site using a map or GPS. Information regarding any special hazards associated with getting to the site or the site itself should be identified in advance. Current, in-depth information should be available regarding the site prior to the event, and every attempt should be made to visit a site prior to conducting the activity.

B. Weather and Climate

Weather should be assessed carefully prior to an activity, particularly an outdoor activity or one that requires travel. Being prepared for a change in weather during an activity is also extremely important. It is far better to be prepared for the worst-case scenario and to operate on the conservative or safe side.

C. Routes

Activities that involve travel or moving from one place to another should be precisely described in the program plan, particularly when a trip of several days or more is planned. Emergency escape routes should be considered and communicated along with possible lodging sites, locations for food and liquids, and locations of medical facilities or services.

D. Facilities

Facilities that are to be used for an activity should be fully described. Directions should be provided if the facility is located away from the home organization. All facilities should be carefully inspected, especially those with high potential for risk, such as ropes courses, swimming pools, gyms, and playing fields. When visiting lakes, streams, or oceans, it is imperative to understand the tide movement, strength of the currents, the depth of the water, the presence of dangerous wildlife, and any unusual occurrences associated with that particular aquatic area.

Proper plans for fire emergencies are important for activities in buildings. Fire alarms need to be continually tested, and a fire emergency exit plan needs to be established and practiced. Periodic inspections of building systems, like electrical and air conditioning, must be a priority. Other equipment that should be formally inspected as the risk management committee dictates includes diving boards, gymnastic equipment, swimming pool chemical and filter systems, and any other equipment or structure that might present a risk.

V. Transportation

A. Mode of Transportation

Transportation plans for activities need to be clearly devised and communicated. If a charter bus is chosen for a ski trip, the company providing the bus should be carefully checked out for its overall safety record, screening of drivers, training requirements for drivers, insurance coverage, and scheduling procedures. An understanding of equipment maintenance records is important. Buses, vans, and cars that are maintained by the organization must also be properly serviced and documented. Drivers should be carefully screened, trained, and monitored.

B. Routes, Distance, and Time

Participants should understand prior to an activity that involves transportation which routes are going to be used, the distance to be traveled, and the time involved, as it can best be projected. Alternative routes and times should be discussed, as should emergency action plans. Often, the transportation of participants and staff members is the most dangerous part of an activity, yet it is too often considered an afterthought. The risk management plan for transportation needs to be reviewed and followed diligently.

VI. Participants

A. Number

Most events will have both a maximum and a minimum number of participants established in advance. Minimum numbers are often set so that resources are not spent on events with little interest, and maximum numbers are set to ensure quality and often to meet guidelines for space accommodation and safety. Both are valid concerns, but flexibility is important when possible and appropriate.

B. Skill Level

Participants should be aware in advance of what skill levels, if any, correlate with a program activity. In many instances, the terms *beginning*, *novice*, *intermediate*, *advanced*, and *expert level* are assigned to different activities and each will have a different skill requirement and a different risk management strategy.

C. Characteristics

Participant characteristics have to do with specific, individual attributes, such as whether a participant is an adult or a child, male or female, and in some cases disabled, highly fit, or just starting a fitness program. Knowing as many characteristics as possible regarding the participants makes it easier for program staff to assign the right kind of supervision. It also allows the participant a chance to understand more about the challenges of a particular activity. For instance, a 10-mile hike or a climb through a hillside covered with rocks would not work for a novice, but might be fine for an intermediate-level participant.

Developing a participant profile helps to prevent mismatching lower level skills or other attributes with an activity that is too challenging.

VII. Leaders

A. Number and Roles

Describing the criteria necessary for activity leaders in the program plan is a wise concept, as is listing the number of leaders required for each activity. Most organizations have a required ratio of staff-to-participants for quality assurance and risk management purposes. Program staff members are usually the most expensive part of a program budget, but generally the more qualified staff an activity has, the better and the safer the event.

B. Qualifications

It is important to maintain a current list of qualifications and years of experience of individual staff members. Hiring standards and requirements for staff members should be at least as stringent as those of comparable organizations in the region.

VIII. Equipment

A. Type and Amount

Listing the various types of equipment involved in an activity and certifying that the equipment meets acceptable guidelines indicates that activity leaders are making every effort to keep risk to a minimum. Maintaining the right number of tumbling mats, for instance, is important, because having a lesser number could raise a concern for safety.

B. Control of Equipment

A system for controlling and maintaining equipment is essential to be certain it is kept clean, dry, and in good condition for the next usage. Equipment should be checked, both when it is returned and when it is checked out again, to maintain the best condition possible and to avoid any unpleasant surprises during an activity.

IX. Conduct of the Program Activity

A. Pre-Activity Preparations

Pre-activity meetings should be included in the risk management plan for all activities to promote a culture that expects the plan to be integrated with the program implementation process.

B. Group Control and Communication

How communication will occur within a group activity, including attendance keeping, should be included in the risk management plan. This, of course, includes any and all safety instructions, as well as a detailed account of who is responsible to whom and for what.

C. Teaching Strategy

Teaching strategies for developing various skills should be documented and notes kept on any variation from non-standard methods, with reasons for the variations. Teaching strategies affect risk levels, so they need to be understood and documented appropriately.

D. Time Management Plan

Setting beginning and ending times and dates for activities, along with times and dates for specific parts of the activity schedule, provides guidance for what is to happen, when it happens, and how long each part is scheduled to last. This provides the program team valuable information for overall program development and is essential for good risk management.

X. Emergency Preparedness

Developing strategies for program emergencies is a critical part of any risk management plan. Plans for fires, storms, floods, first aid, missing persons, transportation breakdowns, and other emergency situations should be developed and documented.

Each program and activity plan should also have a place to include emergency help numbers and emergency numbers for participants in case of an incident. If health forms are necessary, they should be current and attached to the plan. The risk management guidelines for specific programs described in the last section address most components of program activities and can be used as standard operating procedures for similar types of activities. Standard operating procedures or guidelines, as such, can be easily inserted in the overall risk management plan. Release forms and waivers will be discussed in the next section.

REPORTS, FORMS, WAIVERS, AND RELEASES

There are a number of reports and forms that can help in planning and organizing programs and activities. These forms can be prepared by the administrative and program staff, but they should be reviewed by the organizational legal counsel to help make sure that the information needed for legal issues and effective risk management is being collected. Examples of forms include the following (Weis & Muller, 2015):

► **Agreements.** Specific agreements can be developed between collaborating organizations, so that expectations are clear regarding which organization is responsible for specific aspects of the undertaking. These kinds of agreements clarify roles and make managing risk much easier.

▶ **Participation Agreement.** Sometimes called **Assumptions of Risk Agreements**, the document is developed to accurately reflect that the participant understands the risks, agrees to abide by safety rules, and agrees to abide by established behavior codes.

▶ **Accident Reports.** Accident reports should be completed on any incident that occurs during a program or activity supported by the organization and details of any injury that results. The report must include a detailed description of what happened, a list of the parties involved, and an account of what was done to alleviate any pain or suffering.

▶ **Incident Reports.** Incidents that are out of the ordinary which pose potential risk to individuals, property, finances, or reputation should be recorded and any disposition noted.

▶ **Personal Health Forms.** Health forms might be required of all participants in the programs and activities of an organization, or they might be required to complete a form prior to specific activities. Health forms should include relevant information such as the participant's limitations, medications, allergies, disabilities, and health status.

▶ **Waivers/Releases.** These two terms are used interchangeably here, and each implies that the participants agree not to hold the organization responsible. For minor children, this form is only valid when signed by an adult, and parents or guardians **can never sign away the rights of children under the legal age of majority**, as previously mentioned in Chapter 5. Signing such a form for children indicates intent, but does not have a strong legal basis.

Signing a waiver does not eliminate the potential of being sued for negligence. Most U.S. courts have ruled that organizations providing a public service cannot absolve themselves from liability to the public whom they are providing a service, particularly in cases of negligence. Regardless, it is important that organizations protect themselves and their members as much as possible by providing waivers to participants.

Waivers indicate that the participant has at least stated that he or she will not hold the organization responsible and understands the risk involved in undertaking the activity, which might dissuade the participant from pursuing legal resolution. Release forms also remind participants of potential risks and make them more alert to hazards associated with activities. They are, therefore, well worth the effort of creating, completing, and filing.

INSURANCE

One method of reducing the financial risk for an organization is to purchase insurance. Maintaining insurance coverage does not eliminate risk; it just transfers some of the financial responsibility for risk to the insurance company in exchange for a premium. Purchasing insurance does not reduce the possibility that an accident or some other mishap will occur; it simply provides a method of payment for any damages or compensation.

Insurance is usually divided into property and liability coverage (Herman, 2005). **Property insurance** typically covers tangible assets such as furniture, buildings, computers, documents, and equipment. This type of coverage will often replace the losses. It can also pay the cost of a temporary office, if one is needed until a more permanent space can be provided, and it can cover loss of income during periods when programs and activities are not possible. **Liability insurance** provides protection from claims and lawsuits against the organization. It also provides financial relief if the organization is found to be negligent and that negligence has caused damages to another person or organization. These general liability insurance policies—usually referred to as **commercial general liability**—do not cover all losses, particularly those arising from board decisions and the delivery of professional services. These types of claims can generally be protected by purchasing **directors' and officers' policies**, which provide financial relief in the event the organization and/or its officers and staff are sued regarding a loss as a result of a board decision or of a service provided (Weis & Muller, 2015). These are commonly known as D&O policies.

Every nonprofit organization, especially if it occupies a physical space, should purchase general liability insurance. This covers the organization if clients or visitors fall down stairs or a bookcase falls on them. For added protection it would be good practice to add employees and board members as additional insured entities to these policies. The organization should also consider purchasing Non-Owned Auto Coverage, which protects when an employee is driving a family or rental car for business reasons. This type of coverage is usually contained in a general liability policy.

Nonprofits that employ professionals who see clients (e.g., health and social services) should ensure that these employees are covered with professional liability insurance, either individually or as provided by the organization, and that the nonprofit is named as an additional insured entity.

Organizations that move large amounts of money should have additional protection called fidelity coverage to guard against possible criminal acts. These types of losses are specifically excluded from D&O insurance. Areas of loss that fidelity coverage includes are theft, robbery, burglary, forgery, and general shenanigans involving computers. D&O coverage might protect the board from failure to implement proper controls that would have prevented the losses from the exposures covered under fidelity. It is recommended to discuss this with an insurance agent and get your questions answered in writing on the insurance company's letterhead to document the explanation (McNamara, 2013).

The booklet, Nonprofit Board's Role in Risk Management, outlines that D&O insurance typically does not cover fines or penalties imposed by law, libel, and slander; failure to procure or maintain insurance; dishonesty; personal profit; bodily injury; and property damage claims, pollution claims, and suits by one board member against another (BoardSource, 2012, p. 211). The larger the nonprofit and the wealthier the board members, the greater the need for D&O insurance coverage. This coverage is very expensive, making it prohibitive for smaller organizations. It is recommended to work with your agent to create a coverage plan that provides limited coverage for what you are realistically risking. If the organization management team decides to purchase D&O insurance, you should have the proposal reviewed by an insurance professional other than the agent selling it prior to purchasing the policy.

As a final point about D&O insurance, unless the organization's bylaws specify otherwise, it is typically presumed that the nonprofit organization will indemnify an employee or board member for actions taken, as long as no actual malfeasance was involved. Remember that indemnification is not worth much if the organization has limited assets and/or insurance (McNamara, 2013).

Nonprofit organizations are vulnerable to losses stemming from accidents or negligence. Purchasing insurance is one way of mitigating risk to prevent excessive or possibly devastating financial loss to an agency or entity (Weis & Muller, 2015). Insurance policies assure the availability of some of the needed funds to pay for damages and to compensate victims following a loss. Although insurance is important, it is not the only mechanism of protection available to a nonprofit organization. Other options include setting aside reserve funds to pay for potential losses, or establishing a line of credit with a financial institution to cover something that might go wrong down the road. Both of these additional options need to be calculated with the cost of insurance versus the loss of readily available money through the establishment of a reserve fund, or the loss of money to cover a credit owed.

Because of the many different kinds of insurance needs and the number of types of insurance policies available, a committee consisting of administrative and program staff members, board members, and experts in insurance should be formed to help determine the extent of coverage needed. Often, insurance is either mandated by law and/or by the organization's national affiliate. Many times, branches of the same organization or organizations with similar missions and programs will band together to purchase less expensive group insurance policies. In addition, state and regional associations of nonprofit organizations provide the opportunity for nonprofits to participate in group insurance programs. The National Council of Nonprofits (www.councilofnonprofits.org) is a good place to find links to these types of group support systems. In most cases, it is far better to have adequate insurance coverage for all potential losses than to rely on other sources of relief.

SUMMARY

A risk could be anything that is deemed a threat to an organization's accomplishing its mission. Threats usually take the form of potential risk to people, property, income, and reputation in the community. Risk can never be fully managed away, but organizations can develop ways to deal with risk effectively. Maintaining insurance transfers some of the financial responsibility for risk to insurance companies in exchange for a premium, but does not eliminate risk.

Risk management is a plan for dealing with potential risks. There are a number of reasons for developing organizational risk management plans, all of which are aimed at protecting individuals, income, property, and reputation.

There are a number of different strategies for managing risk, and they generally include identifying, evaluating, and handling risk. Experts at the Risk Management Center propose other strategies, including avoidance, modification, retention, and sharing, all of which make it easier for an organization to manage risk.

The development of an organizational risk management plan should be undertaken by a risk management committee made up of board members, staff leaders, constituents, and experts in the field of risk management. Developing a good risk management plan involves four steps:

1. Developing risk management goals and a policy statement.

2. Determining responsibility of the risk management program.

3. Developing a working plan for the program.

4. Documenting, implementing, and monitoring the program.

Certain program activities might require more specific guidelines. In a sense, these guidelines become a plan within the overall organizational risk management plan. They include a general description and details of the program, including dates, times, goals, objectives, location, transportation, participants, leaders, equipment, activities, and emergency processes. Planning and assessing these details in advance adds a great deal of strength to reducing risks in each program activity.

There are a number of reports and forms that can help to plan and organize program activities and help to minimize risk. These include agreements between collaborating organizations, agreements for program participants, accident and incident reports, personal health forms, and waivers and releases.

Insurance is a way to transfer some of the financial responsibility for risk to the insurance company in exchange for a premium. Insurance is the typical way of handling risk to prevent excessive or possibly devastating financial loss to an agency or entity. Because of the many different kinds of insurance needs and the number of insurance policies, a leadership committee should examine the best possible coverage for the organization.

This chapter addressed, in part, the Nonprofit Leadership Alliance Certification Competency Requirements of Nonprofit Risk Management.

REFLECTION AND APPLICATION

1. Relying on the definition of risk provided in the second page of this chapter, describe the three key risks involved in a program activity in which you have recently participated:

   _____

   _____

   _____

   _____

   _____

2. Describe the five steps in the typical risk management process:

   _____

   _____

   _____

   _____

   _____

3. In one paragraph, summarize the 10 reasons the Nonprofit Risk Management Center provides as justifications to have a risk management plan.

   _____

   _____

   _____

   _____

4. What is the importance of a policy statement and how might it be used?

   _____

   _____

   _____

   _____

   _____

5. List and give reasons for including specific members on the risk management committee:

_____

_____

_____

_____

_____

6. Write a brief description of the process for determining risk management priorities:

_____

_____

_____

_____

_____

7. Why is it important to have risk management guidelines for specific program activities? Give two examples of how these guidelines might help reduce risks.

_____

_____

_____

_____

8. What is the role of insurance in managing risk, and what is the process for determining the right kind of insurance for an organization?

_____

_____

_____

_____

_____

_____

REFERENCES

Beaumier, C., & DeLoach, J. (2011). Risk oversight: Should your board have a separate risk committee? *Protiviti,* Issue 24. *Director Notes.* Retrieved from https://www.conference-board.org/retrievefile.cfm?filename=TCB-DN-V4N1-12.pdf&type=subsite

Belmont, D. (2015). Redefining the risk waterfall. Insight Online, Summer 2015. Retrieved from https://www.commonfund.org/wp-content/uploads/2015/12/Insight_Summer2015_Belmont.pdf

BoardSource. (2012). *The nonprofit board answer book: A practical guide for board members and chief executives* (3rd ed.). Washington, DC.

Brinckerhoff, P. C. (2009). *Mission-based management: Leading your not-for-profit* (3rd ed.) Hoboken, NJ: John Wiley & Sons, Inc.

Edginton, C., Hudson, S., & Ford, P. (1999). *Leadership in recreation and leisure service organizations.* Champaign, IL: Sagamore Publishing.

Herman, M. (2005). *Risk management.* Robert D. Herman (Ed.) (2nd ed.) The Jossey-Bass handbook of nonprofit leadership and management. Hoboken, NJ: John Wiley & Sons, Inc.

Herman, M., and Head, G. (2002). *Enlightened risk taking: A guide to strategic risk management for nonprofits.* Washington, DC: Nonprofit Risk Management Center.

Jackson, M., White, L., & Herman, M. (1997). *Mission accomplished: The workbook.* Washington, DC: Nonprofit Risk Management Center.

Jackson, M., White, L., & Herman, M. (1999). *Mission accomplished: A practical guide to risk management for nonprofits* (2nd ed.). Washington, DC: Nonprofit Risk Management Center.

Jackson, P. (2006). *Sarbanes-Oxley for nonprofit boards: A new governance paradigm.* Hoboken, NJ: John Wiley & Sons Publisher.

Katz, D., & McIntosh, L. (2015). The changing dynamics of governance and engagement. *New York Law Journal,* July 23, 2015.

McNamara, C. (2013). *Insurance against liabilities* in Davidson, C. Reducing risk/protecting people: An annotated guide to 40 free online risk management resources.

Roberts, D., Wyman, O., Morris, G., Wyman O., MacIntosh, J., & Millenson, D. (2016). *Risk management for nonprofits.* Oliver Wyman.com. Retrieved from seachangecap.org/.../2016/03/SeaChange-Oliver-Wyman-Risk-Report.pdf

Weis, R., & Muller, S. (2015). *Leading and managing nonprofit organizations* (2nd ed.). Peosta, IA: eddie bowers publishing co., inc.

Worth, M. J. (2017). *Nonprofit management: Principles and practice* (4th ed.). Thousand Oaks, CA: Sage Publications, Inc.

8

ORGANIZATIONAL DEVELOPMENT: BUILDING CAPACITY, IMPACT, AND SUSTAINABILITY

Organizational development is the application of all of the principles and practices presented in the preceding chapters. Leaders need to understand the nonprofit context, the characteristics of quality organizations, and what can be done to make them more effective and efficient. Organizational development means building and improving the various components of the system so that each works as desired and they work well together. Improving the representation of needed skills and perspectives on the board is organizational development. Putting effective financial management controls in place is organizational development. Conducting a comprehensive financial development plan is organizational development. By comparison, **capacity building** includes all that the organization does to improve the impact of its programs and services in the community. It can include work being done to improve human resources and skills, systems and structures, strategies, and program and service approaches. As each of these areas of the organization's work are extended, expanded, and improved, capacity is built to increase and sustain impact on the issues and goals that are aligned with the organization's mission.

A great deal has been written about how to develop healthy and effective nonprofit organizations that are engaged in serving the needs of their communities and constituents. Many approaches to organizational development start with creating and improving the component parts of the system with the expectation that they improve the capacity of the organization to pursue its mission (Worth, 2017). Developing leadership, improving human resources, integrating human development, refining programming, growing finances, and attending to issues such as risk management all serve to make nonprofit organizations more effective (Weis & Muller, 2015).

Nonprofits have traditionally been viewed primarily as mission-driven organizations; while this remains true the pressure for them to function more like traditional businesses has increased tremendously over the past decade. Current measures of success concentrate on an organization's impact, by examining how much it influenced the Human Development Index (HDI) in their target population (Measure of America, 2016). As business enterprises, nonprofits are built on an underlying model that serves to make the programs and organizations operate and succeed. The economic recession of 2008 placed a strain on many nonprofits and led many to question the sustainability of traditional nonprofit models. Christine, William, and Grossman (1999) address the issue of nonprofits resisting the idea of building organizational capacity. Many in the nonprofit sector are drawn to it because of their passion for a specific cause, which involves delivering services. These folks often believe that spending time and energy focusing on market share and fundraising might detract from the mission. These authors make the case that building organizational capacity that can allow for adaptation is the best way to create value for the communities they serve (Christine, William, & Grossman, 1999, p. 24).

According to Light and Hubbard (2004), philanthropic interest in nonprofit capacity building has grown steadily over the past decade. In conducting their research on the topic of capacity building, these authors reported that funds tended to be available in these categories:

▶ Direct response programs—provide funds or services to address defined short-term capacity building needs, such as board training, new financial management systems, or strategic planning.

▶ Capacity building long-term organizational effectiveness—initiatives that address a broad range of issues across multiple aspects of organizational life.

▶ Sector-strengthening programs—support knowledge development through research and educational institutions, knowledge delivery, and knowledge exchange through conferences and meetings.

To prepare for the task of building organizational capacity, leaders of nonprofits must carefully assess the effectiveness of their particular structure and consider moving their organization to operating under a different approach. The Nonprofits Assistance Fund (2014) recommends the following steps when preparing for this type of organizational change:

1. Understand the current operating model;

2. Diagnose any critical weaknesses;

3. Forecast and plan a structure that will address the weaknesses and be effective in the short- and midterm future;

4. Implement the needed, and possibly difficult, changes.

The financial structure of nonprofits is composed of program costs, infrastructure, capital structure, and revenue mix. These work together to define the business model used by the nonprofit organization. These four components are interrelated and changes in one will impact the other three. Step one begins with inquiries and analysis of these elements to understand the current business model. Diagnosing any critical weaknesses necessitates an accurate assessment of external economic factors, past organizational policies, decisions, and activities. Predicting and planning might bring about significant changes in essential processes and programs. Assess the current condition of each component of the business model. Develop a forecast and plan to implement the changes that are needed for the next steps.

Revenue diversification is recognized as a sound method to reduce risk in nonprofit financial planning. Most nonprofits recognize that it is difficult to generate multiple revenue streams, because each different type of income requires the operation of a different line of business. Seeking and managing funding from government contracts, private donors, and charitable foundations often requires different expertise and infrastructure. Therefore, most nonprofit organizations are limited to one or two dominant sources of revenue. These might be supplemented by a couple of secondary sources of funds, but typically do not play a major financial role in sustaining the organization.

Growing revenue is achieved by obtaining reliable systems and fostering relationships that develop those funding sources. The need to diversify funding resources has become evident over the past decade as many social service nonprofits that once relied heavily upon public funding now are forced to find alternative sources or face bankruptcy.

Review your revenue sources. What are your dominant sources of funding? How is the availability of that funding evolving or changing? Do you have secondary funding sources that can be developed to supplement the primary sources? If there is a need to create new revenue streams, are there funds and the capacity to invest to accomplish this task?

Nonprofits have been reducing costs and cutting staff for the past decade. Most organizations have tried to restrict their cuts to administrative expenses in an effort to preserve program services. The long-term health of nonprofit organizations is dependent upon the stability of their leadership, governance, management, and fundraising. After cutting the excess, leadership now has to examine how they have operated in the past and find ways to change the expense structure while maintaining the core infrastructure. One way that organizations have attempted this is with a shift to zero-based budgeting, which forces every department to justify each expense rather than rely on funds that have traditionally come their way. With personnel typically accounting for more than half of the entire budget, a total financial review should include a thorough examination of staff roles and responsibilities, going position by position (Murray, 2005). This might not result in a reduction of positions, but a reallocation of positions to different areas to better serve the target population.

Figure out where the organization's largest expense types are located. Determine whether there is a way to evaluate the effectiveness of these costs in regard to carrying out strategies.

Determine if there are other alternative structures or options to deliver similar programs and services. Identify the strengths and weaknesses of the organization's current infrastructure. Devise a plan to strengthen those areas where weaknesses are found.

It is essential for the ED and the board to assess all financial information to understand the true costs associated with delivering products and services to the target population. Program cost includes all direct costs attributed to the program as well as allocations for common costs such as office expenses, communications, and indirect administrative support. These costs should be shared by programs using a formula derived from the office of the CFO. The actual costs of programs might be different from those itemized in contracts, and are often not accounted for when seeking funding. The difference between these actual costs and the price placed upon the services is subsidized by the organization. The nonprofit must raise funds to cover these costs. Nonprofits often use contributions, earned income, and their reserves to cover these expenses. Decisions about how to best allocate available funds is an important decision and should be made in an informed manner that is based on the organization's strategies, mission, and desired impact.

Capital at nonprofits is usually accumulated through fundraising, capital campaigns, and accumulating budget surpluses when financial times are good. An organization's capital structure is revealed by examining their asset composition. Many nonprofits have substantial assets but practically no liquidity. This is due to most of their assets being investments in buildings, long-term endowments, and restricted cash. There has been a trend toward underemphasized capital within the nonprofit sector for many years. Numerous organizations were solely focused on mission and paid little attention to balance sheets or net assets.

With all of the funding and accountability changes within the nonprofit sector, the importance of appropriate capital structure has never been more obvious. It has become apparent that unrestricted working capital is needed to create capacity. This is required for the organization to invest in changes including new programs, fundraising initiatives, branding, and marketing. The nonprofit organization's financial obligations also reflect capital such as mortgages and other liabilities. The structure and requirements of these obligations have a tremendous influence on financial flexibility and cash flow.

Many approaches to organizational development start with the end in mind by considering the strategic design and integration of all the component parts with the focus first and foremost on the intended impact of the organization's mission. As with travel, the destination informs the journey! This means focusing more on the impact or outcomes of the various services of the organization rather than the organization's entire mission statement. Such approaches move deliberately from internally focused organizational development to strategic capacity building that targets improved impact within the community. This capacity building framework is promoted throughout this text. Each chapter builds on the previous, and can be linked together in the applications associated with building the capacity of the organization to enhance impact that can be sustained.

Nonprofit organizations experience a great deal of pressure to demonstrate the quality of the results of their efforts. In tight economic times, individuals and institutions providing financial support tend to ask more often for evidence of impact on the quality of life among target populations. Being able to demonstrate the relevance of the organization's efforts is increasingly important to funders and to the public in general (Mattessich, 2003). It is not enough to demonstrate that an organization is run efficiently. With the widespread acknowledgment of inequalities across the globe and the push for social justice, more and more questions are being asked by all supporters about results as they decide where to place money, time, support, and related efforts. The changing roles and relationships among the government, business, and nonprofit sectors discussed in Chapter 6 further illustrate the importance of focusing on building the capacity of nonprofit organizations to become more effective in serving the needs of communities. Therein lies the case for learning more about capacity building for nonprofit organizations. This chapter explores capacity building, planning for its applications, and links to resources that support effective practice.

BUILDING CAPACITY

Capacity describes the skills and ability to make and execute decisions in a manner that achieves effective and efficient results, while capacity building is the process of developing those skills and ability (Raynor, Cardona, Knowlton, Mittenthal, & Simpson, 2014). A nonprofit organization can view nearly everything it owns and does so in pursuit of its mission as capacity building. Capacity building has traditionally occurred primarily at the organizational level. Nonprofit organizations have received assistance from a funder to develop their abilities in some way such as enhancing financial management practices or improving fundraising capabilities. DeVita, Fleming, and Twombly (2001) suggest that nonprofit capacity might be conceptualized in collective terms.

Capacity building strategies for intervention can be approached from several different perspectives: the organization, nonprofit sector, or the community. According to Worth (2017), it is probably more useful to approach capacity by thinking about its various component parts. That way an organization can consider what activities might need to be undertaken to improve specific areas. One useful way to approach this is to break down a nonprofit organization's capacity into five components: vision and mission, leadership, resources, outreach, and products and services. These factors are interrelated and reciprocally dependent upon one another. It is not likely, that each of these five factors is equally present in any given organization. Different organizations will emphasize one factor over another, but a good blend of these five components is essential for an organization to flourish and grow. Any of these factors might be an intervention point for improving organizational capacity (DeVita et al., 2001).

The mission has a strong influence on capacity building. The vision and mission influence the ability of a nonprofit to attract and retain leaders who share its goals. These leaders are entrusted to maintain or redirect the mission of the organization. When the organization seeks resources, the vision and mission of the organization influence who the potential donors might be and the types of organizations that they will be competing or collaborating with. Potential donors must find a reassuring match between their interests and the organization's vision and mission. In addition, the guiding principles of the mission statement will influence the organization's strategies and outreach activities. The mission answers the question of why an organization is building capacity.

Building capacity in the leadership component of nonprofit organizations requires enhancing existing developing new leadership. Existing leadership can be enhanced via administrative and procedural policy review, updating to improve operations and better serve staff and target population needs. Professional development sessions can be offered to staff and volunteers to upgrade skills and promote collaboration. The ED can develop a strategy to review the functions of the board members to help individuals to better understand and accomplish their responsibilities.

Identifying and developing new leadership is essential for sustaining the organization. If this is ignored, the current leadership risks becoming outdated. Not only must new leaders be brought into an organization periodically to stimulate and invigorate the work, but also current leadership should play an essential role in mentoring this next cohort of leaders. This renewal and mentoring process will lead to greater diversity within the leadership positions within the nonprofit sector as organizations more closely mirror the people and communities that they serve. Organizations pass through developmental cycles as they grow and mature. It is essential that younger workers move into leadership roles early on to permit adequate time for mentoring so that an organization always has knowledgeable, reliable leadership.

Traditionally, efforts to build nonprofit capacity centered on expanding an organization's resources. In the late 1990s there was an increased interest in building capacity of nonprofit organizations. This interest was generated within the industry by several articles that were published on the topic. These works pointed out that nonprofit organizations had historically depended upon grants to fund specific programs and services. These funding sources required that nonprofits maintain low levels of infrastructure and internal resources to maintain funding (Worth, 2017).

When the recession hit in late 2007, funding for services and programs became more difficult to obtain. This fueled a shift toward nonprofit leaders pursuing ways to build the capacity of their organizations so that there would be less reliance on one-time grants to fund programs and services offered by their organization. By 2012, capacity building relying predominantly upon internal resources had become well established within the nonprofit sector. According to Raynor et al. (2014), capacity building within the nonprofit industry is here to stay.

Strategies for capacity building consist of finding ways to secure more money, staff, and equipment. This alone is not the only answer to the challenges faced by today's nonprofit organizations. The efficient and effective implementation of these resources are also critical factors.

With technology rapidly changing the working environment, it is imperative that training is provided for staff, volunteers, and board members to upgrade skills and revamp established procedures. This can increase the efficient use of the organization's resources.

There are numerous ways to address the resource needs of nonprofit organizations, but there are two areas receiving considerable attention: fundraising and financial management. Nonprofit organizations generate income in different and more numerous ways than for-profit firms and therefore require more complex tracking and reporting systems. As nonprofits are asked to show greater transparency and accountability in their financial operations, the need to improve accounting and reporting systems becomes more pressing.

Nonprofit organizations have been pressured to model their programs and operating procedures after for-profit business models. To accomplish this requires either more formalized methods of monitoring finances, clients, and program outcomes to deliver better accountability or more loosely organized practices that provide enhanced flexibility to capitalize on new opportunities or service delivery practices. These two approaches might not be incompatible, but they are challenging to achieve simultaneously. Because nonprofit organizations usually have numerous constituents, responding to mandates for better accountability can be quite complicated (DeVita et al., 2001).

Outreach is essential to capacity building within community-based organizations. This might take different forms including marketing, public relations, community education and advocacy, collaborations, alliances, partnerships, and networking. These examples reveal that outreach is focused on building social capital and is the way to build a base of support. Even nonprofits that provide confidential services, such as family planning or counseling services, must utilize some type of outreach to increase awareness among community members regarding programs and services they offer. Larger networking efforts and greater outreach result in the nonprofit having access to a larger pool of people. This has another capacity building effect in that the more people who know about the nonprofit organization, the greater the chance to attract people to the organization in various capacities. Therefore, outreach and networking activities can actually have multiple purposes.

There is pressure for nonprofit organizations to demonstrate that their products and services are making an impact and that resources are being used efficiently. This not only increases the need to build capacity to enhance the organization's impact, but also to have the capability to measure and evaluate their products and services so that they can demonstrate their effectiveness to the public. A nonprofit organization's outcomes are the product of the cumulative interactions of their mission, leadership, resources, and outreach efforts. These components work together to generate effective products and services for the communities served. Each of the outputs and outcomes informs other factors associated with capacity and can enhance or diminish their availability. Poorly designed or delivered products or services, for example, might result in fewer financial resources for the organization to sustain operations, which would indicate the need to change leadership. In contrast, designing and delivering high-quality products or services might increase access to resources, generate larger networks, and provide more visibility to the organization, thus strengthening current leadership while building capacity.

To build capacity, there is a logical sequence of actions that if followed, will help increase the organization's potential. (1) Identify a very specific impact of the organization's mission to focus the capacity building effort. It should be an impact that if improved, the ability of the organization to fulfill its mission will be enhanced. (2) Select aspects of the programs and services that target the specific impact. (3) Choose element(s) of the organization's capacities that if improved, increased, or enhanced, would create a reasonable expectation that the selected aspect of programs and services will be more effective in advancing the targeted impact. (4) The measure of effective capacity building results in impacts that are sustained over time with the quality of life in the community enhanced as a result.

In addition to sustainable impacts of one capacity building effort, nonprofit capacity needs to be considered in collective terms. As DeVita et al. (2001) report, "This new vision of nonprofit development is based on nurturing and growing the sector's capacity as a whole." The old 1960s social activist expression "act locally and think globally" has become popular again with new application and potential for social good that comes from the positive contributions of any one nonprofit mission, let alone the systematic connection of the work of many organizations.

A CASE FOR BROADER IMPACT

Imagine the leaders of a local youth sports program that get excited about becoming a part of a new national childhood obesity initiative being promoted by the White House. For years, their developmental objectives included improving sports skills, leadership development, group cooperation, and general fitness. Over time the primary focus shifted to the sports skills objective, which influenced the program model, the coaches' preparation and support, and youth practices. Similar to many youth sports programs, the attention was on producing skilled athletes, with winning as the primary measure of success. Their assumption was that the other objectives were being addressed by giving youth a quality team sports experience.

In order for the program to have any impact on the central goal of the new initiative, the organization has to clarify the specific impact being pursued and build a new set of program supports to work toward these outcomes. Nearly every aspect of the program needs some modification. New objectives might include health-related indicators such as body mass index, heart health, or dietary modifications. New training regimens and related coaches' education programs would have to be instituted to include specific exercises. New rules for practices and games would have to be put into place that promote specific levels and types of activity for each individual. The overall attitude will likely have to shift from winning to ensuring that everyone participates so that all participants gain the desired health benefits. The new approach would have to be aggressively marketed across the community to help ensure that participation and support continued and was embraced by parents. This might require some educational programming to explain the new paradigm. A new set of partners in the community who are concerned about childhood obesity need to be cultivated and incorporated into the work of the program. This all needs to be done in a way that will still be viewed as fun by the participating youth.

Once all of this work is completed and the newly framed program is operating effectively, the organization can measure performance indicators to see if it is having the desired impact on the targeted issue of childhood obesity. As the leaders gather evidence by measuring the parameters selected when setting their goals, in an effort to show positive impact, they will increase the likelihood that they can sustain the program. This type of positive impact will also help encourage support among the community which will help to sustain the operation of the program.

Building the new program framework in conjunction with a national initiative will include alignment with the work of other youth sports programs around the country. Being a part of this larger network will allow the impact of one program to be added to that of other programs, improving the quality of youth health on the national level. The collective impact has the added benefit of helping the local community see itself within a larger context, which again will help encourage support to sustain the program and encourage participation.

This simple example is offered to show the difference in the work of nonprofits when they choose specific new impact targets that have to do with critical issues in their communities, and by doing so in conjunction with other organizations. These choices lead to greater potential for impact and sustainability.

PLANNING FOR EFFECTIVE APPLICATION

Connolly and Lukas (2002) provide a comprehensive framework that can help with the analysis of a situation and planning a strategic capacity building response. It includes five (5) elements of capacity a nonprofit organization should consider when designing a capacity building effort:

1. Mission, vision, and strategy

2. Governance and leadership

3. Ability to deliver programs and ensure the impact of programs

4. Strategic external relationships

5. Internal systems and management

McKinsey and Company (2001) provide a framework of seven (7) elements of nonprofit capacity to help guide the analysis when considering capacity building effort. These authors break down the nonprofit organization into human resources, systems and infrastructure, organizational structure, organizations skills, strategies, aspirations, and culture. The case is made that each element is critical to understanding what needs to be done to increase capacity and how best to accomplish the goal. Conducting the resulting analysis would provide a deep understanding of the current state of affairs in each area and influence how that might impact capacity building. The potential constraints of organizational culture, the limits of current staff skills, the level of support from the system, and the resistance to change among the staff all must be considered when designing major modifications to programming.

Building capacity can be a way of thinking about improving the overall effectiveness of an organization and reducing risk. An *effective and efficient organization* can more fully accomplish its own mission and meet the targeted needs of its constituency. Letts, Ryan, and Grossman (1998) describe how the results of strategic capacity building can be viewed at three levels: (1) improvement in the capacity of the organization to do what it already does (**program delivery capacity**), (2) improvement in the organization's capacity to grow (**program expansion capacity**), and (3) improvement in the organization's ability to sense needs for change and respond to them with program improvements or innovations (**adaptive capacity**). All three types of capacity building are needed if the organization is to perform effectively and efficiently for the long term.

Once the specific focus of a capacity building effort has been determined, the next step is to decide how to go about improving or expanding the work of the organization within the targeted area. Light and Hubbard (2004) examined how foundations that support capacity building typically invest their money in strengthening organizations. They report that funders promote capacity building through three types of interventions: (1) **consultation** that is focused on assessment or process issues, such as building a new program plan focused on the newly targeted area of the mission, (2) **training** that involves small-group seminars or classes in which staff or board members learn specific skills to improve their abilities to work on the issues associated with the targeted area, and (3) **technical assistance** that is a more hands-on process in which the nonprofit is provided support for a project, program, or problem-solving process. Whether the impetus for the capacity building comes from an external source, such as a funder or a national initiative, or from an internal source, such as a board that is pushing for expanding programs, selecting the types of actions to take is the most critical part of the process. Limited money and time, pressure to continue existing programs and services, and the challenges of making change of any kind in the organization should be considered when designing a capacity building effort. There are some important cautions to consider when developing a capacity building effort. These types of perspectives can serve as guiding principles that support the group process of planning and implementing effective capacity building activities (Long, 2010):

▶ First and foremost, do no harm. Be sure that the risks of any particular action have been taken into account before implementation. It is important to take risks, but they need to be calculated risks where any resulting problems are known and managed.

▶ Guard against being overly prescriptive or top-down in the process and implementation. Engaging each of the different groups potentially impacted by the effort will both gain their creative contributions to the design and help ensure their support for any resulting changes. Without the support of constituents, board members, and key staff, the process might be limited or more likely to fail.

▶ Use caution in selecting external resources to support capacity building. To do effective capacity building, an external resource must take into account all of the forces that shape an organization: its mission, its values, and its organizational culture; the environment in which it has to navigate; and the culture(s) and circumstances of its constituents. Look for an intermediary with a solid track record of collaboration with and support of the targeted constituencies.

▶ Recognize the multidimensional roles of nonprofit organizations. They often have important roles to play within their communities beyond delivering services, as a part of the local fabric of support for the area in which they work. Any capacity building work that is undertaken will likely influence other aspects of the organization.

▶ Have clear expectations about the potential outcomes of capacity building:

   ▶ there must be agreement among all involved groups on the targeted results
   ▶ do not push beyond the capacity to assimilate learning and undertake changes while still carrying on its daily business
   ▶ develop clear and manageable communication and reporting procedures to help track the process
   ▶ keep a flexible timeline so that adjustments can be made and time is available for reflections and learning

The report, *Strengthening Nonprofit Capacity*, by the Grantmakers for Effective Organizations (2015) defines capacity building as helping nonprofits develop skills, knowledge, capabilities, and resources to make their work more effective. This report points to three essential capacity building principles referred to as the 3 C's:

▶ **Contextual:** Contextualize capacity building efforts to better meet the unique characteristics and needs of each organization.

▶ **Continuous:** The process is continuous, so a long-term view must be taken with an organization or across a group of funders because the need capacity building never goes away.

▶ **Collective:** A collective approach helps with getting buy-in, networking, and extending the reach of leadership.

There are a lot of resources available to help plan quality capacity building efforts in non-profit organizations. In addition to those referenced above, the Human Interaction Research Institute hosts a searchable database of capacity building resources being carried out by U.S. foundations at www.humaninteract.org/reports/pcbrdatabase.asp.

CHALLENGES AND OPPORTUNITIES

When considering a capacity building effort in a nonprofit organization, there are a number of important factors that will influence the decision and the resulting plan of action. Taking some time to explore such factors before the decision is made or time is spent in planning, will enable leaders to avoid potential challenges and take advantage of opportunities. To promote this sort of advanced thinking, three will be explored here: **readiness, building on strengths, and adequate resources.**

Readiness. It is important to think about whether or not an organization is ready and willing to undertake capacity building work before the process begins. There is a lot to consider. It all starts with a clearly identified problem that, if addressed, will increase the organization's capacity to have an impact on its mission. If that is clear, there needs to be a high level of commitment to the related changes among the staff, board, volunteers, and constituents. Key organization members must believe that capacity building will help to further the mission, particularly senior level leadership (ED and board chair in particular). Among those, it helps to have champions who help promote the process. With each group having the appropriate opportunity to participate in the design process, both the quality and level of support will develop.

With support and commitment in hand, attention needs to turn to the goals, intended outcomes, approach being taken, and plan of action. They should all line up to offer everyone involved a strong sense that the goals can be achieved in the time allotted. In addition, it is important to know that the board and staff leadership have committed the funding and time needed to do the job effectively. Finally, it is important to know that the organization has the expertise needed for the activity or has access and funding support to bring into the effort.

Build on strengths. Most of the time capacity building efforts focus on problems that seem to be limiting the success of the organization's mission. A deficit-based or problem-solving approach may limit the design and implementation (Block, 2008). Imagine the difference that might occur if the efforts were framed on focusing, sustaining, and renewing areas that are strong, and using those internal organization strengths to address areas that are weak or need to be developed further. Referring to the Creative Tension Model in Chapter 2, rather than focusing on "what we do not want," focus instead on "what we want" for the future. Building on an organization's strengths can have a very positive impact on all aspects of capacity building, from the quality of the support and positive energy from each group involved in the process to the resources and commitment to sustaining the resulting changes.

Adequate resources. It is important to balance expectations with the budget, time, and human resources needed for capacity building. While organizational effectiveness can improve with small investments in such things as technical assistance (i.e., board training), it takes more money, time, and commitment to have lasting and substantive impacts on issues of importance to the organization's mission. Organizations require ongoing support and continuing education to sustain any gains in capacity. Time is money, and commitment to sustaining the changes that occur through capacity building efforts involve both. At the core of an effective balance of resources to support capacity building are quality relationships that promote shared learning. Effective leaders and organizations understand this and work to develop three kinds of learning relationships that help sustain the change: (1) networks of colleagues and peers who share their commitments, (2) coaches or mentors who help develop their potential, and (3) experts who provide specialized and objective assistance (Newman, 2001). All of these relationships are important resources for successful capacity building.

> *"To make the greatest impact on society*
> *requires first and foremost*
> *a great organization,*
> *not just a great program."*
>
> **Jim Collins**
> (Author, *From Good to Great*)

SUSTAINING RESULTS

There are strategic points in the life of nonprofit organizations where capacity building makes sense and might be more effectively implemented and the results sustained. Within each, there are some specific considerations that will help with capacity building design and continuation of the resulting changes in the organization (Long, 2010).

Executive transition. Whenever there is a change in executive leadership, there is an opportunity to consider capacity building. A board can look at an upcoming transition as a chance to make changes in its mission and goals and incorporate those desired changes into the search process when looking for new leadership. A new Executive Director can use the transition as an opportunity to engage the organization in developing a new shared vision for the future and to entertain any associated capacity building. Transitions, when appropriately supported and managed, provide powerful opportunities for nonprofit organizations to grow new leadership, make important strategic decisions about the future, and build the capacity needed to realize that future (Teegarden, 2005). Well-planned change can breathe new life into an organization, re-energize staff and volunteers, and renew and build commitments with supporters.

Periods of growth and change. Responding to a desired change in mission and its impacts with a capacity building effort can produce growth in the organization. Growth can be disruptive and have a negative impact on an organization. It can be difficult to pay for the ongoing improvements necessary to maintain effective and efficient operations *without* growth, since a large proportion of funding often comes from fees and contracts for programs and services. The challenge is that the money usually comes after the growth occurs and there are inadequate funds to get to that point in operations. One response to this situation is to raise funds to support the costs of the fundraising, planning, and financial management skills that come with growth. Investing in this type of capacity building can make all the difference when growth and change occur. Capacity building efforts can also require changes to programs that require shifts in staffing, organizational structure, and administrative systems. Training and planning assistance can be crucial in these times, but there are associated costs to consider. It is important to understand that program expansion requires a greater budget for the entire organization, not just for programs.

Times of crisis. Any crisis can be an opportunity for change within the organization. However, organizations in trouble typically have outdated programs, poor morale, or limited funding. Regardless of what is driving the crisis, these types of symptoms might need to be addressed before the organization can work on bigger issues of long-term impact and mission. This situation poses a dilemma because it might be difficult to improve any of these types of conditions without first finding a stronger link between the mission and the current reality of its constituents and community needs.

Keeping organizations strong. A quality, mature organization needs to continually evaluate its work to ensure that its mission is relevant to the changing context of the community and its constituents. A strategic planning process that supports the needed adjustments in programs and services is essential. Quality evaluations can provide important information to periods of transition, growth, organizational development, and change. Having these core processes in place supports effective capacity building.

Stagnant organizations. Even successful nonprofit organizations can become complacent if they are not using quality processes to stay current and relevant in their communities. The staff might not know that their work is no longer meeting evolving needs. Awareness of the situation must be followed with thorough and meaningful assessment and planning to use capacity building to move from stagnation to an effective and relevant future.

Capacity building is just like everything else that a nonprofit organization undertakes. It needs to be developed through an effective planning process, as presented for program planning in Chapter 5. The simple cycle of planning, implementation, and evaluation will bring a deliberate and intentional tone to the work.

FINAL THOUGHTS

In order to have the broadest possible impacts with capacity building efforts, it is helpful to show progress by a different set of indicators than simple measurements of inputs and outputs, such as trainings conducted and new processes implemented or new program designs and numbers of new participants. For any single nonprofit organization or a group of nonprofits working on the same issue, it is important to be able to show evidence of positive impacts on the issue and sustainability of these impacts over time. Evidence that demonstrates key roles that the organization is playing in the group of nonprofits and across the large social system as a result of capacity building is also valued. Demonstrating that the collective effort is having a positive impact is also important to funders.

Together, this type of evidence goes a long way toward building support among all types of funding sources including private donors, foundations, and government agencies with responsibilities for the issue. A nonprofit organization that operates in this collaborative way to have an intentional collective impact on important community issues is demonstrating the six practices of high-impact nonprofits presented in Chapter 2 when describing quality nonprofit leadership. Crutchfield and McLeod-Grant (2008) report that great nonprofit sector organizations do these six things:

- ▶ advocate and serve
- ▶ make markets work
- ▶ inspire evangelists
- ▶ nurture nonprofit networks
- ▶ master the art of adaptation
- ▶ share leadership

There are many resources available to help nonprofit organizations help themselves with capacity building work. It is important to make sure that evaluation is incorporated into the process in order to both inform its development and implementation and to help determine its long-term effectiveness. *The Nonprofit Good Practice Guide* offers links to many useful tools at www.npgoodpractice.org. *Grantmakers for Effective Organizations* also offers a range of useful resources at www.geofunders.org. Finally, the *National Council of Nonprofit Organizations* is a repository of enormous amounts of experience with organizational development and capacity building, through its own resource collection as well as through its network of state associations of nonprofits. More information can be found at www.councilofnonprofits.org.

SUMMARY

Nonprofit organizations must continue to develop in order to stay current and engaged in valuable relationships with the community they serve. As the context and needs of the community continue to evolve, it is the responsibility of nonprofit leadership to make sure that the organization develops to stay relevant and able to positively impact the quality of life in the community. This is accomplished by constantly developing the component parts of the organization so that they are efficient and effective and align with each other to support a quality enterprise.

Beyond this work to continually develop the organization, leadership must pay attention to building capacity to have positive impacts on life in the community and achieve the mission. **Capacity building** includes all that the organization does to improve the impact of its programs and services in the community. Challenging times and circumstances can press nonprofit organizations to improve their capacity to serve the community. However, nonprofit leaders need to consider capacity building as an important part of their regular responsibilities. The case is strong for connecting capacity building to the work of other related organizations so that the collective impact may be more significant in the community and sustainable.

A simple framework for developing a capacity building plan should include steps that ensure thoughtful consideration of the specific targeted impact, selected aspects of the programs and services that need to change or develop, elements of the organization to improve, and the ability to track progress. The chapter offers another element to the framework by focusing on the broader impact of capacity building to promote greater impact and sustainability of strategic partnerships and collaborations among organizations that are committed to the same results. To do this work effectively, five elements need to be considered: (1) mission, vision, and strategy; (2) governance and leadership; (3) ability to deliver programs and services to ensure the impact of programs; (4) strategic external relationships; and (5) internal systems and management. In order to be successful with capacity building efforts, there are a number of factors to consider. The level of readiness in the organization, a commitment to building on the strengths of the organization, and access to adequate resources must be taken into account during the initial planning activity. Planning is also effected by a variety of situations and conditions that can influence the effectiveness and sustainability of capacity building, including executive transitions, periods of growth and change, times of crisis, commitments to keeping the organization strong, and dealing with stagnation within the organization.

Capacity building is an essential part of long-term organizational development that helps ensure the relevance and value the organization will have in the community. If done well in partnership with a group of committed related organizations, the impact in the community can be significant and long-lasting.

This chapter addresses, in part, the Nonprofit Academic Centers Council Competency Requirements of Nonprofit Management and Program Planning, Implementation, and Evaluation.

REFLECTION AND APPLICATION

1. Describe the differences between organizational development activities and capacity building efforts:

   _____

   _____

   _____

   _____

   _____

   _____

2. What are the recommended steps to take in developing a capacity building plan?

   _____

   _____

   _____

   _____

   _____

   _____

3. List the five elements of a nonprofit organization that should be considered when developing a capacity building effort:

   _____

   _____

   _____

   _____

   _____

   _____

4. Define the three types of capacity that can be built in nonprofit organizations:

   _____

   _____

   _____

   _____

   _____

   _____

   _____

5. Describe how readiness, building on strengths, and adequate resources are involved in the decision to conduct capacity building in nonprofit organizations:

   _____

   _____

   _____

   _____

   _____

   _____

   _____

6. Develop a list of the strategic points in the life of a nonprofit organization where capacity building makes sense to undertake:

   _____

   _____

   _____

   _____

   _____

   _____

   _____

   _____

REFERENCES

Block, P. (2008). *Community: The structure of belonging.* San Francisco, CA: Berritt-Koehler Publishing, Inc.

Christine W. L., William P. R., & Grossman, A. (1999). *High performance nonprofit organizations: Managing upstream for greater impact.* New York: John Wiley & Sons, 1999.

Connolly, P., & Lukas, C. (2002). *Strengthening nonprofit performance: A funder's guide to capacity building.* Saint Paul, MN: Amherst H. Wilder Foundation/Grantmakers for Effective Organizations.

Crutchfield, L., McLeod-Grant, H. (2008). *Forces for good: The six practices of high-impact nonprofits.* Jossey-Bass.

Grantmakers for Effective Organizations. (2015). *Strengthening nonprofit capacity.* Retrieved from http://www.geofunders.org/resource-forms/resource-form-capacitybuilding

Letts, C. W., Ryan, W. P., & Grossman, A. (1998). *High performance nonprofit organizations: Managing upstream for greater impact.* John Wiley & Sons.

Light, P. C., & Hubbard, E. T. (2004). *The capacity building challenge: A research perspective.* Foundation Center. Retrieved from http://foundationcenter.org.

Long, R. F. (2010). *Advanced grant portfolio management* (2nd ed.). Johnson Center on Philanthropy, Grand Valley State University.

Mattessich, P. W. (2003). *The manager's guide to program evaluation.* Saint Paul, MN: Fieldstone Alliance Publishing Center.

McKinsey & Company. (2001). *Effective capacity building in nonprofit organizations*, Venture Philanthropy Partners.

Measure of America. (2016). About human development. Social Science Research Council. Retrieved from http://www.measureofamerica.org/human-development/

Murray, V. (2005). *Evaluating the effectiveness of nonprofit organizations.* Robert D. Herman (Ed.) (2nd ed.). The Jossey-Bass handbook of nonprofit leadership and management.

Newman, A. (2001). *Built to change: Catalytic capacity building in nonprofit organizations.* The David and Lucile Packard Foundation. Retrieved from http://www.packard.org.

Nonprofits Assistance Fund. (2014). Transforming nonprofit business models. Retrieved from https://nonprofitsassistancefund.org/resources/item/transforming-nonprofit-business-models

Raynor, J., Cardona, C., Knowlton, T., Mittenthal, R., & Simpson, J. (2014). Capacity building 3.0: How to strengthen the social ecosystem. TCC Group: NY.

Teegarden, P. H. (April, 2005). Leadership change in nonprofit Milwaukee: Making transitions work. *Research and Opinion, 18*(1). University of Wisconsin.

Weis, R., & Muller, S. (2015). Leading and managing nonprofit organizations (2nd ed.). Peosta, IA: eddie bowers publishing co., inc.

Worth, M. J. (2017). *Nonprofit management: Principles and practice* (4th ed.). Thousand Oaks, CA: Sage Publications, Inc.

9

CAREER PLANNING AND PROFESSIONAL DEVELOPMENT

> *Life isn't about finding yourself.*
> *Life is about creating yourself.*
>
> **— Author Unknown**

The need for qualified professionals in the nonprofit sector is growing at a very fast rate and is expected to continue for years to come. Working in a nonprofit organization and developing programs that enhance people's lives is one of the most important and exhilarating careers imaginable. Deciding which organization to work with, then obtaining a position with that organization, however, can sometimes be confusing and frustrating.

This chapter helps anyone assess his/her interests and skills relevant to nonprofit organizations and learn about specific nonprofit organizations, and then, learn a process for developing effective résumés, refined networking skills, compelling cover letters, dynamic interviewing skills, and strategies for assessing job offers. There are two critical aspects of career development and exploration. One centers on individual needs for a clear career plan and a view toward the future. The other revolves around organizational needs for specific and general skills and knowledge. In addition, this chapter will explore both individual and organizational issues related to career preparation and planning, as well as how to look to the future and be prepared to alter career paths both for individuals and an organization. Finally, this chapter's content can also assist students and current agency employees in organizing professional development strategies to meet short-term and long-term career goals.

What a person values largely determines how he or she will approach career development and career options. Is salary more important than what is being done? Is making a difference in the life of just one person enough? Is helping people more important than the pay scale? Arthur Ashe, tennis professional and founder of the Arthur Ashe Institute for Urban Health, put the issue in these words, "From what we get, we can make a living; what we give, however, makes a life."

The one preeminent word in finding and excelling in a career is: <u>**connectedness**</u> (Weis & Muller, 2015). A person must know or discover the connection between and among the following four areas:

1. **Abilities**—These are the things a person does well, their natural skills. They could include the ability to talk with anyone, the ability to help people avoid conflict, the ability to show compassion for people who are hurting, the ability to run fast, or the ability to speak in public with little fear of failure.

2. **Interests**—These are the things a person enjoys doing. These items could include enjoying working outdoors, working with your hands, working alone, working with people, working in stressful situations, working in a highly predictable position, or working at night.

3. **Learned skills**—These are the things a person has learned to do well. They could include anything from the abilities list which does not come naturally. A person can learn public speaking skills, learn to show compassion, or learn to help people manage conflict. In addition, people can learn budgeting skills, programming skills, fundraising skills, or other technical skills.

4. **Interaction styles**—This is the way people like to communicate, the way they like for others to communicate with them. The consequences of a person's style determine how effective a person is as judged by others.

All four of these areas, along with all written correspondence, the résumé, networking contacts, and interview content must be connected in order to "**tell your story**." The competition is often fierce and you have to convince potential employers they should hire you instead of someone else (Dahlstrom, 2009). All the steps and materials prepared to support all applications for employment must be connected to each other. It is in this **connectedness** that an applicant gains power over those who see each step as an individual activity.

Abilities provide the natural base for any career. They set the stage for any success. What a person can't do limits options just as what a person can do creates options. A person with no compassion for the plight of the poor is ill-advised to look at careers in the nonprofit sector. It should also be noted that because a person is good at something does not mean they would be happy doing that for a career. A person who runs fast may not like training well enough to commit to the preparation necessary to become an Olympic class athlete. For that reason, abilities must be combined with other qualities to determine the best career match for each person.

Interests should drive a person's search for a challenging career path. The other three factors are very important, but if a person has little genuine interest in an area of work, there will be little real reward. A statement attributed to Confucius offers sage advice, "Choose a job you love, and you will never work a day in your life."

Learned skills emerge from the knowledge of what a person **needs** to be able to do in order to combine natural abilities and interests to insure greater chances of success in a desired career. These skills are learned through career-related experience and specific, focused training.

Interaction styles reflect how a person prefers to communicate and interact with others. It is clear to anyone who has lived more than a few years that not everyone likes to give and receive information in the same way. Some people find teasing as a sign they are liked by others and some people are offended by any teasing. Some people desire the blunt, straightforward presentation of messages—make it clear. Some people want messages presented diplomatically and indirectly. There are several tools for assessing interaction styles and the implications of each style. Some of those tools are discussed later in this chapter (Weis & Muller, 2015).

THE CAREER DECISION PROCESS

It's important to understand the decision-making process relevant to career planning and develop a strategy for making effective decisions. The *Flowchart for Career Planning* in Figure 9.1 can assist anyone in making informed career decisions. In order to minimize the *confusion and frustration*, substantial *career research* is required. There are two major areas in which to develop and assimilate information for an effective career decision. The *Self-Assessment Profile* area should include information regarding abilities, values, and lifestyle, interests, and interaction style. The *Organizational Exploration* area should include information on professional settings and qualifications for positions in various nonprofit organizations (Weis & Muller, 2015).

It is also important to select someone who is knowledgeable in career planning to assist in the assessment process. This individual should be an academic advisor; a counselor with career services; a coordinator of youth, human service, or service learning programs; or any individual who is skilled in the area of career development. For students, the chair of an academic department or dean of an academic college should be contacted for suggestions on the appropriate advisor. For nonprofit professionals, contact a person who has been successful in nonprofit work. It is critical to choose a person who will take the necessary time to advise, review drafts of written work, and assist in planning for interviews.

Figure 9.1

Flowchart for Career Planning

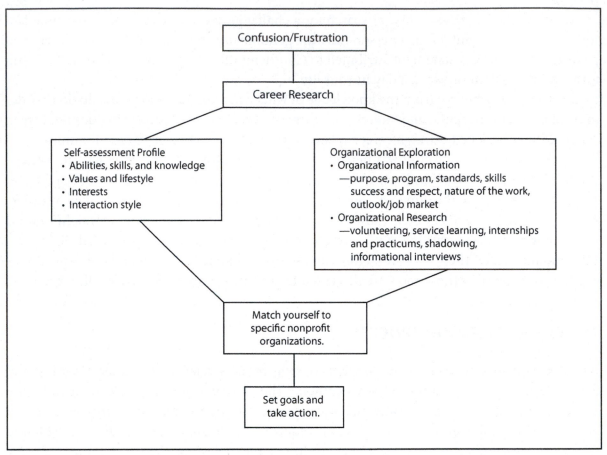

©Roger Weis

Using the *Flowchart for Career Planning* reduces confusion and frustration, provides a structure for career research and allows for informed decisions based on specific goals and clear action steps. The process works! As stated earlier, the two major stages in the career research process are the self-assessment profile and organizational exploration.

Self-Assessment Profile

Like anything worthwhile, choosing a career path requires a good deal of time and commitment. Self-assessment processes can be useful in determining the right career path. Many of the following assessments can be taken at college and university career planning and placement centers, or student development offices. Some of the more popular and useful self-assessment processes include the following:

A.   **Personality Mosaic**—Based on the work of psychologist and vocational counselor John Holland, the Personality Mosaic is an assessment tool that takes approximately an hour to complete. It takes about 30 minutes to complete its 90 questions and another 30 minutes to interpret the results.

Holland theorizes there are six major personality types, or a combination of two or more types and the Personality Mosaic provides a profile of a person based on these results. The Personality Mosaic is a simple assessment, and students generally report the instrument is accurate based on personal observation.

The assessment is included in the career handbook, *Coming Alive from Nine to Five*, by Betty Neville Michelozzi (1992). (Check college or university libraries before purchasing a copy.)

B.   **Strong-Campbell Interest Inventory (SCCI)**—The SCCI is also based on the work of John Holland. It contains over 300 items requiring a "like," "indifferent," or "dislike" response. These items are then divided into groups of professional occupations, academic disciplines, activities, amusements, and types of people.

The individual results are compared to successful individuals in over 70 occupations. Occupations are grouped into the same six categories used by the Personality Mosaic: Realistic, Investigative, Artistic, Social, Enterprising, and Conventional. Because individual responses are mailed to a testing firm for computerized results, an appointment is generally necessary with the campus career counselor for an interpretation of the results.

C.   **Discover**—This is a computer-based planning and information system that includes an interest inventory and activities to help identify individual abilities, experience, and values. These variables are then considered relevant to various occupations. The Discover system also contains modules on exploring various occupations, making educational choices, planning careers, and making career transitions.

D.   **Personal Profile (DiSC)**—The DiSC is an interaction styles analysis tool. It is available through Inscape Publishing. This and other tools can be obtained from a number of independent consultants. One of these is Resources Unlimited (on-line at www. resourcesunlimited.com).

By choosing the adjective which is most like you when you interact with people in a given situation and the adjective which is least like you in the same situation from several sets of adjectives, a profile is shaped. That profile then suggests the consequences of your style of interaction. The profiles allow a person to see not only the consequences of his or her interaction style but also allows for an understanding of the consequences of others' style when the two are working together or in a relationship.

E. **Myers-Briggs Type Indicator (MBTI)**—The MBTI is an excellent assessment which places individuals in 1 of 16 different personality types based on responses to various questions. The MBTI then describes different variables involved, for each personality type, with respect to activities such as choosing a major, studying, playing, and relaxing.

The MBTI includes a list of careers most often chosen by individuals from each of the sixteen personality types along with a list of careers chosen the least by each personality type.

Each of the assessment tools above can provide valuable information for self-assessment. The results from each assessment should be discussed with someone who is experienced and competent in interpreting the results. The more self-knowledge a person is able to assemble the better prepared that person is to "**tell his or her story**." Everyone works best in a situation where there is a match between the person and the organization.

Organizational Exploration

There are a number of effective ways to research and assimilate career information for youth, human service, and other nonprofit organizations. The exploration process that follows concentrates on direct, experience-based techniques for gathering information regarding various careers in nonprofit organizations.

As the examination of different kinds of organizations begins, it's important for students or nonprofit professionals to have some sense of who they are and the kinds of professional goals each hopes to accomplish. Exploring various organizations can help in understanding their purpose and the kinds of activities professional staff members engage in on a daily basis. Firsthand exploration will provide opportunities to see how organizations really operate. This section of the flowchart concentrates on processes for researching organizational information and activities.

ORGANIZATIONAL INFORMATION

A. **Purpose**—One of the most important aspects of any organization is its purpose—what the organization stands for. The purpose of each organization varies, but generally speaking all are designed to enhance the quality of life for specific individuals in specific communities through some sort of program or process. Identifying with the purpose of an organization is one of the essential elements of being comfortable and successful with a career within that organization.

B. **Programs**—Nonprofit organizations will have a number of programs designed to achieve their purpose. It is equally important to have an idea of the kinds of programs organizations implement to determine if they are the kinds of programs that would be interesting and challenging to work with.

C. **Standards, qualifications, and skills**—One should be aware of what an organization expects in the area of educational requirements, certifications, skills, and experience in order to prepare to be a viable candidate for a position. One should also be aware of these expectations because the standards and qualifications an organization maintains provides an indication of the level of quality of the organization.

D. **Success and respect**—Organizations that are consistently successful in achieving their goals in an effective and professional manner maintain a high level of respect in the community. This is an important consideration for employment.

E. **Nature of work**—Being aware of an organization's mission and programs and having an awareness of the work individuals do daily to help the organization achieve its mission is essential.

F. **Outlook/job market**—According to news reports and government and organizational reports, the need for professionals in the youth and human service field increases substantially each year. It is important, however, to research the need for specific positions in certain nonprofit organizations as well as in specific geographical areas.

The Nonprofit Career Field

Today, more than ever before, nonprofit organizations are a mix of vibrant enterprises including universities (Harvard), medical organizations (Doctors Without Borders), and a myriad of religious, financial, social, and legal entities just to mention a few areas (Busse & Joiner, 2008). Because the lines between nonprofit, for-profit (i.e., TOMs Shoes), and government sectors are beginning to blur, there is an increasing call for entrepreneurial, creative, and visionary individuals to fill leadership positions in the nonprofit world.

That said, it is important to look at both the *advantages* and possible *disadvantages* of a career path in the nonprofit sector:

ADVANTAGES

▶ The chance to do **meaningful work** in the community with potential to change the lives of many in a positive way.

▶ **Hands-on** work that provides you the opportunity to experience the results of your work firsthand.

- ▶ **Casual work environment** with the opportunity to wear several hats and be flexible.
- ▶ Working with both staff and people in the community brings a strong need for high levels of **responsibility** to meet the needs of those involved.
- ▶ Nonprofits are always looking for quality leaders and so **job advancement** could be more numerous and faster than other work sectors.
- ▶ Most individuals working in the nonprofit sector have a **culture of like-mindedness,** most always striving to make a difference in the lives of others.
- ▶ Since nonprofit salaries are not always quite as high as for-profit, the difference is often made up in **generous benefits** such as health care, pension plans, and other perks such as vacation to balance things out.
- ▶ Nonprofits are not as tightly regulated as a government organization and may therefore be able to **act more quickly** to community needs (Busse & Joiner, 2008).

DISADVANTAGES

- ▶ Because nonprofits often address the needs of those in need and receive little if any government support, **lower than average wages** are sometimes a concern.
- ▶ Because of sometimes extreme working conditions and long hours, **burnout** is a possibility.
- ▶ **Turnover** in the nonprofit sector can sometimes be high due to lower than average paying jobs, intense job experience, and long hours as examples.
- ▶ Nonprofits are too often **lacking in resources** because of being under funded. This scenario varies of course from location to location and from organization to organization.
- ▶ The nonprofit sector is **still emerging as a credible sector** despite the fact that the sector has been at the forefront of social change that has taken place in this country throughout history (Busse & Joiner, 2008).

After information about what any organization claims to do is collected, it is time to get information about how the organization actually works on a day-to-day basis. This is best done by hands-on contact with the organization. The following suggestions help conduct the most important organizational exploration.

ORGANIZATIONAL RESEARCH

A. **Volunteering**—Volunteering in a nonprofit organization has numerous benefits. Most importantly, a service is provided to a population in the community who needs assistance. At the same time, it's also one of the most direct and effective methods of gaining information relevant to a particular organization. Volunteer opportunities can usually be found through the campus volunteer center or student development office.

B. **Service learning**—More and more campuses are developing service learning course work in which students work in community service projects that incorporate learning objectives. Check with an academic counselor or the office of academic affairs to determine which courses these might be. Service learning is a structured and effective way to provide service, learn course content, and receive college credit.

C. **Internships and practicums**—Internships and practicums are excellent ways to learn about an organization. Select an organization that could be of interest as a career choice to initiate an internship or practicum.

D. **Shadowing**—Another way to gain information about an organization is to follow one or several of the employees around for a day or more. This can be an excellent way to determine what individuals do on a daily basis without a large commitment of time. Organizational leaders are usually willing to accommodate these kinds of requests.

E. **Informational interviews**—It can be helpful to contact an organizational leader and request an interview to obtain information regarding the organization prior to getting involved. Informational interviews are generally more successful when they are done in person, but a phone interview can also be effective if a personal interview is not possible. Potential questions for an interview are listed below:

   ► What is the mission of the organization?
   ► Could you tell me a little about the programs?
   ► How successful has the organization been in accomplishing goals?
   ► How did you become interested in this field?
   ► What do you like best about your job? Least?
   ► What sort of qualities and qualifications do you look for when hiring employees?
   ► What is the outlook for employment within this organization?

NOTE: The informational interview also gives you a chance to get your "foot in the door" so to speak for future employment possibilities. Always send a thank-you note to the person who granted the interview

MATCH AND ACT

Once an individual's interests and skills have been assessed and specific nonprofit organizations researched carefully, it's time to choose target organizations, set goals, and design a plan of action. Which organizations are the best matches for your interests and skills? Which organization missions best match your values and style of interaction? What is the best way to approach each organization chosen? Can others help in the process? What is next?

The most important document for career planning is the résumé! What should go in a résumé? How should it look?

The résumé is a one- or two-page summary of educational, service, and work history. In conjunction with the cover letter, it's the document employers typically use to determine if an individual's qualifications match those of a specific position in their organization. It will determine who they invite for interviews.

Generally, there are two types of résumés: a **chronological résumé** in which various activities are listed by date with the most recently held position listed first, and a **functional résumé** in which skills and supporting activities are presented in segments (there is no emphasis on dates). Since it is the most commonly used, this text concentrates on the preparation of a chronological résumé.

THE RÉSUMÉ

Résumés should be divided into three main sections: header information, basic information, support information. There should be a good deal of white space in the margins to allow an interviewer to make notes. Paper needs to be white, gray, or off-white and at least 50% rag content. This is not the time to use cheap paper. These sections should be included in the résumé in the order they are listed (Figure 9.2). A sample of an effective résumé is included as Figure 9.4 and should be referred to periodically as various sections of a résumé are discussed.

Figure 9.2

Basic Résumé Structure

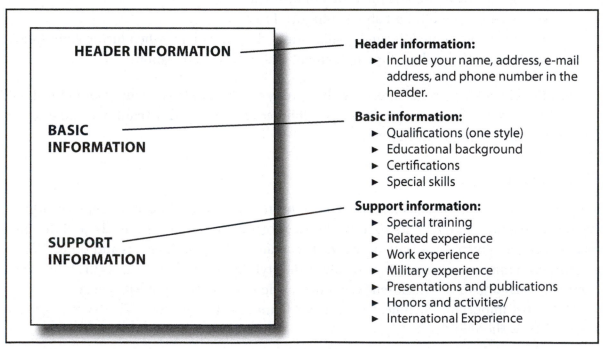

©Roger Weis

Header Information

Header information is contact information. It must be correct and current. Never list a phone number that will not usually be answered or does not have an answering machine or voice mail. If an e-mail address is listed, check for messages two to three times a day.

The perception of a person's professionalism starts at the top. Font size and style for contact information must be professional. Very large fonts and very graphic or ornate styles detract from the message of a professional image. Get some feedback from people who read résumés if you doubt this advice.

Basic Information

This may be the most important section of the résumé because it's what employers see first. The quality and impact of this section may determine whether an employer continues reviewing a résumé further. Research indicates that a résumé will receive a 10-second glance to see if it deserves further attention (Dahlstrom, 2009). Many résumés begin with a Summary of Qualifications, or Education.

Instead of a Career Objective list a Summary of Qualifications that should include skills one has developed that match up with the employers' needs, for example:

SUMMARY OF QUALIFICATIONS

—Confident leader with decisions and problem solving skills
—Effective communicator and team builder with proven success
—Creative program coordinator and motivational achiever
—Proficient in Power Point, Microsoft Word, and Excel

Either a Summary of Qualifications or Educational experiences is effective in keeping a prospective employer interested from the beginning.

EDUCATION

Educational experiences should be included in the basic information portion of the résumé. The following areas are suggested for the education section (Weis & Muller, 2015):

—The institution being attended (or graduated from)
—Location of the institution (city and state only)
—The degree that is being sought or has been acquired
—The date of graduation (or anticipated date of graduation)
—Major and minor fields of study

—Overall grade point average and/or the grade point average in a major—if the GPA is above 3.0 on a 4.0 scale (most career counselors recommend including these averages if they are above a 3.0).

—Any academic honors that are outstanding (for example, graduating Magna Cum Laude or being selected senior of the year in a department).

Although special honors are also included in the Honors/Activities section of the résumé, it's important to list them here as well because it will attract attention sooner and provide more reason to consider a candidacy. Samples of how educational experiences should be listed are as follows:

If someone has graduated from one institution, here's how it should be listed on a résumé:

EDUCATION

Murray State University, Murray, KY
Bachelor of Science, May 20XX
Nonprofit Leadership Studies major and Health minor

GPA 3.93/4.00
GPA in major: 4.00/4.00

Graduated Magna Cum Laude

If a student is graduating in the near future:

EDUCATION

Missouri Valley College, Marshall, MO
Bachelor of Arts, Expected in May 20XX
Health major, Human Services minor

GPA 3.50/4.00
GPA in major: 3.65/4.00

If the applicant has attended two different schools:

EDUCATION

University of Houston, Houston, TX
Bachelor of Science, May 20XX
Education major
GPA 3.21/4.00

Perry Community College, Perry, KY
Associates degree, May 20XX
Social Services emphasis

If the applicant has two degrees from the same institution:

EDUCATION

Clemson University, Clemson, SC
Master of Arts in Recreation, May 20XX

Bachelor of Science, May 20XX
Recreation Major

CERTIFICATIONS

Being certified in areas of proficiency relevant to nonprofit organizations is important and should be included on the résumé. Often, certification in various areas is required for a particular job, and prospective employers always look upon this favorably when choosing employees. A list of example certifications is included below:

CERTIFIED NONPROFIT PROFESSIONAL (CNP)

American Red Cross Basic Life Support (CPR)
American Red Cross Advanced Lifesaving and Water Safety
Certified North Carolina Emergency Medical Technician
State of California Provisional Certification, Grades K–12
Certified Therapeutic Recreation Specialist
American Canoe Association Certification

Certifications should be included on the résumé as follows:

CERTIFICATIONS

Certified Nonprofit Professional (CNP)
American Red Cross Basic Life Support (CPR)

Since certification is so important to some agencies, it's never too late to become certified in a certain area if it's important or required for a position.

Support Information

This section should include support information regarding any special training, related experience, work experience, military experience, presentations and publications, and honors and activities. All entries should reflect achievements and accomplishments to the degree possible. Show a potential employer what to expect based on past performance and accomplishments.

When listing various experiences, begin each descriptive statement with an action verb (see Figure 9.3). Each statement should describe an aspect of an experience and should express a level of responsibility, skill, initiative, and/or success. Include two to three statements for each experience, beginning with the most important to the least important.

Figure 9.3

Common Action Verbs Used in Résumés

Accelerated	Created	Initiated	Reported
Accomplished	Designed	Inspected	Researched
Acquired	Developed	Maintained	Reviewed
Administered	Directed	Managed	Scheduled
Analyzed	Distributed	Minimized	Selected
Appointed	Edited	Modified	Serviced
Arranged	Engineered	Monitored	Started
Assisted	Equipped	Operated	Supervised
Attended	Established	Organized	Surveyed
Combined	Evaluated	Originated	Taught
Completed	Expanded	Planned	Tested
Composed	Facilitated	Prepared	Trained
Conducted	Generated	Presented	Used
Constructed	Guided	Produced	Worked
Controlled	Helped	Recorded	Wrote
Coordinated	Implemented		

©Roger Weis

Special Training

This section should include specific knowledge and skill areas that have been acquired through workshops, seminars, special projects, conferences, or lecture series. Special training in customer relations, leadership, public relations, finance, first aid, risk management, computer technology, or any area relevant to a field of interest should be included. Each descriptive phrase should begin with an action verb. For example:

SPECIAL TRAINING:

American Red Cross, Tempe, AZ
Disaster Relief Workshop, Spring 20XX
Student participant:

- ▶ Attended lectures on community disaster preparedness and relief strategies
- ▶ Participated in simulated community-wide disaster preparedness and relief activities
- ▶ Awarded competency certificates in disaster preparedness and relief strategies

Related Experience

Career-related experiences are those experiences that relate to future professional directions and include experiences from class projects, internships, service learning and volunteer work, and part-time or summer jobs. An example is listed below:

RELATED EXPERIENCE:

YMCA Camp Lakewood, Potosi, MO
Youth Agency Intern/Leadership
Development Coordinator, Summer 20XX

- ▶ Planned and implemented leadership programs for over 500 campers
- ▶ Coordinated the activities of counselors in the delivery of leadership programs
- ▶ Developed evaluation processes to assess camper satisfaction and skill development

Work Experience

Jobs held during the collegiate experience may not be directly related to future professional experiences, but they do represent responsibility and should be included in the résumé. An example is listed below:

WORK EXPERIENCE:

Red Lobster Restaurant, Shreveport, LA
Cashier, Summer 20XX

► Provided customer service and handled financial transactions
► Initiated and developed a customer assessment process that provided important service information

Military

Military experience may be directly related to a future career direction. It is important to include on a résumé even if it is not directly related to current career plans:

MILITARY EXPERIENCE:

U.S. Army, Ft. Monmouth, NJ
Specialist, 4th Class, 20XX–20XX

► Supervised a staff of six in the development of monthly newsletters
► Created a special section advising service men and women of educational opportunities in the community

Presentations and Publications

Presenting formally, conducting research, and/or being published indicates a high level of achievement and should be included on the résumé following work experience. For example:

PRESENTATIONS:

Smart, Amy S. (20XX). **The Implications of Service Projects for Student Development in Higher Education.** Presented at the American Humanics Management Institute, Orlando, FL.

PUBLICATIONS:

Smart, Amy S. (20XX). A comparison of the grades of students involved in service learning projects with those not involved. *Journal of Leadership for Youth and Human Services, 8*, p. 4.

Honors and Activities

Employers want to know about student activities beyond the classroom and if those activities have been successful. Listed below are areas from which activities and honors should be considered:

SOCIAL AND SERVICE ORGANIZATIONS	ACADEMIC ACTIVITIES AND AWARDS
Student government	Athletic activities and awards
Student organizations	Service and volunteer activities
Class projects	Service awards
Dean's list	Leadership roles

Honors and activities should not be repeated if they appear elsewhere in the résumé. The ones included in this section should be listed in the order of importance, as indicated in the example below:

HONORS AND ACTIVITIES:

Girl Scouts of the U.S.A.—Gold Award
Dean's List—six semesters
Nonprofit Leadership Studies—Senior of the Year
All-Greek 4.0 Award
Social Work Club
Alpha Delta Pi Social Sorority

Personal information should not be included in the résumé. A person can unwittingly supply information that is not required or is illegal for the potential employer to ask about. While personal information can be used to establish connection with the interviewer, it can also give the person a reason for disqualification. Most often a résumé is used to knock people out of consideration. The reviewer is looking for a reason to reduce the pile of résumés.

There is also no need to take up space on the résumé to tell the reader that "references are available upon request." This is understood. Use the space for positive information which will increase the value of the résumé to the organization. Although Figure 9.4 is an example of a two-page resume, some organizations may prefer one page so it is important to understand what an organization expects prior to sending your resume.

Figure 9.4

Sample Résumé

AMY S. SMART

Present Address	*Permanent Address*
1405 Sycamore St.	1721 Quarry Lane
Murray, KY 42071	Bath, ME 24112
(270) 759-1833	(213) 475-4678
e-mail: amy.smart@murraystate.edu	

**QUALIFICATIONS
SUMMARY:**   Confident leader with decisions and problem solving skills
Effective communicator and team builder with proven success
Creative program coordinator and motivational achiever
Proficient in Power Point, Microsoft Word, and Excel

EDUCATION: **Murray State University, Murray, KY**
Degree: Bachelor of Science, May 20XX
Major: Nonprofit Leadership Studies
Minor: Recreation

Grade Point Average: 3.93/4.00
Grade Point Average in Major: 4.00/4.00

Graduated Magna Cum Laude

CERTIFICATION: Certified Nonprofit Professional
American Red Cross Basic Life Support (CPR)

SPECIAL SKILLS: Familiar with Power Point and EXCEL

SPECIAL TRAINING: **Murray Family YMCA, Murray, KY**
Risk Management Workshop, Fall 20XX
Student Participant

▶ Attended lectures on all aspects of reducing and managing health and
safety risks
▶ Participated in simulated high-risk scenarios and developed risk management
plan

Figure 9.4

Sample Résumé Continued

AMY S. SMART   **Page 2**

**RELATED
EXPERIENCE:**   **Camp Wyman, Eureka, MO**
                       Human Services Internship, Summer 20XX
                       Leadership-Challenge Coordinator

                       ▶ Developed leadership-challenge programs for 500 inner-city children
                       ▶ Directed the activities of support staff and counselors in delivery of services
                       ▶ Designed Leadership-Challenge Program Manual as a guide for future staff

                       Boy Scout Camp, Murray, KY
                       Recreation Internship, Summer 20XX
                       Challenge Course Coordinator

                       ▶ Planned and implemented team-building activities related to high ropes
                          challenge course
                       ▶ Developed team-building activities to enhance high ropes experience
                       ▶ Supervised five part-time and full-time challenge course leaders

**WORK
EXPERIENCE:**   **Office of Alumni Affairs, Murray, KY**
                       Murray State University, 20XX–20XX
                       Student Worker

                       ▶ Coordinated alumni-faculty scholarship meetings
                       ▶ Organized functions and meetings involving the Board of Trustees and
                          the Alumni

PRESENTATIONS: Smart, Amy S. (20XX). **The Implications of Service Projects For Student
                       Development in Higher Education**. Presented at The American Humanics
                       Management Institute, Orlando, Florida.

**HONORS AND
ACTIVITIES:**   Nonprofit Leadership Studies Senior of the Year
                       Dean's List—six semesters
                       All Greek 4.0 award
                       Sigma Delta Honorary Fraternity
                       Nonprofit Leadership Studies Student Recruitment—Chair
                       Girl Scouts of the U.S.A., 4-H, and YMCA—Volunteer
                       Recreation Club
                       Alpha Delta Pi Social Sorority

Developing a résumé is challenging, but it is an important step in starting a career. Once a résumé is developed, keeping it updated is much easier. The same basic format used for the **Sample Résumé** in Figure 9.4 can be used over and over again, although the "Related Experience" section should be renamed "Professional Experience." Various skills, experiences, and certifications will change and will need to be updated as well.

NETWORKING

With the self-assessment profile and organizational exploration complete and the résumé in-hand, it is time to consider the most critical step of making productive use of your network to take the next step in the career process. A personal network is crucial.

Often college students are selected for a position from campus interviews or internships, but most individuals must establish a networking and job search campaign to connect with individuals in organizations (Weis & Muller, 2015). Establishing a system of friends, family, and professional acquaintances for encouragement and guidance is of critical importance. Since over 75% of all positions are not advertised, it very important that anyone seeking employment focus the greatest effort in the area where the unadvertised positions can be found—the network. Networking, simply stated, means using every contact the candidate knows and everyone each contact knows to find the hidden jobs. The following step-by-step approach to networking and job seeking can be helpful.

STEP 1—UNDERSTAND AND PREPARE FOR THE TASK AHEAD

Networking is the process of developing individual connections within professional settings and promoting your potential as an effective candidate for vacancies. Networking is helping people to get to know someone as a professional candidate, so they can support that candidate for a position within their organization or someone else's organization. Networking is not actually applying for a job but campaigning for a position that may be open sometime in the future. Candidates must be prepared for a job search that can be long, frustrating, and expensive. Finding a job is a full-time job.

STEP 2—DEVELOP A LIST OF PEOPLE AND SERVICES

Developing a list of people and services with potential for providing ideas, strategies, or leads on career opportunities can be very helpful. The following list of people should be considered for contact:

Category I—People

Faculty members
Nonprofit academic leaders

Organizational leaders
Board of director members
Friends and classmates
Family members
Former employers
College and university administrators
Linkedin
Facebook
Twitter
Networking contacts generated from other person listed above

Category II—Services and Lists

University/College career planning and placement office
Organizational vacancy lists (YMCA, Boys and Girls Clubs, etc.)
Chamber of Commerce
United Way
Professional placement services
Association Directories
Chronicle of Philanthropy
Bridgespan Group
Nonprofit Times
National Council of Organizations
The Internet (Hot Jobs, etc.)
Newspaper—Classified Ads

STEP 3—ORGANIZE A NETWORKING NOTEBOOK

One of the most important tools a job candidate can have is a networking notebook, designed to keep records of all the people and organizations contacted during a job search. The notebook can be of immense help in organizing the job search and for future job searches in the years to come. It is also useful when memory fails. Record important data like who has been called, who has a résumé, who has provided other contacts, etc.

A thick, lined spiral notebook can be divided into categories of **People** and **Services** (listed in Step 2). Record keeping should include names, addresses, e-mail addresses, phone numbers, dates, and information on the results of the contact. A loose-leaf, three-ring binder could be used since it makes it easy to move information around to generate a section of "hot" prospects. Or, it can be kept electronically.

STEP 4—MAKING THE CONNECTION

Once the networking notebook is organized, contacts should be made with those individuals or services that are most likely to have information on available professional opportunities. Introductory phone calls should be made explaining that you are beginning a career search and would like to meet with them to get some ideas on a career direction. Sending résumés prior to meeting can be helpful, but it is essential that copies of your résumé be taken with you and shared with any and all network contacts. Face-to-face meetings are generally best, but a phone or e-mail meeting can also be helpful. A candidate should try to get the names and addresses of at least three people who might be helpful in the job search and these names and addresses should be recorded in the networking notebook. A thank-you note should always be sent to the contact person after the meeting.

STEP 5—DEVELOPING A SUPPORT SYSTEM

Since job searches can be long, frustrating, and expensive, it's important to develop a support system from the outset. A candidate must realize the process can be daunting and that determination is essential. Temporary jobs are sometimes necessary and should be selected with flexibility so interviews can be scheduled when needed. Family members and friends should be informed of the situation and recruited for support and encouragement. Faculty members, college administrators, career advisors, and organizational leaders should also be recruited into the support group. It is important to remain focused and to recognize the process is normal and that we all survive it.

REFERENCES

Successful organizations carefully screen potential employees by reviewing letters of recommendation and calling references. Potential references should always be asked if they are willing to be a reference and if they are willing to write a letter of recommendation. Provide each person who agrees to be a reference with a copy of your résumé. It is very appropriate for you to draft a letter which describes how the person knows you, items from your résumé which are related to the job for which you are applying, and personal characteristics the potential employer can expect from you as an employee. This reduces the risk that a reference might produce a bad reference and increases **connectedness**.

References may come from a number of areas, including:

Professors	Advisors
Employers	Administrators
Co-workers	Organizational leaders
Coaches	

Thank-you notes or letters should **always** be sent to individuals who agree to serve as a reference. It is never a waste of time to send a thank-you note. Handwritten is best, but a typed one is better than nothing.

The names of references are never included on résumés, but a list of references should be a part of every job search toolkit. Take a list of references with name, address, phone number, and the nature of their relationship. Four or five is enough. No more than one personal reference is necessary. Most employers are interested in professional associations.

COVER LETTERS

The cover letter has several purposes. It serves as a letter of introduction for a résumé, informs individuals in organizations which position a candidate is interested in, and provides insight regarding a candidate's experiences and skills. Cover letters should be written specifically for the position that is being applied for. In other words, it should reflect the educational and career-related experiences a candidate has had that are relevant to a particular position.

The cover letter is the first document a prospective employer reads and it should be well written and error free. There are three main paragraphs that make up the content of the cover letter.

In the first paragraph a candidate should:

► Explain the résumé is being submitted for review.
► Describe the specific position being applied for.
► Identify oneself in terms of the position.
► Indicate interest in the organization.

The second paragraph is generally the most detailed of the three paragraphs and describes:

► Related experiences and educational experiences relevant to the position and taken from the résumé.
► Levels of responsibility, leadership, initiative, and successes a candidate may have had with these experiences.

The third paragraph is the concluding paragraph and should:

► Reiterate interest in this type of organization.
► Thank the individual reviewing the material.

The cover letter should include the return address, e-mail address if applicable, telephone number, and the date as well as the name, title, and address of the person to whom the letter is directed. A salutation (greeting) should be used before jumping to the body of the letter. See Figure 9.5 for a sample cover letter.

Tips for Cover Letters

- ► The same quality and color of paper should be used for the cover letter and the résumé.
- ► Take every opportunity to **connect** the content of the résumé with the cover letter content.
- ► The cover letter and résumé should be sent as soon as a position becomes vacant or a network lead is received.
- ► Contacting the individual to whom the cover letter and résumé were sent to in 7 to 10 days after the material was sent will help insure receipt of the material.
- ► If possible, set a specific date and time to contact the person to arrange an interview.

INTERVIEWING

The purpose of creating effective cover letters and résumés is to be offered an interview for a position that is of interest. With practice an interview can be as natural as having a conversation with a friend. Without practice an interview can be a professionally devastating experience. A person should prepare for an interview as she or he would for an important exam.

There are two main goals of an interview:

1. First, members of the selection committee or interviewer want to see if a candidate is as promising in person as they seem to be on paper. Interviewers generally take note of dress and appearance, body language and voice, and even a candidate's handshake. As a matter of fact, the first few minutes of an interview are very important in establishing a positive impression. Interviewers are trying to determine if a candidate seems like someone who can do the job and someone they might like to work with.

2. An interview also provides the candidate with a chance to discover if the position and the people who work for the organization are right for him or her. A candidate should ask questions that will help determine if this position is the right position at the right time. The interview is a two-way street, it's just as important for the candidate to be comfortable with the situation and the personnel as it is the others to be comfortable with the candidate.

Figure 9.5

Sample Cover Letter

2207 Carol Drive
Murray, KY 42071
(270) 371-9897

August 30, 20XX

Mr. Brad Simmons
Executive Director
Wilmington YMCA
Wilmington, NC 47501

Dear Mr. Simmons:

I would like to submit my résumé for your consideration for the position of Program Coordinator which recently appeared in the YMCA Vacancy List. I graduated in May of this year from Murray State University with a major in Nonprofit Leadership Studies and a minor in Organizational Communication. I am very interested in working for a youth and human service organization.

I believe my educational and career-related experience is ideally suited for this position. As an intern for the YMCA of Jeffersonville, Indiana, I was responsible for supervising the Counselors-In-Training (CIT) program. This program was so successful that I was asked to write the operating manual for the CIT program. I have also had successful program and supervisory experience with the Murray Family YMCA and the Nonprofit Leadership Studies program at Murray State University (MSU). As the Program Chair for College Day, I successfully organized fellow students in the planning and implementation of a complete day of activities for eight grade students on the MSU campus. I was recently honored for my accomplishments by being selected the Nonprofit Leadership Studies Student of the Year. The enclosed résumé lists my qualifications in more detail.

I am very interested in making a career with the YMCA. I am certainly interested in being considered for this position and working with the Wilmington YMCA. Thank you for your consideration, and I look forward to hearing from you in the near future.

Sincerely,

Jeffrey A. Student

Enclosure

Preparation

One of the biggest mistakes most people make is not preparing adequately for the interview. The more an individual knows about the position, the organization and the people who work there, personal goals and interests, and the interview process, the better chance the individual has of making a positive impression that will result in a job offer. Use a library or the Internet to research an organization before going for an interview.

Exploring the Position

Some information regarding the position is already available if the response was to a vacancy notice. Good organizations have clear and comprehensive job descriptions for each position and are usually willing to share these with candidates. A request can be made for a clarification of the job description from the individual(s) who are conducting the interviews. Asking for more information lets employers know a candidate is interested in a position, and provides the candidate with valuable information.

Exploring the Organization

It is important to find out as much as possible about the organization and the people who work there to assist a candidate in deciding if the organization is worthy of individual commitment. It is important to gather information regarding an organization to be knowledgeable in the decision-making process and to indicate to employers a candidate is taking the position seriously enough to spend time researching the organization. There are several ways to gather information regarding a specific organization:

- ▶ Ask for and review a copy of the organization's annual report to get an idea of its goals, programs, and level of support and success.
- ▶ Contact the local United Way and ask for information on the organization.
- ▶ Contact someone who has received services from or has worked for the organization in the past and ask his/her opinion of the organization.

Common Interview Considerations

Making the cut to the interview is a major accomplishment in and of itself. It's normal to be nervous at an interview. One of the best ways to calm down before and during an interview is to breathe deeply and slowly. If perspiration under stressful conditions is a concern, bring a handkerchief to the interview. Be aware of nervous habits (like running fingers through the hair or clicking a pen) and eliminate these practices from the interview. Throughout the interview, interviewers need to know the candidate is enthusiastic about the organization (without being overly zealous) and excited to be considered for the position.

The following categories of information can be helpful in making the interview process a success.

A. **Dress**—Dress should almost always be conservative. Men should wear suits or sport coats and be conservative with the length of their hair and facial hair. Women should wear business suits or a skirt and blouse, and be conservative with make-up, jewelry, lotions, and perfumes. This is not the time to express a rebellious side or a creative flare.

B. **Interview Etiquette**—Copies of résumés should be brought to the interview for everyone even though they may already have copies. Candidates should arrive at the interview 15 to 20 minutes early. The following etiquette is suggested (Dahlstrom, 2009; Weis and Muller, 2015):

   ► Shake hands firmly (without excessive force) with each person involved in the interview. Be extra courteous and friendly.
   ► Always make eye contact when speaking with someone.
   ► Sit straight (yet comfortably) in a chair and occasionally lean forward when emphasizing important points.
   ► Speak clearly and distinctly.
   ► Always express respect for the interviewers and the organization.

C. **Questions That May Be Asked**—There is no rule on the number of questions that screening committee members can ask so a candidate should be prepared to answer almost anything. Employers will sometimes present questions based on a specific problem scenario and ask how it can be solved. It is important to answer questions honestly, clearly, and as intelligently as possible. The following are standard questions asked in interviews.

   ► Tell me a little about yourself.
   ► Why do you want to work for this organization?
   ► What experience have you had that prepares you for this position?
   ► In what areas would you need to improve to be successful in this position?
   ► Describe a problem you've had in a career-related situation and tell us how you solved it.
   ► What would you hope to accomplish in this position?
   ► Why should we hire you for this position rather than someone else?
   ► What would you like to be doing professionally five years from now?

The first question in the list above is the most common and potentially the most-deadly question asked in an interview. It is easily answered. It is an opportunity to focus the rest of the interview. It is an opportunity often squandered. An answer for this question should be practiced over and over. The question should be answered with a two- to four-minute response containing the following items:

▶ **The candidate's early history** (especially point to anything that relates to the position being applied for such as interests and skills developed or nurtured)

▶ **Education** (with special focus on job related aspects—internships, etc.)

▶ **A brief description of career-related experience** (as much as possible, connect to the position being applied for)

▶ **How that experience qualifies the candidate for the position** (explain why you are a good match for the job)

▶ **Close the answer with a thank you for the opportunity to interview** (if it is the first or second question asked).

Too many people give their whole life history or say "there isn't much to tell." Neither response gets jobs. A carefully thought out answer **connects** the interviewee's training and experience with the job qualifications.

D. **Questions a Candidate May Wish to Ask**—It is important for a candidate to ask good questions in order to have as much information as possible and to express a sense of knowledge and organization to the screening committee. The following questions should be considered during the interview:

▶ Why is this position open?

▶ What were the strong points of the person who last held the position?

▶ What exactly would be my responsibilities in this position?

▶ Who will be my supervisor?

▶ Could you describe his/her/your leadership style?

▶ Will I be supervising anyone, and if so, whom?

▶ Would you explain what a typical day would be like?

▶ What kind of person are you looking for?

▶ Would I have some flexibility to create new programs?

▶ Do you anticipate any changes for the organization in the future?

▶ What resources are available to me to do my job?

▶ Is further training and/or education available?

▶ How and when will I be evaluated?

▶ When can I expect to hear from you?

Questions regarding salary and benefits should never be mentioned in a first interview unless the subject is introduced by someone else. There will be an appropriate time to do this.

E. **Practice, Practice, Practice**—No one ever did anything really well without a lot of practice, and interviewing is no different. Simulated interviews with a teacher or administrator can be very helpful.

F. **Following the Interview**—A thank-you letter should be sent to the screening committee chair immediately following the interview. If the screening committee does not make contact within the designated time frame, a phone call may be appropriate.

ASSESSING JOB OFFERS

An effective networking and job search campaign eventually culminates in job offers. The tendency for many people is to accept the first offer they receive. But accepting an offer without carefully evaluating it could be a major mistake. Create a list of all the important variables to consider in choosing a position. Assign weight to each variable in keeping with your values and of those affected by your choice. As offers come in, evaluate each offer objectively in light of the list. This will produce a better decision. There are several areas to resolve before a job offer is finalized:

— **Salary and Benefits**—Key benefits often included in a traditional benefits package include health insurance, life insurance, vacation and sick leave, a pension plan, tax shelters, and continued training and educational opportunities. Other benefits may include dental care, eye care, day care, and discounted or free facility use, if a facility is involved. When discussing benefits such as health/life insurance, candidates should ask what percentage of the costs they pay for versus what the employer pays.

— **Salary Negotiation**—If the demands of the job appear to outmatch the salary, or if someone thinks they should receive more money for their skills and experience, a candidate may decide to negotiate for a higher salary. This can be done by explaining they will accept the position at the salary offered, but that a higher salary (specific) would be more desirable for whatever the reason. Another option is to explain to the employer that the offer is appreciated, but it can only be accepted at a higher salary (again, be specific). This second option is obviously a risky strategy, and the candidate should be prepared for the possibility of the offer being withdrawn.

Responding to Job Offers

Once a job has been offered and accepted, it is wise to send an acceptance letter. Acceptance letters are important because they provide written documentation regarding the acceptance of the job offer. They also provide an opportunity for clarification of the job offer. Besides, following up with a written letter of acceptance is the expected and courteous thing to do.

If a decision is made to turn down a job offer, it's also important to send a letter of rejection. This expresses consideration to the employer, and it helps keep the door open for future possibilities.

PROFESSIONAL DEVELOPMENT

Training and Education

One of the most important aspects of developing professionally is to involve oneself in as many training and educational opportunities as possible. Good organizations offer numerous in-service training workshops or provide opportunities to attend training workshops elsewhere. Good organizations also encourage employees to continue their formal education, and some even pay for all or part of advanced educational pursuits. In the final analysis, training and education are not job benefits, they are personal necessities. It must be done whether the organization provides it or it comes at personal expense.

Professional Associations

Professional associations can be extremely helpful. They frequently offer support through a number of educational and informational workshops. They can also be helpful for career advancement opportunities. A person is not a professional if he or she is not connected with other professionals. Again, professional associates are not an option, they are a necessity.

Community Responsibility

Nonprofit leaders should always strive to have the best organization, with the best programs, and the best support systems possible. Of equal importance, strive to have the best relationships with colleagues, organizational members, volunteers, and other community members (Weis & Muller, 2015).

Leaders should also become involved in as many activities sponsored by the organization as possible. Most organizations are like big families. It's important to get know and understand people in the organization and to let them know you.

Always consider becoming involved with other organizations as a volunteer or as an interested community member. "Practice what you preach" and offer assistance to organizations other than your own. It's rewarding and fun, and it will ultimately benefit your organization and career as well.

Just as it's important to continue learning and growing professionally, it's also important to balance professional pursuits with personal activities and responsibilities. Reserving quality time for oneself, family, and friends is important. It helps to provide the support and strength needed to be a successful, professional leader.

An appropriate concluding statement for this chapter is found in another of those Successories motivational posters: "Great achievements are not born from a single vision but from the combination of many distinctive viewpoints. Diversity challenges assumptions, opens minds and unlocks potential to solve any problem we may face."

A wise person will spend 5% of every day preparing for the next step in his or her career—promotion, new employer, career change, or retirement. Abraham Lincoln reportedly passed along this insight, "I do not think much of a man who is not wiser today than he was yesterday." To be totally content with today is to be foolish. The wise person positions himself or herself for the next bend in the road. A curve in a person's career path is not a disaster unless he or she fails to make the turn (Weis & Muller, 2015).

SUMMARY

Success in career planning begins with a thorough knowledge of self. Without self-knowledge and understanding planning a career and find a job is confusing and frustrating. The *Flowchart for Career Planning* reduces the confusion. The process begins with the construction of a *Self-Assessment Profile,* ideally, using more than one assessment tool. The next step involves organizational exploration by first collecting organizational information regarding purpose and scope, followed by organizational research which includes data collection from volunteering, service learning experiences, internships, staff shadowing, or informational interviews.

With a specific direction in mind and potential target organizations chosen, the next step is résumé construction. This is usually the most important step in the process. A résumé is a one- to two-page document to provide a summary of education and experience. An effective résumé helps get an interview. It must be error free and completed before any other steps are taken.

The next step is personal and professional networking. This involves using contacts to locate potential positions and developing leads for open positions. Each person needs a copy of your résumé.

References need to be contacted based on their knowledge of the candidate's work experience and training. It is helpful for each reference to receive a résumé and a draft of a letter they might be comfortable sending on behalf of the candidate. References often come from a person's professional network.

With a résumé constructed and contacts from networking activities, cover letters can be constructed to convey to potential employers how the candidate can meet the needs of the targeted organizations. These letters are specific but contain three basic paragraphs: a personal introduction of the candidate; an indication of which position is of interest and how the candidate qualifies for that position; and an expression of interest in moving forward with the employment process and a thank you for the agency's consideration. This too must be carefully written and error free.

If all goes well, the next step is the interview. If effective preparation occurs, an interview can be an enjoyable experience. Carefully collect background information on the target organization, prepare answers to commonly asked questions, select questions to be answered by organizational members, dress appropriately, control nervous habits, and give people a firm handshake.

A successful interview frequently results in a job offer. Don't accept the first offer unless it meets all the requirements of a dream job. Be knowledgeable regarding the job market conditions, salary ranges and benefits packages for positions of interest. Be realistic. Be prepared to negotiate for the things most important for a reasonable career progression.

The last section of this chapter discussed the role of professional development in the life of nonprofit staff members. Take every opportunity to gain additional educational credentials, acquire new skills, and update old skills. In addition, seek every occasion to work with appropriate professional associations and community projects in order to expand network contacts for that next job search.

This chapter addressed, in part, the Nonprofit Academic Centers Council (NACC) Competency Requirements of Employability Skills and Career Development and Exploration.

REFLECTION AND APPLICATION

1. Discuss ways in which you plan to use the *Flowchart for Career Planning* in your career search.

    _____

    _____

    _____

    _____

2. Discuss the value of self-assessment. How can others help in the process?

    _____

    _____

    _____

    _____

3. Discuss the skills you have developed that could be important for most careers in the nonprofit sector.

    _____

    _____

    _____

    _____

4. Select a campus or community leader to host a simulated interview for you. Be sure to prepare for the interview by studying the suggestions in that section of the chapter and incorporate the Interview Simulation Critique Form (Appendix ?) in the process then discuss your results.

    _____

    _____

    _____

    _____

    _____

5. How can any and all work experience be valuable for your résumé and for your career path?

_____

_____

_____

_____

_____

6. Write a 2–3 page paper discussing your dream career path.

7. Choose a nonprofit organization in the community and plan and secure permission for a day of *shadowing*. What did you learn with this experience?

_____

_____

_____

_____

_____

8. Write a personal vision statement for 5 years from now, 10 years from now, and 15 years from now.

_____

_____

_____

_____

_____

9. Create a *networking* list of 20–25 individuals or organizational contacts.

_____

_____

_____

_____

_____

REFERENCES

Busse, M., & Joiner, S. (2008). *The idealist guide to nonprofit careers:* New York, NY: Action Without Borders.

Dahlstrom, H. (2009). *The job hunting handbook.* Holliston, MA: Dahlstrom and Company, Inc.

Michelozzi, B. N. (1992). *Coming alive from nine to five.* Mountain View, CA: Mayfield Printing Company.

Weis, R, & Muller, S. (2015). *Leading and managing nonprofit organizations* (2nd ed.). Peosta, IA: eddie bowers publishing co., inc.

INDEX

CPSIA information can be obtained
at www.ICGtesting.com
Printed in the USA
LVOW02s0222090317
526623LV00003B/6/P